THE MAGIC OF A NAME
THE ROLLS-ROYCE STORY

I was fortunate enough to make the acquaintance of Mr. Royce and in him I found the man I had been looking for for years.

The Hon. C.S. Rolls

I not only admired him, I was one of the few people who were genuinely fond of him . . . Henry Royce ruled the lives of the people around him, claimed their body and soul, even when they were asleep.

Ivan Evernden

Everyone who rode with Rolls testifies to the quickness of his reaction, and to the sensation that he was at one with his steed.

Lord Montagu of Beaulieu

The real genius responsible for the wide fame of the Rolls-Royce car is C.J.

Lord Birkenhead

I can say with all sincerity that those who are best able to judge would put you among a very few men whom the country has to thank above all others for our survival in this war.

Air Chief Marshal Sir Charles Portal
[in a letter to Ernest Hives]

THE MAGIC OF A NAME
THE ROLLS-ROYCE STORY
THE FIRST 40 YEARS

Peter Pugh

ICON BOOKS UK
TOTEM BOOKS USA

Published in the UK in 2000 by Icon Books Ltd.,
Grange Road, Duxford, Cambridge CB2 4QF
e-mail: icon@mistral.co.uk
www.iconbooks.co.uk

Distributed in the UK, Europe, Canada, South Africa
and Asia by the Penguin Group: Penguin Books Ltd.,
27 Wrights Lane, London W8 5TZ

Published in Australia in 2000 by Allen & Unwin Pty. Ltd.,
PO Box 8500, 9 Atchison Street, St. Leonards NSW 2065

Published in the USA in 2000 by Totem Books
Inquiries to: PO Box 223, Canal Street Station
New York, NY 10013

In the United States, distributed to the trade by
National Book Network Inc., 4720 Boston Way,
Lanham, Maryland 20706

Library of Congress Cataloging in Publication number:
99–076897

ISBN: 1 84046 151 9

Typesetting by Hands Fotoset, Woodthorpe, Nottingham

Design and layout by Christos Kondeatis

Printed and bound in the UK by Biddles Ltd.,
Guildford and King's Lynn

Contents

INTRODUCTION

Many books have been written about Rolls-Royce over the years. The Bibliography on pages 325 to 329 shows nearly fifty specifically on Rolls-Royce cars or aero engines or both, and there are hundreds more which devote many words to Rolls-Royce's products and their importance. However, most of these books are either biographies of the leading personalities, or works that tackle specific aspects of the cars or the aero engines.

The last publication to attempt a comprehensive history of Rolls-Royce was Harold Nockolds's *The Magic of a Name*, published by Foulis in 1938 and reprinted several times until a third edition was finally printed in 1972. This book and its sequel, to be published in 2001, is the first attempt since Nockolds to cover comprehensively the story of Rolls-Royce from its earliest days until the present. The Rolls-Royce name *is* magic, made so by the calibre of its people and its products, and the title *The Magic of a Name* is singularly appropriate. Foulis, now owned by Haynes Publishing, has kindly allowed us to use the title again.

When I was asked three years ago to undertake the task of researching and writing the story of Rolls-Royce I was extremely excited at the prospect. It was surely a great story. In fact, as I soon found out, it is much more than that: it is several great stories. The genius and dedication of Royce, allied to the flair for publicity of Rolls, led to the production and worldwide sales of the best car in the world, the Silver Ghost. Shortly afterwards, Royce's skill as a designer quickly produced the leading aero engine of the First World War, the Eagle.

By the 1920s, Royce's reputation was such that he was asked, almost ordered, by the Government to design an engine for Britain to retain the Schneider Trophy. This association with the inspired aircraft designer, R.J. Mitchell, led on to the Spitfire and Rolls-Royce's Merlin engines. It is safe to say that, without the Spitfire and the Hurricane, *and* the Merlins that powered them, the Battle of Britain would have been lost. Finally, in this book, we look at the advent of the jet engine and how Ernest (later Lord) Hives realised its importance for the future of air travel and backed Sir Frank Whittle's development to the hilt.

Rolls-Royce has become world-famous above all for the quality of its products and these have been analysed in great detail elsewhere. This book is not a technical one. It attempts to put Rolls-Royce products and Rolls-Royce people in their context. Royce and Rolls set the highest standards, and when you have read this book I think you will agree that the tradition has been carried on faithfully by all who have been lucky enough to work with them and after them in Rolls-Royce.

Peter Pugh
November 1999

The value of money

In a book about a business, we cannot ignore the changing value of money, and – with the exception of the inter-war years – the twentieth century has been inflationary. There is no magic formula for translating 1900 prices into those of 1999. Some items have exploded in price, others have declined. We have to choose some criterion of measurement, and I have chosen the average working wage.

The Victorian age was one of stable prices, but prices started to rise just before the First World War, and rose sharply at the end of it. (Wars are always inflationary, because they distort supply and demand.) Immediately after the war, prices were more than twice as high as in 1914, and although they declined somewhat in the depressed economic conditions of the 1920s and 30s, they remained about twice as high as those before the war.

Price controls and rationing were imposed in the Second World War, but as these were withdrawn, prices again doubled. Inflation continued at about 3 per cent a year through the 1950s and 60s, but then rose sharply, almost catastrophically, in the 1970s. Although it was brought under control by the end of that decade, there were two more nasty upward blips in the early and late 1980s before the more stable 1990s.

I have used the following formula:
Late nineteenth century – multiply by 110 to equate with today's prices
Early twentieth century – multiply by 100 to equate with today's prices
1918–45 – multiply by 50 to equate with today's prices

AUTHOR'S ACKNOWLEDGEMENTS

In researching this book on Rolls-Royce I have read all of the books mentioned in the bibliography, and quoted from several of them. I am grateful to the authors and to the publishers. I have interviewed many people, some of them several times, and I am grateful to them too. Most of the interviews took place in Britain, but I travelled to the USA several times, both to research the archives held at Gilbert, Segall and Young, Rolls-Royce's legal advisers in New York, and those at Rolls-Royce Allison in Indianapolis, and also to interview a number of people who had been in close contact with Rolls-Royce. I also travelled to Australia to interview a number of people there.

I would like to mention especially: Roy Anderson, John Blatchley, Geoffrey Bone, Martin Bourne, Tom Bowling, Walter Boyne, Bill Castle, John Coplin, Roger Cra'ster, David Davies, Gordon Dawson, Sir George Edwards, Cyril Elliot, Ernest Eltis, Mac Fisher, Sir Ian Fraser, Lloyd Frisbee, Dick Garner, Phil Gilbert, Sir Arnold Hall, Fred Hardy, Ronnie Harker, Rhoddie Harvey-Bailey, Lionel Haworth, Alex Henshaw, Sam Higginbottom, Ronnie Hooker, Sir David Huddie, Mike Hudson, John Jones, Lord Keith, Lord Kings Norton, Kevin Kirby, Jock Knight, Carl Kotchian, Gordon Lewis, Sir Douglas Lowe, Jackson McGowen, Sir Arthur Marshall, Sir Peter Masefield, Sir Robin Maxwell-Hislop, Tom Metcalfe, Stewart Miller, Dr. Gordon Mitchell, Fred Morley, Sir Ian Morrow, Michael Neale, Tom Neville, Alan Newton, Rex Nicholson, Don Pepper, David Pickerill, Sir David Plastow,

Tim Rigby, Jim Rigg, Ian Rimmer, Cliff Rogers, Philip Ruffles, Trevor Salt, Brian Slatter, Sir John Smith, Reg Spencer, Gordon Strangeways, Joe Sutter, Alan Swinden, Bill Thomas, Lord Tombs, Geoff Wilde, T. Wilson, John White, Ian Whittle, Andy Wood, Jimmy Wood, Paul Wood, John Woodward, John Wragg, Ken Wright.

Unfortunately, since I interviewed them, a number have died – Sir David Huddie, Lord Kings Norton, T. Wilson, Ronnie Harker and Stewart Miller. All made a great contribution to both Rolls-Royce and the aircraft industry.

I received constant help from Sir Ralph Robins, the Chairman of Rolls-Royce plc, and from Dave Piggott, a former Rolls-Royce engineer who held my hand through the writing on the development of the Kestrel, the Buzzard, the 'R' engine, the Merlin and the Griffon.

Dave Newill looked after me magnificently when I visited Rolls-Royce Allison in Indianapolis. Both Dave Newill and Dave Piggott are senior members of the Rolls-Royce Heritage Trust.

Philip Hall, curator of the Sir Henry Royce Memorial Foundation at The Hunt House, Paulerspury, gave me full access to the archives held there and was also kind enough to read the manuscript. Peter Baines, General Secretary of the Rolls-Royce Enthusiasts' Club, also read the final manuscript and corrected us on some vital details.

Above all, my undying gratitude goes to Mike Evans, the Chairman of the Rolls-Royce Heritage Trust, without whose guidance and assistance I would not have been prepared to offer the book for publication. Mike Evans joined Rolls-Royce in 1959 from Cambridge as a graduate apprentice, and was inspired by his tutor, Bill Morton, to take an interest in the company's history. He was surprised that there was no museum, and proposed to David Huddie, then general manager, that one should be created. Huddie gained the approval of the board, and Evans was put in charge of the project in 1961. His work on preserving the company's heritage increased during the 1960s and, at the time of the Receivership in 1971, on advice from Divisional directors, he did the only thing he could to preserve his work on the heritage. He bought all of the engines, documents, books, files and photographs he had collected and, as far as was possible, moved them to the cowsheds behind his home.

In the mid-1970s, Evans and the director of engineering in Derby, Roy Heathcote, proposed the launch of the Rolls-Royce Heritage Trust to the Managing Director, Dennis Head. The proposal was supported and the Trust launched with Evans as Chairman, a post he still holds today.

Ably assisted by Richard Haigh, the Trust's Chief Executive, and their secretary, Julie Wood, Mike Evans has given unstinting help to me for the last two and a half years.

Peter Pugh
November 1999

NAMES IN ROLLS-ROYCE

Many aspects of Rolls-Royce were idiosyncratic. It was part of the company's mystique. One of them was the form of address which had been instituted by Royce and used since the earliest days. The names of all departmental heads were abbreviated. Hence, Royce was known as R, Hives as Hs, A.G. Elliott as E, R.W.H. Bailey as By, A.F. Sidgreaves as Sg and so on. The aim of this practice was to remove inhibition caused by titles within the company. Below is a list, by no means comprehensive, of some of the abbreviations used. The practice persisted right up into the 1990s but has recently been discontinued. In the text of the book it was decided not to use the abbreviations.

Sir Henry Royce	R	R.W.H. Bailey	By
The Hon. Charles Rolls	CSR	Ernest W. (later Lord) Hives	Hs
Claude Johnson	CJ	Dr. Stanley Hooker	SGH
T. Broome	TB	W. Lappin	Lp
John De Looze	D	A.C. Lovesey	Lov
R.H. Coverley	RHC	Dr. Llewellyn-Smith	LS
W. Cowen	C	J.H. Maddocks	Mx
Eric Platford	EP	Ivan Evernden	Ev
B.I. Day	Da	Sir Denning Pearson	Psn
Captain Hallam	Hm	W.A. Robotham	Rm

A.G. Elliott	E	Bill Hardy	Hdy
A.A. Rubbra	Rbr	Lord Herbert Scott	LHS
J.E. Ellor	Lr	A.F. Sidgreaves	Sg
Basil Johnson	BJ	A.W. Sleator	Sr
S.H. Grylls	Gry	H. Swift	Sft
Maurice Olley	Oy	A. Wormald	Wor
T.S. Haldenby	Hy		

Many of the personalities mentioned in the book performed several different tasks and occupied a variety of positions in Rolls-Royce and, in order to put each one in context without interrupting the flow of the book, we have compiled a set of short biographies between pages 293 and 324.

CHAPTER ONE

THE PRIME MOVERS

'BOTH MEN TOOK TO EACH OTHER'
THE GODFATHER
HENRY ROYCE
THE HON. C.S. ROLLS
THE HYPHEN IN ROLLS-ROYCE
ERNEST CLAREMONT

'BOTH MEN TOOK TO EACH OTHER'

THE HISTORIC FIRST MEETING OF Henry Royce with the Hon. C.S. Rolls took place on 4 May 1904 at the Midland Hotel in Manchester (now the Holiday Inn Crowne Plaza, Midland, Manchester).

The two men could hardly have come from more different backgrounds. The Hon. C.S. Rolls (his father had been raised to the peerage in 1892 as Baron Llangattock of the Hendre) had been educated at Eton and Cambridge, and moved comfortably in London society among his aristocratic and wealthy friends. Henry Royce had known poverty and hardship all his life and, in that well-worn phrase, the only university he had graduated from was the one of ''ard knocks'. The one characteristic they had in common was a certain prickliness, perhaps in both cases born of shyness rather than arrogance. How would the two react to each other?

It was not a casual meeting, but one which had only been arranged after much planning and persuasion by Henry Edmunds, who came to be known as 'the Godfather' of Rolls-Royce. Edmunds was to say some time later in his *Reminiscences*:

Mr. Rolls accompanied me to Manchester, to which I was then a frequent visitor, as I had to look after several business concerns there and held a trader's ticket between

1

London and Manchester. I well remember the conversation I had in the dining-car of the train with Mr. Rolls, who said it was his ambition to have a motor car connected with his name so that in the future it might be a household word, just as much as 'Broadwood' or 'Steinway' in connection with pianos; or 'Chubbs' in connection with safes. I am sure neither of us at that time could foresee the wonderful development of the car which resulted from my introduction of these two gentlemen to each other. I remember we went to the Great Central Hotel at Manchester and lunched together. I think both men took to each other at first sight and they eagerly discussed the prospects and requirements of the automobile industry which was still in its early infancy. Mr. Rolls then went to see for himself the Royce car; and after considerable discussions and negotiations on both sides it was decided to form a separate concern in which the name of Rolls was conjoined with that of Royce, forming the compound which is held in the highest regard today. [Edmunds refers to the Great Central Hotel but there was no such hotel in Manchester. The Midland Hotel was next to Central Station, and he must have been confused.]

There have been a number of imaginative accounts of the conversations between Rolls and Royce at this first meeting but, as C.W. Morton pointed out in his *History of Rolls-Royce Motor Cars* Vol. 1, no reliable evidence has come to light as to precisely what was said or what business arrangements were made. Edmunds gave the occasion only a few sentences in his *Reminiscences of a Pioneer* and Sir Max Pemberton, who lived close to Royce in his latter years in West Wittering, wrote *The Life of Sir Henry Royce* and talked to Royce, unfortunately did not record a first-hand account from the great man himself. Indeed, Rolls only spoke publicly once about the meeting. At a dinner given by Rolls-Royce to mark the achievement of Percy Northey, the driver of one of the company's first 'Light 20 hp' cars, in coming second in the first Tourist Trophy race run in 1905 on the Isle of Man, he said:

You may ask yourselves how it was that I came to be associated with Mr. Royce and Mr. Royce with me. Well, for a considerable number of years I had been actively engaged in the sale of foreign cars, and the reason for this was that I wanted to be able to recommend and sell the best cars in the world, irrespective of origin . . . the cars I sold were, I believe, the best that could be got at that time, but somehow I always had a sort of feeling that I should prefer to be selling English instead of foreign goods. In addition I could distinctly notice a growing desire on the part of my clients to purchase English-made cars; yet I was disinclined to embark in a factory and manufacture myself, firstly on account of my own incompetence and inexperience in such matters, and secondly on account of the enormous risks involved, and at the same time I could not come across any English-made car that I really liked . . . eventually, however, I was fortunate enough to make the acquaintance of Mr. Royce and in him I found the man I had been looking for for years.

Pemberton maintained that Rolls's business partner, Claude Johnson (the hyphen in Rolls-Royce, of whom much more later), accompanied Rolls to Manchester to meet Royce. This is very unlikely. Edmunds would surely have mentioned it in his *Reminiscences*, and Wilton J. Oldham in his biography of Johnson, *The Hyphen in Rolls-Royce*, said:

[Rolls] returned to London full of enthusiasm and went straight to C.J.'s flat to tell him about his trip to Manchester, saying, 'I have found the greatest engineer in the world' . . . Claude Johnson was as enthusiastic as his partner when he, too, had inspected the 10 hp Royce car and met its designer; so it was quickly arranged that the firm of C.S. Rolls & Co. would have the sole selling rights of the marque, one of the conditions being that the car would be sold under the name Rolls-Royce.

In a later book Oldham maintained that Rolls had persuaded Royce to have a car sent down to London by train. Rolls collected it and drove it round to Johnson's flat at midnight, knocked him up and said: 'I have found the greatest engineer in the world.'

He then insisted Johnson get dressed, and drove him round the deserted London streets. (Johnson was living at this time in St. James's Court facing Buckingham Gate, by coincidence exactly opposite the current location of Rolls-Royce's head office.)

Paul Tritton, a dedicated scholar of the early years of Rolls-Royce, wrote in his book *The Godfather of Rolls-Royce*:

These stories [the ones told by Wilton Oldham and John Rowland giving details of conversations between Rolls and Johnson] have plenty of entertainment value . . . but are not taken literally by Rolls-Royce scholars!

In Tritton's view it is likely that Rolls had certainly seen, and probably driven, the first Royce 10 which was in the south of England in April and May 1904 for the Side Slip trials. He could well have driven Johnson round London late at night *before* he went up to Manchester to meet Royce. While in Manchester he probably drove in the second Royce 10 which was allocated to Ernest Claremont.

What is not in doubt is Rolls's excitement about the car. As Harold Nockolds wrote in his famous book, *The Magic of a Name*, first published in 1938:

Rolls at this time had a prejudice against two-cylinder engines and he climbed into the high passenger seat of the little Royce prepared for all the vibration and roughness that were usually associated with the type. To his amazement he found that the car had the smoothness and even pull of the average 'four' allied to a quite phenomenal degree of silence. He came, he rode, and was conquered.

3

THE GODFATHER

Who was Henry Edmunds, the man who introduced Rolls to Royce? Paul Tritton wrote a book, *The Godfather of Rolls-Royce – the life and times of Henry Edmunds, MICE, MIEE, Science of Technology's Forgotten Pioneer*, which served to place Edmunds in his correct place in the history of technological development in this country, and to give more substance to his place in the history of Rolls-Royce.

Edmunds was born in Halifax in 1853 into a middle-class family. His father was a partner in Edmunds and Hookway, a firm of engineers and iron merchants. Edmunds was educated at private schools until he was 15, when he joined his father's firm. By the time he was 18 he had designed an oil engine, and in 1873 he and two friends patented an oil vapour lamp which could light and heat a cottage or generate steam for a marine or locomotive engine. For the next twenty years Edmunds was to enjoy several adventures while establishing himself in the electrical industry, including a meeting with Thomas Edison, apparently at the very moment of the first reproduction of mechanically recorded speech. In 1893, Edmunds became the Managing Director of W.T. Glover of Salford, Manchester, one of Britain's largest manufacturers of electricity cables.

Later in the 1890s other directors joined W.T. Glover, including Ernest Claremont, Henry Royce's partner at F.H. Royce & Co. Ltd. of Cooke Street, Manchester. Claremont became an important link between the two companies as F.H. Royce & Co. Ltd. (later Royce Ltd.), already well-established as a manufacturer of electric motors and dynamos, had recently developed electric cranes. (Royce's companies went through three different legal entities. From 1884–94 the company was F.H. Royce & Co., from 1894–99 F.H. Royce & Co. Ltd., and after 1899 Royce Ltd.) While this association with Royce Ltd. was developing, Edmunds also became friendly with Rolls and Johnson through his interest in cars and his joining the Automobile Club, where he served on the committee alongside Rolls. And, of course, Johnson was the RAC's first secretary. He donated the Henry Edmunds Hill-Climbing Trophy.

In 1902 Henry Royce began to work on a DeDion Quad, and in 1903 on a second-hand Decauville (George Clegg, an employee at Cooke Street in 1902, remembered that the Decauville arrived by train and was pushed by employees round to Cooke Street) – convinced that he could improve on it. At this time, Edmunds became more closely involved with Royce Ltd. He gave Ernest Claremont some of his shares in W.T. Glover in exchange for a block of his shares in Royce Ltd. Helping Royce make the decision to build the three prototype motor cars in the autumn of 1903, apart from Edmunds's encouragement, was the post-Boer War slump which left Royce

4

Ltd., along with many others, with spare capacity. Royce, mindful of the survival of his company and faced with declining orders and prices, felt that motor cars could be a new product on which he could use his talents as an electrical and mechanical engineer.

While Royce was experimenting and building his cars (he had already built a rockery at the end of his garden to prevent the embarrassment of plunging into his neighbour's garden in the DeDion Quad if the brakes failed) Rolls was asking Edmunds if he knew of a source of new cars.

I wish you could give me any information you may get hold of relating to improvements in the building of motor cars. I have some ideas of my own which I should like to follow out; and there are many opportunities of doing so.

Edmunds was now determined to bring Rolls and Royce together, and on Saturday 26 March 1904 he wrote to Royce:

I saw Mr. Rolls yesterday, after telephoning to you: and he said it would be much more convenient if you could see him in London, as he is so very much occupied; and, further, that several other houses are now in negotiation with him, wishing to do the whole or part of his work. What he is looking for is a good high-class quality of car to replace the Panhard; preferably of three or four cylinders. He has some personal dislike to two-cylinder cars. I will do all I can to bring about this arrangement with Mr. Rolls; for I think your car deserves well; and ought to take its place when it is once recognised by the public on its merits.

On the same day he wrote to Rolls:

I have pleasure in enclosing you photographs and specification of the Royce car, which I think you will agree with me looks very promising. I have written them asking if they can make an early appointment to meet you in London; and also whether they can arrange to send up a car for your inspection and trial. The point that impressed me most, however, is this. The people have worked out their designs in their own office, and knowing as I do the skill of Mr. Royce as a practical mechanical engineer, I feel one is very safe in taking up any work his firm may produce. Trusting this matter may lead to business to our mutual interest in the future.

Six days later, on 1 April 1904 (it was officially recorded as 31 March to avoid April Fool jokes), the first Royce 10 hp made its first run, and later in the month was involved in the Side Slip Trials. On Monday 18 April, the endurance trials began with the 145 miles from London to Margate and back. Edmunds drove and was accompanied by Goody, who normally acted as his chauffeur but in this instance went along as his mechanic, and also by the official observer, Massac Buist, and a reporter from the *Morning Post*. The car performed well, as it did the next day on a journey to Marlborough and the day after on two trips to Slough and Beaconsfield.

As we have seen, Royce and Rolls finally came together on 4 May 1904. Edmunds helped the negotiations between them following this meeting which he had arranged, negotiations which culminated in the famous agreement of 23 December 1904.

Clearly, Edmunds's advice was requested. Royce wrote to him on 8 August 1904.

With reference to Mr. Rolls taking our manufactures, he has at present in his possession an agreement we have got out on these lines, and with reference to his suggestion that you should be named as umpire, I should be most happy to agree to this as I know your anxiety would be for everything to be quite fair on each side. I must thank you for your introduction, which is promising well, and I think we ought to be of great service to each other.

In the agreement, Rolls contracted to take all the cars built by Royce Ltd., who agreed to deliver a range of two-, three-, four- and six-cylinder chassis rated between 10 and 30 hp.

Thereafter, Edmunds was not much involved, although he was a guest of honour at the formal opening of the firm's factory in Derby in 1908, and it was on this occasion that he was first referred to publicly as 'the Godfather of Rolls-Royce'. He continued to act as a director of W.T. Glover, which pioneered urban electrical distribution and electrical installation in mines, and was already Managing Director of Parsons, a manufacturer of non-skid chains. As far as we know, he was not involved further with Rolls-Royce Limited, but without him the company might never have come to exist.

Who were the two men that Edmunds brought together?

HENRY ROYCE

Frederick Henry Royce was born on 27 March 1863 in the village of Alwalton near Peterborough. He was descended from generations of farmers and millers, and his grandfather had been a pioneer in the installation of steam power in water mills. His father, James, in the family tradition, trained to be a farmer before moving on to milling, renting a mill at Castor, Northamptonshire in 1852. He had just married Mary King, the daughter of a large-scale farmer in Luffenham, Rutlandshire. In 1858 they moved to the mill at Alwalton with their first son and three daughters.

James proved to be unreliable and seemed unable to apply himself consistently, probably due to his suffering from Hodgkin's disease. By the time

Henry Royce was born in 1863 he was in financial trouble, and was forced to mortgage the Alwalton Mill lease to the London Flour Company. In 1867 he moved to London to work for this company, taking both his sons with him but leaving his daughters with his wife in Alwalton. He died in 1872 in a poor house, at the age of only forty-one. He proved the exception in a family of prosperous farmers and millers.

Henry Royce therefore knew poverty in his early life, and even before he was four he was earning money birdscaring in the fields near Alwalton. After his father died, he sold newspapers for W.H. Smith and also delivered telegrams in the Mayfair area. Royce's grandfather had taken most of the Royce clan to Canada, leaving few relatives in Britain to give support to James's widow and children. Fortunately, when he was fourteen an aunt on his mother's side agreed to pay £20 a year (about £2,200 in today's terms) for him to be an apprentice at the Great Northern Railway works at Peterborough. He lodged with a Mr. and Mrs. Yarrow, went to evening classes in English and mathematics, and learned a great deal about machining and fitting in the workshop in Mr. Yarrow's garden. At the same time he continued to earn money by delivering newspapers.

After three years, the aunt felt unable to continue her support. This was a serious setback for Royce, since failure to complete his premium apprenticeship denied him 'skilled status'. However, Royce found work as a toolmaker with the Leeds engineering firm, Greenwood and Batley. Although it did not take long for Royce to secure this job, it was a very worrying time. As Pemberton says in his biography:

Unfortunately, at that time there was one of our periodical seasons of trade depression. Henry Royce tramped, as he told me himself, many weary miles upon a vain quest. His powerful recommendations opened no doors. Great houses were discharging, not engaging, men. He must have come very near despair in those fateful days before he found employment.

He was paid 11 shillings (55p or £60 in today's terms) for a fifty-four-hour week. Royce told Pemberton that for several months he worked from 6am until 10pm and all through Friday night. This was the type of dedication he expected from his employees once he founded his own business.

His interest in electricity led to a job with the Electric Light and Power Company in London, and he progressed well enough to be sent as first electrician to the associated company, Lancashire Maxim and Weston Electric Company, which was engaged in theatre and street lighting in Liverpool. Just before Royce's twenty-first birthday in 1884, Liverpool Corporation accepted a contract to install a complete lighting system for several streets, and Royce was given the technical responsibility.

However, by the end of May 1884, the company went into liquidation and Royce, who had saved £20, set up a business, F.H. Royce & Co., in Blake Street, Manchester. Some months later Ernest Claremont, another with electrical training, joined him, investing £50 into the business (a recent biography of Claremont by Tom Clarke suggests that Claremont's £50 was borrowed from his father and Claremont in turn lent it to Royce). They moved within a short time to 1a Cooke Street, Manchester.

At this time gas was still the main source of lighting, both public and private. It was only five years earlier that Swan had made his first successful carbon filament electric light bulb, and there were still very few public supplies of electricity. If any organisation wanted electricity it would almost certainly have to install and operate its own generating plant. F.H. Royce & Co. started with small items for individual sales such as an electric bell-set, and quickly moved into sub-contract work producing bulb holders, switches, fuses and filaments as well as complete bulbs and registering instruments. But they soon moved on to complete installations. Later, Royce said of his skills at this time:

In dynamo work, in spite of insufficient ordinary and technical education, I managed to conceive the importance of sparkless commutation, the superiority of the drum-wound armature for continuous current dynamos. Royce and Co. Ltd. of Manchester became famous for continuous current dynamos which had sparkless commutation in the days before carbon brushes. While at Liverpool from 1882 to 1883, I conceived the value of the three-wire system of conductor in efficiency and economy of distribution of electricity, and also, afterwards, the scheme of maintaining a constant potential at a distant point. Both of these I successfully applied. In the early days I discovered and demonstrated the cause of broken wires in dynamos through the deflection of the shafts by weight and magnetism.

This ability to observe, think about and then improve on existing machines and instruments was to be a consistent theme throughout Royce's life.

Profits were fed back into the business, which developed and eventually produced dynamos, motors, winches and cranes. Claremont concerned himself with sales, finance and virtually everything of a non-technical nature. As with most small businesses, life was precarious. Royce told the *News Chronicle* in an interview many years later:

For many years I worked hard to keep the company going through its very difficult days of pioneering, personally keeping our few machine tools working on Saturday afternoons when men did not wish to work, and I remember many times our position was so precarious that it seemed hopeless to continue. Then, owing to the great demand for the lighting dynamos we made for cotton mills, ships and other lighting plants, we enjoyed a period of prosperity.

In the early struggling years, Royce and Claremont lived together in a room over the workshop. According to Harold Nockolds:

[T]heir only diversion at this time was a card game called 'Grab', which appears to have been a combination of all-in wrestling and strip poker. At any rate they both wore tightly-buttoned overalls when playing the game, which generally ended in their rolling about on the floor, fighting like a couple of puppies.

What the business needed was a steady stream of straightforward work to cover the overheads while Royce could give free rein to his creative genius. Certainly he became obsessed with work, often staying late into the night and even all through the night. On a number of occasions those arriving next morning would find him at a work-bench asleep with his head on his arms.

By the end of the 1880s the firm was sufficiently prosperous for Royce and Claremont to consider other matters besides the next item of production and the next source of income.

Most of the early biographies of Royce assumed that both Royce and Claremont married in the same year. However, this was not so. Official records show that on 19 January 1889 Claremont married Edith Punt (born 1864) who was then living at 147 Euston Road, London, at Old St. Pancras Church, Euston Road. Royce married Edith's sister, Minnie Grace, then of 20 Grosvenor Gardens, Willesden, London in March 1893, at the Church of St. Andrew, Willesden.

The Royces moved into a house called Eastbourne, 2 Holland Park Road (now Zetland Road), Chorlton-cum-Hardy, and Royce found his mother a house nearby. (In 1889 he had brought her up from Tunbridge Wells to live with him in 45 Barton Street, Moss Side. They employed a fifteen-year-old servant girl, Patricia Brady.) Royce visited his mother almost every night on his way home from work. Frequently this was, of course, very late, and he would find her propped up in bed knitting socks for him. Mrs. Royce finally died in 1904 and was buried at the District Council Cemetery in Knutsford.

Also in 1893, Royce had the good fortune to acquire the services of John De Looze as cashier and accountant. He was able to relieve Royce and Claremont of much of the administration, and also took on the thankless task of trying to ensure that Royce took some nourishment during the day. He would send small boys chasing after him with glasses of milk, with instructions not to return until Royce had drunk them.

The same year the partnership of Royce and Claremont was converted into a limited company with the title F.H. Royce & Co. Ltd., Electrical and Mechanical Engineers, and Manufacturers of Dynamos, Motors and Kindred Articles. The directors were Royce, Claremont and a friend of Claremont, James P. Whitehead, who provided extra capital to cope with the demand for dynamos. John De Looze was named secretary, a position he occupied in F.H. Royce & Co. Ltd., then Royce Ltd., and finally Rolls-Royce Limited until he retired in 1943.

The next year the partners decided that further capital would be required to cope with expected expansion and, as a result, a valuation of the business was carried out. From the valuation document we can see that the business was now quite substantial, with a turning and fitting shop, capstan lathe shop, lamp store room, brass finishing room, store room, boiler house, packing shop and yard, pattern room, dynamo room, girls' workroom, cook house, instrument room, general office, private office, showroom, staircase and entrance. The inventory included fifty-three machines, of which thirty were lathes, seven drilling machines and five milling machines or planes. There was also plant at the Manchester Ship Canal Contract owned by the company. (Royce had carried out considerable sub-contract work on the canal, which was built between 1887 and 1894.) The valuation put on the business, excluding premises which were rented, work in progress and finished products, was £2,721 18s 4^d (about £300,000 in today's terms).

The next major project was a series of electrical cranes. By October 1897, the firm had £6,000 worth of orders (about £660,000 today). By February 1899 the figure was £20,000. Further working capital was required, and in 1899 a prospectus was issued seeking £30,000 (over £3 million today) in new share capital. At the same time F.H. Royce & Co. Ltd. became Royce Ltd. (the former was wound up as the latter was formed). Some £20,000 was needed for additional works, and £10,000 for the 'general requirements of the business', what would be called working capital today. At this time, the net value of assets was stated as £20,664, or nearly ten times the figure of 1894. (The valuation of the business in 1894 looks a little unsophisticated. For example, work in progress is surely an asset of the company.)

The flotation was successful and Trafford Park Industrial Estate was chosen as the site for a new factory, the design of which was largely undertaken by Royce himself. It was situated immediately across the road from W.T. Glover, and the relationship between Henry Edmunds (by this time running Glover's following Walter Glover's death in 1893) and Royce Limited became closer. The new factory was occupied in 1901 with the transfer of the iron foundry and crane manufacture from Cooke Street. This was the same industrial estate where Henry Ford assembled the first Model Ts in Europe in 1912, and where Ford built the Rolls-Royce Merlin engines in the Second World War.

The Royce electric crane became legendary for its longevity and reliability and in due course was exported throughout the world, including Japan. The Japanese Imperial Navy installed one in their dockyard at Kobe, and when Royce's agents subsequently visited the yard to see if the crane was performing satisfactorily, they found that the Navy had paid it the ultimate compliment. The copy also had a Royce nameplate!

The success of the cranes and the business generally allowed Royce the luxury of building his own house in the fashionable Legh Road, Knutsford. It was a large house, but for some reason the Royces called it Brae Cottage. The house was set in a substantial garden, in which Royce characteristically worked extremely hard.

One of Royce's colleagues was to say later:

His one recreation was gardening. He was a great believer in root pruning, and kept his apple and pear trees very small, but they always bore plenty of the most beautiful fruit. He also went in largely for roses, and though he never sent any to a show I feel sure they would have won prizes if he had done so. He was a great lover of the country and no one enjoyed a drive more than he did. He was always most careful to clear up any mess after a picnic.

Unfortunately, the prosperity of the business was short-lived. The Boer War caused a general slump in trade, and more specifically, cheaper dynamos and cranes arrived in Britain from Germany, while subsidiaries of United States companies, such as Westinghouse, started up production in Britain. The resulting over-capacity brought downward pressure on prices. Royce's colleagues probably suggested a cheapening of their products to make them more competitive, but the perfectionist Royce would not hear of it. The early 1900s were difficult for Royce Ltd., and as we have seen, Royce turned his attention to motor cars as a potential new product for the company. Claremont was not enthusiastic, preferring to try to ride out the recession.

At weekends Royce would drive his car round the Cheshire lanes, and on Monday morning would put two young apprentices, Platford and Haldenby, to work on improvements he had devised. Frustrated with the inadequacies of the Decauville (although in many ways by the standards of the day it was advanced, and therefore he saw he could build on it), Royce decided in the spring of 1903 to make a prototype car of his own.

Some have tried to give the impression that it was almost by chance that Royce became involved in designing a motor car. Royce was not a man to rely on chance. He saw that the motor car had a great future, and that it would be an ideal product for his business, by this time suffering from cheaper, competitive products which in some cases were using his patents without payment of a royalty.

The experimental car would have a 10 hp two-cylinder engine with a bore of 95 mm and a stroke of 127 mm, with overhead inlet and side exhaust valves. By giving it ample water-cooling spaces, Royce hoped to avoid the overheating problems which plagued so many early cars. There were very few accessory makers, and anyway Royce would have found their products unsatisfactory. Initially he had to use a French Longuemare carburettor until

11

he had designed his own and, with his electrical experience, found no problem with ignition, designing his own trembler coil and distributor. Whereas the average clutch at the time provided only two positions, in and out, which made a smooth start almost impossible, Royce's clutch provided a progressive engagement, allowing a smooth take-off.

There was nothing revolutionary about Royce's car. He had taken the best of current automobile design and improved on every aspect of it.

Frank Lord was to write the following about Royce's first car in an obituary in *Autocar* after Royce's death:

In 1904 he produced the first Royce car: this was before he had met the late Hon. C.S. Rolls. The car was a 10 hp. two-cylinder, and was a revelation for its date, having properly lubricated joints to the shaft drive. As he could not buy a satisfactory coil for the ignition, he designed one, fitting very large points of the purest platinum, which, although expensive in the first place, never seemed to want adjusting or cleaning. The coil itself was as nearly perfect as possible, thus from the very first making the car reliable in a part in which, with most cars, there was endless trouble.

I had the great pleasure and privilege of going with him on the first trial run the car ever made. We left Knutsford one morning shortly after eleven, and arrived in Abergale, about eighty miles away, for lunch, and then drove on to Beaumaris on the Menai Straits. The next day we ran on through Barmouth to Aberystwyth, driving back to Knutsford on the day following, through Shrewsbury. During the whole three days' trial we never had a stop of any sort from any fault of the car, a pretty good performance for a car designed by a man who had never designed one before; yet only what you could expect from one designed by Mr. Royce.

Arthur Wormald, later works manager at Rolls-Royce, Derby, said of Royce's early work on motor cars:

I do not think that Sir Henry did anything of a revolutionary nature in his work on motor cars in the early days; he did, however, do much important development and a considerable amount of re-designing of existing devices and apparatus, so that his motor cars were far and away better than anyone else's motor cars.

I cannot say there was any outstanding original invention incorporated in the 10 hp two-cylinder cars, but I can say that every unit of that car was of a better and sounder design than was to be found in contemporary makes. He paid great attention to the smallest detail and the result of his personal consideration to every little thing resulted in the whole assembly being of a very high standard of perfection.

It is rather to Sir Henry's thoroughness and attention to even the smallest detail than to any revolutionary invention that his products have the superlative qualities that we all know so well. The overhead valve was not an innovation of Sir Henry's; others had it but Sir Henry's method of applying it was years ahead of the rest. In the same way Sir Henry was not the first to adopt shaft drive in place of chains, but here again his shaft drive cut out many weaknesses in the then existing designs.

One major weakness of existing cars was noise, and Royce concentrated on making his car as quiet as possible. He paid close attention to the valve gear, exhaust manifold, carburettor intake and silencer, as well ensuring that every part was meticulously made and assembled to eliminate every cause of noise and rattle. The result was a quietness that stood in sharp contrast to the noise of other makes.

But none of this was achieved lightly. If Royce had driven himself before, he now became almost fanatical in his desire to produce the best motor car. As Nockolds said:

To many he would have seemed a hard task-master in those hectic days, but it is only fair to add that he drove no one harder than himself. In order to solve one particularly knotty problem he did not leave the works for three days and nights, his only rest being a few hours' sleep on a bench.

Fortunately, Platford and Haldenby became equally inspired and worked almost the same punishing hours, up to a hundred hours a week and for just five shillings (25p or £25 in today's terms). Platford was to become Rolls-Royce's chief tester until he died prematurely in 1938. After his death, Ernest Hives, by then general manager and a director, decreed that no one else would ever have the title. Haldenby went on to become assistant works manager by the outbreak of the Second World War, and deputy general works manager later. We shall see that the great climax to his career was the design and supervision of the building of the Crewe and Glasgow factories at the beginning of the Second World War. Both Platford and Haldenby attributed their dedication, and that of others, to the respect they all held for Royce because of his ability for hard work and the fact that he could do every man's job better than the man himself. One employee, Ivan Evernden, said later:

I not only admired him, I was one of the few people who were genuinely fond of him . . . Henry Royce ruled the lives of the people around him, claimed their body and soul, even when they were asleep.

The first cars were not made without a certain amount of friction within the Cooke Street works. To begin with, Claremont did not initially share Royce's enthusiasm for the new project and he would ask Royce how his 'two guinea an ounce' job was progressing. The works manager, Hulley, found himself fighting to keep the mechanics working on the day-to-day business of producing dynamos, winches and so on while Royce was inclined to switch them over to work on his cars. And Royce's perfectionist approach was paramount.

As the first car approached completion, a mechanic bent the front axle 'cold' in order to overcome a half-inch discrepancy. Royce was outraged at 'this foul practice', denouncing it both for its bad workmanship and for its lowering of the safety margin. Platford would recall later how Royce scrapped the whole axle, even though it delayed the eagerly awaited first trial run.

Ian Lloyd, in his research for his trilogy on Rolls-Royce, unearthed Ernest Wooler, a retired engineer living in the USA, who had served his apprenticeship under Royce in 1903. In Wooler's view, it entitled him to claim that he was the first premium apprentice in the British motor industry. He wrote to Lloyd in 1948:

Royce, Claremont and De Looze often visited our home when I was a child so it was only natural I became the first premium apprentice in the motor-car industry in 1903 at 6/- a week, if I was on time, 6.00am till 5.30pm, and lots of overtime for and with Mr. Royce, at 2d per hour. After we got the sketches of the Decauville car they were used by the draughtsmen, two 'experienced' auto designers, Adams and Shipley, to design the Royce 2 cyl. car. But 'Old man Royce' did the designing . . . every little detail, all calculated out and each and every one with Royce's mechanical genius standing out all over it. The radiator design, not for beauty but mechanically correct which gave it mechanical beauty and class etc. etc. I helped assemble the first car and Royce worked right along with us in overalls at times. He wanted a leather washer or gasket one day – or rather night. Nothing in the stock room was suitable or at least I could not find anything. Impatiently he tore off one of his leather leggings he wore occasionally in those days and threw it at me to 'make it out of that quickly'. He sometimes came to the works with only one legging on, or without a tie. Motor cars on his mind all the time . . . Royce's personal interest in everyone's work was very gratifying. He'd rush through his electrical work to get on to his plaything – as we thought the Royce car, especially in the Drawing office, much to the disgust of the electrical department and the delight of the few favoured ones on motor-car work.

We sure missed Mr. Royce when we went to Derby. He never came down while we were building the works and very little afterwards. He was too busy and interested in the engineering in Manchester.

My favourite story of Rolls-Royce workmanship – design and quality to Americans when they ask me about it, as they often do – is the use of taper bolts instead of rivets. I remember Royce carefully explaining to me as a child how a hot rivet never filled a hole when it cooled. A cold rivet was punishing the metal too much. So we made taper bolts fitted perfectly in a hand-reamed hole. It is such details that explain the difference between Rolls-Royce and other cars and Rolls-Royce quality. Also Royce himself, who taught us all the principles which carried on in the whole organisation.

The first car was completed in the spring of 1904 and was used personally by Royce. The second was driven by Claremont but was also used to try out various modifications. As a result it was not consistently reliable and Claremont would have a hansom cab follow him. Whenever the car broke down, Claremont would abandon it, send a telegram to Cooke Street, and resume his journey in the hansom. This unreliability was a source of some embarrassment, and he put up a notice in front of his passengers which read: 'If the car breaks down please don't ask a lot of silly questions.'

This first car, like its successors, was not revolutionary in any single part but in the excellence of the whole. However, the battery and trembler coil ignition system had benefited from Royce's electrical background, and there was a new carburettor, along with a well-designed exhaust system with a huge silencer. The engine had two cylinders, and drove the rear wheels through a cone clutch and three-speed gearbox, propeller shaft and differential on the rear axle. Maximum speed was about 30 mph and the car weighed 14.5 cwt.

THE HON. C.S. ROLLS

The Hon. Charles Rolls's significance in the history of Rolls-Royce has been the subject of considerable debate. Those keen to downgrade it have pointed to the fact that he died only six years after meeting Henry Royce and that, during this period, his interest seemed to move on from selling motor cars to flying aeroplanes. Others, most notably Lord Montagu of Beaulieu, whose book *Rolls of Rolls-Royce* was published by Cassell in 1966, have sought to establish his importance in the early days of the company.

Charles Stewart Rolls was born on 27 August 1877, at 35 Hill Street, Berkeley Square, London, a house rented by his father, John Allan Rolls, Justice of the Peace for Monmouthshire and recently High Sheriff for the county. Some historians have liked to speculate that Henry Royce, then a messenger with the Post Office in the Mayfair area, might have delivered telegrams of congratulations to 35 Hill Street. Gordon Bruce, who wrote *Charlie Rolls – pioneer aviator* for the Rolls-Royce Heritage Trust, wondered also whether Royce was a Rolls tenant when, as he said, he 'lived in a third floor flat in the Old Kent Road' while he worked at the Bankside Power Station in 1881 and 1882.

The Rolls family fortune had been founded by his great, great grandfather John (1735–1801), a dairy farmer who had bought freeholds and leaseholds on both sides of the Old Kent Road. In 1767 John married Sarah Coysh and this expanded the family's holdings into Bermondsey, Camberwell, Newington and Southwark. It also brought sufficiently large estates in Monmouthshire to warrant his appointment as High Sheriff in 1794. John also expanded his business interests by building houses, first for the gentry, and then for London's growing artisan population.

15

His son John (1776–1837) nearly gambled the family fortune away. In 1806 the press reported that a 'dashing Cow-Keeper's son in the Kent Road has, during the past summer, been pigeoned of near £60,000 [nearly £7 million in today's terms]'. John lived more quietly after this and his son, John Etherington Welch Rolls (1807–70) based himself at The Hendre, a farmhouse near Monmouth, part of the dowry of Sarah Coysh. John Etherington and his son, John Allan Rolls (1837–1912) built a mansion at The Hendre and concentrated on the family's agricultural estates in Monmouthshire while, at the same time, completing the family's residential developments in London.

In 1892, when John Allan Rolls was raised to the peerage as Baron Llangattock of The Hendre, the Surrey properties were yielding £33,900 (about £3.39 million today) in rent. Llangattock owned 6,100 acres in Monmouthshire and his London estates housed '60,000 of the working class'. Shortly after the birth of his son, Charles, John Allan Rolls bought South Lodge, Rutland Gate, Knightsbridge, which gave the family a London base as well as their estate in Monmouthshire.

Charles received a conventional upper-class education. After Mortimer Vicarage Preparatory School in Berkshire, he followed his father and elder brothers, John and Henry, to Eton. While still at Eton he installed a dynamo at The Hendre and wired part of the house for electricity. His early interest in things mechanical and electrical earned him the nickname 'dirty Rolls' at Eton. In 1894 Charles moved on to Herbert Pigg's private crammer at Norwich House, Panton Street, Cambridge, with the aim of being accepted by Trinity College, Cambridge. His enthusiasm for individualism, science and speed was satisfied for the moment by the bicycle and cycling. History says that he won a half-blue for cycling but, as G.R.N. Minchin wrote in his book *Under My Bonnet*, published by G.T. Foulis in 1950:

Lady Shelley-Rolls (Rolls' sister) was not certain of this. I very much doubt if 'Blues' or even 'Half-Blues' were ever awarded for cycling. They certainly were not in my day.

Rolls's enthusiasm for the new 'autocar' seems to have been fired by a weekend spent at the house of Sir David Salomons, an early pioneer of motoring in Britain, in February 1896. Rolls wrote to his father:

I intend going in for one of these some time and have been saving up for a considerable time for the purpose.

In the history of motoring, as well as in the history of Rolls-Royce, Charles Rolls is important as one of the early popularisers of motoring and as one of

16

those prepared to stand up to the defenders of the *status quo* who wanted to resist the progress and development of the 'infernal machine'. He joined the Self-Propelled Traffic Association which had been founded by Sir David Salomons and Harry Lawson in December 1895 to repeal the legal restrictions on road vehicles, became a member of the Automobile Club of France, also founded in 1895, and was a founder member, and on the committee until 1908, of the Automobile Club of Great Britain and Ireland (later the RAC).

Rolls also participated in almost every major 'goggles and dust' race and trial that time would permit. In the Thousand Mile Reliability Trial, London to Edinburgh, of 1900, driving a 12 hp Panhard, he won the Automobile Club's gold medal for the best amateur performance. In 1905 he was the British representative in the race in France for the International Trophy offered by James Gordon Bennett (1841–1918), proprietor of the *New York Herald*. And in October 1896 Charles went to Paris and spent all his savings, as well as a loan from his father, on a second-hand 3¾ hp Peugeot Phaeton. This was believed to be the first car ever based in Cambridge. It was soon followed by two mechanical tricycles, a DeDion and a Bollee. Charles used the university engineering laboratories to work on these vehicles. According to Minchin, Rolls decided to be the first undergraduate to go up to Cambridge in a motor-propelled vehicle.

'Our family happened to know the Chief Constables of Hertfordshire and Cambridgeshire,' Lady Shelley-Rolls said, 'and my brother, who always asked for – and generally got – anything he wanted, went boldly to them and extracted promises that in view of his pioneer journey, they would instruct their men to close their eyes when he passed.' This encouraged him to start his first journey from London to Cambridge. He and a companion left in the evening and as far as Potters Bar they conformed to the law, each taking it in turn to carry the red lantern. Rolls happened to be walking in front at the time when he got into conversation with a policeman. It was about two o' clock in the morning.

'Evening,' said the policeman, 'one of these 'ere 'orseless carriages?'

'Yes,' Rolls replied.

'Don't see many o' them things about 'ere, but I should like to 'ave a ride in one.'

'Jump up, then,' said Rolls, and they both got into the car.

'Now you can just let 'er go 'ow you please down this 'ill for there ain't no one else on the beat for some miles further on.'

So away they went in the bright moonlight, touching the fearful speed of perhaps 20 miles an hour, the policeman holding on like grim death till the engine got too hot to go further. Although water-cooled, there were no radiators in those days and ten miles was the very maximum that could be done without getting more water. As the water began to give out it was necessary to ascertain if the pump was working by putting a hand under a pipe in a box behind. This was the job of the passenger and the water was generally boiling. In order to escape being burnt he (or she) usually said 'yes' when asking if the water was flowing, which untruth often led to disastrous results.

This pioneer run, almost certainly the first from London to Cambridge, ended at Cambridge about 10 a.m. the next day. Approximate time 12 hours, average 4½ miles per hour. A very good average, however, for an 1895 touring car.

Rolls graduated in June 1898 with a degree in Mechanism and Applied Science, and began a career in practical engineering following his acceptance as a student member of the Institution of Civil Engineers. In the autumn of 1898 he worked as a third engineer on the family's steam yacht, *Santa Maria*, and he also enjoyed a brief spell in the workshops of the London and North Western Railway in Crewe (interesting in view of later developments). By 1899 he had set up his own workshop at South Lodge, with drilling and milling machines. But Rolls was not a designer or an innovator. Rather, he was a pioneer of action, and his pioneering over the next few years was concentrated on motoring.

Lord Montagu relates many of his early adventures, including driving down to Monmouth while he was still an undergraduate:

[H]e determined to celebrate Christmas by driving down from South Lodge to the Hendre in the Peugeot. To moderns, to embark on such an adventure in winter with primitive brakes which overheated at the least provocation appears sheer lunacy . . . such pneumatic tyres as were available were treadless and thus incapable of any degree of grip. Anti-freeze was unknown, and one thawed out one's cooling system by lighting fires under the car.

On the journey they had to cope with the 1-in-6 descent of Birdlip Hill.

Birdlip all but proved their Waterloo. The side-brake expired on the steepest part of the hill, while the foot-brake linkage bent under the constant pressure, and the pedal went flat to the floor, leaving the Peugeot careering downhill towards a light which appeared to be a vehicle in the road, but was fortunately a lantern in a cottage window. They narrowly missed heaps of stones but reached the foot of the hill in safety.

Montagu said of Rolls:

Among his contemporaries, Rolls stands out by virtue of his understanding of the motor-car and its workings. He could never have matched my father's appreciation of its social significance; he never went to such lengths in his publicity campaigns as did Edge, nor had he Claude Johnson's organising ability . . . But everyone who rode with Rolls testifies to the quickness of his reaction, and to the sensation that he was at one with his steed.

Rolls was not an easy man to work for. According to Minchin:

Rolls was a man of very fixed ideas and he was in some ways erratic. For example, he disliked going to a restaurant during a motor run and preferred to eat his meals in the open, often to the great discomfort of his passengers. He had an utter disregard for appearance and on certain occasions this created embarrassment to his friends, particularly as he would always go to the most expensive hotels. Another trouble was that Rolls never had any baggage. The possession of luggage is looked on by hotels as a sort of guarantee or hostage. Without any it was always possible for a visitor to go for a stroll after dinner and to be sufficiently absent-minded as to forget to return!

Two of Rolls' friends told me they had constant trouble with him over this question of baggage. Apparently Rolls carried only a razor, a few handkerchiefs and some socks in his pockets! On long trips abroad he did take an extra flannel shirt and a celluloid collar, but in spite of this additional wardrobe a friend suffered badly when Rolls would go to the smartest hotel in Biarritz, at the height of the season. 'It is a pity you did not stay longer at Eton where you might have become civilized,' he was told by his friend.

And this is what his friend, Moore-Brabazon, later Lord Brabazon of Tara, wrote about him:

Charlie Rolls was the strangest of men and one of the most lovable [sic]. He was tall and rather thin, and his eyes stood out of their sockets rather more than is normal. He was rather fond of a Norfolk jacket – a thing you seldom see nowadays – and always wore a very high, stiff, white collar. He'd look a bit odd today, but at that time this kit was in no way absurd. While motoring he would turn his cap back to front.

He was greatly imaginative, almost prophetic, possessing a very sound knowledge of mechanics. He was of course a very good driver, and early inculcated in me the maxim that the first thing a driver had to do in a race was to concentrate on getting the car home. Nothing else was so important as to finish. Wise words, and no one was better at carrying out his own advice than Charlie Rolls. He had a wonderful sympathy with machinery – 'hands' I suppose one would call it in horsey language.

Away from his own subjects he never tried to take part in a conversation, but he had many subjects and was clever at turning the conversation along his chosen line. He did not suffer fools gladly and his sense of humour was rather crude – rather like that of the Japanese, who roar with laughter when someone trips over a carpet and nearly breaks his neck. Subtleties and sly digs passed right over him, and he was always a bit aloof, for he was not a good mixer; but to his real friends, who were few, he was a good companion if you were both interested in the same thing. Incidentally, he was a snob too: the way he used his superb powers of salesmanship to float early Rolls-Royce cars on the aristocracy of England left every other firm an 'also ran'.

When Royce and Rolls came together, Royce provided the original engineering but Rolls's contribution both in market intelligence and in the use of his contacts was vital to the early and critical days of the joint venture. When Rolls first went to Manchester to meet Royce he had been looking for a three- or four-cylinder car to sell to his clients. Nevertheless, he was so impressed with Royce's two-cylinder car that he knew he could sell it as it was.

It was Rolls's name that was stressed in the early advertising. The 1905 catalogue mentioned Messrs. Royce Ltd. on page three as the manufacturer of the car exclusively for C.S. Rolls & Co. The catalogue, with its twenty pages, contained comprehensive details of the range of cars, a large number of testimonials from the small number of owners, and biographies (including photographs) of Rolls and Johnson, but ignoring Royce altogether. Up to August 1905, Rolls continued to divide his advertising equally between Rolls-Royce, Minerva and Orleans. But his efforts were increasingly concentrated on Rolls-Royce.

While the agreement between C.S. Rolls and Royce Ltd. was still being drafted, Rolls included a display of Rolls-Royce chassis and engines on the Rolls stand at the Paris salon in December 1904. A Royce two-cylinder 10 hp and a Rolls-Royce two-cylinder 10 hp were also at the show, in order to give rides to prospective buyers. Rolls had been looking for a British replacement for his French Peugeots and Belgian Minervas, and in Royce's car he felt he had found it. When it was awarded a gold medal at the salon he felt his confidence was justified. Outside the salon he gave demonstrations in a 10 hp car to as many journalists and prospective customers as possible. The silent running seemed to impress them most. The motoring correspondent of *The Times* wrote:

When the engine is running one can neither hear nor feel it, and pedestrians never seemed to hear the car's approach.

Country Life was even more eulogistic:

It [the 10 hp] was, in a single word, a revelation . . . never before have I been in a car which made so little noise, vibrated so little, ran so smoothly or could be turned about so easily and readily in a maze of traffic.

It went on to sound a note of caution:

Indeed, the conclusion I reached then and there was that the car was too silent and too ghost-like to be safe. That the engine could be set running while the car was at rest without any noise or vibration perceptible to the occupants of the car was good; that the car in motion should overtake numerous wayfarers without their giving any indication of their having heard it, so that the horn had frequently to be called into use, was almost carrying excellence too far.

When he returned to England, Rolls passed on the comments of the prospective customers to Royce. It was silence and smoothness that most seemed to want. Royce needed little persuading, as these two attributes appealed to him on technical grounds anyway.

And in Britain both Rolls and Johnson were doing all they could to publicise the excellence of Royce's cars. At the end of 1904, Rolls was due to meet at Folkestone HRH the Duke of Connaught, one of Queen Victoria's sons and Commander-in-Chief of the British land forces. Rolls was hoping to convince the Duke that some of his officers should be in cars, not on horses. He made sure many people knew that such was his faith in the reliability of his 10 hp Royce that he would not leave London the day before, but would leave on the same morning of the meeting. He duly met the Duke on time, took him along the south coast and returned to London the same day, after completing 220 miles.

He worked hard on journalists, taking Foster Pedley of Lord Montagu's *Car Illustrated* as his mechanic on the Twenty's preliminary trials in the Isle of Man. He also took W. Worby Beaumont, engineer to the Automobile Club of Great Britain, to the Motor Union's rally at the Duke of Westminster's home, Eaton Hall, Chester, in July 1905. When the headmaster of Eton retired, Rolls did not miss the opportunity to suggest to old Etonians that a Rolls-Royce would make a most suitable leaving present.

At the end of 1906, Charles Rolls travelled to the USA to promote the new Rolls-Royces. He exhibited at the Association of Licensed Automobile Manufacturers' Show in New York's Madison Square Garden in January 1907. The *Manchester Evening Chronicle* described 'Manchester's record order for America' when Rolls persuaded Walter Martin, the newly appointed concessionaire in New York, to commit to taking seventeen cars in 1906 and fifty in 1908. (Rolls's real reason for going to the USA was to meet the Wright brothers as he was, by this time, hooked on the new flying craze. He was successful in this mission.)

Rolls also won a Silver Trophy in a five-mile race at the Empire City Track, New York. (The track still exists and is used for horse-racing. A picture of Rolls is on display.) He drove a Light Twenty and covered the five miles in five minutes 52 seconds, apparently resisting all attempts by the US drivers to jockey him out of the way. He completed the course faster than a 30 hp Packard, a 45 hp Peerless, a 60 hp Renault and a 45 hp Westinghouse.

In 1906, Rolls took Massac Buist, a contemporary at Cambridge, in a Twenty on an attempt to break the Monte Carlo to London record, which stood at 37.5 hours. This is Buist's account of the hectic drive:

In checking over the provisions after 'C.S.R.' had gone to bed on the eve of the attempt, I discovered that there were two half bottles of champagne and much cold tea. On enquiring the scheme of this Mr. Rolls explained quite seriously that the champagne was for himself and that the tea was for the rest of us . . .

In the middle of the night we ran into a driving rain storm, which made the going heavy and greatly increased our difficulties in seeing the road. The car had no latter-day 'all-weather' equipment and I had to thrust the marked route in front of the oil side lamp and try to make out my notes, which 'also ran', the whole book becoming more and more pulp-like. At one level crossing, the gates of which we foreknew would have to be closed at the time we were timed to approach, because an express train would also be due, we had speculated 10 francs on the way down as a tip to the man to be ready to open the gates instantly and momentarily at the sound of our horn – rather a dramatic effect, I had fondly hoped. Because of the storm, however, the wretch assumed we should not turn up, so kept snug in bed. It took us a quarter of an hour to rouse him. Having got him to open the gates we had to look out for an important dividing of the ways a kilometre or so further on. The driver, however, who was so excited by the needless delay and the heavy going, feeling that all the trouble was for naught, forged ahead furiously. Soon we were unmistakably on the wrong road, having shot past the fork while I was struggling with the map under the feeble flicker of the lamp in a high wind and rain that fell like steel rods. We had better turn back. But C.S.R. would not do so, wherefore we drove on. It was impossible to read any road signs, and at that speed it would have been even in a blaze of sunshine! I remember approaching Dijon towards dawn, when we were about two hours behind the record.

But the car never faltered; nor did the British-made tyres let us down . . .

Of course, with the coming of the sunlight and the passing of the stormy and chilly night, we were all as blithe as birds. Thereafter everything went even better than our most sanguine expectations. To see that little car recover those lost two hours and begin beating the record a second time as the day advanced was a heartening revelation. We reached Boulogne – 771 miles from the start, traversed in 28 hours 14 minutes, including all stops, loss of direction and the night storm – and had 3 hours 11 minutes to wait on Boulogne Quay before preparations for departure commenced.

In spite of the long wait they broke the record, but only just – by one and a half minutes!

As the Rolls-Royce partnership progressed and moved towards a fully fledged company, Rolls's attention turned towards flying. He had always been interested in ballooning (he shared this interest with one of his closest friends from Cambridge days, John Theodore Cuthbert Moore-Brabazon, who eventually became Lord Brabazon of Tara and chaired the eponymous committee in the Second World War which looked at the prospects for civil aviation after the war), but when Rolls was in the USA promoting Rolls-Royce cars in 1906, as we have seen, he secured an introduction to the Wright brothers. When he met them again in France in 1908 and flew with them, he said:

After experiencing every sort of locomotion, including cycling and motor racing, a voyage in a French army dirigible and over 130 trips in an ordinary balloon, there is nothing so fascinating or exhilarating as flying.

According to Wilton J. Oldham in *The Hyphen in Rolls-Royce,* Ernest Claremont applied his rigorous attention to costs to the activities of Rolls' London depot once it became part of Rolls-Royce Limited. He was appalled to find that Rolls was employing men in the depot to work on Colonel Capper's airship *Nulli Secundus* instead of on customers' cars. Oldham wrote:

. . . the Directors were not very pleased and there was a row. This was the last straw for Rolls, always a bad loser.

Claremont, never keen for Rolls-Royce to become involved with aircraft or aero engines, had probably become disenchanted with Rolls after he found that C.S. Rolls & Co. had some bad debts when it was absorbed into Rolls-Royce Limited in 1907, a disenchantment fuelled by Rolls's reluctance to remove his name from the business at Lillie Hall, Fulham, where he had set up as an automobile agent in 1903, and by his wanting to continue to trade in the accessories he had sold as C.S. Rolls & Co.

Rolls, a founder member of the Aero Club, had tried to persuade Royce to design an aero engine but Royce had shown little interest, believing that the commercial market was too limited. However, through Rolls, Royce did act as a consultant to the Army on the airship being developed at Farnborough. And Claude Johnson was associated with flying in his capacity as founder secretary of the Aero Club. The one person who was definitely opposed to involvement in aero engines was Claremont. He refused to allow Rolls-Royce to take a licence to manufacture the Wright Flier which Rolls had advocated.

Now, Rolls turned his attention almost fully to flying. He told *The Times* in October 1908:

The sensation of flight was delightful and novel, and the fact of accomplishing what several eminent scientists have 'proved' impossible gave also an added satisfaction.

Before powered aircraft were available to him, Rolls's interest in flight was focused on ballooning. This is what his close friend, Moore-Brabazon, wrote about those pioneering days in his book, *The Brabazon Story*:

In these early days of ballooning Charlie Rolls was again my greatest friend and collaborator. We were both discontented with the type of balloon made by Spencer Brothers, who almost had the monopoly in those days. We discovered two delightful young brothers named Short, who were doing ballooning shows, and we asked them if, after they had studied balloon manufacture in France, they would make us a balloon. This they did after a sojourn in France to pick up the latest technique. They took a place in Battersea under the arches of the railway at the bottom of Lower Sloane Street, and there they made their first balloon for Charlie Rolls and myself. It was called the *Venus*, and we made many very satisfactory flights in it. Incidentally, it was the first spherical balloon made in England.

It seems clear that Rolls was not only interested in flying but also in becoming involved in the whole aeroplane business. He bought one of the six Wright biplanes that were built under licence by Short Brothers and, in May 1909, *Flight* magazine reported that he had

generously placed his [Wright] machine at the disposal of the War Office. A shed is being erected for it by the military authorities, and a suitable ground for testing purposes has been provided.

And in February 1910 *Flight* again reported:

A large shed is being erected on Hounslow Heath, which is, we understand, to accommodate the Wright flyer to be used by the army officers for their aeroplane training. It is probable that the Hon. C.S. Rolls will be actively identified with the initial training of the first flying pilots of the British Army.

Lord Montagu, in his book *Rolls of Rolls-Royce,* disagrees with Oldham about Rolls's loss of interest in Rolls-Royce:

It is fashionable to regard Rolls in these later years as paying only lip-service to Rolls-Royce Ltd. This is far from the truth. The work was unexciting – a steady round of meetings and demonstrations, and not at all the life to be expected of one who had been the Golden Boy of British motoring . . . There were no more dashes down the routes nationales, for these were unnecessary . . . Nevertheless, Rolls was tirelessly demonstrating Rolls-Royces up and down the country.

But even Montagu has to concede that by 1909 his contribution, if not negligible, had become erratic:

Rolls kept irregular hours. Miss Caswell remembers his disconcerting habit of appearing without warning, even at times when he had announced his intention of being absent for three weeks. He would forget appointments with the demonstration car, and his secretary would make frantic telephone calls to South Lodge . . . His office hours became even more erratic when he took up flying in 1909. But he carried on until the conflict of interests became irreconcilable, both to himself and his fellow-directors.

At the end of 1909, Rolls relinquished his position as technical director and moved out of Conduit Street. He remained a non-executive director.

Rolls flew his Wright biplane for the first time in early October 1909 but an accident which necessitated repair work meant he did not fly regularly until 1 November. Between then and the end of February 1910 he made more than 200 flights, some with passengers, in the two Wrights he now owned. One had been built in France, the other by Short Brothers. In March he towed the dismantled Wright behind his car to exhibit it on the Royal Aero Club stand at the Olympia Aero Show. During the show, Rolls sold the aeroplane to the War Office for £1,000 (about £100,000 today) and it was taken first to Eastchurch and then to Farnborough.

Flying was still a very new development. Nevertheless, as Montagu wrote:

1910 promised to be an auspicious year for the new movement. Already the calendar was filling up with a whole new series of important meetings. In France alone, Biarritz, Cannes, Nice, Bordeaux, Lyons, Vichy and Deauville were said to be planning aviation weeks; the Aero Club de France had given its blessing to another event at Heliopolis in Egypt; while Berlin, Budapest, Milan and St. Petersburg had announced their intention of getting into the act . . . Already two British municipalities – Wolverhampton and Bournemouth – were advertising aviation weeks, the latter's to form the centrepiece of the town's centenary celebrations.

Rolls's main ambition in early 1910 was to emulate Bleriot's feat of flying across the Channel. He established himself in a field near Dover in May but was constantly frustrated by the weather, either thick cloud or drifting fog. Finally, on 2 June, he made the journey not only there but back as well, and became a national hero. He was the first person to fly from England to France and the first to complete the two-way flight. The Royal Aero Club presented him with a Gold Medal, King George V sent a telegram of con-gratulations, and Madame Tussaud's set in train the creation of a wax model. The press were ecstatic. The *Daily Mail* said:

This double crossing of the Channel is an encouraging indication that this country is waking up to the real importance of airmanship.

The *Daily Chronicle*, after referring to 'a daring feat brilliantly performed', wrote:

Mr. Rolls has wiped out a reproach which attached to us as a nation for our backwardness in the new art of aviation. [By this time, both De Lesseps and Bleriot had flown from France to England.]

The town of Dover erected a statue of Rolls on the seafront looking out towards France, sculpted by the wife of Scott of the Antarctic. (When it was unveiled in 1912, although her husband had already perished, the news had not yet reached her.)

Rolls moved on to Bournemouth, where he was due to compete with the finest aviators from Britain (Moore-Brabazon, Cecil Grace, S.F. Cody, Claude Grahame-White and Alec Ogilvie), from France (Morane, later to become famous as a builder of high-speed military aircraft, the racing driver Louis Wagner and Edmond Audemars), and from Belgium (Jean Christians, who had also made his name in motor-racing).

Rolls, while making his preparations, spoke of his plans for the future. He had been asked to train army pilots at Farnborough (the War Office was beginning to show interest in this new invention which could pose a military threat). He was planning another trip to the USA, where he expected to meet his mentors, the Wright Brothers, again. He had also discussed with friends the possibility of forming a company to build the Rolls Powered Glider, which he had designed.

But, as we know, none of this was to happen. On 12 July 1910, in a manoeuvre which necessitated landing on a chalked-out circle in front of the grandstand, Rolls brought his French-built Wright aircraft down in a steep glide and pulled the nose up sharply. His experimental tail-plane could not take the strain and disintegrated. The aeroplane plunged into the ground and Rolls died within minutes.

THE HYPHEN IN ROLLS-ROYCE

As Wilton J. Oldham said in his biography of Claude Johnson, *The Hyphen in Rolls-Royce* (the title was suggested to Oldham by Mike Evans, Chairman of the Rolls-Royce Heritage Trust):

In every book that deals with the early history of motoring, the name Claude Goodman Johnson appears.

Johnson was born on 24 October 1864 at Datchet in Buckinghamshire, the younger son of William Goodman Johnson who, at that time, was in the glove trade. He was one of a family of seven. After several attempts to make a business in various trades, his father eventually worked in the Science and Art department of the South Kensington Museum for a very low salary. He remained there for thirty years and, according to Oldham, 'became an expert in the knowledge of art and many well-known connoisseurs thought highly of him'. Once established, he moved his growing family to Ealing, and to supplement his income acted as a watchman at the museum in Bethnal Green.

After school at St. Paul's (as St. Paul's was an expensive private school, it is likely that he won a scholarship), Claude Johnson went to the Royal College of Art. He soon realised he was no artist, but it was here that he met Sir Philip Cunliffe-Owen, who gave him his first job as a clerk at the Imperial Institute at the age of nineteen. Johnson maintained an eye for the ladies throughout his life, and he began his romantic career by eloping with Fanny Mary Morrieson. Both sets of parents were extremely angry, probably with justification, as the marriage did not work out well.

Under Cunliffe-Owen, Johnson organised a number of exhibitions, including one for Francis Galton, the cousin of Charles Darwin. (Galton, through his probability research, was one of the founders of modern theories on psychology.) Finally in 1896, the Prince of Wales, interested in these new-fangled motor cars, decided that the Imperial Institute was the place for an International Exhibition of Motors and their Appliances, and that Johnson was just the man to organise it. It was at this exhibition that the Prince enjoyed his first ride in a motor car, driven by the Hon. Evelyn Ellis. The success of the exhibition brought Johnson to the attention of the leading figures of the motoring world, and when (as we shall see later) Frederick Simms founded his Automobile Club of Great Britain (now the RAC), Johnson became the temporary secretary at a salary of £5 per week, plus ten shillings commission for each new member (this would be about £28,600 a year and £55 commission per member in today's terms).

In the first year of the club's existence it proved difficult to persuade people to join, despite the reduction of the annual subscription from four guineas to three (£420 to £315 in today's terms. The annual subscription in 2000 is £670). Perhaps the club was too fussy as to whom it would take as members. As Piers Brendon put it in his book, *The Motoring Century: The Story of the Royal Automobile Club*:

Before the First World War motor cars were luxuries that only the prosperous could afford, so the Automobile Club attracted affluent members – an open secret of its success. 'I doubt,' wrote an Edwardian journalist, 'if there be collectively a wealthier club in the world.' But even in an age that was given to the 'worship of wealth', cash was supposed to be matched by cachet. The Automobile Club was a gentleman's club. As its first full-time Secretary, Claude Johnson, said, 'Anyone interested in automobilism is eligible for membership, though, naturally enough, we observe some social restrictions.' This meant that candidates were blackballed if they came from the wrong side of the class divide – lacked the correct 'background', were too obviously 'in trade', had a 'common' appearance, 'ran out of aitches' and so on. Thus the Club decided that 'a working manager was not eligible for election'. It also refused to admit 'professional cycle riders', one of whom was proposed by founder member S.F. Edge. Yet, as if to prove that the restrictions were elastic, Edge himself had been a professional bicycle rider (and a pugilist) before going into the car business and becoming a victorious motor-racing driver.

One of the founder members was Charles Rolls, who would sometimes take his own sandwiches into the Club dining-room. The Club retaliated by making a sixpenny table charge. Another early member was Alfred Harmsworth (later Lord Northcliffe) who, through his *Daily Mail*, did so much to champion motoring in its early days. He was supportive both of the Club and of Johnson, declaring that he 'as much as any man, developed motoring in Great Britain'.

As the Club began to prosper (by the end of the century there were 540 members) and Johnson's salary was raised to £1,000 a year, his organising ability was appreciated by everyone and he dressed the part of a successful man. Brendon wrote:

Well over six feet tall, with a cliff-like forehead, a luxuriant moustache, large capable hands and an intimidatingly taciturn air, Johnson was an impressive figure. Although never a dandy, he was very clothes-conscious and, earning ten shillings per new member on top of an annual salary that rose to £1,000, he dressed impeccably. His eldest daughter remembered 'ginger Harris or off-white hairy tweed, white socks, silkiest of shirts, flowing yellow-and-white silk ties and, more often than not, red morocco slippers when not walking or golfing'. Johnson's wavy brown hair was perfectly groomed and he always smelled of bay rum or eau-de-Cologne. He wore his bowler hat at a slightly rakish angle.

He and his equally handsome friend, Harmsworth, worked in tandem to promote motoring. The *Daily Mail* ran a series of articles in which motor cars were held up as the vehicles of the future. Johnson gave the newspaper general information but would not take payment, feeling it necessary to maintain the independence of the Club. However, in return, the *Mail* praised the Club and would only write about cars that submitted themselves to the Club's tests. Harmsworth also helped Johnson with his Thousand Mile Trial, guaranteeing it financially and offering £450 in prizes. Harmsworth said later that Johnson was 'always modest, never seeking the limelight' and had 'worked untiringly' to organise 'the first great tour of Great Britain, which did so much to prove to the public what a change was soon coming over the deserted state of our roads'.

In 1903 Johnson resigned to pursue a more lucrative career, eventually with Charles Rolls and Rolls-Royce. Brendon listed his achievements.

His powerful hand had not only held the Club together, but had driven it forward into new areas of endeavour. Johnson had negotiated agreements with foreign countries whereby members who obtained 'triptyche' forms could avoid complex customs formalities. He had secured the Irish Automobile Club as 'an affiliated branch' in 1901. He had instituted a system of vetting and licensing hotels suitable for motorists, which could display the Automobile Club sign. He had set up an Engineer's Department to give help to members, especially those buying cars or falling victim to the new breed of 'repairing sharks', and to turn coachmen into chauffeurs. In 1903, too, the Touring Department was instituted to give members information about routes and places of interest. Finally, the dynamic Secretary had begun a programme (towards which Harmsworth, preoccupied by the hazard of 'side-slips', i.e. skids, contributed £100) of erecting green and white, diamond-shaped Control Boards at danger spots.

The partnership of Rolls and Johnson worked well when Johnson joined C.S. Rolls & Co., a company set up by Charles Rolls to sell cars. Both knew the motoring world as well as anyone else in the country, and both had excellent contacts amongst the gentry and aristocracy. As we have seen, Johnson was also a brilliant organiser. On one subject – women drivers – they agreed to differ. Rolls was in favour and was happy to give lessons to a prospective client. Johnson maintained that women's place was in the home, and that driving was hazardous enough without adding women drivers. This was an attitude held by most male drivers for the next hundred years!

ERNEST CLAREMONT

Ernest Claremont is important in the history of Rolls-Royce in that he was Henry Royce's first partner. Indeed, he was Royce's *only* partner, as neither Rolls nor Johnson were partners of Royce in the strict sense of the word – they were co-directors in a limited company.

Claremont came from a completely different background from Royce or indeed from Rolls and Johnson. His was a large, genteel, Victorian, professional middle-class family. His father, Claude Clarke Claremont, was a surgeon, and Ernest was one of ten children born between 1853 and 1869. He was the seventh child, born on 3 February 1863 at 1 Thorney Place, Oakley Square, Camden. He was educated privately and went to University College London, though there is no evidence that he graduated. From 1880 he served as an apprentice for three years at Anglo-American Brush Electric Light Corporation, finally breaking his apprenticeship after an argument with a foreman. He may have met Henry Edmunds at Brush, as Edmunds spent some time promoting its electrical equipment. It is generally believed that Claremont met Royce in London some time in either 1881 or 1882, when Royce was working for the Electric Lighting and Power Generator Company at Bankside on the Thames. Paul Tritton, in his book *The Godfather of Rolls-Royce*, speculated that they may have met at Professor William Ayrton's technical classes at the Finsbury Institute, or possibly at Ayrton's electrical demonstrations elsewhere.

Originally, it was thought that Royce and Claremont came together in 1884 to found F.H. Royce & Co. Tom Clarke points out in his book, *Ernest Claremont*, that it is more likely that Royce founded the business and that Claremont came in with his £50 almost as a rescue operation. Claremont himself said that he worked at a company called Cordner, Allen & Co. in Wandsworth until the end of 1884 and Pemberton says in his biography of Royce that Claremont 'increased subsequently by £50' Royce's capital. Tom Clarke also challenges the long-held belief that F.H. Royce & Co. operated immediately from Cooke Street, and shows that study of local directories suggests that the firm originally rented space in Blake Street. Those games of 'Grab' that we read about earlier probably took place in rooms above the Blake Street premises, as well as at Cooke Street where Royce and Claremont rigged up hammocks and cooked their meals in enamelling stoves, a practice that Claremont was to claim caused the gastric troubles that both he and Royce suffered from later in life.

Once on board, Claremont's responsibilities were sales, contracts, payments and deliveries, although, if needed, he would help at the bench. With him and Royce were six young women assembling the lamps and bells, and a little later Tom Jones acted as their first journeyman. To keep the business ticking over they would take in almost anything, including the repair of sewing machines.

Tom Clarke noted that an amendment in the 1888 Poor Rate records shows that on 3 December 1888 F.H. Royce & Co. moved to the workshops at number 1 and the house at number 3 Cooke Street. The company built its first Cooke Street works extension into the west side of Blake Street in the middle of 1894. A second extension was made in 1895 and a third in 1898/9.

As we have seen, Claremont (in 1889) and Royce (in 1893) married sisters, Edith and Minnie, and in either 1895 or 1896 both took on another family responsibility.

Walter, brother of Edith and Minnie, had moved to South Africa with his wife Helena. They had two children, Violet Helena (1887–1988) and Errol (1889–1967), but shortly after Errol was born Helena died and the two children were sent to England to be cared for by grandmother Punt. When she could no longer cope, Claremont and Edith took in Errol, and the Royces, Violet. Errol did not much enjoy being with the Claremonts.

Mrs. Claremont was recalled by Errol's son, Patrick, as a rather Victorian figure with little sense of humour, no warmth and somewhat anti social. Violet's daughter Mary, on the other hand, certainly recalled her as prudish and easily shocked but not without a sense of fun . . . From 1898, when the Royces moved into their new house in Knutsford, Errol spent much more time with them at Brae Cottage. He came to worship Royce and in his later years rarely mentioned the Claremonts.

Claremont, dapper, proud of his military bearing and fitness, began in the 1890s to look at other business possibilities. He became a director of W.T. Glover in 1899 at £500 (£50,000 in today's terms) per annum. This was doubled to £1,000 in 1902. He replaced Henry Edmunds as Managing Director in 1903 when Edmunds became Chairman. At the same time, they swapped shares in Glover and Royce Ltd. As we have seen, Glover and Royce had built new works opposite each other in the new Trafford Park industrial estate in 1901. Royce Ltd. kept on the Cooke Street premises, which were leased until 1910, and concentrated on cranes at the Trafford Park site. In their 1968 centenary booklet, Glovers noted that Claremont had 'a tremendous influence on the affairs of the company over the next twenty years'. He probably spent more time at Glover than at Royce, and also became a director of Trafford Park Power and Light Company and Howard Conduit Company.

It seems almost certain that Claremont was becoming increasingly disenchanted with Royce's diversifications. He probably did not like the move into cranes, and in the 1899 flotation document the words 'the Directors have no intention of launching out into unfamiliar business' were inserted. As for Royce's move into car manufacture, Claremont was horrified, referring to it as 'the two guinea an ounce job'. Nevertheless, he was assigned an early model, although, as we have seen, he issued instructions for a hansom cab to follow him in case of breakdown. He may not have loved cars or driving, but he still invented a screen-wiper (hand-operated by pulleys), and also a sun visor.

Claremont was not present at the initial meeting between Royce and Rolls, and seems not to have been involved in the subsequent negotiations between the two. When Rolls-Royce Ltd. was formed in March 1906, Claremont, reluctant to leave Manchester, did not become Chairman, as he had been of Royce Ltd. He was described as a 'commercial adviser'.

Nevertheless, he was involved with his brother Albert, solicitor to Rolls-Royce, and Claude Johnson, during the rest of 1906 in drawing up plans for offering shares to the public. He became Chairman in 1907, but did not move to the new works in Derby in 1908. In fact, he tried to resign as Chairman in December 1907 but his resignation was not accepted. He was never as 'hands-on' a Chairman at Rolls-Royce as he was at Glover, a fact reflected in his low remuneration at Rolls-Royce of £250 per annum (raised to £400 in 1910).

Perhaps Claremont's main contribution to Rolls-Royce was his conservative prudence, which acted as a necessary balance to the more adventurous approach of his fellow directors. Furthermore, he never forgot the directors' responsibility to the shareholders.

His other contributions to Rolls-Royce were peripheral, but none the less interesting for that. His relationship with his wife, Edith, became as tricky as those of Royce with his wife, Minnie. Both Edith and Minnie were uncomfortable with the physical aspects of human relationships, and both Claremont and Royce were forced to seek solace elsewhere. In Claremont's case, his most durable relationship outside his marriage was with Clara McKnight. He left the same annuity (£500 a year) to Clara and her sister Harriet as he did to his wife. Royce's solace was Nurse Ethel T. 'Auby' Aubin (1885–1967), his full-time nurse from 1912 until his death. The Claremont entanglement with Royce Ltd. continued after the deaths of both Claremont in 1921 and Royce in 1933. Albert Claremont had taken on the Chairmanship of Royce Ltd. after his brother's death, and after he died, George Henry Richards Tildesley, a partner in Claremont Haynes, took over. In early 1935 he married Nurse Aubin, although the two separated as early as 1937 thanks, according to Tom Clarke, to Tildesley's 'latent homosexuality'.

Errol, the nephew originally billeted with Ernest Claremont, seems to have been almost abandoned by both Claremont and Royce, and indeed neither he nor Violet were mentioned in Royce's will. However, Errol enjoyed a long career with the company. He had joined the Army in 1914 and survived the whole war. Demobilised in 1919, he decided to stay in France, where he joined the company's French operation. He handled Rolls-Royce's liaison with French coachbuilders, and stayed with the French company until he was forced to flee the invading German army in 1940, escaping 'by the skin of my teeth in just what I stood up in plus a small haversack'. He moved to Clan Foundry in Belper and, after a spell with R.W.H. Bailey, whom he had known in Paris, worked for his son, Alec.

CHAPTER TWO

'THE MOST PERFECT CARS'

THE EARLY DAYS
BACKGROUND TO MOTORING IN THE EARLY 1900S
ROYCE'S ILLNESS
THE REPUTATION SPREADS
THE SPIRIT OF ECSTASY
THE COMPETITION

THE EARLY DAYS

THE AGREEMENT BETWEEN Royce Ltd. and the Hon. C.S. Rolls was finally signed on 23 December 1904. It was understood that Royce Ltd. would supply C.S. Rolls with four different types of chassis – a 10 hp two-cylinder model to sell at £395 (£39,500 in today's terms), a 15 hp three-cylinder model at £500, a 20 hp four-cylinder model at £650 and a 30 hp six-cylinder model at £890, all of which would carry the name 'Rolls-Royce'.

These prices were not high by contemporary standards. A 60 hp Mercedes cost no less than £2,500 (£250,000 today) and the six-cylinder Napier, perhaps Rolls-Royce's most formidable early competitor, cost £1,050.

The agreement did not preclude Rolls from selling other cars. Indeed, we know that he continued to act as a distributor for other makes and accessories into 1905 and 1906 and even, as far as accessories were concerned, into 1907. And from Rolls's point of view, it prevented Royce from making cars for anyone else.

As well as driving cars, Charles Rolls had gone into business to sell them, and in January 1903 C.S. Rolls & Co. was set up as an automobile agent with premises at Lillie Hall, Fulham. Apart from Rolls's mission to promote the motor car, he would also have felt the need to help finance his own motoring activities. Rolls's basic allowance was £500 (£50,000) a year, but tyres alone for his car (a set would last only about 2,000 miles) would probably cost about £200. He was not the only Old Etonian in the trade. Claude Watney was also selling Panhards and Mercedes from showrooms in Wardour Street. Lord Montagu's father wrote in his magazine, *Car Illustrated*, in June 1903:

Both these young men, with no need, so far as money is concerned, to work, are throwing themselves heart and soul into the business of this great automobile movement. Both of them were at Eton with me, and several other old Etonians are also interested in the motor trade in one way and another.

To launch this business, Rolls relied on his father to provide £6,600, a sum to be deducted from the £20,000 to be paid to Rolls upon his father's death.

By the time the agreement was signed, the first Rolls-Royce two-cylinder cars had been delivered. Already some improvements had been made to the car Rolls had seen in the spring. Drum brakes had replaced the externally contracting band brakes, the engine had been lengthened and the two-bearing crankshaft now had a third, centre main, bearing. The radiator had also taken on the classic shape that became so famous. The badge that also became famous appeared some time in 1905 to replace an oval brass plaque which said 'The Rolls Royce Radiator', and which had first been used in early 1905.

Royce Ltd. immediately began the manufacture of twenty 10 hp two-cylinder cars. Reliability was the strongest feature of these cars. One of them, sold to a customer in Aberdeenshire, was returned in 1923 in perfect running order after 100,000 miles run over the hilly roads of Scotland. Registration number SU13, this car belongs to Rolls-Royce and is kept at the factory in Crewe. Development work continued, and the first Heavy Twenty was demonstrated at the Olympia Motor Show in 1905.

Royce's constant striving for improvement was tested by the need for a lighter chassis. As motorists demanded more comfort and room, a stronger (and therefore heavier) chassis was needed. This was no problem for the 20 hp car, but Royce increased his metallurgical research to try to find a lighter chassis of equal strength.

A sympathiser was Yorkshire businessman Arthur Briggs, the first purchaser of a Heavy Twenty. Briggs was a believer in the value of racing to improve the quality of cars, and he suggested that Rolls-Royce should compete in the first Tourist Trophy (TT) race being organised in September 1905 by the Automobile Club. The race was to be held in the Isle of Man, and Rolls duly entered two 20 hp Rolls-Royces, the first entries received.

The Tourist Trophy race was not just a simple race. The rules were framed with the intention of encouraging economy of running costs without sacrificing too much in the way of speed or comfort. Fuel consumption had to be one gallon for every 25 miles on an average road, the chassis had to weigh between 1,300 and 1,600 lbs, and a total weight of 950 lbs had to be carried. Finally, the coachwork had to be properly finished and equipped. The 20 hp Rolls-Royce fitted these conditions perfectly.

All three Rolls-Royce partners entered the spirit of the race. Royce went over the design with a fine-tooth comb throughout the summer of 1905 (it did not prevent him completing the 30 hp six-cylinder model). Claude Johnson gave his full support, including the loan of a new 30 hp Rolls-Royce to the Automobile Club officials at the race, while Rolls took one of the cars over to the Isle of Man as early as May to establish the most suitable gear-ratios to conform with a fuel consumption of 25 miles to the gallon.

When the cars were considered to be ready, one of them was tested on the London–Oxford road. The car was given exactly two gallons of petrol, and it ran for 55.5 miles. It was then driven for 500 miles, twice the length of the race, without a stop.

In the race itself, Charles Rolls was forced to retire after completing only a few of the 208 miles. In *The Magic of a Name,* Harold Nockolds described the incident as follows:

Rolls, carrying Number One, was the first away. Percy Northey, driving the second Rolls-Royce, was Number 22. The clear road before him enhanced Rolls's chance of success, but it was not to be. It appeared that a few miles from the start, while coasting down a hill in neutral, he heard a most appalling clatter in the gear-box. Subsequent investigation revealed stripped gears, and the various theories accounting for this mysterious phenomenon formed a never-failing topic of conversation in motor-racing circles for some time to come. It is only fair to add that it was universally agreed that whoever or whatever was to blame, it was not the 20 hp Rolls-Royce!

Some, perhaps especially Rolls himself, thought there might have been sabotage, and parts of the gearbox were searched for evidence. *Autocar* recorded the deed in capital letters: 'There was a CRACK, AND THE GEARS HAD PARTED.'

Rolls, of course, was furious, but the truth was probably that the fault was his in trying to put the car into gear while coasting downhill, and without matching the engine revs to the road speed.

Fortunately for the reputation of Rolls-Royce, Percy Northey's was the first car home although, as the cars had started at different times, he was deemed to have come second behind an Arrol-Johnston. Nevertheless, the Rolls-Royce had achieved the fastest non-stop run, since the Arrol-Johnston had stopped *en route.*

According to Nockolds, the performance of the 20 hp Rolls-Royce in the 1905 Tourist Trophy race was critical for the future of the Rolls and Royce partnership. Rolls and Johnson were still selling Minerva and New Orleans cars, and Rolls was still racing other cars. For example, he was chosen as one of Britain's three drivers for the Gordon Bennett race, driving a Wolseley. But the TT race confirmed the qualities of the Rolls-Royce car, and Arthur Briggs stepped in again to provide funds following the formation of Rolls-Royce Limited, formally registered on 15 March 1906.

One of the first major decisions of the new company was that new premises must be found for the production of the motor cars. After research, the choice narrowed to Stretford Road in Manchester, Coventry, Bradford and Leicester. Leicester seemed to be the cheapest, and was chosen, but Derby's council stepped in and made the company a very attractive offer. When Derby offered electrical power at especially low rates, a site of 12.7 acres was acquired and Royce, though he was deeply engaged in the development of a six-cylinder car, still found time to design most of the factory buildings himself. Nightingale Road was acquired on the basis of a rental agreement, with the proviso that it could be turned into a freehold purchase. The new factory was opened on Thursday 9 July 1908 by Sir John, later Lord, Montagu. This was the formal opening. The factory had already been operating for several months.

Speaking at the opening, Charles Rolls outlined the company's policy of hastening by going slowly:

Instead of turning out cars in huge quantities at a low price, we are turning out comparatively a small number of cars by the very best and most careful methods of manufacture. It is, in fact, the comparison between the ordinary watch and an English lever.

Asked why the company did not aim to produce thousands rather than just hundreds of cars, Rolls replied:

In the first place the class of man who would be quite acceptable in ordinary engineering works would be unsuitable for us and for our standard of work. To produce the most perfect cars you must have the most perfect workmen, and having got these workmen, it is then our aim to educate them up so that each man in these works can do his particular work better than anyone else in the world . . . We have always believed that the construction of a motor car which, while possessing every degree of necessary rigidity and strength, was of less weight than other similar cars, is largely a metal question. We consider that the success of the Rolls-Royce and its extraordinary durability and low cost of upkeep, as exemplified in the 15,000 miles trial of last year, is entirely due to scientific design, to the original research work and close study of metals which has been made by Mr. Royce and his assistants in the Physical Laboratory of this Company. We regard this as perhaps the most important department in the works.

A painting by Ray Tootall depicting the
introduction of Rolls and Royce by Henry Edmunds on
4 May 1904 at the Midland Hotel, Manchester.

Henry Edmunds, the engineering pioneer who brought about
the meeting of Rolls and Royce at the Midland Hotel,
Manchester in early May 1904. Edmunds has long been referred
to as 'the Godfather' of Rolls-Royce.

A portrait of Ernest Claremont taken in 1907. Claremont
had joined Royce as a business partner shortly after F.H. Royce
& Co. had been established in 1884. He became the first
Chairman of Rolls-Royce Limited.

Claude Goodman Johnson, founder secretary of the
Royal Automobile Club, organiser and publicist extraordinaire.
He joined Rolls in 1903 and became Commercial Managing
Director of Rolls-Royce Limited in its first year. From 1909
until his death in 1926, he served as General Managing
Director, with great distinction.

OPPOSITE TOP: An electric motor produced by F.H. Royce & Co.
Ltd. between its inception in 1894 and its relaunch as
Royce Ltd. in 1899. The motor was discovered by the Southern
Electricity Board while standardising voltages in the
Southampton area. It was in a shoemaker's shop and had been
in daily use since its purchase, second hand, shortly after
the turn of the century. In that time, it had reportedly been
given one new set of brushes and an occasional drop of oil.
It is now preserved in the Wedgewood Museum of electrical
engineering, near Bournemouth.

OPPOSITE BOTTOM: One of many varieties of crane produced by
Royce Ltd. This photograph shows a glass paperweight
used by the company for publicity purposes.

"ROYCE" ELECTRICAL CRANES.

ROYCE LIMITED, WORKS:- TRAFFORD PARK, MANCHESTER

A photograph of the first two-cylinder chassis taken by
Royce Ltd. early in 1904. There is a strong likelihood that this
was among those taken to persuade the Hon. C.S. Rolls that
a journey to Manchester would be worthwhile.

OPPOSITE: The Hon. C.S. Rolls, pioneer motorist and aviator. He
established C.S. Rolls & Co. in 1902, to sell the best motor cars
he could find to fellow members of the nobility and gentry.

The first Royce car outside the front door of Royce Ltd.
on 1 April 1904, the date of its first run. For a long time, it was
believed that the date of its first run was 31 March,
because 1 April 1904 was not only April Fool's Day, but also
Good Friday, and for both those reasons the company
thought it would be better to give the date as 31 March.

OPPOSITE: A portrait photograph of Henry Royce taken in
1907 for use in the publicity which followed the 15,000-mile
run of the original Silver Ghost.

TOP: The first internal combustion engine built by Henry Royce. The little two-cylinder engine is seen on test in the late autumn of 1903 in the old stable yard at the Blake Street rear entrance to the Manchester factory. The location of this testing was lost to history until the insurance files of the period were found in the 1970s. The photograph itself was found in the bottom drawer of an old desk at Rolls-Royce in 1979. A Royce dynamo absorbed the power, and can be seen on the right.

BOTTOM: From the outset, the Rolls-Royce motor car was characterised by the now-famous radiator. (Strictly speaking, the first two Rolls-Royce cars had Royce-type radiators.) After the first few cars, an oval plaque was used, on which was stamped 'The Rolls Royce Radiator'. The badge as we know it today was introduced in 1905 and has remained substantially unchanged ever since, except that the enamel was altered from red to black in 1933. This change was authorised by Henry Royce and was not, as many believe, introduced as a mark of respect after his death.

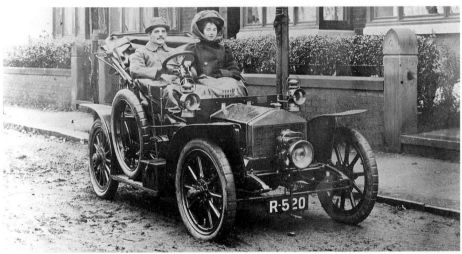

TOP: At the end of 1904, Rolls was due to meet at Folkestone HRH the Duke of Connaught, one of Queen Victoria's sons and Commander-in-Chief of the British land forces. Rolls was hoping to convince the Duke that some of his officers should be in cars, not on horses. He made sure many people knew that such was his faith in the reliability of his 10 hp Royce that he would not leave London the day before, but would leave on the same morning of the meeting. He duly met the Duke on time, took him along the south coast and returned to London the same day, after completing 220 miles. Standing at the front of the car is Rolls's friend, Moore-Brabazon, later Lord Brabazon of Tara.

BOTTOM: Eric Platford and his bride setting off on their honeymoon in 1908 in a 10 hp two-cylinder Rolls-Royce. This was Henry Royce's personal car, which he lent to Platford as a reward for all his hard work preparing cars for the Scottish Reliability Trials of 1908.

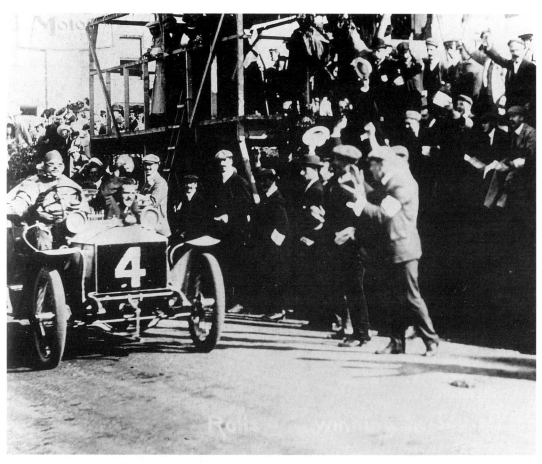

The most successful of the original range of cars was the
four-cylinder 20 hp. The picture shows Rolls winning
the second-ever Tourist Trophy race on the Isle of Man in
1906. He is driving a 'Light Twenty', with Eric
Platford riding as mechanic.

Rolls concluded by saying that the guests would understand that he could not show them the laboratory, as the work there was still under wraps. (The truth was that all the junk and scrap had been hidden there for the day.)

Such a move meant that a considerable increase in capital would be necessary. The nominal capital of the company was increased to £200,000, and £100,000 of shares were offered to the public on 6 December 1906, with the stipulation that unless £50,000 was subscribed within a certain time, the flotation would be abandoned. As the day drew near, only £41,000 had been subscribed, £10,000 by Rolls himself. Then De Looze remembered Arthur Briggs. He went to Harrogate and persuaded Briggs to invest the necessary £10,000. So grateful were the company that when Briggs died in 1919, company secretary De Looze insisted that the annual report be edged in black. C.S. Rolls & Co. was bought out by Rolls-Royce Limited in 1907. The electrical side of Royce Ltd. continued to operate, and did so with mixed fortunes until after Royce's death, while the motor side went into the new company.

The prospectus offering shares also gave the directors' remuneration. Royce, as chief engineer and works director, received £1,250 and 4 per cent of the profits in excess of £10,000. Rolls, as technical managing director, received £750 and also 4 per cent of the surplus profits, while Ernest Claremont, Royce's original partner, was Chairman and commercial adviser, receiving £250 and 2 per cent of the surplus profits.

The other vital early decision made by the new company was to concentrate on one model. Claude Johnson had long seen the potential of the six-cylinder market – Brooke, Napier, Sunbeam and Spyker were all specialising in this type – and now that Royce had produced a model demonstrably superior to all its rivals, he carried a policy at a board meeting on 8 March 1908 that Rolls-Royce would devote its energies exclusively to this model. During 1907, a new six-cylinder model to sell in parallel with the existing six-cylinder version had been considered. It is believed that Royce himself was not wholly in agreement, but he and his fellow directors were persuaded by Johnson of the commercial sense. Instead of diluting his skills over three or four models, Royce could concentrate on bringing one model to perfection.

And this was Royce's *new* model. The previous two-, three-, four- and six-cylinder models were all based on the experience of the Decauville, but manufactured to Royce's standards. Royce knew by this time that the 30 hp six was a dead end. His 40/50 hp was revolutionary in every way, and there are those who say that the new six-cylinder Rolls-Royce, the Silver Ghost, is the most famous car ever made. It first appeared in 1906, and 6,000 were produced over the following twenty years. Initially, there was only *one* Silver Ghost, but the name caught on with the public (though not with Rolls-Royce until after the launch of the New Phantom).

Autocar was immediately unstinting in its praise:

The running of this car at slow speeds is the smoothest thing we have experienced while for the silence the engine beneath the bonnet might be a sewing machine . . . At whatever speed this car is being driven on its direct third, there is <u>no</u> engine as far as sensation goes, nor are one's auditory nerves troubled driving or standing by a fuller sound than emanates from an eight day clock. There is no realisation of driving propulsion; the feeling as the passenger sits either at the front or the back of the vehicle is one of being wafted through the landscape.

To prove its smoothness and lack of vibration, a penny would be placed on its end on the chassis while the engine was running, or a glass brim full of water placed on the bonnet, while the engine was taken up to 1600 revolutions per minute, and not a drop spilt.

This was a golden opportunity for a man of Claude Johnson's marketing skills. He showed its hill-climbing powers by carrying four passengers up Netherhall Gardens in Hampstead (gradient one in seven) in second gear, and the Silver Ghost then achieved 42 mph on the flat in the same gear. It then tackled the test hill in Richmond Park (also one in seven) and, using only third gear, achieved 53 mph. (This was all at a time when the British speed limit was still 20 mph!)

However, the big test was the non-stop reliability run. The world record, 7,089 miles, was held by Siddeley. A team of drivers, including Charles Rolls, Claude Johnson and Eric Platford, drove the Silver Ghost non-stop between London and Glasgow until 15,000 miles had been completed. The engine was always kept running, except on Sundays when it was locked in a garage. When the 15,000 miles had been completed, Johnson invited the RAC supervisors to strip down the chassis and engine and recommend which parts needed replacing to make the car as good as new. The engine was passed as perfect, but one or two parts of the steering showed very slight wear, about one-thousandth of an inch, which the committee considered not as good as new.

The small universal joints in the magneto drive were also worn, and the water pump glands needed repacking. The total bill for replacements was £2 2s 7ᵈ (about £213 in today's terms). Several new tyres had been needed, but even with this expense the cost of running the car had come to 4.5 pence per mile.

It was a standard of reliability none of Rolls-Royce's competitors could come near to emulating, and Johnson broadcast it everywhere. He had already christened the car the Silver Ghost. The precedent was the Grey Ghost, a name given to a four-cylinder 20 hp car produced in 1905.

Not that Johnson did not worry about competition. In a letter to Claremont on 24 September 1908, he wrote:

It is quite difficult to know how far the new Daimler valveless engine is going to affect us. The engine is wonderfully silent. Its drawbacks are unknown, but the Daimler Company, I am inclined to think, would not have put it on the market unless they had thoroughly tested it.

In the same letter, Johnson was also worrying whether the 40/50 was too expensive.

It is quite certain that before long we must drop the price of our car in order to accord with the general range of prices. I do not by this mean that we should come down to the price of inferior chassis, but I do not think that we can hope to keep up the present price for very much longer, and our agents, in fact, are urging us that they could sell six of our cars at a lower price where they are only selling one at the present price.

BACKGROUND TO MOTORING IN THE EARLY 1900s

The British came late to the world of the motor car. Siegfried Marcus had produced a petrol-engined car in Vienna in 1865, and by 1888 Benz was selling his cars in Germany and France. In the 1890s, the French companies DeDion and Panhard et Levassor were forging ahead with manufacture. However, in Britain, development was held back by laws designed to protect a former way of life and, thanks to a powerful lobby in the Houses of Parliament, the interests of the railway companies. The 1865 Locomotives Act stated, *inter alia*, that:

- at least three persons had to be employed to drive a self-propelled vehicle
- while the vehicle was in motion, one of the three passengers was required to precede the vehicle on foot by at least 20 yards
- drivers had to give way to all other traffic, which was empowered to stop self-propelled vehicles by simply raising a hand
- the speed limit was 4 mph, or 2 mph in towns and villages
- there was a licence fee of £10 (over £1,000 in today's terms) per county in which the vehicle was used.

Faced with these restrictions, early motoring pioneers were forced to spend time trying to have such laws repealed, rather than on the development of cars. The legal situation did not encourage the development of the nascent motor industry in Britain, and no less a person than Thomas Edison wrote in 1901:

The motor car ought to have been British. You first invented it in the 1830s. You have roads only second to those of France. You have hundreds of thousands of skilled mechanics in your midst, but you have lost your trade by the same kind of stupid legislation and prejudice that have put you back in many departments of the electrical field.

Meanwhile, Germany and especially France forged ahead. Benz and Daimler put cars on the road in 1886, and Panhard-Levassor and Peugeot cars were produced in France in 1891. By 1894 there were enough different cars in France for a trial to be run between Paris and Rouen to evaluate the best designs. In Britain, the 'Red Flag Act' proved a great deterrent to would-be motor car producers in that it effectively prohibited road-tests. Nevertheless, a few brave, pioneering spirits were determined to show that this new method of propulsion was the means of future transport and, after much lobbying, in 1896 a new Locomotives on Highways Act disposed of the need for a man to walk in front of every car. (The 1878 Act dispensed with the flag.) The maximum speed limit was raised to 14 miles per hour, although the Local Government Board immediately reduced this to 12 mph. Further legislation followed with the Locomotive Act in 1898, the Motor Car Act in 1903, the Motor Cars Order in 1904 and the Royal Commission on Motor Cars in 1905. The motor car was obviously here to stay.

As it happens, 1896 stands out as a birth year for several other developments which were to dominate the social scene in the twentieth century. Asa (now Lord) Briggs, perhaps the leading historian of nineteenth- and twentieth-century Britain, wrote:

Alfred Harmsworth founded the first really popular national newspaper, the *Daily Mail*. Guglielmo Marconi arrived in Great Britain with his pioneer wireless equipment to demonstrate to the post office how he could send signals by wireless for a hundred yards. The first moving picture show was presented in London's West End at the Regent Street Polytechnic and was so successful that it had to be transferred to the Empire Music Hall, Leicester Square. The British Government recognized the existence of the motor car, and increased the speed limit on the roads from four miles per hour to twelve.

The full implications of each of these developments were not clear to people until the middle of the 20th century. Journalism was not transformed overnight by Harmsworth, who followed up the *Daily Mail* with the *Daily Mirror* in 1903. Wireless was for a long time thought of as a substitute for point-to-point communication by wire rather than as a medium of communication: indeed, the fact that broadcast messages could be picked up by people for whom they were not intended was thought to be a drawback rather than an advantage. It was not until 1908 that the first building specially designed for film shows was opened – not in the West End, but in Colne, Lancashire – although six years later there were 3,500 cinemas in Great Britain. As for motor cars, during the first decade of their existence they were thought of primarily as symbols of status. When J.H. Knight, 'a well-known scientific man . . .

and one of the first to work at motor cars', spoke to the Camera Club of London in 1897 about 'two years' progress in mechanical traction', he raised a laugh by saying that he hoped as soon as possible to see the horse abolished or 'found only, perhaps, in the hunting field and the parks'.

Selwyn Edge, who became famous as the test and racing driver of Napier cars, wrote about the prejudice against the motor car:

On more than one occasion I have had drivers of horse-drawn vehicles slash at me with their whips as I have passed them on the road. I have had stones hurled at my head and broken glass bottles deliberately placed in front of motor tricycles I have been riding . . . In driving through London, for example, one was bombarded by jeers and insults from practically every bus-driver and cab-driver one met, and this bombardment increased tenfold if a car or motor-cycle happened to need adjustment, or should break down at the roadside. And Queen Victoria, after seeing her son drive a car, said, I hope you will never allow any of those horrible machines to be used in my stables. I am told that they smell exceedingly nasty and are very shaky and disagreeable conveyances altogether.

Undeterred, the enthusiasts pressed on. To celebrate the repeal of the Red Flag Act, the Motor Car Club (recently founded by Frederick R. Simms, a talented engineer) and entrepreneur Harry J. Lawson organised an 'Emancipation Run' for self-propelled carriages from London to Brighton. As Piers Brendon wrote in his admirable *The Motoring Century: The Story of the Royal Automobile Club,* published in 1997:

Some thirty-two motor vehicles assembled, perhaps as many as half of all those in the country at that time. They presented a weird and novel spectacle. There were bizarre contraptions like the 'Britannia' bath chair, the red parcels van which looked as though it would collapse if loaded with anything heavier than a hatbox, and the Pennington four-seater tricycle which eventually reached Brighton by train. There were Bollee tandems resembling 'land torpedoes', whose exhausts sounded like naval guns. There were machines whose hot-tube ignition burners caught fire when lit by flares, giving a lurid aspect to the scene. There were dogcarts, phaetons, victorias and landaus, which bucked and shied without benefit of horses. Such 'oil cans', 'steam kettles' and 'skeletons on wheels' provoked good-natured chaff from the onlookers. But fears lay behind the jeers. The rumour spread that 'an organised massacre of cab-horses was contemplated'. 'Bill,' shouted one cabby to another, 'my old gee's off to the knacker's yard afore the year's out, blest if she won't.' Other spectators, though, admired the modern mode of travel. 'No fellow would ride behind a 'bus horse while he could glide along like that,' exclaimed a City gentleman. Many who stood in the rain that day felt that they were witnessing the dawn of an era, the beginning of a 'great and beneficial . . . revolution in the life of habits and methods of Locomotion of the people'.

Lawson and Simms became partners in a number of enterprises designed to promote the motor car, but Simms gradually became disillusioned with Lawson's questionable business practices. In 1897 Simms divorced himself from the Motor Car Club, and in July of that year set up the Automobile Club of Great Britain ('and Ireland' was added later), announcing that its headquarters would be at 4 Whitehall Place, London. The inaugural meeting took place in December, and after a lunch at the Hotel Metropole overlooking the Thames at the corner of Whitehall Place and Northumberland Avenue (now offices), some members who possessed motor cars demonstrated them along the Embankment to Battersea. There were two Arnold carriages powered by Benz motors, two electric omnibuses, several Daimlers, and finally a Panhard 6 with a Daimler-Phoenix four-cylinder engine, owned and driven by the Hon. C.S. Rolls.

Progress was slow but assured, although the industry – it if could be called such at this stage – was fragmented and could not agree on basic questions of design. Should the cars have steering wheels or tillers? Should the engines be cooled by air or water? Should the ignition be electric or hot tube? Should the tyres be solid or pneumatic, and indeed should the engines be powered by petrol or steam? The journalist St. John Nixon wrote in 1899:

The industry is highly unstable; hundreds of thousands of people [surely millions?] have still to see a motor car for the first time.

But in the same year, Alfred Harmsworth proposed a 1,000-mile endurance run from London to Edinburgh and back to test the cars and to publicise motoring. St. John Nixon, who participated in the run, wrote:

It was the means of deciding many points of design. Tube ignition received its *coup de grace*, as did tiller steering. Water cooling became universal and the necessity of improving pneumatic tyres rather than extending the use of solids became apparent.

The first decade of the new century saw the fledgling industry burst into life. Over two hundred companies were formed between 1901 and 1905. Few survived. Indeed, few had the good fortune of Rolls and Royce to find a man of vision with the marketing ability of Claude Johnson. Fred Lanchester, an early motor company founder, said:

The difficulties of management were very great, partly owing to the fact that no ancillary trades had been developed, and we had to do everything ourselves – chassis, magneto, wheels, bodywork etc., everything except the tyres. Moreover for many years I had personally to train my labour.

Lanchester, lacking the commercial brain to go with his engineering brilliance, was forced to put his company into receivership in 1904, and it was reformed as the Lanchester Motor Company. Fred left the running of the company to his brother George, and applied his engineering skills to Daimler. After a shaky financial start – in spite of the fact that the Prince of Wales's first car in 1900 was a chocolate and black Daimler phaeton – Daimler prospered under the aegis of the Birmingham Small Arms company. By 1914, Daimler employed 4,000 people and was producing 1,000 cars a year. Only the subsidiary of the American company, Ford, and Wolseley, Rover and Singer were larger, while Austin and Morris were about the same size.

Demand was growing rapidly. In May 1906 the Royal Commission on Motor Cars reported that the number of cars on the road had increased by 80 per cent in sixteen months, to 44,908. The report went on to say that there had been

a great advance in the use of motor cars for trade purposes such as the carrying of goods in light vans or heavy lorries and for professional purposes, e.g. by medical men and by surveyors and public officials whose duties include the inspection of large districts. Moreover horses have rapidly become familiarized with cars in places where they are much used and it may fairly be said that in London and its neighbourhood, motor cars and even the noisy omnibuses have ceased to be a special cause of alarm to the horse-drawn traffic.

Sir Harry Ricardo, who, as we shall see later, became a close friend of Henry Royce and a consultant to the company from the 1920s onwards, was one of the early experts on the technology of the petrol-driven internal combustion engine. Writing in the *Automobile Engineer* in 1960, he looked back on the first decade of the century as the most stimulating and creative in the history of the motor car. He saw it as the age of invention and elimination. In his view, it saw the best creative work of Royce and Lanchester and, at the same time, the elimination of the steam and electric cars, to be replaced by the four- and six-cylinder in-line petrol engines. In those ten years the horseless carriage became the motor car.

And private car registrations, required by the 1903 Act, grew inexorably.

Year	Registrations	Year	Registrations
1904	8,465	1911	72,106
1906	23,192	1912	88,265
1907	32,451	1913	105,734
1909	48,109	1914	132,015
1910	53,169		

ROYCE'S ILLNESS

Following Rolls's death in 1910, another calamity struck the following year when Royce himself was taken seriously ill. Long years of overwork and neglect of the needs of his body in terms of regular meals finally took their toll. Doctors were pessimistic about his chances of survival. Johnson, terrified for the future of the company without its design genius, took Royce on an extended holiday. He left the works at Derby in the hands of Wormald and Haldenby, with quality control to be checked by the dependable Platford. In London, his own position was assumed by Lord Herbert Scott, who had joined as a director in 1907 when Johnson had felt that a member of the aristocracy would bring respectability to the company and help with the raising of any extra capital that may have been necessary. (Lord Herbert Scott was a cousin of Sir John, later Lord, Montagu.)

Johnson took Royce to Europe, driving across France and Italy to spend the winter in Egypt. On the return journey in the spring, they were travelling along the Côte d'Azur when they arrived at the tiny hamlet of Le Canadel. Overlooking the bay from the top of a hill, Royce said: 'I would like to build a house here.'

Both were mindful of the doctors' words about rest and recuperation in a warm climate, and Johnson immediately organised the construction of a house before Royce could change his mind. Far from changing his mind, Royce designed the house himself.

They returned to England in the early summer, and Royce took up residence at Crowborough in Sussex. Johnson realised that Royce should never live in Derby again, and worked out how he could surround him with his most trusted engineers, in the south of England in summer and the south of France in winter.

As early as 1908, Johnson had felt that Royce should be moved away from Derby. In a letter to Claremont on 24 September of that year, he wrote:

This brings me to the point that one cannot help wishing that a portion of Mr. Royce's time should be spent right away from the works, so that his brain might have the chance of producing for Rolls-Royce a somewhat similar but better departure. So long as he insists on being worried with all the small, petty-fogging, irritating details which must inevitably surround him so long as he superintends the works, his time and the value of his brains to our Shareholders must to some extent be lost. That is to say, his brain is undoubtedly valuable at the works, but its most valuable property, namely, invention, has not sufficient chance to be exercised.

The new system worked well. As Nockolds put it in *The Magic of a Name*:

His mind undistracted by the management of the factory, Royce kept his staff busy with a continual stream of ideas from his fertile brain . . . Often his health kept him in bed all morning, and this was the period of his greatest mental activity. Without making a single note, he would design a new component in his head. After lunch he would explain his plan to an assistant, and when the latter had put it on the drawing board, it was invariably found to be mathematically correct. Blue-prints would be sent to Derby and finished parts would come back. Royce would turn them over in his sensitive hands, criticise them, and generally re-design them . . . Executives from Derby and London would visit Le Canadel or St. Margaret's Bay [Johnson had found him a house near his own at Kingsdown, near Dover] to discuss some point which required the great man's decision. Platford, of course, was a frequent visitor, often bringing with him a chassis incorporating some proposed modification, and in later years, a completely experimental car.

R.W.H. Bailey, in writing notes about his career, was to say:

When R was comfortably installed at Le Canadel arrangements were made for the leading officials at Derby to pay regular visits in order to discuss their various problems, the real object CJ had in view in all this was to ensure not only that R would have full and complete control of the works as he had when living and working in Derby but to convince R that this was really the case so that he could settle down to the new conditions with the assurance that he was still the hub of the whole of RR activities.

And Royce was not averse to keeping his leading engineers with him at Le Canadel for much longer periods than was strictly necessary. R.W.H. Bailey remembered going to visit him in early January 1912 to discuss the new four-speed gear box, which in his view should have necessitated a stay of perhaps ten days. He wrote later:

I found myself at the end of thirteen weeks still there. I had taken with me the complete design for the new box but R was quite unpredictable. When dealing with his designers, one found that R was a law unto himself and so, instead of appreciating the urgency of the matter I had come about I found myself doing designs for both the other sections . . . I had the utmost difficulty to get R interested although the new box was a necessity for the three cars entered for the 1913 Austrian Trials.

Royce also used Bailey to help him organise buildings on his land at Le Canadel. This was no easy matter, for the whole coastline was a dense mass of pines grown for the production of pit props. Bailey soon found his time being taken up negotiating with a local builder and organising construction of the buildings Royce wanted. Claude Johnson would have been concerned that Bailey's valuable design abilities were not being used in Derby, but on the other hand pleased that Royce was being kept happy in Le Canadel. A Rolls-Royce colony developed around Villa Mimosa (Royce's villa was originally going to be named Villa Cypress, until someone pointed out that cypress trees usually grow in graveyards), with a drawing office known as Le Bureau, and a house for the designers, Villa Rossignol.

The land that Royce had bought was to acquire significant historical value, apart from the fact that Royce lived there. In 1944, the first soldier of the Free French Army was supposed to have set foot in France at that point. As Bailey wrote later:

There is now, quite close to the garage I designed for R, a large monument erected by the French Government recording that at 4am on the morning of August 7th 1944 the first soldier of the Free French set his foot again on French soil in the final effort to liberate France.

Bailey also made some comments about his joining Rolls-Royce, which give an insight into the somewhat chaotic management style of Royce and Johnson. He had been interviewed by Johnson and taken on without meeting Royce.

CJ, as I knew him later, asked me much about my previous work and then finally, off his own bat, offered me a job as one of the three chief designers to work under Mr. F.H. Royce. As a chief designer I would control a number of draughtsmen . . . The appointment was peculiar. We had agreed on a salary and a five year agreement with an increase every year but before this came into force I was to work three months on trial on the understanding that if I was not found to be suitable at the end of the three months I should be paid up and finish without any further claim on the company.

In spite of this appointment to a senior position in the company, when Bailey arrived at the Derby works Royce was away for a few days, and no one seemed to know anything about him.

No one was expecting me and I had to produce a letter from Mr. Claude Johnson before anyone bestirred themselves and then it was only to find myself ushered into an office accommodating some half a dozen draughtsmen and shown a vacant board and desk at which I could work if so inclined.

After some days of frustration for Bailey, Royce appeared.

At the end of ten days or so a tall well built man with a beard came into the office and walked thro to Mr. Moon [J.A. Moon, who was in charge of the jig and tool office] where there were some heated remarks about the jigs which were submitted. I left for lunch leaving the visitor still criticising the jig design in the background and upon my return was informed by Moon that the visitor was Mr. Royce.

I naturally expected Mr. Royce would come and see me and explain what he wanted me to do, but no, for a fortnight visits were paid by Mr. Royce to Moon to criticise or pass the various jig designs but I might not have existed so far as Mr. Royce was concerned, until one morning after some rather biting criticism of the designs submitted there was silence.

Bailey had been working on a jig design, which he had given to Moon. When Royce saw it he realised Moon had not done it, and inquired who had. When Moon told him, Royce still did not approach him in the office, but when Bailey was leaving at the end of the day Royce drew up alongside him on a chassis and offered him a lift. Royce asked if he had found a house, and Bailey said he had not. As he wrote later:

This certainly surprised me, as my peculiar experiences at the works had convinced me that there was a serious difference of opinion between Mr. Claude Johnson and Mr. F.H. Royce with whom I was supposed to work, it seemed to me the former was anxious to have capable men working as understudies to be available in the event of the latter being ill again while the latter would have none of it, otherwise why should I be completely ignored as I had been.

Bailey indicated to Royce that he thought he was the unfortunate victim of some scheme hatched by Claude Johnson, of which Mr. Royce was not aware.

Mr. Royce looked very distressed and said I was all wrong. CJ had engaged me at R's special request and the only reason he had appeared to ignore me was his own personal shyness and excessive sensitivity for which he apologised saying he hoped I would stay with him and set out at once to find a house as he understood from CJ I was married.

Mr. Royce then went on to explain that he was not satisfied with the ability of his present assistants, that it was his intention to make me sectional chief for the transmission which included the clutch, the gear box, brakes and back axle as his present man was leaving at the end of his agreement which would determine itself in the course of another two or three weeks.

After this difficult start, Bailey went on to enjoy a long and productive career in the company, as did his son, Alec Harvey-Bailey. Bailey's recruitment was part of a plan by Johnson to make sure that there would be able successors to Royce. Perhaps we could also surmise that Johnson wanted to lure away the best engineers from Rolls-Royce's competition. Hence, Elliott, Hives, Rowledge and Sidgreaves all came from Napier, and Day from Sheffield Simplex. A number of attempts were also made to recruit Roy Fedden, who, as we shall see, built himself a formidable reputation.

THE REPUTATION SPREADS

While Johnson was coping with Royce's illness and the setting up of the new system whereby Royce could continue to work in congenial surroundings, the business of consolidating the Rolls-Royce as the best car in the world continued.

Napier had been insinuating to the world at large that Rolls-Royces were cars for 'old ladies'. In 1911, in response to a similar run by Napier, a Silver Ghost (chassis no. 1701) travelled from London to Edinburgh in top gear and achieved a better miles-per-gallon rate than the Napier. The car was then fitted with the 'bathtub' body and, driven by Hives, achieved 100 mph at Brooklands, the first car to do so on the Brooklands circuit.

The most valuable marketing achievement of 1911 was N.C. 'Fatty' Neill's winning of the Prince Henry Tour. The tour lasted for several weeks and was sponsored by HRH Prince Henry of Prussia, who had conceived the idea of a 'goodwill' tour of British and German clubs (the press in Germany and Britain had been engaged in a propaganda war for several years). Royalty was heavily involved. Prince Henry himself competed, and additional awards were presented by King George V and Queen Mary, as well as the Kaiser and the German Empress.

The tour began at Homburg in the Taunus mountains and, after several days' driving in Germany, the entrants crossed the Channel to Southampton before driving to Scotland, from where they returned to Brooklands after negotiating many famous test hills. Both in Germany and Britain there were many receptions, speeches and professions of goodwill. Four Rolls-Royces entered, and the one driven by Neill (with the well-known motoring journalist Thornton Rutter as his co-driver and navigator) was judged to have given the best all-round performance on the tour. Johnson, Royce and everyone at Derby were delighted.

In the summer of the following year, the Austrian Automobile Club staged an eight-day trial over the Austrian Alps, designed to be the toughest and most testing of any trial yet held in Europe. Jimmy Radley, the pilot who had been the first to reach Charles Rolls after his fatal air-crash at Bournemouth, entered his Rolls-Royce. Radley was considered one of the best drivers in the country, but nevertheless a shock was in store both for him and the company.

The news that his car had failed to climb the Katschberg Pass on the very first day of the trial came as a bombshell. Claude Johnson could hardly believe the telegram he received from Charles Freeston reporting on what had happened. On the steepest section of the Katschberg, reputedly one of the toughest mountain roads in Austria, Radley's car simply came to rest and could only continue after two passengers had dismounted. Radley lost points in the judging of the car's performance, and the name of Rolls-Royce was disgraced.

Only one remedy was possible if Rolls-Royce was not to lose its reputation. The cars entered the following year must be seen to be clearly ahead of their rivals. The Rolls-Royce thoroughness was brought into play. Several cars were sent out to the Alps under Platford's supervision to obtain accurate information on the length and severity of the passes, the altitude and atmospheric conditions and the angles on the hairpin bends. The rougher continental roads and the severity of the *canivaux* (drainage ditches) also suggested a strengthening of the suspension would be needed.

Royce made various modifications, and in order to test them he designed a 'bumping machine', which gave the effect of thousands of miles of road in the space of a few days. A four-speed gearbox developed by R.W.H. Bailey was re-introduced, and a radiator with a larger block and header tank replaced the existing radiator. The whole chassis was given greater ground clearance. The radiator was also ball-mounted so that it did not crack when the chassis twisted. Johnson called this modified version the Continental Rolls-Royce, but they became universally known as Alpine Eagles.

Although Claude Johnson had christened the twelfth 40/50 hp car the Silver Ghost, and the public came to know all the 40/50s as Silver Ghosts, others, especially those in and close to the company, referred to the cars as the London to Edinburgh type, the Continental type, the Alpine Eagle and so on. It was after the 40/50 hp New Phantom was launched in 1925 that the name Silver Ghost was applied generally and retrospectively to all previous 40/50s.

The 1913 Austrian Alpine Trial assumed great significance for the company in the light of the apparent 'failure' in 1912. Johnson nominated three drivers for the Rolls-Royce official team – Friese, Sinclair and Hives, of whom much, much more later. These were augmented by Jimmy Radley, who had driven the car that failed to climb the hill the previous year, and who was now lent 'Tubby' Ward as his riding mechanic in a purpose-built new Alpine Eagle. Radley was a worthy pioneer for Rolls-Royce, and a man of great stamina. As Nockolds pointed out in his book:

Long runs were Radley's delight. A day or two before the start of the trial he was talking to some competitors and officials in a Viennese café. Not without justification he boasted of the powers of his beloved Rolls-Royce. Someone casually remarked that he would bet a thousand crowns [Austrian presumably] that Radley could not drive to Klagenfurt and back, a distance of 400 miles, between the hours of sunrise and sunset.

'Done!' said Radley. 'Let's stay up now, and I'll start as soon as it gets properly light.'

He took three people with him. They stopped for breakfast and lunch, and for one hour to give a sick passenger a breather. They were back in Vienna in 13 hours, in time for dinner, winning the wager with the greatest of ease.

The trial this time was a triumph for Rolls-Royce. The four cars swept all before them. Charles Freeston wrote in *Autocar*:

The Rolls-Royces came past in great style, and I am bound to say that I have never seen anything more beautiful in the way of locomotion than the way in which they flew up the pass; we all know what a fast car is like on the level; but the sight of a group of cars running up a mountain road at high speed, with a superbly easy motion to which each little variation in the surface gave the semblance of a greyhound in its stride, was inspiring to a degree . . . It was a spectacle, indeed, worth going many a long mile to see.

Success in Austria was soon followed by success in the Spanish Grand Prix, organised in the Guadarrama Mountains by King Alfonso, and by Radley – who else! – setting up the record for driving from London to Monte Carlo in 26 hours 4 minutes, including the Channel crossing.

Rolls-Royce's reputation soared, and by 1914 showrooms had been opened on the Champs Elysées in Paris and service and repair depots established in New York and Toronto, staffed by Derby-trained mechanics. Rolls-Royce India was formed in India in 1912 and Rolls-Royce de España in 1913. In May 1914, the Paris branch supplied two cars to Tsar Nicholas II in Russia.

Sir Arthur Marshall, who built the famous Marshall engineering company in Cambridge and who has enjoyed a long association with Rolls-Royce, remembers, as a boy, Rolls-Royce chassis arriving at Cambridge station, from where they were taken to Windovers, a coachbuilder in Huntingdon: 'When you started the car, you couldn't hear the engine.'

Claude Johnson had long been friendly with Lord Northcliffe, owner of the *Daily Mail*, who became an enormous fan of both the cars produced by Rolls-Royce and of Johnson and Royce themselves. In 1912, Northcliffe wrote:

The six-cylinder Rolls-Royce is taking the place of the railway train as the most luxurious form of travel in town, or between town and country, or for cross-country journeys etc.

The special system of suspension, combined with the Rolls-Royce patent shock absorber, makes travel on rough roads more luxurious than travel in a Pullman car on the railroad.

The beautiful suppleness of the six-cylinder engine, with its powers of rapid acceleration, transforms progress into a smooth, shockless, vibrationless glide.

The gear on which the car can be driven behind a crawling four-wheeler in London, viz: the top or direct drive, will carry the car and its load up Dashwood Hill, the Test Hill in Richmond Park, and from London to Glasgow.

Although the chassis is sufficiently long to carry a large luxurious body, the steering lock is so designed as to enable it to manoeuvre in traffic and road corners better than many far shorter and far less comfortable cars.

The lubrication is odourless and smokeless under all conditions owing to the Rolls-Royce patent lubricating system.

Its trustworthiness has been proved by an official trial in which the car ran 14,371 miles without an involuntary stop.

Its durability (which means economy in upkeep) has not only been proved to be extraordinary beyond all precedent by an official trial of 15,000 miles, but the evidence of disinterested private owners shows that this remarkable record is confirmed by the performance of cars in private service.

It is the Car de Luxe. Everyone who buys the best things from the best people buys only Rolls-Royce Motor Cars. The lady who goes to Paquin or Jay's for her dresses, Tiffany's for her jewels, the Maison Lewis for her hats, goes to Rolls-Royce Limited for her Motor Car, for use in town or country. The man who goes to Poole's for his clothes, Purdey for his guns and Hardy for his rods, goes to Rolls-Royce Limited for his Car. [The 1912 40/50 hp brochure includes many photographs with the car outside these famous 'houses'.]

Disinterested experts, who have tried every other make of car, after driving the Rolls-Royce always admit that it is a revelation of suppleness, luxury of suspension, silence, smokelessness and all-round excellence.

Northcliffe peppered Johnson with advice, writing to him in 1913: 'Is it not time you fitted a self-starter?'

Johnson replied:

We dare not fit anything which will ever go wrong, and we have not yet come across a self-starter which is good enough for Rolls-Royce. Royce is devoting himself entirely to the question of self-starters, but this one is surrounded with difficulty.

After many problems, Rolls-Royce fitted self-starters in 1914. Unless the Silver Ghost was cold, a self-starter was not necessary anyway. The driver switched on the ignition and moved the timing lever in the centre of the steering wheel from 'early' to 'late' or vice versa (everyone else called it 'advance' and 'retard', but Royce liked plain English, hence 'early' and 'late'). The spark ignited the gas in the cylinder of the stationary engine and off it went.

Northcliffe continued with a stream of ideas, sending Johnson a 'memo for 1913': 'Give electric light, insist on safety doors, have some new talking points.' (Electric lighting and starters were standard equipment in Cadillacs by 1912.) He also suggested the advertising slogan used by the company for many years: 'The Best car in the World.' (As we shall see, this slogan was also used by Napier for a time, and the press had used 'The best six-cylinder car in the world' to describe the Rolls-Royce 30 hp six-cylinder car in 1906.)

But amid all this battery of advice, Johnson became concerned at the share buying of another of the dynamic businessmen of the first half of the twentieth century – Max Aitken, later Lord Beaverbrook, proprietor of the *Daily* and *Sunday Express*, who, by acquiring C.S. Rolls's shareholding after his death, had bought a substantial holding in Rolls-Royce.

Northcliffe was prepared to speak highly of Aitken: 'He is one of the straightest men in the company.' Aitken was operating in conjunction with Lord Selborne (who described himself in the 1913 *Who's Who* as Second Earl Selborne; the first Earl was a very eminent lawyer and Lord Chancellor 1872–74 and 1880–85). This Lord Selborne had gained a first class History degree at Oxford, and had been First Lord of the Admiralty from 1900 until 1905 and Governor of Transvaal and High Commissioner for South Africa between 1905 and 1910. Presumably a partnership with him bestowed great respectability on Aitken, who, in spite of Northcliffe's high regard, had not yet established himself completely in British society (although he was already the Member of Parliament for Ashton-under-Lyme, and had been knighted in 1911). Aitken had left his native Canada after a somewhat buccaneering career in which his company, Royal Securities Corporation, had involved itself in mergers affecting almost every section of Canadian industry.

Throughout 1912, Aitken caused Johnson considerable anxiety. He had already suggested in September 1911 that he and his associates might find the extra working capital that Rolls-Royce Limited needed, but Johnson and Claremont were wary. Aitken wanted to be elected to the board, but changed his mind and put forward two associates, Edward Goulding and Geoffrey Rowe, both of whom were duly elected in the spring of 1912.

Aitken continued to interfere in Rolls-Royce affairs, and in early January 1913 Johnson met Northcliffe in Paris and asked him to intervene with Aitken on Rolls-Royce's behalf. As a result, Northcliffe wrote to Aitken on 15 January 1913:

The day before yesterday, Claude Johnson, of the Rolls-Royce Company, told me that you and Selborne had bought many shares in the Company and seemed anxious to convert it into a larger enterprise. My interest in the automobile is that of a pioneer,

TOP: The Cooke Street factory near Hulme in Manchester. The two-storey building in the middle of the picture was used from the mid-1880s, Henry Royce and Ernest Claremont initially living on the upper floor. The three-storey building to its right was erected in the early 1890s, its upper floor being the design office. This view remained unchanged until a German bomb destroyed the offices during the Second World War, and the remainder of the building was bulldozed down in 1965.

BOTTOM: The Cooke Street location served Henry Royce well for over twenty years. The fitting shop shown here had been used since the early days of F.H. Royce & Co. in the mid-1880s. Expansion took place in the early 1890s when a large crane shop was erected through the pillars on the left. At the head of the stairs on the right is the area in which Royce and Claremont originally lived. By the time of the photograph, it contained offices – including Royce's. The factory was located behind rows of terrace houses and could not be expanded to meet the growing demand for Rolls-Royce cars.

As can be seen, the 30 hp six-cylinder engine effectively
comprised three two-cylinder 10 hp cylinder blocks
on a common crankcase. This allowed little room for an
adequate centre-main bearing on the crankshaft,
which in itself initially retained the two-cylinder 10 hp
journal diameters. The six-cylinder in-line engine was new,
and all manufacturers found themselves having to deal
with the potentially destructive natural vibrations of
six-cylinder crankshafts.

The Hon. C.S. Rolls (front passenger) in a 1905 Short 30 hp
2637 Barker Roi-des-Belges tourer in May 1906.
The others are: Prince Jaime de Bourbon, decorated by the Tsar
for his services in the Russo-Japanese War, at the wheel, Lady
Mary Savile and Viscount and Viscountess de Veance,
a Mr. Oswald, Captain Brandt and Baron de Korwin, an
Austrian aeronaut (seated on the step beneath the Prince).
In the background is Rolls's chauffeur/mechanic,
Reginald Macready.

TOP: Royce's 120° V8 engine designed for the Landaulette Par Excellence and Legalimit. It pioneered features subsequently found in the 40/50 six-cylinder engine.

BOTTOM: In addition to the range of in-line two-, three-, four- and six-cylinder cars, Royce launched two models with a V8 engine at the request of Rolls. The one illustrated here sought to compete with the then-popular electric town carriages, and the other, the Legalimit, was designed so that it would not exceed the maximum 20 mph speed limit.

Four very early 40/50 hp cars at the Cat and Fiddle public house on the road from Manchester to Buxton. The cars had been driven from Manchester in direct drive gear only, to demonstrate their flexibility to motoring journalists. On the left is the Silver Ghost, chassis 60551, with Claude Johnson at the wheel. Next to him is AX 205 (three of the cars are registered in Rolls's home county, Monmouthshire – the fourth has a Manchester trade plate) with the Hon. Charles Rolls at the wheel. The photograph was taken on 21 June 1907.
AX 201 and AX 205 still exist. The latter, chassis 60552, was the first 40/50 hp to be exported to the United States.
Despite extensive improvement, the climb from Stockport to the Cat and Fiddle remains a tortuous drive to this day.

By 1906, Royce had amassed a great deal of first-hand experience with motor cars. He had learnt about the problems with six-cylinder crankshafts, how to make engines run smoothly and smoke-free, and what mattered in terms of accessibility for routine maintenance. He had realised that the 30 hp six-cylinder did not offer a way forward, and therefore designed the world-beating 40/50 hp engine for the top chassis of the range. (The version shown here is a post-First World War engine.)

The twelfth 40/50 chassis to be built at Cooke Street, 60551, was provided with coachwork, painted in silver, and all its brightwork was plated in real silver. The car was used as a demonstrator by the company and was given the name Silver Ghost. In 1907 it won a gold medal in the Scottish 2,000-mile trial. It was run thereafter from Scotland to London and back until a total of 15,000 miles had been covered, whereupon it was handed to the RAC for detailed checking.
The RAC reported formally that the total cost of replacing parts on which there was any sign of wear and tear was £2 2s 7$^\mathrm{d}$ (about £213 in today's terms). This single act consolidated the reputation of Rolls-Royce, then only a year old, as the maker of the best car in the world.

TOP: Sir John Montagu and other dignitaries arriving at
Number One Gate, Nightingale Road, for the formal opening
of the works on 9 July 1908.

BOTTOM: The Rolls-Royce factory built in Derby as it
appeared in 1908. The opening ceremony took place in the
building on the right. Although now vastly bigger,
the factory still incorporates these original buildings,
which are in daily use.

Charles Rolls took the closest interest in the achievements
of Orville and Wilbur Wright. Having first met them in New
York in 1906, he is seen here with them in a Silver Ghost
while acting as their official host on behalf of the Aero Club
during their visit to England in spring 1909.

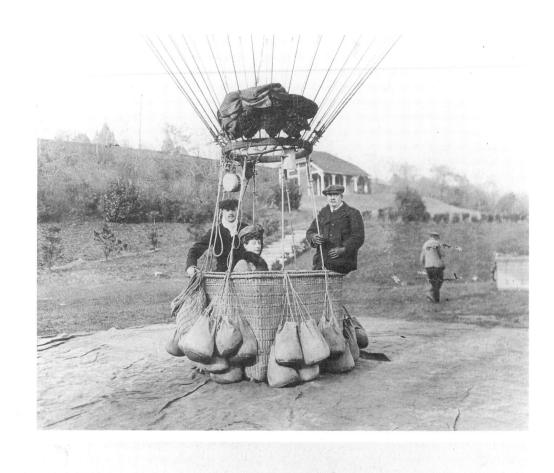

One of Britain's pioneering aviators,
Rolls is seen here waiting for the weather to improve before
making his greatest flight, his two-way
crossing of the English Channel on 2 June 1910.

OPPOSITE TOP: Charles Rolls with Frank Hedges Butler and his
daughter, Vera, co-founders with Rolls of the Aero Club.

OPPOSITE BOTTOM: Charles Rolls died tragically at the age of
thirty-two, while flying his own aeroplane in an
air show at Bournemouth on 12 July 1910. The crash was
the result of a structural failure of components added to
his original Wright aeroplane.

In response to a challenge from Napier in 1911, one of the
latest 40/50 chassis, 1701, was driven in top gear only
from London to Edinburgh, beating the performance of Napier
comfortably. At the wheel is Ernest Hives.

Following the London to Edinburgh run, a minimal body
was placed on chassis 1701 and Hives drove it at the
Brooklands race circuit, where it exceeded 100 mph.
Following these two achievements, little more was heard
of the company making cars for old ladies.

Henry Royce and friends at Claude Johnson's house in 1913.
LEFT TO RIGHT: Count don Carlos de Salamanca (Rolls-Royce's
agent in Spain from 1913 until the 1960s), Mrs. Wigs (Claude
Johnson's second wife), Henry Royce and Lord Northcliffe.

OPPOSITE TOP: Following the embarrassing incident in the first
Alpine Trial in 1912 when James Radley failed to re-start
his Silver Ghost through lack of a low enough gear, Rolls-Royce
responded by entering a works team in 1913. The three
works cars, plus a fourth private entry driven by Radley,
dominated the trials that year.

OPPOSITE BOTTOM: Ernest Hives led the works team in the
Austrian Alpine Trials, and is seen here at the finish with other
members of the Rolls-Royce team.

Following his major illness in 1911, Royce never worked in Derby again. From 1912, the war years excepted, he made his winter home at Le Canadel on the French Riviera, where he designed his own house, Villa Mimosa. The Rolls-Royce colony comprised Claude Johnson's Villa Jaune (top right of group), Royce's Villa Mimosa (next to it), the design office, Le Bureau (below Royce's Villa), Villa Rossignol (in front of Le Bureau and almost obscuring it) where the designers lived while working with Royce, and the garage (below Villa Rossignol) which incorporated a generator for the colony. The villa top left belonged to the Michelin family, and the building on the extreme right was the local hotel.

and in Rolls-Royce a platonic admiration for somebody else's beautiful garden. The Rolls-Royce business is a delicate orchid which owes its success entirely to Johnson, who previously, as you know, organized the Royal Automobile Club, bringing it from bankruptcy to, I think I am right in saying, seven or eight thousand members. My head chauffeur, who is an engineer with English, French and American experience, tells me that at Derby they have assembled the finest mechanics in the world.

Johnson asked me to write to you on the matter, but I told him that I did not interfere in other people's business or disputes. Having said this I have done with it.

But Johnson was still concerned about Aitken, fearing he was trying to win control of the company. He wrote to Northcliffe:

He is artful enough to cry 'Peace!' when there is no peace . . . I am continuing to build up defences on the supposition that he is quietly acquiring shares and proxies.

And indeed, Johnson approached Rolls's father, Lord Llangattock, and tried to buy his 30,000 shares. Llangattock would not sell, but assured Johnson of his support. Meanwhile, Northcliffe gently reprimanded Johnson:

In view of what you tell me, you must not mind my saying that you have been lacking in foresight and forethought in not obtaining control of the company, a perfectly easy thing to do. Control is essential to the peace of mind not only of the head of a business but of the humblest employee.

Aitken gradually became disillusioned with the company as Johnson seemed disinclined to take his advice. In October 1913 he sold his holding to the American tobacco magnate, J.B. Duke, saying to Goulding on 11 October, 'I expect to be all out of Rolls-Royce by the 15th of this month', and telling Goulding that he could inform the board that he had sold his shares 'entirely on account of the fraudulent agreements' (he had earlier written to Johnson about improper contracts whereby 'certain Directors practically constitute themselves permanent Directors'). Goulding could also tell them that 'I am satisfied retribution will overtake them'.

Aitken's nominated man on the board was Edward Goulding, later Lord Wargrave, who became Chairman of the company a few years later. There was considerable acrimony, culminating in De Looze's recording a board resolution as a suggestion, not a resolution. Aitken realised he was not going to win over the hearts and minds of the Derby directors but, as we shall see, his association with the company and his respect for it was to bear fruit at the beginning of the Second World War, when Aitken, by this time Lord Beaverbrook, was appointed Minister for Aircraft Production.

THE SPIRIT OF ECSTASY

While the company directors were striving to publicise the merits of the Rolls-Royce in every way possible, they gave the car a symbol which, along with the radiator and the badge on its background, became a recognisable feature of the car in the ensuing years.

As car production and sales increased, one of those periodic crazes developed which have affected car owners over the years – they began to fit mascots to their radiator caps. They were mostly frivolous, such as toy policemen, black cats and dolls. The Rolls-Royce directors did not like their cars being adorned in such a way, and commissioned the well-known artist Charles Sykes to design a suitably dignified mascot.

At the end of the 1890s, a young lady called Eleanor Thornton went to work under Claude Johnson, later, of course, the General Managing Director of Rolls-Royce, but at this time Secretary of the newly formed Automobile Club of Great Britain and Ireland. Eleanor Thornton would have met all the leading lights of the nascent motoring world, including John Scott-Montagu (later Lord Montagu of Beaulieu) who, in 1902, persuaded her to leave the Automobile Club and join him as his secretary, or in modern terms, personal assistant. In that year, Montagu launched *The Car Illustrated*, Britain's first motoring periodical, and for the next thirteen years Eleanor Thornton helped him with its publication and sale.

No one can be absolutely sure how Sykes conceived the Spirit of Ecstasy. One theory is that Sykes knew Montagu through freelance work for *The Car Illustrated*, that Montagu introduced him to Claude Johnson and that, after a series of meetings and a ride in Montagu's Rolls-Royce, he became inspired by the car's excellence. Where did Eleanor Thornton come into the story? Undoubtedly, Sykes would have known her for a number of years through his work for the magazine, and there is also no doubt that he created a cartoon of her, 'St. Eleanor's Perpetual Prayer'. She also acted as his model for a pastel of Mary Magdalene washing the feet of Christ, and for a statuette of a Sybarite which Sykes submitted for the Royal Academy's Summer Exhibition of 1908. The design for the Rolls-Royce mascot was registered in 1911 as The Spirit of Speed. American-built cars excepted, all Flying Ladies were made by Sykes, and bore his name until the Second World War, when the rights were purchased by Rolls-Royce.

But was Eleanor the model for the Spirit of Ecstasy? Paul Tritton researched the question thoroughly, and quoted the present Lord Montagu as saying, 'I am absolutely certain that Eleanor Thornton was the model'. Apparently, Montagu had been told by Jane Clowes, who worked with Eleanor for many years, that she was the model. Dr. Reggie Ingram, Lord Montagu's doctor, also believed she was, and is reputed to have said, 'They shouldn't have put Eleanor's head on it'.

Others, including Sykes's daughter, Jo Phillips, were not so sure. In her opinion, the pose is such that no person could have adopted the position, with arms swept back, for long enough for any artist to have made a sketch.

Nevertheless, legend has it that Eleanor Thornton was the model, and she was a suitably romantic figure, a woman of grace, beauty and independent spirit – a fitting emblem for the world's most prestigious motor car.

Unfortunately, her life was cut tragically short. She drowned in 1915 when the SS *Persia* was torpedoed off Crete. She had been sailing to Egypt with Montagu who had, it later transpired, been her lover since 1902. A daughter was born in 1903, and although she was brought up by foster parents, Montagu provided for her.

THE COMPETITION

If the Rolls-Royce motor car had a close competitor in its early days, it was undoubtedly Napier. An engineering company that had enjoyed considerable success during much of the nineteenth century, D. Napier & Son was in a poor condition when Montague Stanley Napier took it over in 1895 on the death of his father. Montague Napier had been a keen cyclist in his youth, and, as he worked hard to restore the fortunes of the family firm, also began to take an interest in motor cars.

Just as Royce and the motoring enthusiast, Rolls, were brought together by Edmunds, Napier was introduced to another motoring enthusiast, Selwyn Francis Edge, an Australian who had become the London manager of the Dunlop Pneumatic Tyre Company. Edge became convinced of the great future of the motor car industry, and wanted to organise the building of a British car along the lines of the French Panhard, which he had seen race so successfully (again, the parallel with Charles Rolls is remarkable). Edge drove the Panhard for long distances in order to identify its strengths and weaknesses. One weakness was the tiller steering system, which was tiring to use and failed to give the driver proper control. Walter Munn, a friend of both Edge and Napier, suggested Napier might be able to engineer the necessary modification. Edge visited the works and was unimpressed by Napier's prototype car, but was extremely impressed by Napier's modification to his steering. Edge persuaded Napier to design a new engine. When he saw it, he said:

I was now convinced that in Napier I had the good fortune to alight on a motor engineer of outstanding ability. I saw no reason why he should not design and produce a British car which would be second to none in the world.

At this point Edge convinced the Dunlop Chairman, Harvey du Cros, that this was a venture worth backing. They formed the Motor Power Company with premises in Regent Street, London, and the agency for Gladiator and Clement-Panhard cars, but, most importantly, also for Napier cars. The initial agreement was for the supply of six cars, three with a twin-cylinder engine and three with a four-cylinder engine, all to be delivered by 31 March 1900. Furthermore, the agreement provided for the delivery of 396 cars by the end of 1904 – the time, as we have seen, when Rolls and Royce were finalising their agreement.

The Napier's debut race was Paris–Toulouse–Paris in July 1900, and who should Napier choose to be his riding mechanic? None other than the Hon. Charles Rolls! They were not successful in this event, but Edge continued to race the Napiers and in 1902 won the Gordon Bennett Trophy in the Paris–Vienna race. This brought a flood of orders both for Napier cars and for the commercial vehicles they were making. Expansion was such that the Napier works moved from Vine Street in Lambeth to a greenfield site on the Uxbridge Road in Acton. Orders continued to roll in, and Edge continued to enter all the major races, some with success, some without. D. Napier & Son prospered, and by 1905 they employed 600 men and were ready to expand the factory. By the end of 1906 the work force had doubled to 1,200 and the factory was enlarged yet again, to cover seven acres.

At this time, Napier were using the slogan later adopted by Rolls-Royce, 'The best car in the world'. One of the company's admirers wrote: 'The man of moderate means is not the class of client for whom the Napier motor is intended. It is essentially a rich man's luxury.'

In the autumn of 1906 a rich Surrey landowner, Hugh Locke-King, began the construction of a two-and-three-quarter mile banked racing track on his Brooklands estate near Weybridge. One of those whose advice he sought was Edge, who later booked the track to attempt to drive a car for twenty-four hours at 60 mph. At 6pm on 28 June 1907, three Napiers, one driven by Edge, set off and twenty-four hours later completed the historic run. All three covered over 1,500 miles in the twenty-four hours and, apart from one broken spring, there had been no mechanical troubles. As David Venables put it in his book, *Napier, the first to wear green,* published by Foulis in 1998:

The run had put Napier right back at the forefront, not only of the British motor industry, but also of the world industry . . . in the eyes of the average motorist such a feat was worth a lot more in terms of prestige than a quickly forgotten racing victory.

Nevertheless, Edge and the Napiers continued to race until suddenly, on 22 September 1908, Edge wrote to *The Times*:

Sir,
The views which have been so well expressed in your columns with regard to dangerous motor racing have interested and impressed me greatly.

I feel you will realise the question is a very serious one for the manufacturer. There can be no doubt the rapid development of the automobile has in the past been very largely due to racing and the public undoubtedly then took a great interest in it; but your recent utterances have developed the fact there is now an immense volume of feeling against dangerous racing and that there is a general idea that the automobile is developed and established so sufficiently that racing demonstrations of an extreme kind are no longer necessary.

As one who has been responsible for most of the racing in this country, I think it may perhaps be my duty in deference to public feeling to be the first manufacturer to publicly announce my intention of withdrawing Napier cars from all dangerous competition.

Edge was adept, as Rolls had been, at gaining publicity by writing 'Dear Sir' letters to major newspapers and journals. It proved a lot less expensive than advertising.

Venables surmises in his book that the high moral tone was misleading, and that the true reasons for the withdrawal were the pressures that Edge and Napier were feeling, both from the cost of racing and from competition in the market-place from Rolls-Royce, who were not indulging themselves in racing. Rolls himself had written an article in *The Times* in July 1907 with the headlines: 'The Cost of Motor Racing, AN EXPENSIVE GAME, OF WHICH MANUFACTURERS ARE GETTING TIRED.' Venables concludes:

The great racing years of Napier had ended. The final season had had its share of triumphs and setbacks, but at the end of 1908 Napier was still indisputably one of the great British marques, rivalled only, perhaps, by Rolls-Royce. The bitter rivalry between these two firms was to take many forms over the coming years.

Although the Napier factory was still running flat-out in 1909, by 1911 the competition from Rolls-Royce was beginning to hurt. We have already seen how a Rolls-Royce Silver Ghost triumphed in the RAC London–Edinburgh top gear trial early in 1911, improving on Napier's figures by recording 24.32 miles per gallon. Moreover, few disputed that the Silver Ghosts were better looking than Napiers and, perhaps more important, were sounder from an engineering point of view. Napier had never properly solved the vibration problem with their six-cylinder engine. Edge talked of it as a 'power rattle', but many preferred the quietness of the Silver Ghost which they felt was more appropriate for a luxury car. Furthermore, we have to ask whether people wanted to pay more for a Napier than a Rolls-Royce, and then drive around with the same radiator as on a Napier lorry or Napier taxi.

On top of all this, and perhaps because of it, Edge and Napier began to have differences. Edge wrote in his book, *My Motoring Reminiscences*:

I saw that his [Napier's] interest in Napier cars was beginning to wane; there was not the old enthusiasm and there was a certain air of indifference as regards the class of work that left the factory . . . His chief interest seemed to pass from the drawing office to his own bank pass-book, which was never the case in the early days.

For his part, Napier was irritated by the better margins enjoyed by his distributor, Edge, than he could achieve as a manufacturer. Eventually, Napier started selling cars on his own account, a move that prompted Edge to sue. Fortunately, the two decided that litigation would benefit only lawyers, and Napier bought Edge's business instead. The condition was that Edge would not participate in the motor industry for seven years. It was a sad end to what had been a very effective partnership. And while this wrangle was progressing, Napier's chief designer, Thomas Barrington, left him to work for Rolls-Royce. Barrington was not the only highly talented person to leave Napier for Rolls-Royce. Others included A.G. Elliott, E.W. Hives, Basil Johnson, Arthur Sidgreaves and A.J. Rowledge.

In spite of Napier's problems, new designs were put in hand and were due to be launched in Autumn 1914. However, events on mainland Europe in June, July and August of that year meant that the sale of luxury cars would have to wait for more settled times. As with the directors of Rolls-Royce, the board of Napier thought the war would be a disaster for their company and, as with Rolls-Royce, they could not have been more wrong. In Napier's case it was also aero engines that saved them. In the short term, however, the company survived on the manufacture of lorries, and by November 1918 nearly 2,000 commercial vehicles had been produced.

On 2 August 1915, the Government decreed that the Acton Factory should stop making vehicles and should concentrate solely on the production of aero engines. At first these were designed outside the company, but Napier found this unsatisfactory and asked his chief designer, Arthur Rowledge, to design an aero engine. He designed the Napier Lion, which, although it was too late for the war, was used extensively after it by the RAF.

After the war, Montague Napier, who, like Royce, also moved to the south of France for health reasons, wanted to concentrate on aero engines and abandon cars, but his board disagreed and Rowledge was asked to design a new car. Unfortunately, it was not a great success, largely because of production problems, and Rowledge, blamed by Napier for its failure, resigned and followed Barrington to Rolls-Royce. There he became chief design assistant to Royce, and was a key member of the team that designed the Kestrel and 'R' engines, as well as the air-cooled Exe engine. However, he remained in Derby and did not join the other designers around Royce at West Wittering in Sussex, from where Royce operated in the 1920s. Johnson was looking for a design assistant for Royce, and offers were made to Mark

Birkight of Hispano-Suiza and to Roy Fedden, by this time at Cosmos Engineering. However, it was Rowledge who accepted the position.

The Napier company enjoyed a profitable decade in the 1920s, thanks to the success of the Lion aero engine. They were no longer manufacturing cars. However, by the end of the decade the Lion was becoming obsolete and, although there were new designs on the drawing board, the company was looking to the Government to provide the necessary orders. With a world recession, indeed a depression, breaking, Government contracts were extremely scarce and the Napier board were considering a return to motor car manufacture. To their relief, an existing marque became available when W.O. Bentley's firm fell into the hands of the receiver. As Venables put it succinctly:

Most of the pain and problems of going back to making motor cars could be solved merely by the signing of a cheque. The under-capitalisation which had plagued Bentleys would be a problem no longer.

Napier negotiated a price, and the deal was about to be consummated at the Royal Courts of Justice in the Strand, when a barrister appeared to announce that he had been instructed to intervene on behalf of undisclosed clients. Both sets of counsel appeared in the court before Mr. Justice Markham, and the Napier counsel confirmed their offer of £103,675 (£5 million in today's terms). The other barrister announced that he was acting on behalf of British Central Equitable Trust, and that he had been instructed to offer slightly more than Napier. Napier's counsel requested an adjournment, made a frantic telephone call to Acton, and came back with a higher offer. Counsel for British Central Equitable Trust rose, but before he could speak Mr. Justice Markham said he was not prepared to oversee an auction, and invited the two sides to return at 4.30pm with sealed bids.

When they all returned and the judge opened the envelopes, Napier had bid £104,775 and the Trust £125,256. The Trust turned out to be a nominee of Rolls-Royce, and thus Bentley moved to Derby, not to Acton. Napier abandoned their attempts to re-enter the car market. The company enjoyed an increasingly prosperous decade in the 1930s, thanks to the rearmament programmes. By 1942, satellite factories were operating in Liverpool, Luton and at Park Royal, west London, and the company was employing over 10,000 people. In November of that year it was taken over by the English Electric Company.

Chapter Three

'The achievement of a thinking designer'

'The lights are going out'
The First Flights
The Stimulus of War
Rolls-Royce's First Aero Engine
The Hawk, Falcon and Condor
'To provide a moderate profit'

'THE LIGHTS ARE GOING OUT'

THE NINETEENTH CENTURY IS VIEWED, correctly, as a period of prosperity for Britain, but that did not mean that it was one long boom. There were long recessionary periods – the last twenty years of the century was one – and manufacturers especially had to struggle with a generally overvalued pound sterling. We have seen how Royce met severe competition from the emerging industrial nations, Germany and the USA, in his engineering and electrical business. Nevertheless, there were sufficient wealthy people in the world to make the production of a luxury car a viable commercial proposition – in peace time.

War was a different proposition and, as the confident celebrations of a new century faded, the strains of the changing situation in Europe made war seem a possible, perhaps an inevitable, consequence.

By 1900, the Austro-Hungarian Empire had virtually collapsed, as had that other bulwark of strength in southern Europe and the Middle East, the Turkish Empire. The Russian Empire was looking increasingly unstable, while the new strong man of Europe was the recently united Germany. The architect of German unity, Otto von Bismarck, Prime Minister of Prussia, had not wanted war with his neighbours, and had created a series of complicated alliances to prevent it.

However, following Bismarck's death in 1898, the German Kaiser, Wilhelm II, assumed greater power and influence, and, although he was a grandson of Queen Victoria, Britain (and especially the British Empire) became the object of his envy. From the late 1890s until a general European war broke out in 1914, an increasingly shrill propaganda war was waged between Germany and Britain, with France, initially a bemused onlooker, eventually coming down on the side of the British.

There were several crises before 1914, most notably in the Balkans and at Agadir in Morocco, and in March 1914, giving his final peacetime Naval Estimates to the House of Commons, the young Winston Churchill said:

The causes which might lead to a general war have not been removed and often remind us of their presence. There has not been the slightest abatement of naval and military preparation. On the contrary, we are witnessing this year increases of expenditure by Continental powers on armaments beyond all previous expenditure. The world is arming as it has never armed before.

All the major powers, and many of the lesser ones, were becoming restless. France was looking for revenge for her defeat by Prussia in 1870, and wanted the return of Alsace and Lorraine. Russia had been defeated by Japan in 1905 and humiliated in the Balkans in 1908, and was not prepared to suffer any further reverses. Austria-Hungary was crumbling, but believed it could stiffen its backbone by overcoming Serbia, and had secured a pledge of support from Germany. The Germans, now feeling severely threatened with encirclement by the Triple Entente (a pact between Britain, France and Russia), were ready for war. Britain itself, somewhat distracted by Ireland, had no ambitions in Europe, but felt threatened by the new German fleet.

The final lighting of the touch-paper to this powder keg was the assassination of the Archduke Franz Ferdinand, heir to the Austro-Hungarian throne, in Sarajevo in Bosnia. This gave the Austrians the excuse they had been looking for to strike against Serbia (in fact the Serbian Government had not been involved, but the assassination plot had been hatched in the Serbian capital, Belgrade). However, the Austrians wanted to be certain that Germany would back them, and the Austrian Ambassador in Berlin delivered a note to the Kaiser which concluded: 'What would German policy be if Austria decided to punish this centre of criminal agitation in Belgrade?'

Initially cautious, the Kaiser came to the conclusion that Russia would not be prepared to go to war over Serbia, and effectively gave his Austrian ally a blank cheque. Indeed, the Germans quickly became more keen on military action than Austria, even though they must have realised that both Russia and France would be dragged into the conflict. Unaware of the determination of the Germans and Austrians to go to war, the allies in the Triple

Entente attempted conciliation. It was useless. The Russians felt obliged to mobilise, which gave the Germans the excuse to declare war on them. The Austrians followed. France and Britain continued to try to negotiate, but on Tuesday 4 August 1914 the German Army crossed the Belgian frontier. The British issued an ultimatum demanding withdrawal by midnight. At midnight, no reply had been received and Britain was at war with Germany. Foreign Secretary Viscount Grey said wearily: 'The lights are going out all over Europe. They will not be lit again in our lifetime.'

For Rolls-Royce Limited as for every other luxury car maker, a prolonged war would be fatal unless their skills could be used in the war effort. The outbreak of war took the company, and indeed many others, by surprise. The profitability, even the survival, of the company was threatened, as R.W.H. Bailey made clear in his autobiographical notes:

The outbreak of war threw the whole works organisation out of gear. It was clearly useless to carry on making the big luxury cars which were our only product and source of income and we were at once instructed from London to discharge one half of the designing and technical staff and, at the same time, the remaining sectional leaders were asked, at least temporarily, to consider if we could accept a reduction in salary and how much.

Employees were advised not to pay their rent and, if evicted, it was made clear that they could bring their families to live in the factory.

The first board meeting after the outbreak authorised Claude Johnson 'to reduce the works wages to about one-fourth by discharging about half the hands and allowing the remainder to work only half time'. More surprisingly, the board decided that the company 'would not avail itself of the opportunity, now possibly arising, of making or assembling aero engines for the British Government'.

We have already seen that Royce, Johnson and Claremont had resisted Rolls's attempts to persuade the company to become involved in the manufacture of aero engines. Indeed, the minutes of a board meeting held on 12 February 1909 show that a motion that 'this Company should acquire the rights for the British Isles to manufacture the Wright aeroplane' was flatly rejected.

Looked at from 1999, the board's initial reaction to becoming involved in aero engine assembly was staggering, but few in August 1914 expected the war to last long. 'Home by Christmas' was the catch-phrase of the hour when discussing how long our lads would be in France.

When war broke out, the staff and employees were taking their annual holiday, and Johnson placed an advertisement in the *Daily Mail* instructing them to return home immediately and 'to observe the most rigid economy'.

He addressed the sales staff at the Conduit Street HQ offices and showroom, telling them that the firm was being run on money borrowed from the bank, an acceptable position in peacetime. In wartime, however, he was not so sure. He told them:

A week ago the Rolls-Royce business and its property were worth a very large sum of money; I cannot say whether when the bank opens again on Friday the bankers may not take the view that the Rolls-Royce business is worth nothing at all, and therefore they may refuse to let us draw another penny from the bank. Anyone with their eyes open can see that the sale of Rolls-Royce cars must be absolutely stopped.

Johnson soon had second thoughts about whether to accept war work. He contacted 'the Flying Factory of the War Office' and heard that

we might possibly tender for the assembling of 30 engines and the making of a further 20, for which designs and specifications will be provided for us. There is a possibility of further orders which may keep our factory extremely busy.

Apparently, some customers and shareholders disapproved of this move into aero engine development, but as Johnson pointed out to shareholders at the eighth annual ordinary meeting on 20 January 1915:

[T]heir trade was largely diminished . . . and they had immediately to find work with which to employ their highly skilled hands or turn them adrift, and lose the value of all the years of training in the special Rolls-Royce methods.

He made contact with the office in charge of transport for the expeditionary force due to leave for France, and offered a hundred chassis at £800 each. De Looze, the company secretary, went to see the bank manager in Derby, who did not take the extreme measures feared by Johnson, but merely suggested that the overdraft facility not be used for the purpose of manufacturing cars for stock.

In spite of the Rolls-Royce board's earlier decision, Royce and Johnson were persuaded by the War Office to tender for the manufacture of fifty aero engines to a design from Renault in France. At the same time as the Rolls-Royce board were deciding not to make aero engines for the Government, Royce was designing the Eagle. Not for the last time, Royce was ignoring what the board had decided in his absence. Johnson, prompted by Arthur Biddulph, superintendent of the night shift, also scoured the country for sub-contract work. He saw it as his business to keep work flowing through the factory, and accepted orders to make the Renault V8 aero engine and the RAF 1A engine, the 40/50 hp chassis for staff cars, ambulances for the Army and armoured cars for the RNAS, shell cases and flechettes (known as 'arrows of death', these were little hand-held darts that were dropped over enemy trenches and quickly reached an incredible speed, fast enough to go through a man's helmet and kill him), parts for torpedoes and, almost, the manufacture under licence of the Danish Madsen automatic rifle.

THE FIRST FLIGHTS

Many books have been written on the first years of flight, incorporating man's early attempts to propel himself through the air. In this book we are concerned with the flight of heavier-than-air craft propelled by engine power, and it was only with the development of the internal combustion engine at the end of the nineteenth century that this became a serious possibility.

In England, an Aeronautical Society was founded as early as 1866, but it was not until 1901 that the Aero Club, later the Royal Aero Club, was formed by C.S. Rolls and Frank and Vera Hedges Butler, with Claude Johnson agreeing to act as secretary *pro tem*. In 1902 Stanley Spencer made the first flight in a British airship, which was 75 feet long, 20 feet in diameter, and with a capacity of 20,000 cubic feet. The power-unit was a Simms water-cooled petrol engine which developed 3.5 hp at a speed of 2,500 rpm, and which drove a single airscrew through a reduction gear. On 22 September, Spencer flew 30 miles in 100 minutes, taking a wandering route from Crystal Palace in south London to Eastcote in Middlesex. At about the same time, both French and German engineers developed and flew airships of differing sizes and power. The Germans in particular invested heavily, seemingly intent on challenging rivals not only on land and at sea, but also in the air.

However, some saw the future of powered air flight not in airships but in machines shaped more like birds. Otto Lilienthal, a German engineer, made more than 2,000 flights in fixed-wing gliders before he stalled and crashed, killing himself, in 1896. However, his exploits received wide coverage in newspapers and periodicals throughout the world, and two American brothers, Wilbur and Orville Wright, bicycle manufacturers in Dayton, Ohio, found them inspirational. It is now accepted that the Wright brothers made the first practical flight powered by an internal combustion engine on 17 December 1903, and that they were the first men to achieve powered, sustained and controlled flights, landing on ground *at the same level* as the take-off point.

In the early 1900s, the brothers built a number of powered aircraft – Flyer, Flyer II and Flyer III – and gradually became convinced that they had developed a valuable asset which could be sold to the United States Army. Unfortunately, the Army showed little interest, and they turned to both the

British and French Governments. Their sales efforts were not helped by their secrecy while their patents were still pending. Slightly disillusioned, they put their machine away in October 1905 and did not make another flight for two and a half years.

However, their American patent was granted in 1906, and the brothers entered into agreements with firms in Britain, France and Germany for the manufacture of their aircraft under licence. In the summer of 1908, Orville submitted a machine to acceptance trials for the US Government, while Wilbur went to Europe to make demonstration flights. Between August and December he made over a hundred flights in France and caused a sensation. Baden-Powell, founder of the Scout Movement and a keen kite flyer, said: 'Wilbur Wright is in possession of a power which controls the fate of nations.'

Ironically, the Wright brothers thought that their invention would mean permanent peace. Orville Wright said in 1917:

When my brother and I built and flew our first man-carrying flying machine, we thought we were introducing into the world an invention which would make further wars practically impossible.

The competitors were spurred into action. In Europe, Henry Farman built a biplane that was more stable than the Wright aeroplane, and in the USA Glenn Curtiss produced a similar machine. The Frenchman Louis Bleriot developed his monoplane, and became a national hero when he made the first cross-Channel flight in a heavier-than-air machine. Developments in Germany, Austria and Italy did not lag far behind.

At this stage, though, Britain *was* lagging behind. It was not until December 1909 that A.V. Roe flew more than half a mile in a British-designed aeroplane, although J.T.C. Moore-Brabazon and the expatriate American S.F. Cody were making progress in aeroplanes designed and built overseas. Early in 1909 Colonel H.S. Massy, late of the Bengal Lancers, and Stephen Marples, a consulting engineer, came together to found the Aerial League of the British Empire (later called the Air League), whose main aim was

educating the citizens of the British Empire as well as the authorities entrusted with the defence of it, to the urgent necessity for the establishment and maintenance of similar superiority in the air to that which we hold on the high seas.

On 19 and 24 February 1916, correspondence was published in *The Times* which showed that an offer of the Wright patents had been made to the British Government in February 1907 by a New York finance company, Flint & Co. On 4 March 1907, the Secretary of State for War, R.B. Haldane, had written to the firm:

The War Office has not the least intention of entering into any agreement as to flying machines with anyone, or of giving them the slightest guarantee.

When the Aerial League was founded at the Carlton Hotel in London in February 1909 it was already well behind similar organisations in France, where the French Aerial League, with 30,000 members, could boast funds of £50,000 (£5 million in today's terms) and Germany, where the German Aerial League had raised nearly £500,000 for the establishment of a national air fleet.

The Aerial League set about rectifying this situation, and in April 1909 the Lord Mayor of London presided over a crowded meeting in support of the League at the Mansion House in the City. Contributing to the speeches on the day were Lord Montagu (a visionary about the future of the aeroplane, just as he was about the motor car), Professor Hele Shaw (later to patent the variable-pitch propeller), the prolific inventor Hiram Maxim, Major Baden-Powell and Admiral Sir Percy Scott. Messages of goodwill were sent by Vice-Admiral Prince Louis of Battenberg, Lord Curzon, Lord Charles Beresford and Winston Churchill. After a lengthy debate, Lord Montagu moved a resolution:

That this meeting of the citizens of London views with considerable anxiety the rapid development of the science and practice of aerial navigation by other nations and deplores the backwardness and apathy shown by this country regarding this new means of communication, which is of vital importance from a commercial as well as from a national defence point of view; and pledges itself heartily to support the objects of the Aerial League of the British Empire.

To support their arguments, the League produced figures that showed Britain's position *vis-à-vis* her European competitors. These showed that compared with Britain's five officers, forty men, no airships and only one aeroplane involved in anything that could be described as a national force, France had twenty-four officers, 432 men, eight airships and ten aeroplanes, Germany twenty officers, 465 men, six airships but no aeroplanes. Russia had no fewer than seventy-nine officers and 3,255 men, but only one airship and no aeroplanes. Further afield, the Government of the USA was as backward in support as Britain, employing only three officers, ten men, one airship and one aeroplane.

Belatedly, the British Government began to take an interest and, following a report from the Committee of Imperial Defence, created a special department for the study of aeronautical problems at the National Physical Laboratory in Teddington. In October 1908, the Committee of Imperial Defence had established a subcommittee on aerial navigation, and C.S. Rolls had testified that 'England will cease to be an island'. The Army Balloon Factory at Farnborough was reorganised to become the Army Aircraft Factory in 1911. (In April 1912 the Army Aircraft Factory was renamed the Royal Aircraft Factory (RAF), and over the next five years a number of aircraft and aero engines under the RAF logo were designed. Most were produced under licence by the growing number of aircraft and engine manufacturers, and official records show that only 533 aircraft were produced at Farnborough itself up to 1918. In June 1918 the factory was renamed the Royal Aircraft Establishment to avoid confusion with the recently formed Royal Air Force.)

In August 1912 about thirty British and foreign aircraft were invited to take part in military trials at Larkhill on Salisbury Plain, for a prize of £5,000. The highest marks were scored by S.F. Cody in his ungainly Type V biplane, powered by a 120 hp Austro-Daimler engine. This engine was produced under licence after 1912 by Beardmore in Glasgow, who developed it into the BHP (Beardmore, Halford, Pullinger). Meanwhile, the Government had brought Armstrong Siddeley into the aero engine manufacturing arena. They did not like the BHP and, having redesigned it, put it into production as the PUMA (the Rolls-Royce Heritage Trust, Coventry branch, have one running). The Government preferred the more elegant and practical B E 2 aeroplane designed and flown by Geoffrey de Havilland, who had been taken on at Farnborough by the superintendent of the factory, Mervyn O'Gorman, himself a distinguished engineer. The B E 2 flew at 70 mph, achieved an initial rate of climb of 365 feet per minute and reached an altitude of 10,000 feet. Although built at the Royal Aircraft Factory, the B E 2 was powered by a 70 hp Renault engine, built in France.

From the B E 2, de Havilland developed the B E 2 C, of which nearly 2,000 were built by various British firms. After 1911, the year of the Agadir Crisis, as the European political situation deteriorated, all governments took more interest in air power and increased their budgets for both aeroplanes and airships. In the spring of 1912, the British Government formed the Royal Flying Corps, consisting of a Military Wing, a Naval Wing, a Central Flying School, the Royal Aircraft Factory and a reserve. The Navy retained a flying school of its own, and in the summer of 1914, as war approached, succeeded in detaching the Naval Wing from the Royal Flying Corps.

THE STIMULUS OF WAR

The more visionary and enlightened in government and the armed forces had appreciated the likely importance of air power in future wars, but what was the state of Britain's air services when war broke out on 4 August 1914? They were still primitive, but at least in a state of formation and expansion.

On 29 July, instructions had been issued to the Royal Naval Air Service (RNAS) to confine itself to home defence and protection of vulnerable points from possible attack by enemy aircraft and airships. This would leave the Royal Flying Corps (RFC) to support the Army. The British Expeditionary Force embarked for France on 9 August, and two days later RFC head-quarters left Farnborough and, via Southampton, arrived in Amiens on 13 August. Numbers 2 and 3 Squadron flew to France on 13 August, as did 4 Squadron from Eastchurch. They were joined on 15 August by 5 Squadron. All were based at Amiens. No. 2 Squadron flew B E 2s, while No. 3 Squadron flew Bleriot monoplanes and Henry Farman biplanes. No. 4 Squadron also flew B E 2s, while No. 5 flew a mixture of Farmans, Avros and B E 8s. The total strength of this RFC force was 105 officers, sixty-three aeroplanes and ninety-five mechanical support vehicles. None of the aircraft carried any armament, whether guns or bombs.

All governments saw reconnaissance as the main function of aircraft. Nevertheless, bombing trials were carried out in most countries before the outbreak of war. Aircraft were first used in battle before the First World War by the Italians in their attack on the Turks in Tripolitania. However, as the Turks did not possess an air force or any anti-aircraft weapons, this could hardly be considered a true test of the efficacy of air power in combat.

This test was to come in the second half of 1914, as the German High Command put Helmuth von Moltke's plan into action. The original German plan for the defeat of France and Russia had been drawn up by Alfred von Schlieffen in response to the Moroccan crisis in 1905, before air power was considered and at a time when British intervention was not expected. How-ever, the development of heavy howitzers and airships meant that the Germans felt they could tackle the strongly fortified Belgian forts at Liège and Namur, enabling them to make a faster and more direct thrust into northern France. When war broke out and the Germans attacked the Belgian forts, airships were used both for reconnaissance and for bombing, but proved vulnerable to fire from the ground.

During August 1914 the Moltke plan worked perfectly, and the British and French Armies were soon in full retreat. Both the British Expeditionary Force and the French Fourth and Fifth Armies retreated behind the River Marne. By the end of August, Paris seemed to be at the mercy of the German Armies, but at this point reconnaissance, aided by aircraft, told Joseph Gallieni, the Military Governor of Paris, that the German First Army's flank was exposed. The British and French attacked, and by 9 September the British realised from their reconnaissance aircraft that Kluck's First Army was in full retreat. Over the following three days, the British Expeditionary Force advanced about thirty miles and the French Fifth Army about twenty. Von Moltke was so disillusioned with the collapse of his plan that he thought

Germany should make peace. The German High Command thought otherwise and, as the retreating German Armies dug in along the River Aisne, a line of opposing trenches was gradually established, stretching from the English Channel to Switzerland. Four years of bloody attrition began.

A stalemate set in, but at the same time both sides hoped for a decisive breakthrough. The only means of gaining intelligence to achieve this was through the capture of prisoners (who in most cases knew little of any significance) or, more importantly, through reconnaissance from the air. Both sides fought not only for mastery of the air but also, by bombardment from the ground, to prevent observation by enemy aircraft. Aeroplanes were forced higher, making observation more difficult, but this limitation was soon offset by the use of photography. Bombing raids on objectives beyond the reach of artillery were soon put in hand, though targets proved more difficult to hit than to identify.

As the war ground on, both sides developed their air power as fast as they could, supporting their massive armies both in defensive and offensive roles. The Germans also made bombing raids on Britain, sending sorties of thirty to forty bombers which killed and injured hundreds of people in London. This prompted Prime Minister David Lloyd George, and Lieutenant-General J.C. Smuts, whom Lloyd George had brought into the War Cabinet, to plan similar raids on German cities.

For such operations, they realised they would need an Air Ministry to bring together the Royal Flying Corps and the Royal Naval Air Service into a unified air force. The post of Secretary of State for Air was offered to Lord Northcliffe, who turned it down; it was taken up by his younger brother, Lord Rothermere, also a newspaper proprietor. Brigadier-General H.M. Trenchard, who had enjoyed a somewhat controversial spell as a front-line commander in the RFC, became Chief of the Air Staff.

ROLLS-ROYCE'S FIRST AERO ENGINE

As we have seen, Rolls-Royce initially declined to become involved in the manufacture of aero engines at the beginning of the First World War.

This reluctance was understandable, knowing Royce's temperament, as the company was initially asked to make engines under licence from the French company, Renault. Harald Penrose* (see footnote overleaf), in his comprehensive series, *British Aviation,* made it clear how the British Government had become complacently reliant on its new-found ally:

Before the war the Government had considered it safe to keep the British aeroplane and aero engine trade ticking over with minimal orders, believing that in emergency the strong French aircraft industry, where there were real factories rather than scattered selections of sheds, could satisfy all needs. Sir Walter Raleigh, in the opening volume of 'The War in the Air' describes what ensued: 'In October 1914 a Flying Corps officer was sent to Paris to organise a department to deal with purchase of French aircraft supplies. The Paris office, which dealt through the French Ministry of War, became known as the British Aviation Supplies Department, and in December a representative joined the Department to watch the interests of the Naval Air Service and place orders on behalf of the Admiralty Air Department. The Paris office did not work smoothly. From the outset the War Office and Admiralty representatives were, by nature of their different allegiance, in competition. Each was there to get all he could for his own Service, and the consequent friction led to disappointments which, because many of the high performance aeroplanes used by the RFC were French, had repercussions in the field. The result was that Major-General Trenchard (at that time Lieutenant-Colonel at Farnborough building up the RFC) found it essential to make many personal visits to the French firms . . . French manufacturers were in no real position to meet British demands . . .'

The initial panic that the bank would withdraw Rolls-Royce's overdraft facilities and that the company would face liquidation was soon transformed into a 'keep everyone working' situation, as Johnson's tireless efforts to secure war-related contracts were successful. When the company quickly reversed its decision on becoming involved in the manufacture of aero engines, and as Royce began the development of his own engine, the state of the aircraft industry (it was hardly large enough to merit such a description) was extremely rudimentary. The hub of the structure, such as it was, was the Royal Aircraft Factory at Farnborough, which had been established as early as 1905 (as the Army Balloon Factory) and was capable of designing and manufacturing its own aircraft and engines. There were also twelve private aircraft-manufacturing companies, but their combined annual output was only about a hundred aircraft. Three of them specialised in seaplanes. Nearly all the aero engines, designed either by Farnborough or by enthusiastic amateurs, were still in the experimental stage, and for completed engines Britain was still totally dependent on France. On the outbreak of war, not a single British aero engine was in production, or anywhere near it. It had only been the year before when Farnborough was authorised to design an engine, and been allocated £5,000 (about £500,000 in today's terms) for the purpose.

Royce was probably enthused about aero engines by the same Jimmy Radley who had driven a Silver Ghost in the Austrian Alpine trial. Radley

---

* Harald Penrose OBE, born in 1903, studied aeronautical engineering at London University before joining Westland in 1926 as a designer-technician. In 1936 he was elected as the youngest-ever member of the Royal Aeronautical Society. During his long career with Westland he flew over 400 types of aircraft, and has written many detailed books on the British aircraft industry.

was a pioneer aviator with his own aircraft works in Huntingdon. On 3 August 1914, one day before war broke out, Johnson prompted Radley to visit Royce in St. Margaret's Bay to talk about the possibilities of aircraft engines. Within two weeks, Royce and Johnson visited Mervyn O'Gorman at the Royal Aircraft Factory, who asked them to make a French V8 air-cooled engine.

Royce was reluctant, as he did not like the design, but Johnson persuaded him to allow the Rolls-Royce factory to manufacture some while Royce designed his own engine. O'Gorman also asked Rolls-Royce and Napier to develop and make a new RAF air-cooled 200 hp design. Royce would not become involved with this, as he felt that air-cooling was not the best way forward. He, Elliott and Maurice Olley set off to design a water-cooled engine, mainly because Royce felt that air-cooling would take too long to get right. His whole experience was in water-cooling.

Once Royce had decided he must design his own aero engine, it was the head of the Admiralty Air Engine Section, Engineer-Commander Wilfred Briggs, who did all he could to help. After consultation with Commodore (later Admiral Sir) Murray Sueter, Commander of the Royal Naval Air Service (who had asked Frederick Handley Page to build the RNAS a giant bomber, 'a bloody paralyser of an aeroplane'), Briggs, with his assistant, Lieutenant W.O. Bentley (later to see his car company sold to Rolls-Royce), drove a Grand Prix Mercedes, with its water-cooled cylinders, to Derby. They gave the car to the works manager, Arthur Wormald, with the suggestion that it might be a useful starting point for the 200 hp engine required for the heavy bomber they had in mind. Accompanying Briggs and Bentley was Roy Fedden, technical director of Brazil Straker. Fedden was probably invited because he had already impressed everyone in the industry by modifying a dangerous batch of Curtiss OX-5 engines shipped from the USA, and Briggs perhaps hoped that he and Rolls-Royce could work together to build a first-class aero engine.

Hives, at the time setting up development testing, tested and dissected the engine. The ultimate decision, of course, was Royce's, and he lived 200 miles away at St. Margaret's Bay in Kent. Royce did use water-cooling and he did use a cylinder similar to that of the Silver Ghost, but other than that he worked closely with A.G. Elliott and Maurice Olley in considering the most appropriate design for each part of the engine.

Some have suggested that Royce almost copied the Mercedes engine. This is incorrect. Royce studied the engine, as he did any engine he thought relevant, but he drew on his own experience with the 40/50 – the Silver Ghost was recognised as the best car in the world – and his study of the Mercedes engine was aimed at avoiding German patents as much as anything else. His 'Bible' (see extracts that follow) makes this clear.

In designing the Eagle engine, what did Royce's own experience and the necessity for swift action tell him? He should be considering safety, cost-effectiveness and what was readily usable. On the Silver Ghost, the crankcase, which was aluminium, crankshaft, gears, lubrication and piston cooling were all the best available, so he used them. How could he achieve the necessary power of 200 hp which the War Office had requested? He felt he could not increase the piston diameter, but could increase the piston travel. As we have seen, he had no experience of air-cooling, so he would have to stick with water-cooling. This development was still not giving the required power, so Royce doubled the number of cylinders to twelve. Still not enough power, so Royce ran the engine faster, at the same time gearing down to ensure that the propeller remained below 1,100 rpm. The RNAS had told Royce that this was essential for prop 'efficiency'. So far so good, but the big cast-iron cylinder blocks were too heavy, and the sidevalves (L-head) were fine for smoothness and silence but not good for performance. Royce therefore used overhead valves driven by an overhead camshaft (used to great effect by Peugeot in their 1913 racer) to reduce the inertia in the system, and also hemispherical heads and gas crossflow with air feed in one side and exhaust out of the other. Finally, to reduce the weight, Royce used pressed-steel water jackets on each cylinder separately.

Drawings were sent up from Kent, and Claude Johnson, basing himself in Derby during this emergency, made sure the parts were made as quickly as possible and sent back for Royce's inspection. Initially, important parts were made in wood so that Royce and his team could shave off parts to reduce weight without losing strength. For example, the crankshaft went backwards and forwards three times before it was made in metal.

In spite of all the constraints imposed by this communication system, Hives had an engine on the test bed in late February 1915. It was expected to give 200 bhp at 1,600 rpm, but allegedly gave 225 bhp on its first run. However, Royce was not satisfied with that. He strove to increase power, reduce weight and fuel consumption and, at the same time, improve reliability. He wrote to Derby Works on 22 March 1915:

Re 200 hp aero engine – short duration tests etc. We presume that you are continuing the tests at high compression and increased speed, first finding out how fast you can run for one or two-hour spells with the lubrication as in the 20 hour test, and then whether the big-end will bear an increase in speed with (1) castor oil (2) cooler oil, or (3) higher pressure.

Royce was testing every part to destruction, and whenever a major increase in power was achieved, a long-endurance test would be run to prove the engine at the higher power. So impressive were the instructions from Royce that in December 1915 Johnson had Royce's memos on the subject printed and bound in a limited edition of a hundred copies. The book was called *The First Aero Engines made by Rolls-Royce*, and in the preface were the words:

In the opinion of the Board of Directors, the Memoranda and letters written by Mr. F.H. Royce, the Engineer-in-Chief, in connection with the design, testing and manufacture of these engines are so admirable as evidence of extreme care, foresight and analytical thought, that the Directors decided to have them printed and bound in order that copies may be available for study and as an example to all grades of Rolls-Royce Engineers, present and future.

The book was marked 'CONFIDENTIAL, not to be shown to anyone without the authority of the Directors'. The following extracts give some flavour of what it contained.

Re Aero Engine Cylinders

With reference to the aero cylinder tools, any way that the first sample cylinders can be produced with temporary tools will please me. It is necessary, however, if we make tools that are at all costly, that they should be made thoroughly well, so as to be lasting and achieve their object without any nursing. This cylinder work is so important that nothing is too good to produce it so that the parts of the engine will go together without hesitation, and be interchangeable.

I am quite willing for you to alter any designs that I send, providing that they will carry out their duties satisfactorily, but I do not think it worth while to alter them seriously because they may, in the form I send them, be thought rather expensive.

Re R.A.F. Aero Engines

Referring to the high-class finish, we are not people that put a high finish on parts unless it is necessary, and I quite agree that on this work no money should be spent on unnecessary finish, but spend all the money and time necessary to make a good and reliable working job of the highest possible efficiency.

Re 200 hp Aero Engine

We do not believe that it is possible to test them to destruction, but we should very much like to do so, if any satisfactory means can be found of repeating the load thousands of times. This we may do later.

Re Aluminium Pistons

This subject will bear investigation, and for your part I recommend that one of the pistons only on an engine be made larger than the other eleven, in fact, so large in the top that you know when the throttle is suddenly opened it will probably pull up the engine with its tightness. We can then let this piston be fitted to an articulated rod, and can pull up the engine a few times with this piston, providing that nothing breaks on the first occasion. Should the piston or connecting rod give way, the experiments will be fairly conclusive and very instructive.

The book became famous as the *Rolls-Royce Bible*, and on 31 December 1919 *The Times* printed a whole article about it, concluding:

The 'Bible' was printed for the purpose of providing those engaged at the works with an example of engineering living, and of impressing upon them the amount of care and thought needed for the design and manufacture of a successful aero engine. During the war its author received a remarkable tribute from a German engineer, who had apparently studied the evolution of the engine from successive captured machines. He described it as a classic example of how a designer can avoid every possible difficulty that can be foreseen in a design, and thus ensure success; and he declared that many details of the engine are undoubtedly not the result of long continued experiments, but the achievement of a thinking designer.

Bill Gunston, in his book *Rolls-Royce, Aero Engines*, published by Patrick Stephens Limited in 1989, wrote:

Under Hives the progress of the engine was nothing short of brilliant. The 'Old Man's' instructions were followed meticulously, and nothing was left to chance. Speed was increased almost immediately to 1800 rpm, and by August 1915 to 2000 rpm, the maximum brake horsepower then reaching 300. After prolonged testing it was decided to clear the engine for production at a rating of 255 hp at 1800 rpm with 1900 permitted for short periods. By this time the engine was being referred to not as 'the 200 hp engine' but by the RNAS and aircraft industry as 'the 250 Rolls-Royce'.

Now committed, Royce displayed his usual drive, and wrote to the Works in Derby on 24 October 1914:

I am very surprised to hear there was any difficulty about finding machines to work on the aero-engine cylinders. I am afraid the position is that we must find machines. We have worried the RFC and the Admiralty. We have also worried and worked continually on the design of this, and there must be no delays put in the way of the progress of the engine, because we must either do the work promptly or abandon the idea of doing it altogether. We cannot possibly have it hanging about, otherwise it will be only a disgrace to us.

During 1916 the Eagle gradually increased in power, from 266 bhp in March, to 284 in July, to 322 by December. By September 1917 it had reached 350 and in February 1918, 360. By 1917 no fewer than eight versions of the

Eagle had been produced, but irrespective of the series number, each engine was a twelve-cylinder, water-cooled, 60-degree vee of 20.32 litres capacity. Each cylinder, with its water-jacket, formed a separate unit. The barrel, machined from a steel forging, was retained by a base flange and studs. Inlet and exhaust ports were machined from solid forgings, welded in at opposite sides of the head, and the water-jacket was fabricated from steel pressings, welded in place. There was one inlet and one exhaust valve for each cylinder, and a single camshaft on each bank of cylinders, carried in a casing above the cylinder heads, operated both inlet and exhaust valves.

The supply of magnetos was a serious problem on the outbreak of war, as most had come from Germany or the USA. Eagles I to V used only one sparking plug per cylinder, with two six-point magnetos. Later models used two sparking plugs per cylinder, with four six-point magnetos. The Eagle I had two carburettors, while Eagles II to VIII had four (the Eagle IV had two duplex).

The company was also a strong advocate of water as a cooling medium, claiming it ensured equalised temperature throughout the cylinder and provided heat dissipating surfaces in a form offering very low air resistance. The Royal Aircraft Factory tended to favour air-cooling, but Royce resisted their efforts of persuasion. Of course, Royce understood the supreme importance of power to weight – the 40/50 had aluminium castings, except for the cylinders, and alloy steels in all important ferrous components – and applied his knowledge and experience in this field in the design of the Eagle.

A unique feature of the Eagle was the epicyclic reduction gear, which had the advantage of creating less strain on the crankcase than was caused by spur gearing. The gear was of fixed sunwheel type, in which an annulus (an internally toothed gearwheel) on the crankshaft meshed with three smaller spur gearwheels on the extremities of three arms formed integrally with the airscrew shaft. The three small gears were connected to three pinions which meshed with the fixed sunwheel, and the airscrew shaft was bolted to the three-armed spider which carried the planet pinion cage. An Oldham coupling provided the anchorage of the sunwheel to the gear casing and allowed the gears to be perfectly aligned.

Olley designed the gear early in 1915 at St. Margaret's Bay. A driving parameter was getting the reduction ratio right. There were worries about sideloads on the crankshaft.

Once proven, Government orders flowed in for the Eagle to such an extent that engineers were sent from Derby to the USA to supervise production of an extra 1,500 engines there. Rolls-Royce's aim was to secure a contract with the US Government for them to organise the building of the Eagle in the USA. Negotiations took place with the US company Pierce Arrow, which nearly led to a merger. However, Eagles were not manufactured in the USA because the US Government backed the Liberty engine. Nevertheless, many US companies manufactured components for assembly in Derby. By the time they started arriving the Armistice had been signed, and the company was faced with some painful cancellation negotiations.

In 1914, the Air Department of the Navy, dissatisfied with the delay in the development of a 200 hp Sunbeam which they had commissioned Louis Coatalen to design, had placed a contract with Rolls-Royce for an engine of 250 hp. The Royal Aircraft Factory gave both Rolls-Royce and Napier all available data to help them.

Harald Penrose wrote in *British Aviation – The Great War and Armistice*:

It was at least due to Farnborough's preliminary design that Henry Royce had commenced work on his first twelve-cylinder vee water-cooled engine, the prototype Eagle, which had been followed by the smaller and lighter twelve-cylinder Falcon with the intention of concurrently supplying both bombers and fighters with suitable powerplants.

This is incorrect. Royce studied Farnborough's preliminary design and made a conscious decision *not* to copy it. The Falcon was a direct scale-down of the Eagle, but with a few strategic bits 'beefed-up'. The design work on the Falcon was carried out at Derby by R.W.H. Bailey and his team.

However, as we would have expected from Henry Royce, he was determined to develop his own engines. *The Final Report of the Judicial Enquiry into the Administration and Command of the RFC*, published at the end of 1915, said:

The Royal Aircraft Factory was designing a 200 hp water-cooled engine before the war and had proceeded some way by 1914. General Henderson, as one of the judges at the engine competition that year, was of opinion that higher-powered engines would be required, but hoped private firms would develop them. He therefore handed the drawings to Rolls-Royce and Napier, but the former declined and independently designed their 250 hp engine of which deliveries are just beginning.

As the historians of the Farnborough enterprise, S. Child and C.F. Caunter, wrote:

Napiers closely followed this design, but that remarkable genius, Henry Royce, proceeded *de novo*.

Royce almost certainly made a good decision in not attempting to work with the Royal Aircraft Factory, as the *Report* went on to say:

Napiers agreed to participate, and the joint effort resulted in a 200 hp engine now under test, the somewhat longer delay inevitably arising from the difficulties of joint collaboration.

The first aircraft to use the Eagle was the giant Handley Page 0/100. Harald Penrose described the debut of this aircraft:

Construction had presented many problems, and specimens of every item – such as spars, struts, undercarriage construction, main fittings – had been tested to destruction in seeking absolute assurance that adequate safety factors had been achieved. From HP [Handley Page] himself to the office boy, every workman and technician had worked on this imposing machine seven days a week, latterly modifying it to take the new Rolls-Royce engine, known as the Eagle, which luckily was now available in early form, rated at 250 hp at 1600 rpm.

Handley Page's later colleague and collaborator, Dr. G.V. Lachmann, recorded that, 'All through 1915 the Handley Page designers and workmen slaved in the old riding school at Cricklewood Lane'. Their number rose to 150, and additional buildings, including the Rolls-Royce repair depot next door, were rented.

On the night of 9 December 1915, this great machine, with wings folded to the fuselage, was slowly pulled by a contingent of bluejackets towards Hendon aerodrome. Small trees barred progress at one point so, calling for steps and saw, HP shinned up and lopped their branches to the alarm of figures in night attire appearing at neighbouring windows. It was a slow, bizarre procession but after several other difficulties such as marginal turns and burst tyres, Hendon was safely reached.

At 1.51 pm on Saturday 18 December, the 0/100 took off and completed a safe flight, the first for a Rolls-Royce aero engine.

The engine was soon to receive praise from the enemy it was aiming to vanquish. A young British airman, instructed to fly to an airfield in France, landed by mistake at a Luftwaffe base near Lille. When the Germans inspected the engine, they said:

One of the most interesting of hostile aero engines, on the highest plane in respect of design, is undoubtedly the Rolls-Royce.

The biggest market for the Eagle was the Handley Page bombers, first the 0/100 and then in late 1917 the 0/400, a heavy night bomber. In 1916 and 1917, the last Airco DH4 day bombers flew with the Eagle III, VI, VII and VIII. Two other users were the Felixstowe series of large flying boats, the F.2 and F.3, and the Fairey Campania float seaplanes. In total, about fifty different aeroplane and airship types used the Eagle. The official number of engines manufactured was 4,681.

After the First World War, nine Eagle engines took part in historic flights. As we shall see, Engines 5244 and 5246 powered the Vickers Vimy in which Alcock and Brown crossed the Atlantic in 1919. Engines 5466 and 5716 powered the Vickers Vimy which left Hounslow, west London, at the end of 1919 and flew in stages to Darwin and on to Sydney, Australia. By the time they reached Darwin, the engines had been in the air for 135 hours without overhaul. And two other Eagle Mark VIIIs powered the Vickers Vimy Silver Queen, which flew from Brooklands on 4 February 1920, crashing at Wadi Halfa. Transferred to Silver Queen II, the same engines powered her until she also crashed, at Bulawayo. At that point the pilots transferred to a DH9 and eventually reached Cape Town.

In 1922, the Portuguese Navy succeeded in making the first flight across the southern Atlantic. They tried with three Fairey 111 floatplanes powered by Rolls-Royce Eagle VIII engines. Two did not make it but the third, the Santa Cruz, with pilots Gago Coutinho and Sacadora Cabral, achieved the crossing.

Also after the First World War, a special Eagle Mark IX was developed for use in commercial airliners. Military Eagles were used by the RAF until 1926 and in some other countries until 1930. Civilian Eagles were used throughout the 1920s, but all had been withdrawn from service by 1931.

THE HAWK, FALCON AND CONDOR

Quickly following the Eagle came the Hawk, designed in 1915 and intended originally for use in training aircraft. Royce was extremely unimpressed by the Renault air-cooled V8s that Rolls-Royce had been asked to make, and he and his team designed an engine (later named the Hawk by Johnson) in the same power class. This six-cylinder engine was designed for reliability above all else, and its operating conditions were not severe. The aim was to achieve 75 hp at 1,370 rpm, and this was achieved on its first test run. But, as with the Eagle, ratings soon increased so that by February 1916 it was giving 91 hp and, by October 1918, 105.

Claude Johnson and his fellow directors approved the Hawk for manufacture under licence by the Bristol-based Brazil Straker, run by technical director Roy Fedden. Orders for the Hawk were limited and, after Rolls-Royce had made the prototypes, Brazil Straker made most of the main run of just over 200. Most of them were made for RNAS non-rigid airships.

For the first two years of the war, indeed even well into 1916, the British war effort in the air suffered from the smallness of its aircraft industry. In 1916 British firms produced only 5,716 aircraft, while a further 917 were imported, mostly from France. The production of aero engines was only 5,363, with a further 1,864 imported, again mostly from France.

Building up engine production for Rolls-Royce and other manufacturers was constrained by the lack of raw materials, machining capacity and trained operatives, and by the need to construct testing facilities. On the materials front, nickel chrome alloys were hard to obtain, and by the summer of 1916 the shortage of magnetos became acute (the original supply from Germany had, needless to say, been cut off in August 1914). The minutes of the Air Board meeting on 7 June 1916 show that Claude Johnson suggested that the Government select a moderate number of engine types and establish central factories with sub-contractors to produce them. However, Brigadier-General David Henderson, on behalf of the Government, countered that this concentration would limit improvement. As John Morrow put it in *The Great War in the Air*:

He was concerned about excessive dependence upon Rolls-Royce and its superlative combat engines, the 275-hp Eagle and the 200-hp Falcon.

Throughout the war, there was overwhelming pressure on aircraft manufacturers and their component suppliers to increase production. None felt it more, because of the quality and reliability of their engines, than Rolls-Royce. However, as Harald Penrose pointed out:

That great company [Rolls-Royce] would not yet sub-contract to anyone except 32 year old Roy Fedden of Brazil Straker, car-builders at Fishponds, Bristol, for they considered other engine builders could not attain their high standard.

As we have seen, Fedden had proved himself by modifying a dangerous batch of Curtiss OX-5 engines shipped from the USA, and had been introduced to Elliott at Rolls-Royce. Fedden said of the company:

When the Ministry of Munitions tried to force Rolls-Royce to get a dozen or so other firms to make their engines, that very great man Claude Johnson took the bold stand that he would tear up every drawing and go to prison rather than agree to risk inferior skills of other companies.

Johnson said that the plan of using other manufacturers was futile and 'would yield nothing but mountains of scrap'. He had his way. Other companies were not licensed and Johnson stayed out of prison. However, it almost led to Rolls-Royce being nationalised. Frustration was mounting and de Havilland expressed his concerns to Trenchard, who wrote to Major-General J.M. Salmond, Director General of Military Aeronautics:

I do not know who is responsible for deciding upon the DH9, but I should have thought that no one would imagine we should be able to carry out long-distance bombing raids by day next year with machines inferior in performance to those we use for this purpose at present. I consider the situation critical and I think every endeavour should be made at once to produce a machine with performance equal at least to the existing 275 hp Rolls-Royce DH4 and to press on with the output with the utmost energy.

There was great admiration for the quality of the Rolls-Royce engines, but also frustration that such quality could take so long to come to fruition. Even by 1917, the planned time from engine design to production was sixty-four weeks. The Air Board and the Ministry of Munitions both became obsessed with the need for standardisation of engine production. While Rolls-Royce was concentrating on increasing the power of the Eagle and the Falcon, the Air Board and the Ministry wanted to organise licensing of the production. As we have seen, Claude Johnson would not countenance this. The Government tried to persuade Johnson to extend the Derby factory. Johnson could see the advantages of this if the war were to continue for several years, but if it ended quickly Rolls-Royce would be encumbered with an extension it did not need. In the end, a compromise was reached. The extension was built, but the Government paid for it.

The Air Board panicked and ordered 10,000 of the untried All British Company (ABC) radial engine, the Dragonfly. The Board was very excited by its claims of producing 300 hp from a weight of 380 lbs, a scarcely believable power/weight ratio.

The Aircraft Inspection Department had issued warnings about relying on untested designs, but was ignored. All production in Britain in 1918 except for Rolls-Royce would be concentrated on the Dragonfly. Exactly 1,000 were produced, none of them achieving the claimed power/weight ratio, and many of them suffering crankshaft failure. The Government returned to production of the W.O. Bentley design, the BR2 rotary. The problem was that everyone wanted Rolls-Royce engines but the company, try as it might, could not produce enough. Rolls-Royce itself suffered manpower shortages, and customers constantly changed their minds about their requirements. Bristol fighters were modified to take Hispano-Suizas, but they too could not supply sufficient quantities, and the alternative – the Sunbeam – was markedly inferior to both the Rolls-Royce and Hispano-Suiza engines. The de Havilland DH4 was forced to use BHPs (Beardmore, Halford, Pullinger) and Fiats, but again these did not give the performance of the Rolls-Royce engines.

The first successful type of British airship built was the SS, more popularly known as the Blimp. They consisted of an aeroplane (BE 2c) fuselage without wings or tail planes slung from an elongated gas envelope, and were fitted with 70–80 hp engines, mainly Rolls-Royce Hawks. A small airship fleet was sent to the Dardanelle Straits in 1915 to support the Navy in Winston Churchill's imaginative but doomed attempt to break the stalemate of trench warfare. Considered the most reliable engine, the Hawk was fitted to all these airships.

In June 1916 the SS was superseded by the SS Zero, and the handbook noted:

The Rolls-Royce Hawk type engine of 75 hp was adopted as possessing a degree of reliability and other properties of particular suitability higher than other makes available.

Of the 55,700 hours flown by British airships, no fewer than 36,000 were powered by Hawk engines. Flights of up to 30 hours were common, and in August 1918 an uninterrupted flight of 50 hours and 55 minutes was made. As well as powering airships, the Hawk was also fitted to the Sage trainer Type III, and a few BE 2es and Avro 504 Fs.

The Hawk was a six-cylinder, ungeared, vertical water-cooled engine with one magneto, plus coil ignition and two carburettors (the Hawk MKI) or one carburettor (the Hawk MKII). Oil consumption was half a gallon per hour, and fuel consumption at normal power was 6.5 gallons per hour. The engine weighed 405 lbs. This is what the company itself said about it:

It is usual, when starting this small engine, to turn it by means of the propeller for filling the cylinders after the induction pipes have been primed. The operation of the hand magneto (also supplied by Rolls-Royce) then starts the engine. The Rolls-Royce Patented Device is supplied for priming. This is a light and simple apparatus, embodying a hand pump, which can be fixed in any convenient position near the pilot's seat, or as desired. One priming device may serve two or more engines with the use of a change-over cock. When required, a starting handle can be supplied, arranged in line with the crankshaft at the timing gearcase end of the engine, and connected thereto by a reduction gear. This apparatus is especially suitable for airship installations.

The Falcon, effectively a scaled-down Eagle largely designed by R.W.H. Bailey, arrived in 1916. As with the Eagle and Hawk, the Falcon's ratings grew almost monthly.

In April 1916 it was developing 205 hp, in May it was 228, by February 1917 it was 247 and in April, 262. All of these were at 1,800 rpm. By November 1917, the output had risen to 278 hp and by July 1918, 285. These were at 2,000 rpm.

The engine was developed from Falcon I to Falcon II to Falcon III, and its most famous application was in the Bristol Fighter F. 2B, in which the Falcon III became standard, remaining in service until the 1930s.

The F. 2B was Britain's most effective two-seater fighter of the First World War. Known as the Brisfit or Biff, the F. 2B could dive faster than any other aircraft, and its all-round strength often enabled it to fly home even when severely damaged. *The Ballad of the Bristol Fighter* included the verses:

> *But few of them know the secret*
> *of making my heart rejoice,*
> *Like a well-rigged Bristol Fighter*
> *With a two-six-five Rolls-Royce.*
>
> *Is there sweeter music,*
> *Or a more contented sound,*
> *Than the purring clop of her broad curved prop*
> *As it gently ticks around?*

The F. 2B flew with other makes of engine, but with the Falcon it became a byword for reliability, often flying a hundred hours in the tough field conditions of the Western Front without an overhaul – roughly three times as long as its rival engines could manage. And none of its rivals had as many cylinders.

It also saw service in the Martinsyde F1, F3 and F4, RE 6 and 7, Armstrong Whitworth FK12, Avro 523c and 529 Pike, Blackburn SP and GP seaplanes, Kangaroo and Sprat, DH4, Fairey F2, Sopwith tractor triplane, Parnell Perch, improved Short 184 and Vickers Vendace. As with the Hawk, the Falcon was also manufactured under licence by Brazil Straker to supplement output from Derby.

In a book written for Rolls-Royce after the end of the First World War, *The Soul of the Aeroplane – The Rolls-Royce Engine*, Boyd Cable made it clear how effective the Eagle and Falcon engines had proved to be.

In the later stages of the air war various types of machines had evolved and were evolving for use on special work. The night bombers were tending more and more to develop in the direction of size and weight-carrying capacity, and the huge multiple-engined bombers were becoming the standard . . . The principal virtues required of the engines for these machines were power to lift the great weights, endurance and an ability to run for many hours on end. In the main the work required was a long distance flight straight out over Hunland and back, practically the whole of the distance over enemy territory . . . It was one more compliment to the recognised ability of the Rolls-Royce engines that by the end of the war they were the standard and in fact, the only type in action on our big night bombers.

But it was not only on night bombers that Rolls-Royce engines were effective. As Boyd Cable made clear, the DH4 (a daylight bomber) and the Bristol Fighter, the two most effective of the offensive two-seaters, were also fitted with Rolls-Royce engines. Their need for speed and power of manoeuvre required the utmost reliability. Here is Boyd Cable again:

In some of the amazing fights put up in these machines, in fact in almost every fight in the air, the pilot, under stress of circumstance, has to handle his engine in a fashion that might well make the hair stand on end on the heads of the engine designers and builders. One instant the engine may be straining to the limit of its power to lift the machine nose up straight into the air, the next it may be racing wildly beyond its laid-down number of 'revs' per minute in an almost perpendicular dive. It may be throttled right down or shut off, and then with a jerk thrown into top speed. It has to keep running at any tilt and any rate of speed on its back, on its side, on its nose or tail, upside down or right side up . . . All these things the Rolls-Royce Falcon and Eagle engines have done time and again.

Boyd Cable gave examples of the outstanding performance of the engines, writing of one bomber, whose radiator and oil sump drained after being hit by enemy gunfire, which managed to fly back over the trenches for thirty minutes before crash-landing. He also wrote of the endurance and reliability of the engines:

One of the 275 hp Falcon engines flew without giving trouble of any sort for 150 hours and was then, in the regular routine, sent for overhaul, although the pilot was positive it was as good as the day it came from the shops. Another Falcon after 120 hours flying was as good as ever; another was only sent for overhaul (without showing any sign of need of it) after 162 hours, 54 minutes flying, and another was still going strong with 123 hours to its credit.

These hours may sound paltry compared with modern engines, or even with car engines of the day, but compared with other aero engines of the First World War they showed a matchless level of reliability. The night bombing raids over Germany were single feats of great endurance. Raids over Frankfurt and Mannheim took five hours. One raid over Cologne, which dropped a ton of bombs, took seven hours.

The Condor, following closely the pattern of the Eagle and Falcon, was released in August 1918, just before the end of the war. A larger engine, the Condor Series 1 developed 550–600 hp and its larger cylinders needed four valves per cylinder rather than two. The valves were operated by a single camshaft on each bank. There were only two carburettors, which were mounted low down on each side of the crankcase in line with the centre bearing. The water pump was transferred to the centre of the engine, and an electric starter could be provided if required. The Series I was succeeded by the IA, which developed 650 hp at 1,900 rpm. The Series II seems to have had a very short life, but the Series III became very well known. The Series III, with its lower weight, spur reduction gear, crossbolted main bearings and fork and blade rods reflected the arrival of A.J. Rowledge from Napier. Like the IA, it developed 650 hp at 1,900 rpm, but it weighed about 300 lbs less. (The earlier Condor proved to be too heavy.) One of its notable features was the fitting of a single-spur reduction gear, carried in a housing bolted to the front end of the crankcase. This made for improved cowling lines, but Royce recognised that higher stresses were set up in the crankcase than with the old epicyclic type. In the new gear, a flange was formed on the front end of the crankshaft. Bolted to this was an internally toothed ring, the teeth of which engaged with similar teeth on the end of a short, hollow shaft. The opposite end of the shaft was formed with splines to transmit the torque to a hollow pinion mounted in roller and ball bearings. In this way, transverse loads were prevented from being transmitted to the crankshaft from the gearing. The pinion engaged with a toothed wheel mounted on, and keyed to, the airscrew shaft, which was supported on roller bearings and fitted with a ball-end-thrust bearing to take the thrust of the airscrew. The engine was cleared to use a metal airscrew, of which the most efficient diameter was about sixteen feet.

Eagerly awaiting the Condor was Handley Page, who wanted maximum horse-power in a twin-engine design. He was assured in 1917 by Royce that it would be ready for the 1918 offensive. Nevertheless, with the experience of delays in development of engines, and aware of Royce's thoroughness, an alternative design using four Eagles was suggested for the new giant V/1500 bomber. This bomber, carrying a crew of six, was the largest British machine flying at the end of the war. It had been designed specifically for the bombing of Berlin from bases in Britain, and the first squadron was ready with loads of 1,650 lb bombs only three days before the signing of the Armistice. The raids were never made, or at least not for another twenty-two years, and then they were still made in aircraft powered by Rolls-Royce engines.

Following the Condor III came the Condor IV, which was generally similar but which employed a direct-drive unit. Apart from the omission of the reduction gear, in the Condor IV the crankcase was fitted with cast feet for the engine bearers instead of ball-joint, front-end mounting and the spring leaf rear mounting previously standardised. This engine gave a normal output of 650 hp at 1,900 rpm and weighed 1,250 lbs. It was designed for the Hawker Hornbill, the fastest fighter of its day.

'TO PROVIDE A MODERATE PROFIT'

To appreciate the contribution that Rolls-Royce made to the war effort, we must remember that until 1914 the company did not make a single aero engine, or even have any plans to do so. Furthermore, it was not a mass-

Silver Ghost chassis were supplied for use as staff cars, ambulances and armoured cars. The Silver Ghost armoured car was at its best in desert conditions. It is seen here with Ford Model T tenders, which also stood up to the arduous conditions in the desert.

The Silver Ghost served brilliantly through two world wars.
Outstanding amongst those who exploited its versatility and
reliability to the full was the legendary Lawrence of Arabia.

OPPOSITE TOP: When war came in 1914, Rolls-Royce soon turned
their hand to manufacture for the armed forces. Among the
earliest products were a number of Renault V8 air-cooled aero
engines. One is seen here on test at Derby.

OPPOSITE BOTTOM: A Wolseley-built B E 2 C that was powered
by the Renault V8 engine.

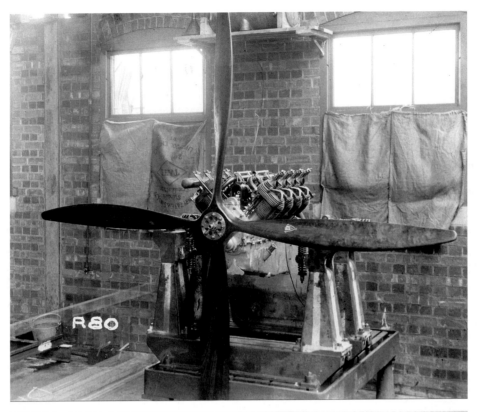

Within days of the outbreak of war in 1914, Henry Royce was
hard at work deciding the optimum features for an aero engine.
Throughout the period in which his first aero engine was
designed, two senior designers, Albert Elliott and Maurice Olley,
worked with him at St. Margaret's Bay. Both would have a great
part to play in the future success of Rolls-Royce.

Royce's first aero engine was the Eagle, shown here on
test in 1915.

TOP: Testing compression on a Rolls-Royce Eagle engine, salvaged from a damaged aircraft, at the aircraft repair depot, Rang du Fleurs, July 1918.

BOTTOM: The ultimate mark of Eagle in the First World War was the Mk VIII shown here. Eagle VIIIs powered the Vimy in which Alcock and Brown made the first non-stop crossing of the Atlantic in 1919, the Vimy of Ross and Keith Smith in their flight from England to Australia shortly afterwards, and finally the Fairey III of the Portuguese Navy in which Coutinho and Cabral first flew the South Atlantic in 1922.

The Rolls-Royce Eagle powered nearly fifty aircraft, flying
boat and airship types. Here are five of them.
TOP LEFT: Vickers Vimy bombers being assembled at Morgans
works, Linslade, Leighton Buzzard.
TOP RIGHT: de Havilland DH9.
BOTTOM LEFT: Felixstowe F.3 flying boat.
BOTTOM RIGHT: Naval airship 23.
CENTRE: Handley Page 0/400 bomber.

The Falcon was a smaller version of the Eagle designed by
R.W.H. Bailey at Derby. It was designed particularly for fighter
applications, of which the most famous was the Bristol
Fighter. The Falcon III was the definitive mark, and many of the
engines were made by Brazil Straker at Fishponds in Bristol.

OPPOSITE: The Rolls-Royce Falcon powered a number
of aircraft. Here are two.
TOP: Bristol F. 2B Fighter, known as the 'Brisfit'.
BOTTOM: Blackburn Kangaroo.

A Porte Felixstowe F.2A of 230 Squadron. This aircraft was
powered by an early version of the Rolls-Royce Eagle engine.
Here it is on patrol in wartime dazzle pattern.

A Bristol F. 2B Fighter of III Squadron. The 'Brisfit' was the
most outstanding aircraft to be powered by the Rolls-Royce
Falcon, and was retained by the RAF after the First World War
longer than any other wartime aircraft.

Effectively half an Eagle but without a propeller reduction
gear, the Hawk was originally designed for trainer aircraft.
Its most distinguished application was in powering non-rigid
airships known as Blimps. Most Hawk engines were
built by Brazil Straker.

The Hawk was first choice of the RNAS to power its
Blimps, which were used to patrol coastal waters and to protect
convoys from U-boat attack.

The Condor was the last and largest of Henry Royce's first
generation of aero engines. It was intended for long-range
bombers, but the Armistice was signed before they could be
used. The Condor III, shown here, reflected the input of Arthur
Rowledge, who had recently arrived from Napier.

OPPOSITE TOP: The Hawker Horsley bomber of the 1920s was a
major application for the Rolls-Royce Condor engine.
This photograph was taken at Hawker's factory airfield – the
banking of the old Brooklands racing track can be seen
quite clearly in the distance.

OPPOSITE BOTTOM: A Hawker Horsley, powered by a Rolls-Royce
Condor III, being prepared at Brooklands in 1927 for an
attempt on the long-distance, non-stop record.

Sir Alan Cobham returning to Britain and landing at
Rochester in a Short Singapore powered by two Rolls-Royce
Condor IIIAs after his round-Africa flight in 1927.

production manufacturer. Throughout the war it found itself under extreme pressure to produce aero engines as quickly as possible, but it refused to compromise its hard-earned reputation for the quality and reliability of its products.

Ever since the under-subscribed flotation in 1906, Rolls-Royce had been short of working capital, and were forced to make hard choices between extending their factory buildings and investing in new machine tools. They went into the First World War with a lot of second-hand and clapped-out machine tools. This would have been intolerable for a mass-producer, but a manufacturer of low-volume, high-quality expensive motor cars could cope with this situation, thanks to the skill of their work force. Once the development work on the aero engines was proceeding smoothly, albeit at a hectic pace, the orders began to flow in. On 3 January 1915 the Admiralty ordered twenty-five of the new 200 hp engine (the Eagle), on 19 April another seventy-five, and before the end of 1915 a further 300, as well as seventy-five of the new Hawk engine. However, confusion was caused at Derby by the War Office also ordering a hundred of the Royal Aircraft Factory eight-cylinder engines. Johnson wrote to the War Office:

If we were to make the RAF engines at the date previously contemplated it would mean that the manufacture of that engine would follow immediately after the manufacture of 25 Rolls-Royce engines of 200 hp and therefore all the tools, machinery, etc., engaged in the manufacture of the Rolls-Royce engine would have to be dismounted in order to be replaced by the tools necessary for the manufacture of the RAF engine. This dismounting of tools and mounting of new tools would, of course, mean a serious loss to the nation, as compared with the far more efficient programme of our continuing to manufacture the 200 hp Rolls-Royce engine for the Admiralty, and we therefore suggest that in this time of the Empire's great need you may be able to arrange to have the 100 RAF engines of 100 hp manufactured in some other firm which is already engaged in the manufacture of these engines, or by some firm which is not at present engaged in the manufacture of engines for the country.

The War Office was not interested in Rolls-Royce's production problems, and insisted on the manufacture of the RAF engines as well as those for the Admiralty. Johnson realised that Rolls-Royce were now effectively under Government control, and that this placed both the company and share-holders in a potentially difficult situation. On 31 March 1915 he wrote to the Chairman, Claremont:

The British military authorities in France and England wish to impress upon the public that the date at which the war will be finished is regulated mainly by the supply of the Munitions of war.

The earlier the war is over, so much the better for Rolls-Royce Ltd., for instance our French Company alone is costing us £1,000 a month.

The Admiralty assures us that the delivery by our Company of 200 hp Rolls-Royce aero-engines is of the greatest importance in connection with the general scheme for the finishing of the war, and in addition to the 25 of these engines already ordered, are anxious for us to make at once 100 of the RAF factory aero-engines, and if we had the equipment would be glad to give us an order for 8 of these engines per week for the whole of 1916.

In the face of this national situation there are two alternative courses which we can take. Firstly we may say that in order to maintain the Rolls-Royce business of motor cars we must insist on making a number of motor cars for pleasure purposes and therefore will only devote a proportion of our works to satisfy the urgent national demand for war engines; or secondly, we may place the whole of our equipment entirely at the disposal of the nation.

I do not think it is possible for any firm of repute to take the first course. Furthermore, I do not believe that it would be to the interests of the shareholders to take the first course. And, if we take it, the Government would force us to do what in my opinion we should do graciously. At present we are adopting the second course. By the end of July our business as motor manufacturers will be suspended except for the manufacture of two chassis per week, which will, it is believed, be required by the Government. Our works will otherwise be devoted to the manufacture of perhaps twelve aero-engines per week.

In this situation, Johnson wrote to the shareholders saying that, in his opinion, he did not feel it was right to extract the highest possible price from the Government.

Personally, I should be very ashamed to stand up before the shareholders and ask them to commend the General Managing Director because he had succeeded in extracting from the pockets of the already over-burdened tax payer a price for war goods which had enabled me to put large profits in the pockets of the shareholders.

He told them that he was quoting prices for war goods which were intended solely to cover 'our established charges at home, but not abroad, and to provide a moderate profit'.

Nevertheless, Johnson knew that when the war ended, Government contracts would cease; he also knew that there was, as yet, no civilian airline business and that the company would again be dependent on the success of its cars. Consequently, he continued to press for the sale of Rolls-Royce cars to the United States right up until the entry of the US into the war in 1917, and when production at Derby ceased, he bought second-hand cars in England, reconditioned them and shipped them to the USA.

And the company's financial dilemma was made worse by the indecision and infighting among various Government departments and the armed services. In response to a public outcry over munitions shortages, the Government set up the Bailhache Committee which recommended the establishment of an Air Board, duly formed in May 1916 under the chairmanship of Lord Curzon. Not that the arguments stopped – Curzon was soon in conflict with the Admiralty over production priorities and allocations. However, at least some of Claude Johnson's recommendations were listened to, most significantly the suggestion of cutting down on the different types of engine in development so that production could be concentrated on those already proved to be successful. Top priority was given to the expansion of air power, and the number of engines given Government contracts was reduced from fifty-one to eight. Four – the Sunbeam 6, the Sunbeam 8 (Arab), the Hispano-Suiza and the BHP – were in the 200 hp water-cooled class. Two were rotaries: the 130 hp Clerget and the Bentley; and two – the Rolls-Royce Eagle and the RAF 4A – were in the higher power class. Substantial orders were placed for all these engines, but only Rolls-Royce and the Hispano-Suiza factory set up by the Admiralty in France produced anything like their quota. Even Rolls-Royce's output was restricted by the company's insistence on carrying out repairs and servicing to its own engines, and by a wrangle with the Government about expenditure on extra buildings to accommodate this work.

Claude Johnson travelled to the United States to see whether production there could ease the backlog. However, he was not prepared to licence a company without guarantees about future production.

We are not prepared to enable any company in the United States to make the Rolls-Royce engine because this would necessitate our imparting to them information which would enable them to become serious competitors, not only in the manufacture of aero engines of a design nearly approaching to that of a Rolls-Royce engine, but in the manufacture of a chassis which might compete with the Rolls-Royce chassis.

Johnson would consider two possibilities. The first was to manufacture at a Government arsenal under Rolls-Royce supervision 'without the fear of inspection by temporary Government officials who hitherto have been and after the war probably will be engaged in the factories of our automobile competitors'. The second was the construction of a factory in the USA in which Rolls-Royce would assemble parts made by sub-contractors.

Protracted negotiations with the US Government finally ran into the sand, partly (perhaps primarily) because the US Government was pinning great hopes on the Liberty engine, which was moving quickly towards quantity production. Nevertheless, Rolls-Royce won deserved praise from the US Government for their unselfish approach. Maurice Olley made many valuable suggestions to Major Vincent, one of the designers of the Liberty, based on his experience with the Eagle and the Falcon. The British Aeronautical Mission to America said:

It should be clearly noted that the design of this gear [reduction gear of the epicyclic-geared engine] has been carried out in the main by Messrs. Rolls-Royce representatives for the Aircraft Production Bureau and it is considered that some very definite mark of appreciation be conveyed to the firm for the generous and wholehearted manner in which they have placed their knowledge at the disposal of the Americans. The officials of the production bureau were loud in their praise of the assistance they had received.

Johnson turned instead to the possibility of a merger with a US company, Pierce Arrow, engaged not only in the manufacture of cars but also of trucks. He could see great benefits for the future: the elimination of competition from the Pierce Arrow car, the use of the Pierce Arrow selling organisation throughout the USA, and the additional income from selling Pierce Arrow trucks in Europe. Johnson could also see the potential for aero engines in the USA once the war was over:

Aero engines must have a great future for commercial use in the United States, the country of long distances, the land where people will embrace and pay for new methods of rapid communication.

The negotiations came to nothing, but Johnson's efforts in the USA led to orders from the Air Board for 2,000 Eagle engines, with the parts for 1,500 to be manufactured in the USA. Unfortunately, as we have seen, these parts arrived after the end of the war, and were all sold for scrap in 1920.

In summary, Johnson's nine months in the USA, from June 1917 until March 1918, when his absence from the UK was sorely missed, would have to be deemed a failure, although it did give Rolls-Royce's representatives excellent experience of American manufacturing methods and conditions, and established relationships with manufacturers such as Wyman Gordon, with whom Rolls-Royce dealt for many years.

CHAPTER FOUR

THE ACME OF REFINEMENT

'A ROLLS . . . WAS ABOVE RUBIES'
POST-WAR RECONSTRUCTION
THE TWENTY AND THE PHANTOM
THE DEATH OF CLAUDE JOHNSON
'THEY WORKED IN MONASTIC SECLUSION'
SPRINGFIELD, MASSACHUSETTS

'A ROLLS . . . WAS ABOVE RUBIES'

THE SUCCESS OF Rolls-Royce cars in the 1913 and 1914 Austrian rallies made it certain that during the First World War the allied forces would want to use them in France and Belgium. The telephone was a useful communications tool, but unsophisticated in those days, and not as useful in the very fluid situation of the early days of the war as it became once the stultifying trench system had become established. Sir John French, Commander-in-Chief of the British forces, used his Rolls-Royce continuously to keep abreast of developments. His Assistant Military Secretary, Lieutenant-Colonel Stanley Barry, wrote to the company on 20 November 1917:

Field Marshal Lord French has had photographed recently the Rolls-Royce which he has used since the commencement of the War. It struck him that a copy of this photograph might be of interest to you. This car was taken by him to France in August 1914, and was used by him the whole time he was engaged in operations in France, including the Retreat. He brought it home to England when he came back and it is now in constant use. It has done thousands of miles and is as good now as when he first had it.

There were many stories of the reliability of the Rolls-Royce. Millerand, the French War Minister, already owned a Rolls-Royce when war broke out. He ordered two more, which covered 20,000 miles between them in three months, often travelling 400 miles a day, and not only on roads but across fields and through woods. Millerand's driver, Edouard Forester, wrote to the company:

After having studied all the makes of cars, other than Rolls-Royce, which have passed through my hands, I wish by this letter to express the satisfaction I have experienced not only with the 40 hp three-speed car of your make which I drove for a year before the war [in fact they were all 40/50 hp], but also with the two 40/50 hp four-speed 1914 models which I induced M. Millerand, War Minister, to purchase.

I travelled with him 35,000 kilometres in three months, all over France but principally at the front. Both our two cars travelled throughout without a single breakdown and always behaved perfectly. We traversed bad roads along deep ruts made by the wheels of heavy artillery, and encountered shell holes where the wheel sank to the axle-box – for instance, in the Woods of Tracy, where we had to pass between trees without the trace of a road. There I fully appreciated the endurance and remarkable suppleness of your cars. It is only necessary to have done the journeys I have in them to be convinced of the quality of your cars.

The French Premier, Georges Clemenceau, also had reason to be thankful to his Rolls-Royce. An attempted assassination was averted by the quick thinking of his chauffeur and the speed of the car.

Rolls-Royce cars were offered and chosen for the King's Messenger service maintained between the Channel ports and British headquarters. The RAC had been asked by the War Office to find four reliable cars and, of course, there was only one possible choice. British headquarters were situated initially at Villeneuve St. George on the outskirts of Paris, but were moved regularly. For two years, the four Rolls-Royces kept up their daily trips and not a single mechanical breakdown occurred, although James Barry did hit a French farm cart in the Type 70 Silver Rogue, which needed to go back to Derby for repair. Thereafter it was used as a lorry, ferrying forgings from Sheffield to Derby.

Rolls-Royces were also chosen for armoured cars that were used in Belgium and France. Three-eighth-inch armour-plating was specified; the engine was to be protected by an armour-plated bonnet, and the radiator by two armoured doors that could be closed at will. The driver was to sit on the floor with his back supported by a sling. He could see through a narrow slit in the armour.

To cope with the five-ton weight, thirteen-leaf springs were fitted at the front and fifteen-leaf at the rear. In spite of this weight, the cars could cruise in formation at 45 mph. (The speed limit on British roads was still 20 mph.) The cars were delivered in squadrons of twelve, with two or three mechanics from Derby attached to each squadron.

Unfortunately, by the time the first squadrons were ready in March 1915, war on the Western Front had settled into trench warfare stalemate, giving little scope for armoured car activity. The squadrons, originally formed by the Royal Naval Air Service, were taken over by the Army, split up into groups of four and sent to distant theatres of war. They saw action against the Turkish Army at Gallipoli and against the Germans in West Africa. The Duke of Westminster, who gave his cars ferocious names such as Bulldog, Biter, Bloodhound and Blast, was particularly active, first in German West Africa and later in Egypt.

The most famous exploits in which Rolls-Royces were involved were those of T.E. Lawrence, 'Lawrence of Arabia'. He wrote about their value to him in his book, *The Seven Pillars of Wisdom*, relating how the cars crossed the vast mudflat at speeds of up to 65 mph:

. . . not bad for cars which had been months ploughing the desert with only such running repairs as the drivers had time and tools to give them . . . Across the sandy neck from the first flat to the second we built a corduroy road of brushwood. When this was ready, the cars came steaming and hissing along it, dangerously fast to avoid getting stuck, rocking over hummocks in a style which looked fatal for the springs. However, we knew it was nearly impossible to break a Rolls-Royce, and so were sorrier for the drivers, Thomas, Rolls and Sanderson. The jolts tore the steering wheel from their grip, and left them breathless with bleeding hands after the crossing.

According to Lawrence's driver, S.C. Rolls (no relation to C.S. Rolls), on one single day Lawrence, with three Rolls-Royce armoured cars, captured two Turkish posts, blew up a bridge, wiped out a Kurdish cavalry regiment, blew up another bridge and ripped up 600 pairs of rails. Lawrence wrote later:

A Rolls in the desert was above rubies . . . Great was Rolls and great was Royce! They were worth hundreds of men to us in those deserts.

By a quirk of coincidence, Lawrence met Royce many years later when, as Aircraftsman Shaw, Lawrence was working at Calshot air base where the Schneider Trophy seaplanes were being tuned. Royce was amazed, saying, 'Who would have thought that little fellow was Lawrence of Arabia?' This sounds slightly dismissive, but apparently Royce felt it a great honour to have met Lawrence.

Mesopotamia was another theatre of war in which the Rolls-Royce armoured cars saw action. Indeed, they were deemed the only vehicles capable of coping with the rough terrain, as is shown by the following notice in *The Times* in September 1920, after the war in Europe was over, but when military action continued elsewhere.

The War Office issued the following statement yesterday.

'Statements have appeared in the Press today to the effect that the Government are buying Rolls-Royce cars, and that the Rolls-Royce company is asking private purchasers to agree to postponement of delivery because the Government wanted cars. In order to remove misapprehension, it should be pointed out that the purchase of Rolls-Royce chassis is necessitated by circumstances in Mesopotamia where through age and heavy wear and tear our armoured cars are rapidly being worn out.

The existing cars there require immediate replacement, and as the Rolls-Royce chassis is of a type which experience has shown can carry the necessary weight of armour and give satisfaction in all circumstances of climate and terrain, it was necessary to make urgent arrangements to supply replacement chassis.

In view of the situation in Mesopotamia and the protection there of our detachments and women and children, it is thought that prospective buyers of Rolls-Royce cars would not object to a very short postponement of delivery in order to promote the safety of those mentioned above.'

POST-WAR RECONSTRUCTION

The return of peace after four years of slaughter, the like of which had never been seen in the world before, brought the directors of Rolls-Royce face to face with the need to plan the whole strategy of the company. Should they continue to manufacture aero engines, should they return to making luxury cars or should they do both?

Clearly, the demand for aero engines would fall dramatically, and although the company had been given a large order for the Condor by the Air Ministry, it was unlikely that they would all be wanted. Cars looked a much better proposition, although nothing new had been developed during the war. However, the magnificent Silver Ghost had been supreme before the war, and just as Rolls-Royce had not been able to continue car development, neither had any of their rivals. Silver Ghosts had been produced for military purposes and commercial exports until the overwhelming need for aero engines meant the cessation of all chassis production in 1917. Now, Silver Ghost production could continue while its successor was developed in the Experimental Department.

The performance of the armoured cars had only served to enhance the Rolls-Royce legend. There had been few breakdowns. As well as the mud of Flanders and the deserts of Arabia, the Russian winter had also been overcome. A British officer, Commander Locker-Lampson, had driven 53,000 miles over the Caucasus mountain range and beyond, sometimes at temperatures 40 degrees below zero. At the end of the journey, only the front springs and a ball-race in one of the front wheels needed replacing. Some of the armoured cars survived to do service in India and Africa in the Second World War, and also served in the Eire Army until 1946.

Immediately after the end of the war, with virtually no new cars available, there was a boom in the value of second-hand cars. Silver Ghosts realised very high prices. The grandmother of Wilton J. Oldham, the author of *The Hyphen in Rolls-Royce*, sold a 1912 Silver Ghost with a Barker Torpedo Cabriolet body to Claude Graham-White for £2,750 (probably £140,000 in today's terms), and Graham-White was expecting to sell it on for a profit.

Rolls-Royce themselves were busy reconditioning pre-war cars and overhauling those that had not been used during the war. The Silver Ghost benefited from experience learnt from the use of the chassis for armoured car work, although the 1919 model was almost identical to that of 1914, except that it now had an electric starter and aluminium pistons. There had, of course, been many improvements from the introduction of the 40/50 in 1906 up until 1914.

- The year 1906 saw the launch of the car with a chassis based largely on the 30 hp six-cylinder. It had platform rear springs and a transmission footbrake, as well as a four-speed gearbox with overdrive fourth.
- The year 1907 brought the 'C' springs and improved transmission brake.
- In 1910 there were improved 'C' springs and the torque tube axle, as well as the three-speed gearbox in place of four-speed with overdrive fourth.
- The year 1911 brought many improvements, including the cantilever springing of the torque tube axle, a bigger stroke to the engine, a bigger bore inlet manifold and carburettor, spring drive to the helical timing gear and a crankshaft torsional damper.
- Rear drum footbrakes (as well as handbrakes which had always been rear drum) were introduced in 1912, and in 1913 there were many changes, including the introduction of a four-speed gearbox with direct-drive fourth, while massive rear brakes were introduced in 1914.

Although heavily engaged on aero engine design during the war, Royce nevertheless found time to think about cars, and in a memo dated 7 July 1917 from West Wittering, he announced that all post-war chassis would have electric self-starters and that he had been studying the Lanchester gearbox. ('Boss' Kettering of Delco had introduced the electric starter to General Motors cars in 1912.)

What would the market be like after the end of the war? The board and senior management of Rolls-Royce were quite optimistic. There was a considerable backlog of pre-war orders, and a number of further orders had been taken. On 21 January 1919 a meeting was held at Royce's new home in West Wittering, at which it was decided to increase the number of chassis to be built per year above the previous limit of 500.

Royce had already begun work on the design of a smaller car before the end of the war – fortuitously, perhaps, because the immediate post-war boom was followed by a slump. Johnson, concerned that not enough people would be able to afford the Silver Ghost, felt that a smaller 20 hp car would be a very useful addition to the company's range. Further influencing his decision was the imposition by the Chancellor of the Exchequer, Winston Churchill, of a road tax on all vehicles of £1 per unit of horsepower. This meant that the Silver Ghost, at 48.6 hp, would cost its owner £49 (about £2,500 in today's terms) per annum.

The board had been asked to consider the possibilities of merging with other British car manufacturers. On 4 April 1917 Claude Johnson had been invited by Sir William Peat, of the accountants Peat Marwick, to come to a meeting to discuss

. . . some form of amalgamation or union of interests between the leading British motor car manufacturers in order more effectively to combat the American and foreign competition which is likely to obtain after the war.

On 17 April 1917 Sir William chaired a meeting which included Claude Johnson, Sir Victor Caillard, a director of Vickers, Ernest Hopwood, the Managing Director of Wolseley, and Edward Manville, the Chairman of Daimler. The Managing Director of Sunbeam had also been invited, but did not attend. Sir William mentioned that a merger would have approval from 'other quarters' (presumably the Government), and would be advantageous for three reasons: overcapacity, too many models and a smaller market.

Sir William also made some detailed suggestions as to how the merger could be put together. Claude Johnson was suspicious, and wrote to his fellow directors:

It appeared to me peculiar that Vickers were represented by three people at the conference, and that one of them, Sir Victor Caillard, should produce from his pocket a typewritten statement of the statistics which each company should supply. I came to the conclusion that Vickers arranged the meeting [This was not correct. The original suggestion came from Siddeley] and that it was to the interest of Vickers (and probably not of Rolls-Royce) that the combination should be formed.

He was concerned that Vickers were trying to buy Rolls-Royce, now world-famous for both cars and aero engines, on the cheap. He continued:

Under the circumstances Vickers would probably desire to swallow up Rolls-Royce as part of a combination which they would control rather than face Rolls-Royce in open markets. Personally, I would sooner risk Rolls-Royce going out of business than be part of a combination in which there would be unholy and dirty elements. This may be short-sighted prejudice. [Just over sixty years later, Vickers did acquire the motor car side of Rolls-Royce but not, of course, the aero engine company, though interestingly there were discussions in 1919 between the two companies with the object of forming Vickers Rolls-Royce Aviation.]

Johnson wanted Royce to continue to concentrate on design, but nevertheless kept him informed of commercial developments. Royce wrote his views to Claremont.

It is difficult to see the position of the luxury car after the war. One has the impression that there will be somewhat limited use for such a car, probably much more limited than before the war. It is from this point of view perhaps that the advantage of amalgamation of the kind mentioned has, of course, enormous economic possibilities, both commercial and manufacturing, and we could be represented in every civilised land, and would have a chance of competition with strong companies, or combinations of companies that will exist in America and Germany. I do not see any objection to giving the necessary figures for the proposed combination, so that we can go in or stay out, according to the character the amalgamation acquires.

And it is almost certainly true that Johnson and Royce wanted to be their own men. Royce admitted it.

From a personal point of view, I prefer to be absolute boss over my own department (even if it was extremely small) rather than to be associated with a much larger technical department over which I had only joint control.

But Royce *was* fearful of the future.

I do not think the present way, that is the multitude of small companies doing a great variety of work, can possibly stand the competition after the war, and I am anxious that our own position should not be equally weak. I feel that something must be done, otherwise the trade of motor manufacturing will leave England.

After several further meetings, plans for amalgamation were shelved and were not brought down and dusted off until after the Second World War, when most of the surviving car companies merged themselves into large groups. *The Economist* pointed out that in 1923 total British output of 37,753 vehicles was produced by no fewer than ninety different companies.

In dealing with the more prosaic matter of production and sales on a day-to-day basis, Rolls-Royce worked hard to satisfy the backlog of orders. Many customers had signed contracts at pre-war prices but these bore no relation

to post-war costs, and lengthy negotiations were necessary with these customers. To preserve goodwill, Johnson conceded that the price would have to
be honoured if the customer would not agree voluntarily to an increase. The
following analysis of the increase in costs shows what Rolls-Royce were
paying for their goodwill. The pre-war works cost of the 40/50 hp chassis
was £506 (made up of £124 for wages, £196 for materials and £186 for
overheads (150 per cent of wages)), and it was estimated that the war had
more than doubled this figure to £1,083 (about £50,000 in today's terms).
The agent's commission was 20 per cent on the sale price of £1,450, which
increased the cost to £1,373. This meant that the company was making only
£77 on each sale through an agent. On direct sales, it saved the commission
and made £367.

The margins were clearly inadequate, and in December 1919 the chassis
price was raised to £1,850, in April 1920 to £2,000, and in June to £2,250.
However, this last increase caused the cancellation of twenty-six of the
current order book of 110, and by November some 48 per cent had
cancelled. It was not surprising that the company received cancellations. The
economic outlook was poor, and it was not helped by what, in retrospect,
were extremely misguided Government and Bank of England policies. After
the Second World War no one wanted to go back to the 1930s, a decade of
depression and high unemployment. By contrast, after the First World War
many people wanted to recreate the conditions of the Victorian and
Edwardian era, considered to be a golden age. One essential was to restore
the value to the pound, which had slumped from US$5.00 to $3.75. In April
1920 Montagu Norman, Governor of the Bank of England, raised the bank
rate to 7 per cent, and kept it there for a year. This had the desired effect of
raising the value of the pound; it also had the less happy effect of raising the
level of unemployment to over two million, which is more or less where it
stayed until the early 1930s, when it rose to over three million.

There were two major problems with the British economy in the 1920s.
Markets for traditional British exports such as coal, cotton textiles and ships
had disappeared during the war. Other countries had built their own
industries, and coal was being replaced by oil. In theory, men who lost their
jobs in these traditional industries should have found jobs in new ones, but
not many new jobs were appearing, and entrepreneurs were not encouraged
by high interest rates and a rising pound. There seemed to be a regular pool
of long-term unemployed and, although the 1911 Unemployment Insurance
scheme was expanded, it still only provided insurance for fifteen weeks in
any one year.

Maynard Keynes, who prescribed the theory that most Western governments eventually adopted to cope with this problem – spend to pump
money back into the economy – was still working on the theory and only

propounded it fully in his *General Theory of Employment, Interest and Money*, which was not published until 1936. The orthodox reaction in 1920 was to cut public expenditure and balance the budget, in the belief that this would restore the health of the economy. The result was a committee set up under Sir Eric Geddes, whose report was so sweeping in its recommended cuts that it became known as the Geddes Axe.

The signs for a luxury car maker were not propitious, bringing pressure for a cheaper car. As we have seen, Royce had been asked to design a 20 hp car, which was codenamed the Goshawk. Royce himself had seen the probable need for a smaller car. He had begun work in the latter stages of the war and had written formally to the board about it in May 1918.

The difficult economic conditions that followed the immediate post-war boom were hurting Rolls-Royce, and many others, by 1921. Trading in 1920 had been good, producing a record profit of £202,000. Nevertheless, with the outlook so uncertain, the board reduced the dividend from 25 to 10 per cent. The bank was not prepared to increase its overdraft facility of £400,000 (£20 million today). The heavy taxation due could only be paid in instalments.

In May, the price of the Silver Ghost chassis was reduced to £1,850 in an attempt to clear stocks. As the economic situation worsened, arrangements were made for customers to purchase on an instalment basis, and negotiations with the suppliers of drop forgings, alloy steels and castings were pursued in an attempt to obtain lower prices.

Fortunately for Rolls-Royce, many of their competitors' prices were also high. The Napier 40/50 hp, their strongest pre-war rival, cost £1,750, Daimler sold three chassis between £1,000 and £1,900, Crossley four from £1,200 to £1,450, Sunbeam seven between £1,125 and £1,650, and Lanchester two at £1,500 and £1,850. Rolls-Royce, of course, until the appearance of the Goshawk in late 1922, concentrated on one model, as did Rover, a policy that allowed *The Economist* to describe them in 1923 as 'our best managed motor concerns'.

As we have seen, Lord Northcliffe had always taken a close interest in Rolls-Royce, and in 1921 he wrote to Johnson advocating more and better advertising.

My dear CJ

I had a long talk with your nice brother about the Rolls-Royce situation.

I wonder if you realise that publicity will inevitably play a greater part in your future than it has in the past.

As you develop the Rolls-Royce so will you be less in a position to rely upon the personal recommendation and prestige which have hitherto stood you in the place of advertising.

I do not hesitate to say that the present advertising of the Rolls-Royce is contemptible. Compare, for example, the advertising of the two best American automobiles with your own publicity. Not only is your advertising bad, but I have often seen it in almost worthless publications. You would have done better to throw the money out of the window in Conduit Street. Some poor man might have picked it up and benefited therefrom.

At a time when people want to save money, many believe what they hear and are deterred from buying a Rolls-Royce by the constantly whispered propaganda that 'the car is not what it used to be – that the 1920 is not as good as the older models'.

An intelligent advertising service agent should call personally, or through skilled and courteous representatives, on every one of the chief purchasers of your 1920 cars, and get each of them to write a testimonial stating, as I will state, that the new 1920 model is as great an advance on the pre-war models as the original Rolls-Royce was on the then existing automobile.

Your brother said that people would not write these letters but of course they would if the man takes with him half a dozen testimonials from people like John Montagu and myself.

The time to spend money in advertising is not when trade is busy but when it is slack. I am spending so much in advertising 'The Daily Mail' and 'The Times' today . . . that I am practically getting all the advertising and sale from my competitors.

British manufacturers rarely understand advertising.

I suggested to your brother that you should consult W.S. Crawford, a young Scotsman who is becoming a leading advertising service agent. Tell him in confidence all that you are going to do. Give him three months to think out the situation. The people who issue the enclosed are also very good. Either would require time to consider the position.

There are so many Rolls down here that some wag suggests that the place should be called 'Monte Rolls' not Monte Carlo. At the lawn tennis club yesterday there were twelve side by side.

It seems to me that, despite many difficulties, the Rolls-Royce cars always have the best position in the modern European market.

By proper publicity you can get the words 'Rolls-Royce' before the world, so that when better times return, there will be a rush for any kind of model that you wish to issue.

And Johnson listened to Northcliffe. The 1920 Rolls-Royce brochure included several favourable comments.

'At the Motor show it was commonly agreed that **THE Rolls-Royce CHASSIS STOOD OUT IN A CLASS OF ITS OWN.**' – *The Times*, Nov. 22nd, 1919.

'Even on the Continent the Rolls-Royce has long been accepted as **THE SUPER-EXCELLENT CAR.**' – *The Autocar*, Sept. 27th, 1919.

'THE WHOLE MOTORING WORLD IS JUSTLY PROUD OF THE Rolls-Royce.'
– *The Sphere*, Nov. 8th, 1919.

'Apart from the aggregate of tyre wear and fuel consumption to be expected from a car of this size and power, a Rolls-Royce is **ACTUALLY A CHEAPER CAR TO RUN THAN MANY A WELL ESTEEMED TWO-SEATER OF 10 HP.**' – *The Auto*, Nov. 6th, 1919.

'Rolls-Royce Cars **OCCUPY A UNIQUE POSITION** in the automobile market all over the world, since they are universally recognised as being **SECOND TO NONE.**' – *The Autocar*, Nov. 8th, 1919.

Northcliffe, like Johnson, was enthusiastic about adding to the range of cars. He wrote suggesting that they might consider charabancs or little cars. As we know, Johnson had long been thinking along these lines himself, and he replied on 26 April 1921:

Private and Confidential
My dear 'N',
Many thanks for your letter. Firstly your letter of 20th concerning motor coach.

Unfortunately, we cannot deal with this business until Royce has finished the designs for a 20 h.p. car, a 15 h.p. car, something like a taxi, and a new 40/50 car, which will be cheaper to manufacture than the existing one. These will occupy him two or three years.

If we were to employ some other engineer to design the charabanc Royce would still insist upon criticising and probably re-drawing every part of the design and, therefore, he would be over-loaded and we should be risking his health.

I quite agree that the demand in the future for a 40/50 h.p. car is going to be very limited. It was for that reason that before the Armistice we asked Royce to design a 20 h.p. car. He did so. It is on the road. But unfortunately, it is too costly in manufacture to enable us to put it on the market and, therefore, he is designing another 20 h.p. car of simpler and less costly design.

All this is, of course, confidential as we are vigorously contradicting rumours which are abroad to the effect that we intend to sell a 20 h.p. car, lest the knowledge might interfere with the sale of our present car.

You need have no fear that anyone on this Company will consider you a busybody because you are good enough to favour us with your suggestions.

On the contrary, all the Directors are deeply grateful to you for the trouble you take in connection with our affairs.

THE TWENTY AND THE PHANTOM

The Twenty was launched in 1922. This was a strategic move, in that it represented a deliberate ending of the 'one-model' policy insisted upon by

Johnson in the early years of the company. The original plan was to sell the chassis for £920, half that of the Silver Ghost, but when it appeared in October the price was set at £1,100. Initially, demand was high, but it fluctuated and the company recruited and laid off workers regularly in line with these demand fluctuations. As a result, it acquired a reputation for a policy called 'Rush 'em and Rest 'em'. In its first year of production, the Twenty accounted for £550,000 of the company's turnover, against £660,000 for the Silver Ghost.

With its three-speed gearbox, American style, some referred to it disparagingly as a 'copy Buick', and indeed it is possible that Royce copied some of the Buick's better features. As we know, he was a great improver of others' efforts. It was also criticised for its lack of power compared with the 40/50. This will not have worried Johnson, who had become irritated by some people's obsession with speed. In a memo following a board meeting on 14 July 1922, he had written:

[N]o orders must be taken for high compression cars. It is considered that the reputation of the Rolls-Royce car was largely made by the fact it had a silkiness and silence and smoothness which could not be found in other cars and that these qualities must not be sacrificed because certain people want to go at 70 miles an hour instead of 60 miles an hour with the low-geared axle.

The serpent of speed and power has entered into this Company and is likely to poison its existence ... Anyone encouraging in any way, the making or selling of high compression cars will be regarded as an unfaithful servant of the Company and his services will be dispensed with.

Bill Morton, who worked on the 20 hp, recalled that they were called 'Sweet Lavinia, the gutless wonder', or 'Cinderella', or even more disparagingly, 'the shite-hawk'.

And, in spite of Royce's successful efforts to keep the chassis light, the Twenty became heavier and more complicated, often because customers would insist on heavier and heavier coachwork.

Did the Twenty have any competitors? The strongest was the Daimler 25/85, costing between £950 and £1,700 for the complete car, and therefore cheaper than the Twenty. At this time, Daimler also enjoyed the attendant prestige of supplying the 'Royal Car'. Another was the 21 hp Lanchester. Lanchester always seemed to offer a chassis price £50 cheaper than Rolls-Royce, and in 1923 they offered the 21 hp in complete tourer form for £1,250. Its performance was probably better than the Twenty, but it never achieved the silence of that model. Nor did it handle as well. In terms of sales, while 2,900 Twenties were sold between 1923 and 1931, only 500 Lanchester 21s were sold in the same period.

The sales of the Twenty were achieved almost *despite* the Sales Department at Conduit Street, rather than because of them. In April 1923 Claude Johnson's brother, Basil, at that time involved with sales in the Conduit Street office, decreed 'that second-hand Rolls-Royces be sold in preference to new 20s', and a memo from the Sales Department on 28 April 1923 said:

The policy is not to push the 20 hp if the 40/50 hp can be sold instead. Rolls-Royce heard that Barkers (coachbuilders) are trying to induce Royalty and other celebrities to go in for the 20 hp, which is just what Rolls-Royce don't want.

As Fasal pointed out:

Bolster, in his entertaining book [*The Upper Crust*], states what can only be implied from Johnson's memo, 'The small Rolls-Royce was not really an upper-crust car.'

Rolls-Royce were aiming the 20 hp at the professional segment of the middle class: the owner-driver doctor, dentist, solicitor and moderately successful industrialist.

Nor was the Twenty exhibited at the 1923 Olympia Motor Show. Arthur Wormald, critical of this policy of not pushing the Twenty, said that this 'gave competitors a good chance of saying that Rolls-Royce were ashamed of it'. There was no doubt that many in the company regarded it as a stop-gap measure until sales of the 40/50 improved. Indeed, Henry Royce had said so himself.

Whatever anyone else thought, Royce's biographer Sir Max Pemberton raved about it:

To:

ROLLS-ROYCE LIMITED

14–15 Conduit St. London W1

Telephone Mayfair 6040

'MY FIRST HUNDRED THOUSAND'

Dear Sirs:

It is with very real pleasure that I write to you about the remarkable performance of the 'Twenty' which I have now driven since the year 1923.

This car has accomplished 100,000 miles, it has done so without any road stop whatsoever and the engine is as quiet as the day it left your factory.

Your 'Twenty' has always been regarded, and deservedly, as the ideal town car for women; but I would like to say that I have driven this particular car for thousands of miles in all conditions of wind, weather and track, and found it no less efficient on the open high road than in London.

101

The late Lord Northcliffe once said to me that as an instrument of advertising British efficiency in industry the Rolls-Royce car was unique. When I reflect upon the performance of the 'Twenty' I have driven now for six years, I am wholly in accord with this opinion.

It is surely one of the World's two great cars. The other is the 'Phantom'.

Yours sincerely
Max Pemberton

Modifications were made during the 1920s, notably the introduction of a four-speed gearbox. These modifications added over 200 lbs to the weight, further reducing performance. Royce instructed Cyril Lovesey to see if more power could be formed through improved induction freeness. Lovesey, who had joined the company after the war (following experience with the RFC and RAF), concluded that only major changes would achieve more power.

Towards the end of the 1920s, sales declined and Royce, with success in the Schneider Trophy under his belt, turned his attention to the Twenty. He wrote a strong memo.

20 HP CHASSIS
Sales, Works and W.W. [West Wittering] are not in complete agreement concerning the 20hp chassis . . . The rate of sales is decreasing, therefore either there is not a market for this model, or our programme is not sufficiently attractive . . . We cannot expect to compete with popular prices. We can, without much extra cost to ourselves, improve:

1. The appearance.
2. The riding qualities – can only be improved by avoiding big bodies.
3. Performance – can only be improved by avoiding heavy bodies and adopting the improvements to the engine which are in sight.
4. An increase in the size of both engine and chassis.

Shall we do either, any, or all of these, or shall we let the 20hp fade away?

I want to make it clear that unless I can do something my responsibilities must stop. I will do my best but if you do not follow my advice, I must not be blamed. I very definitely do not recommend (4.) because it will make our second model compete with Phantom. Therefore we must once and forever cease to fit the large ponderous bodies.

Clearly, Royce was frustrated by the failure, as he saw it, of the sales operation in London to control the size and weight of the bodies fitted to the Derby chassis. Whereas Basil Johnson and Arthur Sidgreaves were all in favour of the stately 'sit up and beg' approach, Royce could always see the attraction of a car with a little more 'fizz' and, therefore, glamour.

In 1929 the last 20 hp chassis was made as the company prepared to launch its replacement, the 20/25 hp. So nervous was the company that anyone might see this replacement, that a memo was issued:

Visitors should be dissuaded from visiting the Works, on the grounds that the Works are about to close for holidays.

The new 20/25 hp had become necessary because owners would insist on fitting heavy coachwork which rendered the Twenty greatly underpowered. Hives had written to Royce in February 1922:

We expect that we shall get beaten for pure speed and hill climbing when we compete against cars with larger engines. We shall be able to put up a very good show but there must be a limit of performance without spoiling the engine in other aspects.

In spite of Claude Johnson's equanimity on this point, the fact was that people did not like being overtaken by what they considered to be inferior cars. The 20/25 became very popular, and in its seven years of production between 1929 and 1936 it exceeded the sales of the Twenty by over 900 chassis. In 1936 its power increased further, and it became the 25/30. In 1938 the small car gained a new chassis with independent front suspension, and took on a more familiar Rolls-Royce name: the Wraith.

As we have seen, the Silver Ghost was constantly improved. Nevertheless, by the 1920s the performance of others had caught up, and in 1922 the directors took the decision to invest in a new car. It may have been a necessary decision but it was, nevertheless, a courageous one. Sales had slumped in 1921 and 1922. In the year before the war, the company had sold 742 chassis, a third of them abroad. In 1922 only 430 were sold, less than a quarter overseas. Turnover for the year was only £1,055,000.

By 1925, the New Phantom (retrospectively called Phantom I when Phantom II was introduced in 1929) was ready. It replaced the Silver Ghost, beating its performance and re-establishing Rolls-Royce's lead as *the* manufacturer of luxury cars. Initially, the only differences between the Silver Ghost and Phantom I were a new engine and a different method of mounting the steering column on the chassis.

Apart from the engine, the chassis with its separate gearbox was the same as the Silver Ghost. However, the engine, of 7.668 litre capacity and with a 4.5 inch bore and 5.5 inch stroke, though smaller and longer respectively than the Ghost, was more powerful. The compact cylinder head with pushrod operated overhead valves was designed by A.G. Elliott, and similar ones were fitted on all Rolls-Royce cars until 1939. The flywheel with a single-plate clutch was enclosed in the crankcase.

The new model had been prepared with great secrecy, and during its development had been codenamed EAC (Eastern Armoured Car). Hives, in charge of development, even left pieces of armour plating around the factory to lend credence to the idea that an armoured car was being developed.

And when the Phantom arrived it was superb. Nockolds told the following story in his book, *The Magic of a Name*.

Perhaps the best story about the Phantom 1 is told by Mr. Maurice Olley, the General Motors engineer who worked for Rolls-Royce in the United States in both wars. [This gives the wrong impression of Maurice Olley's career in the USA. Olley went to the USA with Claude Johnson in 1917 when they were negotiating manufacture of the Eagle engine. He stayed on to become chief engineer at Rolls-Royce's Springfield plant, and was made redundant when the plant stopped making cars in 1930. He joined General Motors in 1931 and, of his own volition, was seconded to Rolls-Royce during the Second World War.] It appears that in 1928, when General Motors opened the 4-mile speed loop at their proving ground at Milford, Michigan, not a single car – whether made by General Motors or any other American manufacturer – could cover more than two laps at full throttle without ruining its big ends. At that moment there arrived on the scene a stately Rolls-Royce Phantom 1 with a massive Barker 7-passenger landaulette body destined for the private use of Mr. Sam McLaughlin, the head of the Canadian Buick company. The Rolls was promptly tried out on the track and, to everyone's amazement, it proceeded to lap at a steady 80 mph without the slightest signs of trouble. The engine was immediately dismantled and examined to discover the Derby 'Know-how', with the result that within two years every American car had durable big ends.

By 1928, the engineers were working on a replacement for the New Phantom. One of the new generation, W.A. Robotham, wrote:

Owing to the improvements made by our competitors – amongst them Buick and Sunbeam – we must really push forward our own progressive development.

And Royce supported him.

I have long considered our present chassis out of date. The back axle, gearbox, frame, springs, have not been seriously altered since 1912. Now we all know it is easier to go on the old way, but I so fear disaster by being out of date, and having a lot of stock left, and by the sales falling off by secrets leaking out, that I must refuse all responsibility for a fatal position unless these improvements in our chassis are arranged to be shown next autumn, and to do this they must be in production soon after midsummer 1929.

In 1929 the new Phantom was replaced by the Phantom II, which was augmented a few months later by the Phantom II Continental. The engine had been redesigned, but the chassis was completely new. The engine and gearbox were now one unit, with the right-hand gear change which had been, and remained, a feature of Rolls-Royce cars for so long.

THE DEATH OF CLAUDE JOHNSON

The year 1926 had brought two serious blows to the company. The first was the death on 11 April of Claude Johnson, without whom the company would not have survived as an independent entity. The second was the General Strike. Beginning as a strike in the coal industry, it spread to railways, road transport, iron and steel, building and printing. Although the so-called General Strike lasted only nine days, the miners stayed out for nearly six months, and widespread (if spasmodic) unrest continued elsewhere in industry. Not only were factories disrupted, but also the whole social atmosphere contributed to caution when people were considering expenditure on such items as luxury cars.

Far, far worse from Rolls-Royce's point of view than the General Strike was the loss of the man who had turned Royce's genius into a commercial proposition, and this perhaps is an appropriate moment to compare the qualities of the two men and to see how they complemented each other. Without Royce, the peerless engineer, there would have been no Rolls-Royce cars and no Eagle aero engines in the First World War – that much is certain. But without Johnson's organising ability and flair for publicity there would probably have been no company to exploit the cars and aero engines.

And Johnson thought not only of external relations, but also of those inside the company. Royce's lack of what today are called inter-personal skills with his managers and employees is well-known, although he engendered quite remarkable loyalty in spite of being a hard taskmaster. For example, almost all of the work force from Manchester moved to Derby between 1907 and 1910, many of them making the journey on foot. However, Johnson was more aware of human relationships, though even he might be dubbed 'paternalistic' by today's standards.

In the works were hung notices exhorting the work force to 'be accurate' and 'be certain', and reminding everyone: 'You are on your honour not to depart from standards.' Johnson also arranged for badges of merit to be given to those who it was felt had earned them. He would arrange for the whole works management to go to the theatre on Monday night, he organised regular medical checks and encouraged all types of sport.

Johnson was also the marketing brains of the company. It was his idea to retain the famous radiator, in spite of the difficulties in producing it. Like the facets of the portico of the Parthenon, those of the Rolls-Royce radiator are slightly curved to give the illusion of straightness. They could not be produced by machine, and the soldering of the sharp corners was only achieved with considerable difficulty. Nor was it particularly efficient. Indeed, Royce wanted to scrap it, but Johnson understood its significance as a symbol. It linked every new model to the achievements of the past. Johnson also insisted on four gears, even though Royce maintained that three were sufficient. There were those who criticised Johnson after the First World War for not imitating Henry Ford's methods of mass production. When he heard this, F.E. Smith, later Lord Birkenhead, commented:

Ford and the world Fords with you,
Rolls and you Rolls alone.

In purely financial terms, Johnson's record speaks for itself. In 1926 Rolls-Royce had capital of £814,000 and made profits of £164,000, a return on capital of 20 per cent. But perhaps Johnson's greatest contribution to Rolls-Royce was his understanding of Royce himself, and his unselfish action in 1911 in taking him on an extended trip through Europe and Egypt which almost certainly saved Royce's life. Johnson also understood that both Royce and his employees would probably function better if they were kept apart. It was a happy coincidence that Royce's doctors prescribed sea air and that Derby, whatever other climatic attributes it offered, could not boast of sea air.

If Royce had stayed in Derby, his obsession with detail might well have hampered the commercial viability of the growing organisation. Even when he was in the south of England or at Le Canadel, he could become obsessed with intricacies of a component that might ultimately not even be used in production. And he would become involved in details that could easily have been left to others. For example, he insisted on designing the tool kits to be fitted into the cars. He could not stand adjustable spanners, and designed a full range of double-ended open spanners. However, these did not satisfy him because each different size of nut required a different degree of leverage. He therefore designed a set of spanners with single ends, but with the length of each spanner exactly appropriate for the size of nut.

Like all businessmen, Johnson made mistakes, though fortunately for Rolls-Royce he did not make many. Spurning work on aero engines at the beginning of the First World War was one mistake, though he quickly realised this and reversed the board's decision. Perhaps his greatest mistake, certainly one that brought him a great deal of anxiety in his last years, was the decision to manufacture Rolls-Royce cars in Springfield, Massachusetts. We shall see how this operation proved to be a failure. Taken as a whole, Johnson's contribution to Rolls-Royce was immense, almost incalculable. Lord Birkenhead had said at the unveiling of the statue of Royce at Derby in 1923, 'the real genius responsible for the wide fame of the Rolls-Royce car is CJ'.

Claude Johnson was succeeded as Managing Director by his brother Basil, whose first task was to implement some severe economy measures to cope not only with the generally unfavourable economic environment but also with a £250,000 (£12.5 million in today's terms) discrepancy in the stock discovered in 1925. Basil Johnson, in a speech to the senior sales staff in December 1926, said:

We now have before us what is always a most objectionable and tiresome task of retrenching and economising. We cannot hope to prosper and make profits until we have tackled this position seriously . . . We are making far less profit per chassis now compared with a few years ago . . . We dare not raise the price of these chassis except as a last resort. We feel we are already at the limit in this respect. We therefore <u>must</u> reduce the cost of manufacturing and selling if we are to show any profits in the future.

'THEY WORKED IN MONASTIC SECLUSION'

The British economy, especially manufacturing industry, had geared itself up to win the war, and there was concern that peace would bring widespread dislocation, especially in the factories that had come to rely on Government contracts. As Lloyd George had predicted, a short-lived boom was followed by a prolonged slump, exacerbated in the winter of 1918–19 by a great influenza epidemic.

Nevertheless, after a war that had come increasingly to rely on the petrol engine, demand for motor cars was sure to be heavy. At the end of the war there were 160,222 vehicles on the road in the United Kingdom (at that time including the whole of Ireland), fewer than in 1912. In 1921 the total of registrations was 478,538.

As Rolls-Royce turned their attention once again to the design and production of luxury cars after wartime concentration on aero engines, how did the organisation function? Royce himself was forced to nurse his health, and Johnson had long ago decided that this meant staying away from Derby and working in the more congenial climate of either the south of England (in summer) or the south of France (in winter). Between 1912 and 1917, Royce's homes were all in the south-east corner of England, apart from the winters of 1912–13 and 1913–14, which he spent in Le Canadel. He was unable to go to France during the First World War, but he went back to Le Canadel for the winter of 1918–19 and every winter until his death, apart from the last one, 1932–33, when he was already too ill to travel. The years 1912 and 1913 found him at Crowborough in Sussex. In 1914 he rented a house called Westward Ho! at St. Margaret's Bay near Dover, which was also near to Johnson's house. After spending the 1914–15 winter in a hotel at

Bognor Regis, he moved back to St. Margaret's Bay, where he bought a house and called it Seaton (his father was buried in Seaton in Rutland). In 1917, Royce and Nurse Aubin found a house and a village, West Wittering, which they liked better. Dover was being subjected to increasing bombardment, and so they had set off in his Bugatti (he had given up his Silver Ghost as an economy measure) armed with estate agents' leaflets. One hundred miles away they found Elm Tree Farm, which they renamed Elmstead. They stayed there in the summer months until Royce's death in April 1933.

Royce and Nurse Aubin established themselves in the main house, and set up a studio on the ground floor where Royce worked with two of his designers. Other designers worked in a studio called Camacha a few hundred yards away. Next door to Elmstead was a barn on a plot called The Piggery, and here Royce garaged his cars and set up a small workshop.

W.A. Robotham, who enjoyed a long and distinguished career in the company, wrote a book, *Silver Ghosts and Silver Dawn* (published by Constable in 1970), and in it he gave a first-hand view of how the company operated in the 1920s.

In 1923 the control of the company was vested in three widely dispersed groups. All designing was carried out at West Wittering in Sussex or Le Canadel in the south of France. All the directors except Royce were based in London, together with the Sales and London Service Departments; and all production emanated from the Derby works, where the Experimental Department was also located. The function of the latter was to make parts to Royce's design, test them, suggest means of eradicating any faults and finally carry out road endurance tests before releasing them for manufacture.

In essence this was correct, although it did not give the full story. There was also a major design office in Derby, albeit under Royce's control. During periods of heavy workload, design schemes were developed here under R.W.H. Bailey – for example, the Falcon, Buzzard and 'R' engines.

Because Royce's word was law throughout the company, the apex of the administrative triangle was undoubtedly the team of designers working under Royce at West Wittering. This team consisted of Elliott, Day, Jenner, Hardy, Evernden and one or two others – all extremely able and competent engineers. They worked in monastic seclusion in a drawing-office called Camacha situated in the middle of the village about a quarter of a mile from Elmstead, Royce's house. To ensure a minimum of distraction the drawing-office was for a number of years forbidden the luxury of a telephone, communication between Camacha and Elmstead being maintained by Marmont (Royce's secretary and, as it happens, a man. Nurse Aubin would probably not have tolerated a woman) riding a bicycle!

It seemed to me that, until his health deteriorated, Royce made the majority of the technical decisions. As I later found to my cost, if one attempted to turn Royce from his chosen path by any arbitrary action, one got into very severe trouble indeed.

. . . On the design side, Elliott's drawings were a delight . . . Day largely concentrated on the chassis components and Jenner on the engine. Hardy was the transmission expert and Evernden had the unenviable task of negotiating the no-man's-land where the body and frame came together. He was also a very competent stylist and, due to his engineering background, was able to help the coachbuilders to improve the mechanical qualities of their products.

This was the team responsible for the design of every car and all their components from 1919 until Royce died in 1933. From the late 1920s they were supported by junior potential successors, A.E. 'Tony' Cook, Don Bastow and H.E. 'Harry' Biraben. Robotham makes it quite clear that

[i]n matters concerning the actual model which eventually went into production, Sir Henry's decision was final, even though the sales department might not always agree that they were getting exactly what they wanted.

In the London office in Conduit Street, the Chairman was Lord Wargrave, but the key decisions were made by Claude Johnson, the Managing Director. Supporting them was William ('Billy') Cowen, who had worked his way up from a junior clerk and who now looked after the administration of the Sales Department, the Repair Department at Cricklewood, and the department that inspected and passed the car once its body had been fitted by a coachbuilder. Major Cox was in charge of the London sales team at Conduit Street, T.E. Bellringer ran the substantial service and repair operation at Cricklewood, and Lee Evans ran the final inspection team.

In Derby, the works manager was Arthur Wormald, who was also a director and who had started with Royce in Manchester; he was supported by the company secretary, John De Looze, who had also started in Manchester. T.S. 'Tommy' Haldenby, another recruit in the earliest days, looked after the factory buildings and maintenance. (He was to play a big part in the planning of the 'shadow factories' at Crewe and Glasgow in the late 1930s.) Captain Hallam, with only one arm, ran the Repair Department and brooked no interference from outside, while R.W.H. Bailey was in charge of technical production, including the production drawing office where Royce's designs were turned into working blueprints. He sailed between the Scilla of convincing Royce that his drawings had been correctly interpreted and the Charybdis of Wormald's view that manufacturing difficulties were caused by the shortcomings of the drawing office. And, of course, there was Hives, who ran the Experimental Department.

Robotham himself moved into Hives's department after completing his premium apprenticeship in 1923, and he has left us with a graphic description of how this scheme worked.

He [Eric Platford – Robotham's mother had met Mrs. Platford, and Platford was telling the young Robotham how Rolls-Royce worked] explained that Rolls-Royce had a training scheme for privileged apprentices, or 'premium apprentices' as they were known in the works. These apprentices normally came straight from public schools. They signed indentures for four years and their parents paid the company a lump sum of £250, in return for which the premium apprentices had the advantage of working in every department in the factory. Platford passed me on to John De Looze, the company secretary, who said that I could start work as soon as my parents had paid £250 and my indentures had been signed. Apparently no technical qualifications whatsoever were required.

Scarcely able to believe my good fortune I returned home and induced my father to post the necessary cheque the same day . . . the reader should remember that in 1919 comprehensive practical and theoretical training schemes simply did not exist in the automobile industry. What I learned, or failed to learn, in my first four years with the company was probably little different from the experience I should have gained had I joined any other motor-car firm. At this point it is worth recording that since 1945, Rolls-Royce have had, in my opinion, one of the finest training schemes in the country.

It should be remembered that £250 would be about £12,500 today, so Mr. Robotham senior was making a considerable investment in his son's future. And indeed, Robotham found the training scheme somewhat patchy in its effectiveness. His four-year scheme was organised by a junior member of the Secretarial Department with no knowledge of engineering. His time was allocated in equal compartments to each section, which meant that Robotham had too little time in some sections and far too much in others. When Hives became general works manager in 1937, he wrote a report for the Chairman, Lord Herbert Scott. Included in the report was a section on the Rolls-Royce apprentice training scheme, which Hives described as hopeless. However, he did say that Robotham was one of the few successes, though Hives thought this was despite, rather than because of, the training scheme.

Robotham worked for Hives as his technical assistant from 1923 until 1933. This was a wonderful position, as Hives was a key man in the organisation, reconciling Royce's fanatical perfectionism with the economic reality of producing cars. It was also Hives's responsibility to make Royce aware of critical comment from customers.

SPRINGFIELD, MASSACHUSETTS

Meanwhile, Rolls-Royce had been struggling to establish themselves in the world's biggest market. Any car manufacturer, especially one of luxury cars, has to look for sales to the wealthiest country in the world, the United States of America. We have already seen that Charles Rolls went to the USA in 1906. A number of cars had been sold there before the First World War, and an even greater number were bought by Americans visiting the UK. Rolls-Royce had set up an import company on Broadway in New York at the end of 1906, and took direct control of sales in the following year. There was also a service garage in New York run by Ernest Caswell, the brother of Florence Caswell who had been a secretary to Charles Rolls and Claude Johnson (she was also part of the team at Le Canadel, and eventually became a companion to Rolls's mother, Lady Llangattock).

After the war, the company seriously contemplated manufacture in the United States and, after protracted negotiations, set up a company in conjunction with the financier, J.E. Aldred, who had successfully financed other large and successful US companies, among them the Montreal Heat, Light and Power Company and the Gillette Safety Razor Company. In October 1919 Aldred issued a prospectus inviting subscription to the preference stock, and this issue was oversubscribed. The prospectus gave the authorised capital as $15 million (the exchange rate at the time was just under $4 to £1; this was therefore £3.75 million, or about £190 million in today's terms), equally divided between preference and ordinary. $3.5 million of preference shares were issued to the public out of a total issue of $7 million, the remaining shares being stock of no declared value.

The products of the English and American companies would be identical and indistinguishable. The English board would act in an advisory capacity and the English company would supply 'prominent technical officials'. The initial production target was 380 chassis a year, but the factory would be designed in such a way that it could be readily expanded. The former Rolls-Royce agent in New York, Robert Schuette, was to be paid $100,000 compensation (ultimately he secured a far larger sum).

It was felt wise to avoid the car-manufacturing area of Detroit, and there was also considerable difficulty over erecting a new factory. In the uncertain economic situation after the war, contractors were reluctant to give firm quotes, due to the fluctuating prices of raw materials. The company settled on the purchase of an existing plant in Springfield, Massachusetts. Springfield had long been a centre for the manufacture of service rifles, a kind of US 'Woolwich Arsenal', and as a result the area boasted a mechanically highly skilled labour force. Part production began in July 1920.

Having successfully set up the company, Claude Johnson returned to England and reported to the board. He asked his US lawyer, Kenneth Mackenzie, to report to him quite separately from the US board. This was not an entirely satisfactory arrangement, and the venture was further jeopardised by the inclination of potential US buyers to consider that an American Rolls-Royce could not be as good as an English one. Americans who had already bought English cars naturally did nothing to dispel this view. And the President of one of the leading American motor manufacturers told *The Times*:

If the American Rolls-Royce is to be made of English material, by English workmen, with English workmanship in the real Rolls-Royce way as if each car were a special order; if, in short, the Derby works are going to be reduplicated exactly over here, then I consider the venture to be a serious menace to the American high-class car. If, however, the car is going to be turned out on real American lines, frankly it does not give me the smallest uneasiness. It won't be a real Rolls-Royce.

The selling price of the American chassis was settled at $11,750, after the Springfield management had suggested $9,300. Johnson said:

I am very glad that you think you can sell chassis in sufficient numbers for $11,750. By all means keep the price up.

Aldred and his partner, H.J. Fuller, visited England in April 1920 to discuss this and other points, and Johnson returned to Springfield in June and found everything to his satisfaction. Shortly after his return, he wrote:

I was much pleased with the spirit of the men and their determination to excel the English quality and not merely to equal it. Surely that is the spirit of Rolls-Royce.

However, in August serious problems arose over the quality of some of the accessories. The American board wanted to fit Bijur starters and Bosch magnetos, complaining that the Watford magnetos and Lucas dynamos were unsatisfactory, and pointing out that several owners had fitted a Bosch magneto at their own expense. Furthermore, Lucas did not have a service operation covering the USA, whereas Bijur did.

Royce himself said Lucas dynamos were poor quality and hopelessly overpriced. Bijur and Bosch were better value, more reliable and could be replaced or repaired almost everywhere in the USA. That was a driving force, because only Rolls-Royce dealers would have had spare Watford magnetos or Lucas parts. Customers in the UK insisted on CAV instead of Lucas. (Perhaps that is why Lucas bought CAV.)

Ernest Hives, by this time chief of the Experimental Department, was sent out to assess the situation, and he visited both the Bosch and the Bijur plants. Both companies offered to put their products through any test Hives required, and he found them competitive in terms of quality and especially price. Hives was impressed with American methods.

There ought to be some scheme developed whereby the costs of Derby and Springfield are constantly compared, not only raw material costs but machining costs, fitting costs, testing costs and office costs. I saw enough in the USA to realise that in all departments there is something to be learned from American methods . . . One of the surprises was the excellence of their custom-built bodies. The best American bodies were better made and better finished than the English. They were made to more practical designs and had better fittings.

Maurice Olley, who had worked closely alongside Elliott with Royce before and during the First World War, became the key man in Rolls-Royce's attempt to manufacture successfully in the USA. In the opinion of many, he was the best engineer Rolls-Royce ever employed. He discovered that conditions in the USA were very different from Britain, and responded accordingly. He soon realised that the electrical products on the cars needed to be of US manufacture so that they could be repaired anywhere. Because the winters were so cold, he found that slats were necessary to protect the radiator and engine (Derby followed his lead in 1922 with the 20 hp, and in 1929 with the Phantom). In the extreme climatic conditions of the US, the British practice of applying twenty to thirty coats of paint to the coachwork proved disastrous. The paint cracked and the colour faded. Olley discovered that a thin coat, preferably black, worked best. (Henry Ford had said: 'They can have any colour they like as long as it's black.' Clearly, this may not only have been for reasons of speedy production.) Coping with the poor roads of the US (there were virtually no decent inter-city roads until the late 1920s), which would freeze and then thaw into very uneven surfaces in the spring, helped Olley to become one of the world's leading experts on car suspension.

Fitting the American Bosch magneto received Royce's approval, but the Springfield operation continued to struggle under the handicaps of importing expensive components from Derby, as well as finding that the Derby chassis was not as well suited to American conditions. The carburation was inadequate to cope with the lower-grade petrol and the greater range of atmospheric temperatures. The car was proving difficult to start, and the imported chassis with its right-hand drive, its petrol tank fillers on the wrong side of the body (with a nozzle too small for the standard American pumps) and its lack of petrol tank gauge was giving enough dissatisfaction for a number of owners to return their cars. (Some Springfield Rolls-Royces did have petrol gauges, but they were in the petrol tank, not on the dashboard.) In the early days of Springfield, all modifications needed sanction from the UK. This process was slow and cumbersome.

These technical problems were subsumed by financial ones. The cost of setting up in the USA had been grossly underestimated. Expenditure on jigs, tools and dies was $848,000, against an estimate of $300,000. (By this time, the pound had declined against the dollar from its pre-war position, and in today's terms $848,000 was probably about £12 million.) Paying off Schuette, the New York agent, cost $239,000, whereas $100,000 had been budgeted. There emerged an unexplained increase of $228,000 on the chassis and body trading account. Working capital requirements also proved much higher than estimated, and in November 1920 Aldred again visited England to tell the board that the American company would require an extra £400,000 (£20 million today) to pull it through the crisis. Aldred felt that he could probably raise the money in the USA, but he would need a guarantee from the English company. Unfortunately, the English company was in no position to give such a guarantee. It was engaged in the process of raising £600,000 to finance its own ventures, and De Looze had been told by the company's bank that any guarantee given to the American company would trigger a corresponding reduction in its overdraft facility.

After a year of constant negotiation and a further exhausting visit for Claude Johnson to the USA, an agreement was finally signed for a debenture issue of $2 million in early 1921. But there were still plenty of difficulties ahead. By the end of March, production had reached only five cars a week against a planned twelve, and sales were averaging only three a week. Sales, although they picked up from these low levels, never reached the targets originally set, and the American company struggled on, handicapped by heavy debt and interest payments and by the conflict of interest between financiers who did not want to become motor car manufacturers and motor car manufacturers who did not want to become financiers.

Selling conditions were very different in the USA, and the English board did not seem to want to understand them. In England, Rolls-Royce's view of the cars' sales appeal was that each car was unique, made specially for each customer, just like the Purdey or Holland and Holland shotgun, or the fishing rod from Hardy. If the customer had to wait eighteen months, so much the better. It would make him feel that the car, gun or rod was being hand-crafted specially for him. In the USA, the approach was completely different. A wealthy American would be prepared to wait for a product manufactured in Europe, but if it was made in the USA he wanted it 'now!' And in the USA, the dealers would almost certainly have to take back the car previously sold if the customer were to buy a new one. Hence, dealers sold second-hand Rolls-Royces alongside new ones, a practice of which the English board strongly disapproved. (In spite of this, the showroom at Conduit Street displayed second-hand Phantoms which, as we have already seen, some sold in preference to new 20 hp models.)

By 1925, more stability had been achieved as sales rose, but when Johnson made what proved to be his final visit to the USA, he wrote on his return:

The difficulties were enormous. One can buy three or four fine American cars for the price of a Rolls-Royce car. The American citizen cannot believe that the Rolls-Royce can possibly be superior to his own cars to this extent and turns his back on the Rolls-Royce. Further, the American citizen has a great fear of being laughed at locally by his neighbours as being a pretentious ass. Our big competitors in America have been most industrious and inventive in rubbing in these views. Consequently the difficulties of making the American citizen believe that in buying a Rolls-Royce he is making a sound investment and that he can afford to laugh at those who buy a new car every year instead of buying the best, have been, and still are, prodigious.

Even with all the difficulties, the American company made a substantial profit in 1926, despite losing nine weeks' production as it changed to the Silver Ghost's replacement, the New Phantom. Throughout 1926 and indeed 1927 and 1928, Aldred was constantly engaged in trying to persuade the English company to sell its interest in the American company. This was stoutly resisted, first by Claude Johnson, and, after his death in April 1926, by his brother Basil, who succeeded him as Managing Director, and by the rest of the English board. By 1928, the American financiers were becoming very concerned and Fuller, the President, wrote to the English board saying that there were few buyers of the shares. He had approached General Motors, Henry Ford, Studebaker and Dodge Brothers, without any success. They all took the view that

the Rolls-Royce car was not worth the price, and that in the way it was designed and constructed it could not be built, even in quantities, at a price which would enable it to become a profitable thing.

By the end of 1928, after Fuller had visited Derby and discussed the situation at length with Basil Johnson and Arthur Sidgreaves, it was decided that production of the full chassis at Springfield should be discontinued. (Basil Johnson had joined Rolls-Royce at his brother's invitation in March 1914, but he left the organisation when war broke out, eventually becoming Commanding Officer of the Admiralty Stores Depot at the White City. He was released from this at very short notice and returned to Rolls-Royce at the Admiralty's request to take over his brother's work. Claude was able to spare

115

him only a few hours to inform him of the state of the company's business before he left for America in 1917.)

The Rolls-Royce board decided that the American company should convert itself into a selling agency. The capital was not available to contemplate re-tooling for the Phantom II at an estimated cost of $1 million. Aldred made another suggestion (he had discussed it once before), and that was that American financial interests should attempt to buy control of the English company as well as the American one. Various important shareholders were approached, with the full knowledge of the English management, and the idea was discussed with several of the leading financial institutions in London. However, the shares were too widely dispersed by this time for the scheme to get off the ground. Furthermore, there was reluctance on the part of several shareholders to sell, knowing that control of the company would pass to the USA.

While Springfield staggered on, both producing its own cars and importing chassis from Derby, world economic events took a turn that threatened to overwhelm all the manufacturers of luxury cars. In the USA, if not in the rest of the world, the 1920s had proved to be a decade of increasing prosperity. Credit was easy and the American public became increasingly confident that they would grow richer and richer. The total output of the economy between the post-war depression of 1920–21 and the end of 1929 increased by some 50 per cent. In the motor car business, trade was booming. The pace-setter, Ford, was hotly pursued by General Motors, which offered no fewer than seven different makes of car: Chevrolet, Oldsmobile, Pontiac, Oakland, Buick, LaSalle and Cadillac. Henry Ford, never one to think small, retaliated by designing a new low-cost car to replace his Model T. The changeover cost him $100 million, as he closed his Detroit factory while work was progressing on the new Model A. American citizens read in their newspapers of the forthcoming new model with its shock absorbers, brakes on all four wheels, windscreen wiper, speedometer and stoplight. Furthermore, there would even be a choice of four colours, not just black. According to an eyewitness:

The preview raised more excitement than a declaration of war. On 2nd December 1927 a million potential buyers filed into the Ford showroom on Broadway. Elsewhere in New York temporary display centres were overwhelmed and Madison Square Garden was hurriedly rented to accommodate the overflow. (A confidence trickster who saw the chance of rapid wealth roamed through the crowd promising immediate delivery for a down payment of 25 dollars. He had collected a small fortune by the time the police caught up with him.)

The eight million cars in the USA of 1920 became twenty-three million by 1929, and by then the car industry was using 15 per cent of the nation's steel

116

and contributing some 13 per cent of the whole national output. At the same time there was a construction boom that transformed the face of every American city. In retrospect, it was obvious that it couldn't last when President Hoover assured his fellow countrymen in 1928: 'We are nearer today to the ideal of the abolition of poverty and fear . . . than ever before in any land.'

One of the weaknesses in the structure was what the great American economist J.K. Galbraith called 'Corporate thimblerigging'. This took a number of forms, the most common of which was the organisation of corporations to hold stock in other corporations, which held stock in yet other corporations. In the case of the railroads and the utilities, the purpose of this pyramid of holding companies was to obtain control of a very large number of operating companies with a very small investment in the ultimate holding company.

In other cases, companies were organised to hold securities in other companies in order to manufacture more securities to sell to the public. A classic example was the investment trust. The general public, attracted by the supposed expertise of the trust management, could buy shares in the trust, which could invest it in the operating companies.

The number of securities in a company that the trust could sell was limited only by the number of new companies it could set up. During 1929, as the bull market reached a frenzy, one investment house, Goldman Sachs & Company, organised and sold nearly a billion dollars' worth of securities in three interconnected investment trusts: Goldman Sachs Trading Corporation, Shenandoah Corporation and Blue Ridge Corporation. All eventually became virtually worthless.

Matching the leap forward in production and consumption was the stock market. By early 1929 the bull market in stocks had lasted four years, and the Dow Jones index, which had stood at 110 in 1924, was now 338.35. For the first nine months of 1929 the market moved higher and higher, and almost everyone seemed to be in on the act. (In fact, there were only about one million investors, but they made enough noise both before and after the Crash to make it seem like almost everyone.)

What made the explosion in prices possible was the trading 'on margin', which meant that buyers of stocks only had to put up a tenth of the value. It was the obvious and easy way to get rich. People could scrape together $1,000. That would not buy them much on the market, but $10,000 would. And when the stock doubles, the $1,000 has become $20,000. While the market was going up and up, few contemplated what would happen if it stopped or, worse, fell. When that happened, the punter realised that he had committed himself to $10,000 and his stock was worth $7,000 – no, sorry, that was yesterday's price, today's is $6,000.

When the turn came, it was very nasty. A leading steel stock, surely the safest investment around, fell from $90 to $12. Within a month, shares fell by a third. They then stabilised, and in April 1930 even rose slightly. But this was a classic 'dead cat bounce', and shares then fell steadily for two years so that, by the middle of 1932, the average industrial share was only 15 per cent of its 1929 level. The effect was felt throughout the land. For once, only the poor escaped. They had been poor in 1929 and they stayed that way. They were joined by many who had thought themselves secure. A few canny ones did escape unscathed. Rockefeller is supposed to have walked into his office a week before the Crash and told his clerk to sell everything he had. When the clerk protested, Rockefeller said: 'Listen! I've just heard two boot-blacks discussing stocks. Who's going to buy from them? Sell!'

Samuel Insull, who had donated the Opera House to Chicago, heard the crowd muttering in the soup queue outside the House, and increased his bodyguard from two to thirty.

Arthur Schlesinger, the economic historian, wrote later:

The national income was half what it had been four short years before. Nearly 13 million Americans – about one quarter of the labour force – were desperately seeking jobs. The machinery for sheltering and feeding the unemployed was breaking down everywhere under a growing burden. On the morning of Roosevelt's inauguration [the beginning of 1933], every bank in America had locked its doors. It was now a matter of seeing whether a representative democracy could conquer economic collapse. It was a matter of staving off violence – even, some thought, revolution.

Clearly, Rolls-Royce was not going to escape this economic turmoil. Mackenzie wrote to the English board on 11 November 1929, just over a month after the initial slump on Wall Street:

The stock market situation has long been a source of anxiety . . . When the change came everyone was surprised at its suddenness and immensity . . . the whole automobile market is in a demoralised condition.

The American board decided to close down the Springfield plant, retaining only a skeleton staff. Half the sales organisation were made redundant. Only an injection of $500,000 by Aldred prevented the American company from going into liquidation. The US venture was a failure, but not because the effort had been half-hearted. Fuller had struggled hard and persuaded some very able men to serve on the board, but the costs of the operation did not work. The volume of sales remained low because there were not enough Americans prepared to pay $8,000–$12,000 more than the cost of the most expensive American car. And these American cars were not of poor quality.

As we have seen, Johnson held them in high regard and Arthur Sidgreaves, the new Managing Director, was equally impressed, especially by the 16-cylinder Cadillac and the Studebaker, when he visited the USA in 1930. The Experimental Department under Hives brought in cars both from the USA and Europe and tested them rigorously. They found, certainly by the mid-1930s, that US component quality was better than that attained in Britain, largely because of the huge research and development programmes of the American component manufacturers. It also became clear that Rolls-Royce would have to introduce the synchromesh gear change, which had become commonplace in the USA by the mid 1930s. When Sidgreaves visited the Studebaker plant, he noted the 'fabulous' amount of money spent on research and development. He also observed that the tests to which the Studebaker car engine was submitted were 'considerably more severe than the hundred-hour type test of our aero-engines'.

Hives followed Sidgreaves to the USA in late 1930, and was depressed by what he saw at the New York Show.

When you see a Cadillac, Packard, Lincoln with a custom built body, as regards general lines, appearance and finish, we can show them nothing very much better. As regards price, one almost hesitates to make a comparison.

The Cadillac was selling for $6,000 and the Packard and Lincoln for $4,000, while the Rolls-Royce was $14,000. Hives noticed the obsession with cost whenever he visited a car plant.

When visiting factories in the USA, it is interesting to note how everyone talks costs. If one is talking to engineers they will always end up with the description of a part by saying how much it costs. If you walk round the works and take special interest in a part the man in charge of that section will tell you how much it costs.

Hives sent a full report of his visit to Royce, who understood only too well the dilemma faced by British companies in trying to compete in the USA. As Ian Lloyd pointed out in his book, *Rolls-Royce – The Years of Endeavour*:

[Royce] made it quite clear that he had no illusions about the relative merits of British industry. In the seventeen volumes of his memoranda which have survived it is the only occasion upon which he used capital letters.

MY GREAT MOTTO FOR GREAT BRITAIN AND OURSELVES IS MASS PRODUCTION WITH QUALITY. UNLESS WE DO THIS WE ARE FATED SO LET US DO IT BEFORE IT IS TOO LATE, BECAUSE AT THE MOMENT ENGLAND CANNOT TRULY BOAST OF EITHER.

The American company struggled on, but as the Depression deepened – Aldreds succumbed, among thousands of others – its prospects became hopeless, and the Springfield plant was sold. The responsibility for Rolls-Royce sales in the USA returned to Derby.

CHAPTER FIVE

'WE MUST NEVER BE SATISFIED'

THE BUYING OF BENTLEY
THE DEATH OF SIR HENRY ROYCE
THE DIFFICULT 1930s
ERNEST HIVES

THE BUYING OF BENTLEY

ECONOMIC DIFFICULTIES WERE NOT confined to the USA. Indeed, they spread like wildfire around the world, as country after country tried to give itself an advantage in a series of competitive devaluations. Businessmen were forced, as always, to cope with current conditions, and those could scarcely have been worse. Nevertheless, Rolls-Royce was still sufficiently well-funded to buy the firm of Bentley Motors Ltd. when it was placed in the hands of the receiver in 1931.

Rolls-Royce had already turned down two acquisition opportunities in 1929. Their old friend and rival, S.F. Edge, had become a major shareholder in AC Cars, and had suggested that Rolls-Royce should manufacture his cars. The company was also offered a controlling interest in the coachbuilder, Barker.

Like a number of other early carmakers (including, of course, Henry Royce), W.O. Bentley had served his apprenticeship in the big railway workshops, in Bentley's case in Doncaster. Both Royce and Bentley worked for the same company, GNR (Great Northern Railway). By the outbreak of the First World War, Bentley had become an agent in London for a French motor company. During the war he developed a highly successful aluminium piston for aero engines. He had used aluminium pistons in the French cars he had raced so successfully before the war, and he suggested to Hives that

Rolls-Royce should use them on the Eagle aero engine. Royce followed this suggestion and, when he turned his attention to cars again at the end of the war, used them on the car engines as well.

Bentley designed two of the First World War's best aero engines for the RNAS, the BR1 and BR2 air-cooled rotaries. At the end of the war, he began to make cars with his brother H.M. Bentley and a designer, F.T. Burgess.

Bentley, described as 'short, stocky, dark, inclining towards ocular fierceness, deliberate, monosyllabic and decidedly dour', later said that trying to construct a new car without substantial capital was like trying to build a house on a desert island with a penknife. When his prototype Bentley burst into life it brought complaints from a nearby nursing home, to which someone replied: 'A happy sound to die to – the exhaust roar of the first three-litre Bentley engine!'

Conceived in an office on the top floor of a building in Conduit Street, not far from the Rolls-Royce London office and showrooms, the first prototype was built in a mews garage just off Baker Street, and the first car was on the road in 1919.

However, it took another two years and the further raising of capital before any cars were sold. The first purchaser was a rich socialite, Noel van Raalte, a racing motorist since his days at Cambridge, and the man who put up the money for KLG plugs. The early Bentleys owed much to Continental influence, and in some ways were racing cars adapted for the road. Ettore Bugatti referred to them as *Le camion plus vite*, the fastest lorry. Bentley himself said: 'I wanted a car that could be driven hard without minding, a car with long legs.' Apparently, the cars he admired were the 1912 Peugeot and the 1914 Grand Prix Mercedes.

Bentley customers were members of the Royal Family, millionaires from the USA, princes from the East and stars from the West End stage, such as Tallulah Bankhead, Gertrude Lawrence and Jack Buchanan. The 'Bentley Boys', as they were dubbed by the press – Woolf Barnato, Sir Henry 'Tim' Birkin, Jack Barclay, Glen Kidston and George Duller – provided some glamour in an otherwise grim world of recession, unemployment and industrial unrest. They raced the cars for glory. And of course there were plenty of Bentley Girls. In 1931, some took part in a race at Brooklands organised by none other than Barbara Cartland, who did not know how to reverse. The dangerous driving apparently horrified spectators.

By 1925 a six-cylinder, six-and-a-half-litre model was added to the three-litre, four-cylinder model, and this was soon followed by a sports derivative known as the Speed Six. In 1927 a four-cylinder, four-and-a-half-litre model was launched. The Bentley Company was seen as a real threat to Rolls-Royce. Indeed, Royce had written from West Wittering as early as 1925: 'Regarding the Bentley, the makers are evidently out to capture some of our trade.'

The real challenge came with the Bentley eight-litre, which was superior to the Phantom II in a number of respects. Royce did not think he would learn much by buying a model.

We can see in which way it can be better than we are ... for high-speed performance, because it has four valves per cylinder. It would appear more costly than ours to produce for equal silence.

A year later, Royce touched on the subject again, writing from Le Canadel that he would like to design 'a high-speed sports car, not expecting much in the way of sales, but for the good of ordinary sales'. And Robotham in his book, *Silver Ghosts and Silver Dawn*, recalled:

My first contact with a 3-litre Bentley was in about 1924. Neville Minchin, one of our oldest customers, brought the car along for us to try. I was much impressed by the general quality of the car and the way it handled; it was to be our most serious competitor for the next seven years.

But by 1930, in spite of the eight-litre, Bentley Cars Ltd. was in severe financial trouble. Participation every year in the Le Mans 24-hour race (in which they were extremely successful, coming first for four successive years from 1927 to 1930), although beneficial in terms of publicity, was extremely expensive; along with development costs, it had brought the company to the brink of bankruptcy. In a fund-raising exercise in 1925, W.O. Bentley had ceded control to Woolf Barnato. Captain Woolf Barnato was enormously rich, thanks to his father, who had left the East End as a pauper and finished up controlling the diamond fields of Kimberley in South Africa alongside Cecil Rhodes. In spite of his wealth, he was self-effacing and modest and, as a Bentley driver, had accepted any car he was asked to drive and had complied with any instruction from the team manager, even though it might deny him the chance to win. He once raced, and beat comfortably, the Blue Train down to the Riviera, a feat that brought him a rebuke from the RAC. At one of his parties, the waiters wore racing kits complete with crash helmets, and the table decor was a miniature Brooklands. A note on each guest's menu said: 'Before parking his or her chassis, each driver should ensure that his or her carburettor is flooded with at least two cocktails.'

At the end of 1930, Barnato put in J.K. Carruth as Managing Director, and in June 1931 Carruth wrote to Sidgreaves effectively suggesting a merger (even Barnato was affected by the world financial crisis). He told Sidgreaves that if Bentley went into receivership a hundred chassis would be dumped on the market, to Rolls-Royce's disadvantage. He suggested a working agreement whereby the companies would have common sales and service operations, and a production arrangement under which Rolls-Royce would make two-thirds of the parts that Bentley usually bought in. In return, Rolls-Royce would be able to use W.O. Bentley as a designer. Carruth told Sidgreaves that Bentley needed £35,000 (about £1.75 million in today's terms) to tide them over. Sidgreaves discussed the idea with Carruth, and the Rolls-Royce board considered the proposition carefully. However, at a board meeting on 23 June they decided against making any such investment. As with all such cases, taking over a company that is nearly bankrupt is risky because the buyer is not aware of the potential liabilities. Once a company is bankrupt, the liabilities are clearly defined.

This was the last chance for Bentley. The principal lender, the London Life Association, called in its loans and a receiver was appointed on 11 July 1931. As we have seen, Napier were contacted by W.O. Bentley and agreed to purchase the company and develop new models. On 14 August, *Autocar* announced, under the headline NAPIER BENTLEY FUSION:

For some weeks past, negotiations have been proceeding between D. Napier and Son Ltd. Acton, the famous aero engine manufacturers and Bentley Motors Ltd. with a view to the Napier Company taking over Bentley Car production. On going to press we learned from Mr. H.T. Vane CBE, managing director of D. Napier and Son Ltd., that negotiations had reached an advanced stage but nothing definite had been settled.

In the event, as we saw, at the last minute Rolls-Royce bid more than Napier for the company, and Bentley became part of Rolls-Royce. During the crisis, production had virtually come to a standstill at Bentley's Cricklewood factory, and Rolls-Royce needed to decide which models to produce and sell. They were not happy with the four-cylinder four-and-a-half-litre model, which then left the four-litre and the eight-litre. The four-litre had not been very successful, due to its adverse power to weight ratio (it was produced quickly in an attempt to stave off bankruptcy, and had a Ricardo rather than a Bentley engine); this left only the eight-litre. However, this was a direct competitor to the Phantom II Continental.

The ideal would be a brand new car that did not compete with any Rolls-Royce model. Cricklewood had already started developing a smaller car to undersell Rolls-Royce's 20/25. Different engine sizes were being considered and time was passing. Meanwhile, the Sales Department was fretful that the value of the Bentley name was being lost.

The Experimental Department was working on another small Rolls-Royce car, the Peregrine, a scaled-down version of the 20/25. Delays were becoming intolerable when Hives proposed putting the 3,669 cc 20/25 Rolls-Royce engine and gearbox into the Peregrine, so that they could achieve the performance acceptable to Bentley owners and the smoothness and silence acceptable to Rolls-Royce owners. The Peregrine had been developed as a smaller car than the 20/25. However, the savings on manufacturing costs had not been enough to allow a significantly lower selling price, and the Peregrine had effectively been put under dust-sheets in 1930. The Experimental Department dragged the cars out and tried a supercharger. But Hives thought this was a perfect application for his development of the 20/25 engine known as the 'JI'. Royce accepted the solution, and this first Rolls-Bentley was one of the successes of the 1930s. Unfortunately, Royce died before he could see a production model, but as Robotham said:

It should be emphasised that all the Peregrine and 20/25 components that went to make the first Rolls-Bentley were designed by Royce. All we did was to rearrange their disposition in the Derby Experimental Department.

Even W.O., who became heavily involved in the testing of the car, wrote to Derby:

Taking all things into consideration, I would rather own this Bentley car than any car produced under that name.

Initially, Sidgreaves, when he tried the car out at Brooklands, complained that it was too silent and did not sound like a Bentley, but when they tried it, the Rolls-Royce agents Pass (of Pass and Joyce) and Jack Barclay were full of praise for the 'Silent Sports Car'.

THE DEATH OF SIR HENRY ROYCE

On 22 April 1933 Sir Henry Royce died at West Wittering. (He had belatedly received a baronetcy in 1930 in recognition of his contribution towards winning the Schneider Trophy in 1929.) There were, of course, large obituary notices in all of the major newspapers, covering the ground that we have already covered in this book. Royce was quite simply a genius, and thanks to a meeting with C.S. Rolls (who fortuitously was in partnership with Claude Johnson), the benefits of his genius were spread and shared by the whole country, indeed by the world at large.

We have noted his belief in hard work. He set the example and expected others to follow. As Ivan Evernden, who worked with him in the 1920s and who continued to serve the company until the early 1960s, observed:

Henry Royce ruled the lives of the people around him, claimed their body and soul, even when they were asleep.

A.G. Elliott joined Rolls-Royce from the company's great rival, Napier, in 1912, rose to be chief engineer, then joint Managing Director and finally Vice Chairman. He served the company for forty-four years, and said of the Silver Ghost, Royce's masterpiece:

When I saw the engine dismantled it revealed new and advanced features of design which astonished me. It was the first six-cylinder engine I had seen fitted with a crankshaft damper, the first expanding carburettor with such effective schemes of jet and air control, the first valve gear with a silent scientifically designed cam and the first high tension jump spark distributor, the last named feature being entirely new to motor car ignition.

Elliott recognised genius at work, and felt compelled to leave Napier and join Rolls-Royce to see how it was done. He said later:

Henry Royce never claimed to be a good draughtsman, but he had a wonderful eye for line and proportion and instinctively knew the right shape for every piece. Nor was he a trained mathematician but he had his own way of doing calculations, by using simplified methods, showing that he had a highly developed sense of the fundamental principles of mathematics.

And of course everyone who worked with him knew that he was a perfectionist. They knew how he would test parts far beyond anything they were likely to have to withstand on the road. Some found his habit of changing and improving designs extremely frustrating. He wanted his designers to be rubbing out and improving all the time. He wanted them to be 'Knights of the Rubber'. In Royce's view, such an approach saved time in the long run. It was obviously going to be much cheaper to change a drawing than to cut metal and then have to make changes. This tradition of obsession with functional perfection long outlived him, and indeed is paramount in both Rolls-Royce companies today.

His near-fatal illnesses in 1911 and 1912 may, from the company's point of view, have been a blessing in disguise although, coming little more than a year after Rolls's death, they gave Claude Johnson some of his most difficult moments. Never one of the world's great man-managers, Royce was able to concentrate on what he knew best. We saw what Harold Nockolds thought of this development:

His mind undistracted by the management of the factory, Royce kept his staff busy with a continual stream of ideas from his fertile brain.

Royce's last memorandum on 'Experimental Car Work and Design Generally', written from Le Canadel on 5 March 1932, serves as a fitting memorial.

It should be clear that I am not an obstructionalist, but wish anything hopeful to be tried that can be bought both for test and special customers.

I have preached for many years the practice of – 'when in trouble find out what others are doing, and that we have enough well educated and inexpensive young men to take a personal interest in any special subject, and give them a chance of showing their ability and ingenuity.' We older engineers will use our experience to pick out that which we think is worth working on, and it must be remembered that time and money will not allow us to try or make everything and someone knowing most of our history is best able to make the choice.

We want to avoid the resources of the Experimental Dept. being crowded by ill-considered, half thought out, schemes, so that things which have had much time and thought are never made, or are pushed aside before they are tested to a finish.

I have no desire to spend the small hours of the morning seeking solution of our difficulties, and features of design, etc., because this practice (forced upon me) has done much to make my life – through ill-health – nearly unbearable.

Royce's striving for perfection in everything he did was epitomised by a comment he made to a local vicar in West Wittering after he had stripped and rebuilt the vicar's lawnmower. The actual words were not recorded, but they inspired the vicar's son, the famous sculptor Eric Gill, to paraphrase them as: 'Whatever is rightly done, however humble, is noble.' Gill obtained access to Royce's house and carved the Latin inscription in a stone mantel-piece: *Quidvis recte factum: quamvis humile praeclarum.*

Clearly his death was going to leave a void in the creative side of Rolls-Royce, but in truth the management of the company was already suffering heavily from the death of Claude Johnson seven years earlier. The period between 1926 and 1936 was a hiatus for the company, spanning the ten years between Johnson's death and the promotion of Hives to general manager and, shortly afterwards, main board director. In spite of the loss of Johnson's drive, Rolls-Royce still chalked up some notable achievements – the launch of the Kestrel and Buzzard, the winning of the Schneider Trophy, the setting of land-, water- and air-speed records, the launching of the Derby Bentley and the beginnings of the development of the Merlin engine.

Royce himself had never 'run' the company, although even as an old man his stream of ideas continued. His influence on company policy remained very strong until the end of his life. He had been Managing Director of the company only from March to December 1906, but thereafter he dictated product ethos and design and steered the commercial philosophy, particu-larly once Claude Johnson began to fade. He overruled the board's refusal to make aero engines and, as we shall see, made sure Basil Johnson resigned when he discovered that Johnson had suppressed Fell's report. Royce decided, against board resistance, that the company should develop an engine for the Schneider Trophy. Until Hives took control, the overall management of the company drifted, with insufficient attention being paid to cost control or profitability. Nor was it a time for being anything but highly efficient. The late 1920s and early 1930s were probably the most difficult years for a manufacturing business in the whole of the twentieth century.

THE DIFFICULT 1930s

Rolls-Royce were never going to be mass-producers of cars, and never wanted to be. However, as we have already seen in looking at the US operation in Springfield, they could not afford to ignore the technological advance being achieved by the large motor car manufacturers in America. The Model T Ford did not worry them, but the excellent cars being produced by Cadillac, Buick, Marmon and Packard gave them food for thought, and indeed models were always bought by the Experimental Department team. Robotham visited the USA in 1932 and was shown great hospitality by all the major car manufacturers. He was massively impressed. Writing years later, he recalled:

Cadillac's were particularly interesting to me because they were developing their new models of motor cars in much the same way as we were. The main difference between the two Design and Development Departments as far as I could see, was that in Detroit the responsibility for the finished product was far more decentralised than at Rolls-Royce. Thus, while Seeholm had the over-all management of the team, each major component such as the engine or suspension would have a group of specialists working on it, led by a very competent engineer. These groups made their own decisions until their product approached finality. Once a development project was getting to the state where it might go into production, the manufacturing team went through it again and again until they were quite convinced either that it could be built at the right price or else that it should be suitably modified – a complete contrast to the way we worked in Derby in 1932.

General Motors possessed five main car divisions: Cadillac, Buick, Pontiac, Oldsmobile and Chevrolet. If one of the divisions made an important technical breakthrough, such as happened with the hydromatic gearbox, there seemed to be no restriction on the others using the same component. Behind the engineering departments of the five divisions lay the General Motors research laboratory – a very large building in the centre of Detroit. This was staffed by highly qualified scientists who were frequently working on advanced projects which might have no practical application for years. Finally, lying in the heart of Michigan and covering many acres of rolling country, there was the General Motors proving-ground. This was a private testing facility with miles and miles of roads of varying surfaces and gradients, as well as a high-speed cambered track which permitted vehicles to be run at speeds in excess of 100 mph for indefinite periods.

In contrast, the centralised system at Rolls-Royce, whereby Royce approved every design, even of the smallest components, meant that progress was slow. Royce had gathered round him a powerful team of designers at West Wittering.

**ELMSTEAD
OFFICE
ENGINE DESIGN WORK**

ENGINEER-IN-CHIEF:
F.H. ROYCE (R)

IN CLOSE LIAISON WITH 'R'
BUT BASED IN DERBY:

SENIOR ENGINE DESIGNER:
A.G. ELLIOT (E)
Came from D. Napier & Son Ltd. in 1912. Headed 'R's personal design team from 1917 until 1932.

ASSIST. CHIEF ENGINEER:
A.J. ROWLEDGE (Rg)
A brilliant designer who had come from D. Napier & Son Ltd. in June 1921. Mainly concerned with aero engines, but also developed the 4-wheel brakes and servo system.

ENGINE DESIGNER:
C.L. JENNER (Jnr)
Came from Phoenix Motors Ltd. in 1911 and came to WW in 1918.

ENGINE DRAUGHTSMAN:
DONALD EYRE (DE)
Joined R-R Derby, Feb. 1920 under R.W.H. Bailey. Came to WW in 1928.

SENIOR DESIGNER TO 'Rg':
S.F. POTTINGER (SFP)
Joined R-R in 1914. Went to WW in 1918 under 'E' but later returned to Derby.

GEARS AND GEARBOXES:
A. JOHN STENT (AJS)
Left in 1925 and went to Argentina.

GENERAL ARRANGEMENTS:
C. CAROLIN (CC)
Left in late 1921.

**CAMACHA
THE STUDIO
CHASSIS DESIGN WORK**

CHASSIS, SUSPENSION, STEERING, AXLES & BRAKES:
B.I. DAY (Da)
Came from Sheffield Simplex Ltd. in 1913. Had formed nucleus of Derby Design Office which kept in contact with 'R' during work on aero engines. Joined the WW staff in 1921.

EXHAUST SYSTEMS, BODY MOUNTINGS & COACHWORK CONCEPTS:
H.I.F. EVERNDEN (Ev)
Joined R-R in January 1916 under 'E' on jig and tool design work. Came to WW in April 1921.

GEARS, GEARBOXES & PROPSHAFT DESIGNS:
W.G. HARDY (Hdy)
Had joined Clement Talbot Ltd. in 1911. Came to R-R in 1919 and to WW in May 1921 to form the 'Camacha' trio.

Two gentlemen also in attendance at WW were R.L. MARMONT (M), 'R's secretary, who kept communication between the office and studio by riding the ¼ mile on his bicycle until Royce agreed to the installation of a telephone; and FRANK DODD (Dd), 'R's driver and mechanic.

[Reproduced from John Fasal's book, *The Rolls-Royce Twenty*]

Royce fully understood the strength of the competition and the strain under which the Experimental Department was working. Occasionally he replied bluntly to his critics, as in September 1930 when, in response to criticism of the delay on development of compression ignition, he wrote:

Believe me we are doing our best to get our work equal to our competitors, and you will realise that it is not easy to produce designs sufficiently good to be worth making; one firm fully engaged against many. Very few indeed care to strive for hours, days, weeks, months, on the drawing board, to produce something worthy of the name of a design. Like our 'dear to memory C.S. Rolls', after a very short time they think it is good, when it is still only worthy of the name of a sketch.

Harry Ricardo, a brilliant consulting engineer who set up his operation at Shoreham in Sussex, not far from Royce at West Wittering, sufficiently impressed Royce with his skills for Rolls-Royce to give him a standing £500-a-year consultancy fee. But correspondence between them and between Ricardo and Hives shows that Royce was reluctant to let anyone outside the company carry out development work for them. Royce was friendly enough with Ricardo to write on 7 June 1922:

Dear Mr. Ricardo,
Many thanks for your very kind and interesting letter of the 1st April.
    I have been away by the doctor's orders in the south of France and only lately returned, or else I had hoped to have seen you earlier this year.
    I shall be very pleased to come over for a short time at the Works, any time that is convenient to you. Saturday, Monday or Tuesday, or any afternoon will suit me, but I may be away in London until Friday evening. Can I bring Miss Aubin, who will keep very quiet in the office?
    Having only just returned we have no satisfactory domestic help, but if we do get some-one soon, I hope you and Major Evans, with your ladies and children, will come and see me, although our garden is not much just now, but it is a nice ride and will make a diversion.
Yours sincerely
H Royce

However, two weeks later, he was writing:

Owing to some changes we are making in the engine design, I should be very pleased if you would allow the matter of our suggestion for you to examine our engine to stand over for about a week, when I will let you know whether it is worth while doing anything with our 40 hp chassis as it is at present.
    I am sure the Company will be most happy to come to some arrangement with you if any invention that you may discover in your extensive experimental research

should prove to be of any advantage in cost or efficiency to the chassis or aero engine production.

I very much regret that we have not in the past been able to use any of the parts that you have been so kind as to show us.

Yours very sincerely

H Royce

Meetings and correspondence continued throughout the 1920s and on into the 1930s, and the work carried out by Ricardo for Rolls-Royce increased in the late 1930s enough for Ricardo to write to Hives in January 1939 requesting a rise in his annual fee from £500 to £1500. Hives replied in characteristic style:

My dear Ricardo,

Thanks for your letter of January 9th.

When I was first given control of Derby it was pointed out to me that for a number of years we had been paying Ricardo & Co. £500 a year and getting very little for it. My answer was that it was our own fault, and since that time I believe with the better contracts we are getting value for money.

As regards your suggestion of increasing the fee from £500 to £1500, I would not like to put that claim forward to my Directors at the present time. I would like to suggest to you that the fees remain at £500, and that we pay you in addition for any additional work which we think is justified.

If you consider you have an extra claim for work done in 1938, we are quite prepared to consider it.

I suggest that we might usefully discuss this with you on your next visit to Derby.

Yours sincerely

E Hives

As the 1930s progressed, the world gradually emerged from the Depression, much of the increase in prosperity regrettably due to rearmament programmes in response to the increasingly belligerent statements and actions of the two dictators in Europe, Hitler and Mussolini, and of the military establishment in Japan. In Britain, there was considerable suffering and heavy unemployment, but it was not all unrelieved misery. As J.B. Priestley wrote in his *English Journey*, published in 1933:

The third England . . . is the England of arterial and by-pass roads, of filling-stations and factories that look like exhibition buildings, of giant cinemas and dance-halls and cafes, bungalows with tiny garages, cocktail bars, Woolworths, motor-coaches, wireless, typing, factory girls looking like actresses, greyhound racing and dirt tracks, swimming-pools, and everything given away for cigarette coupons . . .

Most of Rolls-Royce's customers were rich enough to weather the storms of the early 1930s, but in manufacturing it is always the last 10 per cent of sales that makes most of the profit, and the loss of *any* customers is always keenly felt. Furthermore, Rolls-Royce had abandoned the single model policy laid down by Johnson in 1906, and was now producing three different models, but without an appreciable increase in the total number of cars sold. The implications for the profitability of the car side of the company were not good. Indeed, the car side of Rolls-Royce ceased to be profitable in 1929, and only made money again in the sellers' market after the Second World War. As we shall see, once the market became more competitive in the mid-1950s, profitability again proved elusive.

As the situation in Europe deteriorated and the government's rearmament programme gathered pace, Hives's attention became almost entirely focused on the aero engine side of the business. Robotham spelt it out clearly in his book.

I had several discussions with Hives about the future, but by 1937 the imminence of war was already casting a shadow over the company. Hives accepted that some changes in our car policy were inevitable, but in view of the international situation he could not possibly prejudice his efforts to get the Merlin into production by spending time on long-term plans for motor-cars. It was undoubtedly fortunate for Britain that he took this view.

By 1936 Royce's last car, the 12-cylinder replacement for the Phantom II, was ready and, after considerable boardroom discussion, was called the Phantom III. Sales in the three and a half years up to the outbreak of war in September 1939 were disappointing, although they were only following a trend; sales of the Phantom had been falling since the mid-1920s, when about 450 were sold annually. The Phantom II sales averaged less than 300 per annum, and total production of the Phantom III was only 727 cars.

Hives was heard to say that although Rolls-Royce undoubtedly made the most expensive car in the world – the Phantom II – its pushrod operated overhead valve gear was no longer the quietest or most comfortable on the market. Furthermore, both the Phantom II and Phantom III were slightly cumbersome, and the Phantom III was too large and heavy to be popular as an owner-driver's car. With a production rate of less than 200 a year and no major component common to any other car, the Phantom III stood no chance of being profitable. Arthur Sidgreaves reported after one tour of the USA:

Not only are we not progressing, but we are definitely going back. In other words, we are being surpassed by the Americans in particular respect to those features on which our name and reputation have been built up.

At the end of the First World War, the changing structure of
society brought the need for a smaller Rolls-Royce. It was
launched in 1922 as the 20 hp. This shows a model on the road
at Glencoe in Scotland.

The Silver Ghost was succeeded in 1925 by the Phantom I.
Henry Royce is seen here in 1924 with a prototype Phantom,
chassis no. 46 PK, at Elmstead, his house in West Wittering.

Henry Royce with his long-term companion, Nurse Aubin,
Ernest (later Lord) Hives and Albert Elliott, with the first left-
hand drive Rolls-Royce Phantom II with a Barker Sports
Saloon body.

A group of key Rolls-Royce personnel at Claude
Johnson's memorial service.
FROM LEFT TO RIGHT: Eric Platford, R.W.H. Bailey,
Harry Swift, Arthur Wormald, Arthur Sidgreaves,
William Cowen, Ernest Hives, Captain Hallam,
John De Looze, Tommy Haldenby.

A portrait photograph of Henry Royce, possibly taken when
he was created a baronet in 1930 for his contribution to the
British victory in the Schneider Trophy contest of 1929.

Until 1936, the judge attending the Derby Assizes used a coach and horses to drive to court. However, in September 1936, he used a motor car for the first time. The lead car is an experimental Rolls-Royce Phantom III, 34 EX, with its V12 engine. Behind is a privately-owned Phantom II. Subsequently, 34 EX crossed the Sahara and travelled from Derby to Nairobi and back, covering 12,500 miles in thirty-four days.

Hives was also alarmed: 'In spite of us charging fabulous prices there remains very little profit.' He looked at Rolls-Royce's proud boast that they made all their own parts, and decided to source the radiators from outside. A study of component costs revealed that shock absorbers costing the company £8 to make could be bought for £3, and that the exhaust system costing £13 could be bought for £1 if an American type were used. Hives wrote:

The company has dropped so far behind with major components such as frames, springing, engines, steering, brakes etc. that where we can get help outside we have got to take advantage of it.

And although Rolls-Royce would not see themselves as competing with the likes of Austin, Morris, Ford, Rootes, Vauxhall or Standard, these companies were competing with each other and, aided by technical improvements, were reducing prices. Taking 1924 prices as the equivalent of 100, the average price of cars fell consistently over the following decade, to reach 49 in 1936.

It was clear to Hives that a virulent attack on Rolls-Royce's cost base was absolutely essential. When he was appointed general manager in 1936 he faced the twin tasks of improving quality and profitability. One of his problems was an archaic system of cost control which produced too little information too late to be of any use in making production decisions. Hives was heard to say:

I have always held the view that accountants make just as many mistakes as engineers, but that it is very much more difficult to find them out.

On the quality front, it was clear that the Phantom III had been launched too early in its development, and that the recently launched 4¼ litre Bentley was plagued with bearing problems when driven at high speed on a light throttle, for example on the new German autobahns. Some were impressed, however, as this flowery piece in the *Sunday Pictorial* by the Earl of Cottenham (a well-known motoring journalist of the 1930s and himself once an apprentice at Derby) makes clear.

I lay six to four on Phantom III, an amazing mover by Painstakers out of Derby. And what is it up against; what other cars might claim to be in the same category? Only five that I can recall offhand: the latest Hispano-Suiza, Horch, Mercedes-Benz, and Packard; and the huge 'golden' type Bugatti . . . Other people might suggest other famous machines as well – the biggest Daimler or Delage, the Lancia 'Dilambda', the Isotta Fraschini, the large Cadillac or the Duesenberg. . . .

Some . . . of the names I have mentioned bespeak beautiful 'conveyances', commodious, efficient in a restrained, gentlemanly manner; some, by contrast, bring to one's mind graceful big 'cars', equally commodious, equally efficient, but in a determinedly capable way.

Only the first half-dozen strike me as really possessing twin personalities, those of the town carriage and the sporting car, and of being entirely adequate in either part without overacting the smooth gestures of the first to the point of being indefinite or the virile movements of the second to the pitch of savagery. And the greatest of these six, in my view, is the Rolls-Royce Phantom III, fourth in descent from the famous old Silver Ghost model, as it was called.

And here is an extract from *Autocar* after it had subjected the Phantom III to a road test:

The V twelve-cylinder engine is even quieter than its forebears; undoubtedly it is still more flexible on top gear; certainly also it has a wider range of performance of the kind that counts in modern road conditions, its acceleration being, to say the least, thrilling.

Equally, it shows a great gain in riding comfort, allied in an extraordinary degree with stability on the road at all speeds . . . it is most impressive that such a big car as this, with a capacious body that can only be likened to a carriage, should be capable of travelling at over 90 miles an hour if desired, yet retain in the uttermost degree of the virtues of flexibility, silence, ease of handling and the maximum of road comfort as at present understood . . .

Perhaps most of all one is impressed by the easy way in which the Phantom III handles. There is no sense of great bulk; the car can be put just where one wishes on the road with an accuracy and delicacy of steering that prove how painstaking has been the design . . .

On top gear the twelve-cylinder engine will pull the car at the barest crawl, about 3 mph. Then the throttle pedal can be put straight down, there is a smooth surge of power, and one is aware of no more than that the car is rapidly gaining speed, the speedometer needle moving quickly round its dial. At first it is necessary to refer quite frequently to the instrument to verify the actual speed, for there is no indication of increased effort at 70 as compared with 50 mph, for example . . .

It [the servo-mechanical braking] is a system which shows up to extraordinary advantage. A smooth but utterly sure power grips the car, as it were, from high speeds, and pulls the velocity down, yet the driver is scarcely conscious of having applied the brakes . . .

'Somewhere,' the report concludes, 'is an ultimate in the highest expression of road travel comfort and performance and the Phantom III is beyond question the nearest approach to it as yet.'

Hives decided to split Engineering into two divisions, and put A.G. Elliott, previously in overall charge of Engineering as chief engineer, in charge of

Engineering for the Aero Engine Division. At the same time, he put R.W.H. Bailey in charge of Engineering in the newly formed Chassis Division. This latter appointment was clearly a surprise to many. In his book, *Silver Ghosts and Silver Dawn*, Robotham does not mention it. Indeed, Bailey is not mentioned in the book at all.

Whatever the feelings, the team worked to produce plans that would deliver reductions in cost. As Ken Lea, chief engineer power train at Rolls-Royce Motors in the 1980s, put it in his book for the Rolls-Royce Heritage Trust, *Rolls-Royce – the first cars from Crewe*:

This was to adopt a philosophy of common units being applied across a series of different chassis for each market/model, these also designed to utilise common components such as pressings, suspensions, steering, brakes, instruments and so on. In his [Bailey's] scheme, there was to be a new series of engines code-named the 'B range'. Within the 'Rationalised Range' of cars, for that was its code name, the new engines would be available in 4-, 6- and 8-cylinder in-line form with an added flexibility derived from different cylinder bore sizes.

After consultation with Bailey and his team, the following board plan of rationalisation was put in place.

- Three basic engines of four, six and eight cylinders would be used, being of the same design and having many common parts.
- There would be a few standard wheelbase lengths, with several models sharing each length.
- Bodies would be common to several models.
- Front end dimension (dash to front wheels) would be common to several models.
- More than one size of engine would be possible in each model.

It was decided that the Bentley III, later known as the Bentley V, should form the basis of the rationalised range with the new B range of engines which Robotham was very keen to promote on the grounds of lower cost.

By this time, the company had also become unhappy with the quality of the bodies provided by the coachbuilders, realising that rattles and noises reflected badly on Rolls-Royce itself in the eyes of the customer. The solution was to adopt a standard range of bodies and have them made by one coachbuilder, Park Ward, which Rolls-Royce acquired in 1938.

By September 1939 the new Bentley V and its performance version, the Corniche, had been thoroughly developed and tested. Both were ready for announcement at the 1939 Motor Show, and the Bentley V was already in production. There were also several examples of the rationalised range built and on test, including the Phantom III replacement. However, the outbreak of war meant that the Motor Show was cancelled and the production of cars rapidly ceased. Bailey was transferred back to Merlin engine work and Robotham succeeded him as chief engineer of the Chassis Division.

ERNEST HIVES

In the history of the Rolls-Royce company, there are three key people in its formation – Royce, Rolls and Johnson – and in its progress from the 1930s to the 1960s there is a fourth – Ernest Hives, later Lord Hives. Much has been written of him, and none of it better than that by Alec Harvey-Bailey, son of R.W.H. Bailey, both long-serving and dedicated servants of the company. In his book for the Historical Series published by the Sir Henry Royce Memorial Foundation, *Rolls-Royce – Hives, The Quiet Tiger*, Harvey-Bailey covers Hives's life and contribution comprehensively, and what is written here is effectively a précis of that book. (The Historical Series was conceived by the Rolls-Royce Heritage Trust. After its launch, the Trust suggested that the Sir Henry Royce Memorial Foundation join it in the publishing venture.)

Hives became a nationally known figure by dint of his outstanding achievement in building up and sustaining production of the Merlin engine, to be used in Britain's warplanes and in the American P-51 Mustang during the Second World War. This contribution will be covered later in the book. However, he was also heavily involved in the development and production of Rolls-Royce cars, and it is appropriate to cover this aspect of his work here.

Born in 1886 in Berkshire, Hives began a three-year apprenticeship with an engineering company in Reading when he was still only twelve. He stayed on after hours to learn more from those on the night shift, and taught himself to drive by moving cars in the garage. When he was fourteen he drove on the open road for the first time, while teaching a customer how to drive.

In about 1903 he was hired by Charles Rolls as his personal chauffeur and mechanic. Apparently, Rolls had been impressed by Hives's help when his car was in difficulty on the way back to London from the family home in Monmouth. Hives then worked for a time at C.S. Rolls & Co. at Lillie Hall, before moving on to H.R. Owen and then to Rolls-Royce's great rival, Napier. Having driven for Napier in the 1907/8 Scottish Trials and raced at Brooklands, he joined Rolls-Royce in 1908 as a tester. He was to say later:

When I got to Derby in 1908 and walked out of the station it was raining hard and looking up Midland Road it seemed so drab that I spun a coin to decide whether to go on to Rolls-Royce or catch the next train home.

By 1911, when Rolls-Royce undertook the London to Edinburgh non-stop run in top gear, Hives's skill was appreciated so much that he was chosen as the driver. Later that year he drove the same car with some modifications at Brooklands, and achieved a speed of 101 mph.

We have already seen how Jimmy Radley's failure to negotiate a hill in the Austrian Alpine Trials of 1912 caused considerable anxiety at Rolls-Royce and a determination to restore their reputation in the 1913 Trials. Hives, who had been carrying out development testing for Rolls-Royce from 1910, led the works team of three cars in 1913 and effectively succeeded in doing so.

Hives's first contact with aero engines soon followed, as Royce began developing the Eagle engine after war broke out in 1914. In 1916, at the age of thirty, he was made head of the Experimental Department. By this time the department was made up of a group of development engineers, and work continued throughout the war, not only on the Eagle but on the Hawk, Falcon and Condor and on the armoured car.

After the war, Hives returned to cars and solved, by trial and error, a problem on the aluminium piston in the 40/50. He also supervised Arthur Lidsey carrying out trials of the new 20 hp model in France (Royce was now spending the winter at Le Canadel again). In addition, he was deeply involved in the introduction of four-wheel brakes and the overhead valve Phantom I engine. The development team also looked at the problems of 'shimmy' and front wheel tramp.

As we have seen, he also made visits to Rolls-Royce's US company in Massachusetts, reporting on quality and production issues.

In the late 1920s, Hives headed the development of the 'R' engine which enabled Flying Officer (later Flight Lieutenant) H.R.D. Waghorn to win the Schneider Trophy in 1929, and we shall see more of this later in the book. Hives's next piece of lateral thinking was his suggestion for the engine to be used in the Bentley after Rolls-Royce had acquired the company in 1931. Alec Harvey-Bailey wrote:

Within six weeks of the takeover [Hives] wrote to Wormald suggesting the sports car could be made by combining existing units and that this could be done quickly. However, as recounted in 'Rolls-Royce – The Derby Bentleys', West Wittering considered other avenues, either by super-charging the 2¼ litre Peregrine engine, or designing a new 3 litre straight eight. These engines would be used in what was basically a Peregrine chassis. [Hives] waited patiently, and finally he was instructed to test a blown Peregrine engine giving at least 50 per cent more power than the unblown version then on road test. As he anticipated, the test revealed that there would be many problems to overcome. On 30th September, 1932, he directly challenged Royce's decision, cogently arguing the case for the 3½ litre J1 engine in the proposed chassis. Against the odds he won the day and on 18th January, 1933, was able to report that the 3½ litre Bentley was on the road. Not only was it one of the nicest cars the Company made but it also showed Royce's appreciation of [Hives] as an engineer.

Hives's next task was to continue the development work on the aero engines that Rolls-Royce were making. We have already seen how the company had moved on from the Eagle XVI to the FX, which became the Kestrel. It then made the scale-up, the 'H', which became the Buzzard. The Schneider Trophy had prompted Royce to design the Racing 'H' or 'R' engine, from which was developed the Griffon, incorporating both Buzzard and 'R' engine features into the basic Buzzard. By this time, the power of the engine (at 1,300 hp) was felt to be too big a jump for the RAF from the Kestrel's 500 hp, and Rolls-Royce decided to develop a 1,000 hp engine. Using 'R' engine know-how, the PV12 was developed and, once Government support was forthcoming, this engine evolved into the Merlin.

Both the PV12 and the Merlin were 27-litre engines, but they were nevertheless quite different. On the PV12 the crankcase and cylinder blocks were combined, whereas on the Merlin they were separate. On the PV12 the heads were separate, whereas on the Merlin they were variously separate and combined, while the reduction gear was helical on the PV12 but spur on the Merlin.

Alongside this development, the Kestrel was also produced in steam-cooled form as the Goshawk, the ultimate version of the Kestrel being the Peregrine, with central entry supercharger. No sooner had work started on the PV12 than Royce, the founder and inspiration of the company, died, leaving a huge vacuum at the top of the organisation. Wormald, a director and general works manager, was a sick man, and died in the autumn of 1936. He suggested that Harry Swift, the production manager, should replace him, but Hives was unhappy about this and reached an understanding with another senior and longstanding manager, R.W.H. Bailey. They agreed that Hives would have Bailey's full support if he (Hives) became general works manager, and that both would leave if Swift got the job. Fortunately, it did not come to that. Hives threw his hat into the ring, and while the board considered outside candidates, including Roy Fedden, they appointed Hives general works manager in 1936 and in 1937, a board director.

Hives lost no time in writing a report for his Chairman, Lord Herbert Scott, and his Managing Director, Arthur Sidgreaves. Always a man to say what he thought, Hives pulled no punches. He wrote in his report, dated 18 January 1937:

This report is intended to give my view on the Factory when I took it over in October, 1936. I want to make it clear at the start that I appreciate fully the Company's marvellous record for profits and dividends. This record makes one hesitate to criticise, but nevertheless I intend to give my views, devoid of all sentiment.

PRODUCTS
MOTOR CARS
Our motor car business is dependent on one class of trade, which can only be described as the 'Super-Expensive' class. It is only in England, where these super-expensive cars are sold. In the U.S.A., where they produced, say, 2,000,000 cars last year, only 300 were sold at a price exceeding £800 [£40,000 today]. The expensive car in the U.S.A. has rapidly declined during the last 6 or 7 years.

I cannot do better here than to quote from a memo. I wrote in 1933 on the general car position:-

'We have previously written a report pointing out that we do not consider either the Phantom or 25 HP., which we are producing, are good enough. After my recent trip to the Continent I am more than ever convinced that this is so.'

It is a fact that where we are selling cars against competition there is no outstanding merit in our cars to make a customer desire to possess one. The reputation of Rolls-Royce was built up on silence and smoothness: there are a number of other cars now which are more silent, have less vibration, and a better performance. There is no doubt about this, and it is a point which can easily be confirmed by trying our competitors' cars.

This position we consider we should regard as being most serious, because there is a real danger of Rolls-Royce losing their pre-eminent position of producing 'The Best Car in the World'. The fact that we are selling a very large number of cars at the present time does not alter the position technically. If we look for the reasons why we are selling, we find that 95 per cent (this is a guess) are being sold in the home market where we have no competition, are protected by the tariff and a strong national desire to 'Buy British'. It is certain that even in the home market we shall not be left in this comfortable position with no competition. It is therefore up to us to be prepared to meet it. My own view is that we are not prepared, and are not shaping the right way.

Hives was no more sanguine about the aero engine position:

Our prosperity on aero engines at the present time is entirely due to the Government Expansion Programme. It should be appreciated that although the Rolls-Royce reputation is to a certain extent reflected on the aero engines, it is only on reliability, efficiency and performance that we can meet competition. The seriousness of our aero position is shown up by the fact that we have no Rolls-Royce engines operating on Civil Air Lines. For recognised Aero Engine Manufacturers we are unique in this respect.

In the U.S.A., 50 per cent of the aero engines sold by the principal firms are for civil aircraft. In England at the present time the Bristol Company are selling over 300 engines a year for civil aircraft. The engines we are at present making cannot compete with our competitors on performance and efficiency.

There has got to be a real revival in Rolls-Royce aero engine production to maintain a reasonable share of the business after the expansion programme is completed.

It will therefore be seen that I personally am just as anxious about the aero position as I am with regard to motor cars.

As for the factory, Hives was extremely critical, describing the factory management as 'peculiar', with personalities within the works management never being encouraged. He did not like the fact that at the monthly conferences instituted by Arthur Sidgreaves there were representatives from both the Design and Experimental Departments, but none from the factory. Within the factory, the management, such as foremen and supervisors, had all come from 'elevated mechanics', and in most cases had been promoted on length of service rather than merit. 'Actually,' he wrote, 'the position is that we have relied too much on brawn and craftsmanship, and we have not sufficient brains in the factory.'

He was also critical of the lack of investment in the factory: '50 per cent of the machinery in the factory in October is over 20 years old, and 60 per cent over 15 years old.' And he was not afraid to be critical of the results of Sir Henry Royce's management style:

It has got to be realised that the whole time the late Sir Henry Royce was Chief Engineer of the company he personally made all decisions as regards engineering policy and design. Most of our present staff of designers worked with him at his private house, so that for 20 or 25 years they were never asked or expected to take any responsibility. One can see the result of that today. By not having had to take responsibility in making decisions, we make more mistakes than we should do.

The results show we do not get our designs quickly enough, and they are not sufficiently good or economical when we do get them. Our design organisation was built up when Sir Henry Royce did all the design work with a staff 150 miles away from the factory. It was all planned to suit his exceptional qualifications; therefore one must expect that the same organisation is not going to be successful when he has disappeared. We have got to expect a reorganisation.

He did not stop there. The Purchasing Department's methods were 'out of date', the Experimental Department was 'too big and too expensive'. He concluded:

I am sorry that my review is such a mournful one, but it represents my honest opinion, and I am prepared to substantiate any of these statements.

Following these harsh words, Hives put forward concrete proposals for improvement. First, he wanted to create a different atmosphere.

In the past the outlook has been that we have got the finest factory in the world, the finest brains in the world, and that nobody could teach us anything. If anyone went outside and came back and suggested that we were out of date, he had a very cool reception. The people who came back after a visit to the U.S.A. were always accused of having become Americanised.

The outlook we have got to create is that we must never be satisfied. As soon as we have done a good job and have got good results, we must immediately go over it and find ways of making it better. Throughout the whole organisation it must be realised that no matter what results we obtain we can always do better, and must do better.

Hives had always felt that Rolls-Royce was too introspective, and in the late summer of 1937 arranged for A.G. Elliott, James Ellor and Harry Swift to visit aircraft and aero engine factories in Germany. They went to the four main aero engine factories and two of the leading aircraft plants. With hindsight we may be surprised that as late as 1937 British engineers were allowed to visit German aircraft and aero engine plants, and perhaps can only conclude that, at this stage, Hitler had no intention of going to war with Britain, but wanted to show influential people what a powerful war machine he possessed.

Certainly the Rolls-Royce engineers were impressed, writing in their report on 15 September:

We soon realised that Germany was thinking, planning and acting on a very much larger scale than we are . . . We feel that they are well on the way to possessing the finest air force in the world, both as regards performance, numbers and rapid production.

They went on to say that they were allowed to examine all the engines and machines up to the latest production. Their conclusion was stark.

Generally speaking we formed the opinion that our standard of technical abilities is equal to theirs, that the problems and projects on which we are engaged are similar to theirs but that they are more likely to reach a quicker solution on account of the co-ordination of brains, facilities, drive and a clear realisation of the ultimate object.

We feel that for Rolls-Royce to be on a competitive basis and maintain its supremacy, the thinking capacity must be considerably increased, greater facilities provided to develop important projects, including material investigation and for the production capacity to be planned on a much larger scale.

At about the same time as the Rolls-Royce engineers visited the German aircraft factories, Major G.P. Bulman, assistant to Lieutenant-Colonel L.F.R. Fell at the Air Ministry, attended the International Air Congress in Munich as a representative of the British Government, and he also took the opportunity to visit various German aircraft and aero engine manufacturers. His subsequent report was also chilling from a British perspective. He wrote later:

[The report] reviewed in detail the incredibly quick progress in German aeronautical development; the advanced state of their Daimler-Benz and Junkers 12 cylinder inverted Vee liquid cooled types of 33 litres capacity against the 27 litres of our Merlin, and which though currently rated only at the Merlin's power ought very soon to outstrip it by far, given the same amount of continuous development.

It stressed that the German Air Ministry hitherto organised in four main Departments, of Research, Development, Finance and Supply, each sub-divided into Branches for aircraft, engines, instruments and armaments, was in rapid process of evolution under Milch to become four Departments of Aircraft, Engines, Instruments and Armaments, each subdivided into branches for research, development, and supply. There would be created therefore a co-ordination of all aspects of engine work under one Head directly answerable to Milch. Such Head would be an engine specialist, expected competently to discuss any aspect of engines with anyone, whereas hitherto the individuals responsible for all Research, all Development, all Supply could not be expected to deal effectively with the quite different techniques of modern aircraft, engines, etc.

To quote from my report:

'It may be thought that I have myself become a victim of subtle Nazi propaganda and hypnotism, and that striking though the facts are, the essential quality of German aero engines in performance and serviceability has yet to be demonstrated in Service use.

'. . . that they have troubles with all types of engine is an obvious and admitted fact; some of the same sorts of trouble which every one of our established types is prone to give at times, and also some different ones.

'It was in the discussion of such troubles and in the free exchange of general ideas which I enjoyed with Dr. Sachse and many others that I found myself convinced that whereas in recent years we have regarded America as our pace maker and hot rival we have now to look at Germany.'

Having tackled the factory and split the Aero Engine and Chassis Departments, Hives turned his attention to costings and the Accountancy Department. It will come as no surprise to see that his criticisms were scathing.

After a year I have come to the conclusion that our Accountancy have got to be very definitely livened up. I have always held the view that Accountants make just as many mistakes as engineers, except that it is very much more difficult to find them out. The figures we get served up are merely the addition of certain Order Numbers; the information is so far out of date that it is of very little value, with no intelligent analysis. I know that it is possible to get a complete analysis of the Factory efficiency two or three days after the end of the week, and I shall not be satisfied until that is an established fact.

The first job I intend to give the Efficiency Experts who it has been agreed to call in is to get their advice on dragging out of our Accountants some intelligent figures. The Powers-Samas Mechanical Accountancy will undoubtedly help us, but that is going to take time: we must get some results earlier. I am very anxious next year to budget for all indirect expenses, so that we shall know at the beginning of the year, instead of three months after the end of the year, what those expenses should be.

Again, he attacked the attitude of complacency:

I want the various Chiefs to become 'Cost-Conscious' and to realise that no matter how good they think their job is, it is a complete failure unless it is making money. I have a feeling that our Accountancy feel that as long as they can confuse the accounts so that the Air Ministry Cost Officials cannot understand them, they are doing very well, but unfortunately we suffer from the same confusion. Personally I doubt whether they do deceive anybody. I look upon the Air Ministry Cost people as something like the Income Tax people: they have so much experience of people trying to confuse them that they know all the answers. In any case we have got to recognise that when parts are produced in the Government's own Shadow Factories they will know exactly how much the parts cost to produce.

The board backed Hives, as did the work force. We have already seen earlier in this book what Hives thought of the Rolls-Royce training methods. The premium scheme was abandoned in favour of engineering apprentices, whose parents paid no premium. They were put on a properly organised course with part-time release to take the Higher National Certificate. Hives was responsible for setting up an engineering pupil scheme, the precursor of the graduate apprentice scheme. By January 1938 there were forty, who were to go on to make a valuable contribution by the middle of the Second World War.

During the 1930s, under the lengthening shadow of the coming war, Rolls-Royce's emphasis as a company changed decisively from that of a motor car manufacturer showing some interest in aero engine design and production, into an aero engine designer and producer *par excellence*, with car design and production pursued, not quite as an industrial hobby, but certainly as an adjunct to its aerospace business. The fulcrum year was 1935, when turnover of the aero engine division exceeded that of the chassis division for the first time. By 1938 it was six times as large.

Certainly the motor car division was a cause of great anxiety to Hives. He tried to get Maurice Olley back to Rolls-Royce, writing in his report to the directors:

On the design side we have a difficult problem. It is obvious that when we have made the division in the factory between motor cars and aero engines, and in the Experimental Dept. between cars and aero engines, and in the Test Dept. between cars and aero engines, that this should follow through on the Design side, and some day it must be done. I sent a cable to [Olley], in the U.S.A., asking him whether he would consider the position of taking entire charge of motor car design. The reply I got was that he greatly appreciated my offer, but had made definite promises to the Vauxhall Company which he would have to carry out. This is a great pity, because in my opinion he was the ideal man for the job. He had sufficient training with the late Sir Henry, and experience in Rolls-Royce products to get the right atmosphere. He had gone to the General Motors Organisation and established himself as one of their leading engineers. I have still not given up hope as regards Olley, and am waiting to hear what he says in his letter, and if necessary I will see the Vauxhall people and find out whether they would be willing to release him.

The position still stands that we have got to get a good man on motor cars.

But Olley was adamant that, having given his word to Vauxhall, he would not leave them in the lurch. On 13 January 1937 Hives sent a memo to Sidgreaves, saying:

I have received the following cable from [Olley] –
'Greatly appreciate your offer but have definitely promised Vauxhall. Cannot let them down. Writing.'

This means that we have got to have another think.

He had asked Bailey to design and develop a complete range of models and, at the same time, sort out the quality problems on the Bentley 4¼ and the Phantom III. He said:

The Chassis Division is having a difficult time; in fact, the whole of our motor car business causes great anxiety . . . There is no doubt that the Chassis Division as a whole is grappling with this problem, and it is certain that we are going to get a substantial reduction in costs without any reduction in quality. As most of the improvements have to start with the design, we have got to be patient before we see any results in the current factory costs.

Bailey and Robotham, two strong characters, seemed to be able to work together. As we have seen, Robotham never mentioned Bailey in his book.

This would suggest that Robotham had little time for Bailey, but Alec Harvey-Bailey, in another of his books, *Rolls-Royce – Hives' Turbulent Barons*, maintained that the two men respected each other:

[Hives] chose [Bailey], but was nonetheless anxious that there should be co-operation rather than competition between the strong character of [Bailey] and the equally strong-minded [Robotham], who could well have seen himself in the job. If Derby waited for the clash of Titans, it waited in vain. Both men recognised the problems facing the Division and that they could only be solved by everyone pulling together. They shared the same sense of urgency and it is a tribute to [Robotham] that when there were clashes of priority he accepted [Bailey's] ruling without rancour and got on with the task.

The two men, as well as sorting out the Bentley 4¼ and Phantom III problems, put the Bentley III on the road (as the Bentley V) in the spring of 1938, and launched the Rolls-Royce Wraith at the Motor Show in the autumn of that year. In November, Hives was heard to say: 'The Chassis Division is making very satisfactory progress.' And in January 1939 he reported to his Managing Director, Sidgreaves:

Although in the motor car division we are making considerably fewer cars, we are still maintaining and strengthening the engineering and development side. Although the actual results shown by the figures are nothing like good enough, I am satisfied that we are now on the right road which will enable us to produce motor cars with a reasonable profit. We cannot expect the results very quickly – for the last twenty years I have been present at discussions to produce cheaper Rolls-Royce cars. A considerable amount of money has been sunk on this in the past without achieving any results, but we are now making definite progress.

The years 1939 and 1940 would probably have been good for the motor car division, except that in September 1939 the world was once again plunged into world war. If Viscount Grey thought the lights were going out in August 1914, heaven knows what he would have thought this time. The new Bentley V never appeared at the Motor Show, because it was cancelled; nor did the exciting, high-speed Bentley Corniche. The four straight-eights of the 'rationalised range', ready by autumn 1939, would have to wait for happier times.

CHAPTER SIX

'ARE WE IN THE AERO ENGINE BUSINESS?'

'STILL PLUNGING DOWNWARDS'
'NO MORE CONDORS'
THE SCHNEIDER TROPHY

'STILL PLUNGING DOWNWARDS'

THE VIMY WAS DODGING IN AND OUT of the clouds when quite suddenly, as they emerged into a space of clear air, Alcock and Brown saw a great towering mass of cumulo-nimbus straight ahead, blocking their path like some vast range of black mountains.

There was no time to alter course, the Vimy flew straight into the centre of this storm. A sudden turbulence gripped the machine and tossed it around like a falling leaf in an autumnal gale. All around them swirled thick vapour, hiding the wing tips and, at times, the front of the fuselage. The wings quivered and vibrated, the rigging wires humming in loud sympathy. The dreadful suddenness of the storm caused Alcock and Brown to lose all sense of direction and balance. The rain turned to hail which drove into their faces with cruel violence. The Vimy was completely out of control, plunging like a crazy horse, and throwing the two men around in the cockpit with only their safety-belts to hold them in place. Alcock fought to regain control and keep the machine on the level, but with no horizon to see and his senses knocked out of balance by the violence of the Vimy's plunge, it was impossible. Their instruments became useless, the bubble of the artificial horizon had long since vanished and there was only the pressure of their seats against their backs to show that they were not hanging upside down in space. The lightning flashed around the Vimy...

At this point disaster nearly overtook them and finished off their venture. The storm was at its height with the airspeed indicator jammed, showing a reading of 90 knots. Alcock wrestled with the joystick, trying to force the nose of the Vimy up, but they were moving too slowly for this to be effective. For one sickening moment the Vimy hung motionless in the air, then she stalled, tilting over and dropping in a steep spiral dive towards the Atlantic. Neither man could see anything through the swirling mass of cloud that had swallowed them up, and the lightning so dazzled their eyes that they could not read their instruments . . .

4,000 . . . 3,000 . . . 2,000 feet . . . the Vimy was still plunging downwards, completely out of control with both engines roaring and wings threatening to pull away from the fuselage . . . 2,000 . . . 1,500 . . . 1,000 feet and they were still dropping in a spiral through the black and savage cloud of cumulo-nimbus.

(From *The Flight of Alcock and Brown* by Graham Wallace)

Captain Alcock and Lieutenant Brown only met each other for the first time in the spring of 1919, although their lives had run along similar lines since they had both decided flying was the life for them. By coincidence, both had been brought up in Manchester, although Arthur Whitten Brown, born in 1886, was the son of American parents. His father was an engineer and had been sent to Britain to supervise the building of a factory for Westinghouse. Brown himself qualified as an engineer and then spent two years in South Africa, returning in 1914 just in time to claim British nationality and enlist in the Universities and Public Schools Battalion. During 1915 he saw action on the Somme and at the Second Battle of Ypres. However, his real interest was flying and he successfully put in a request for transfer to the Royal Flying Corps. Acting as an observer, he developed his skills as a navigator before he and his pilot were shot down in November 1915 and taken prisoner. In the crash he severely injured a leg, and would need a stick to walk for the rest of his life.

John Alcock, known to all as Jack, was born in 1892 and also brought up in Manchester. He too joined an engineering company when he left school in 1908. But his real interest was aeroplanes, and when in 1912 an aero engine was sent to his company for repair, Alcock was the man who did the work and who was asked to return it to the owner. This turned out to be the French air 'ace' Maurice Ducrocq, who ran a flying school at Brooklands. As well as being the accepted centre of the motor racing world, Brooklands, with Hendon, had become one of the two headquarters of British aviation. Alcock persuaded Ducrocq to take him on as a mechanic.

He was in heaven. Grouped around the aerodrome were the flying schools, workshops and hangars of the pioneers of British aviation: British and Colonial (later called Bristol), Deperdussin, Avro, Sopwith, Martinsyde and Vickers. And an eager young man could listen to the flying heroes of the day: Tom Sopwith, Freddie Raynham, Gustav Hamel, Howard Pixton, A.V. Roe and Alcock's mentor, Maurice Ducrocq. It was not long before Alcock persuaded Ducrocq to teach him to fly. Not that it took long. Alcock made his first solo flight after only two hours' instruction on the ground and in the air.

Alcock enjoyed two happy years of flying before he too, of course, was caught up in the First World War. He joined the Royal Naval Air Service and, considered too valuable to be risked as a pilot, was sent as a warrant-officer instructor to Eastchurch, where he helped to train pilots for the next two years. However, a man of Alcock's temperament would only be happy if he were in the thick of the action, and he managed to persuade his superiors to transfer him to a front-line squadron in the Eastern Mediterranean. He saw enough action there to satisfy any man, before he was shot down and taken prisoner by the Turks.

Both Alcock and Brown were eventually repatriated and faced, along with hundreds of thousands of others, the tough prospect of finding a job in post-war Britain. As they did so, Lord Northcliffe, the owner of the *Daily Mail*, who had done so much to encourage the development of a British aircraft industry, reaffirmed the offer he had made before the war. On 17 July 1918, the newspaper made a strong re-statement of his offer of £10,000 for the first non-stop Atlantic flight. (When the offer was first made, £10,000 was probably worth about £1 million in today's terms; by 1918, the value had been reduced by wartime inflation to about £500,000.)

This offer was suspended on the outbreak of war, and we now revive it in order to stimulate the production of more powerful engines and more suitable aircraft.

A number of individuals and companies were keen to take up the challenge. Aircraft and engine manufacturers knew that the days of easy orders were over, and that they would now be competing fiercely with each other. The prestige of winning the prize would be a very useful marketing tool.

And Rolls-Royce were very much to the fore. Of the seven realistic British contenders – Vickers Vimy, Sopwith Atlantic, Martinsyde Raymor, Handley Page V/1500, Boulton Page Savory, Short Shamrock and Fairey Special – all but the Savory would be using Rolls-Royce engines. The Savory would use two Napier Lion engines.

Meanwhile, the Americans were not standing idle, and whereas in Britain the Government was not directly involved, in the USA the Navy Department was at the forefront of plans to complete the first transatlantic flight.

Back in Britain, Vickers had selected Captain Alcock as the pilot for the Vimy with which they were going to compete for the prize. Like the Handley Page V/1500, the Vimy had been designed as a bomber capable of flying to Berlin and back. Although smaller than the V/1500, the Vimy nevertheless had a range of 2,440 miles, adequate for a flight measuring just under 1,900 miles from Newfoundland to the west coast of Ireland.

The Vimy's vital statistics were as follows: length 42.7 feet, wingspan 68 feet, height 15.25 feet, weight (empty) about 7,000 lbs, capacity 865 gallons of petrol and 50 gallons of oil, maximum speed 100 mph, cruising speed 90 mph. It was powered by two Rolls-Royce Eagle Mark VIII engines of 360 hp, each engine driving a four-bladed wooden propeller.

While Alcock was making some modifications to the Vimy, such as replacing the bombing gear and spaces with extra petrol tanks, Freddie Raynham and Major C.W.F. Morgan, pilot and navigator of the Martinsyde Raymor, were giving their machine – and especially its Rolls-Royce Falcon engine – a novel endurance test. They sat in the hangar and ran the engine until it either faltered or ran out of fuel. It never faltered, but after 24 hours it did run out of fuel.

Alcock was leaving nothing to chance. He made a point of visiting the Rolls-Royce works in Derby, where he talked at length with Claude Johnson and watched the engines he would use being run in on the test benches. Rolls-Royce made an engineer available for each of the six contestants using their engines. The man assigned to the Vimy was Bob Lyons, a cheerful red-headed northerner. Alcock insisted that Lyons went to Newfoundland with the rest of the Vickers mechanical team. (Eric Platford also went to New-foundland on behalf of Rolls-Royce, but his role was to offer assistance to any of the competitors using Rolls-Royce engines.)

As preparation of the aircraft continued with all possible haste commensurate with the necessary thoroughness, one thing – or rather one person – was missing: a navigator to accompany the pilot. The confident Alcock was prepared to fly alone and act as his own navigator, but even he knew that his chances of success would be improved by having a first-rate navigator with him.

Meanwhile, the semi-crippled Lieutenant Brown was finding it harder than most to find a job – it was not uncommon to see ex-officers working as cabbies or porters, or even hawking their medals in the street – and he was almost in despair when he approached Vickers, having been given an introduction to Maxwell Muller, Vickers's factory manager at Brooklands. Fortunately, he impressed both Muller and Alcock with his quiet manner and manifest knowledge of the art of navigation. The team was complete, and they sailed on 4 May 1919 on the SS *Mauretania* bound for Halifax, Nova Scotia.

Once in Newfoundland they joined other competitors, most notably the Australian Harry Hawker, who was to give his name to one of the most famous British aviation companies, and who was preparing to fly the Sopwith Atlantic; there was also Freddie Raynham who, as we have seen, was leaving nothing to chance in the preparation of his Martinsyde Raymor.

The weather in Newfoundland throughout May 1919 was foul, but eventually on Sunday 18 May both the Atlantic and Raymor were ready to go. The Raymor crashed within 200 yards of take-off, hit by a sudden cross-wind, but Hawker and his navigator, Mackenzie-Grieve, soared away in the Atlantic. All went well for a time, though the weather worsened and they were forced to fly constantly in thick cloud. After several hours they were forced to search for a ship, as they realised that a cooling problem had reduced their quantity of cooling water to a dangerous level. Following a forced landing in high seas, they were picked up by the Danish steamer *Mary*. The steamer did not possess a wireless, and for five days everyone assumed that the two had perished. King George V even sent a message of condolence to Harry Hawker's wife.

When the *Mary* eventually signalled the lighthouse on the Butt of Lewis and the world was told that Hawker and Mackenzie-Grieve had survived, the reaction was startling – certainly to the two airmen, who could scarcely believe that their failure could be treated as a huge success. Naval destroyers were despatched to bring them south. The train journey from Perth to London was punctuated with stops where crowds flocked on to the platforms anxious to see – and possibly touch – the two heroes. At King's Cross, 100,000 people packed into and around the station. Hawker and Mackenzie-Grieve were summoned to Buckingham Palace to receive the Air Force Cross, and Lord Northcliffe presented them with a cheque for £5,000 at a *Daily Mail* luncheon at the Savoy. It made the airmen still in Newfoundland realise what reception might await the crew of an aircraft that made a successful crossing!

1,000 . . . 500 . . . 250 . . . 100 feet. The needle of the altimeter was almost resting on the zero mark when they left the storm as quickly as they had entered it. The Vimy fell out of the cloud only sixty feet above the ocean. But, to the startled eyes of Alcock and Brown, the ocean was not in its customary place below them, it was standing up sideways, almost vertically to them . . . Instinctively Alcock centralised the joystick and rudder. The Vimy responded at once. Alcock opened the throttles wide, the Rolls-Royce engines roared out and they regained their flying speed, skimming the crests of the waves, at times so close that the spray of the white horses beat on the underside of the wings. The danger was past.

(From *The Flight of Alcock and Brown* by Graham Wallace)

When the Vimy reached the west coast of Ireland, Alcock and Brown were faced with a tricky decision. They still had enough fuel on board to reach Brooklands but, on the other hand, they did not know whether the Handley Page aircraft had taken off in Newfoundland, and whether it was just behind them or even ahead of them. The Handley Page V/1500 was based about sixty miles from St. Johns, at Harbour Grace, and it had been difficult for Alcock and Brown to know how preparations were going there. Furthermore, the V/1500 operation was run in a very military manner by the starchy Admiral Mark Kerr (cousin of Lord Montagu), with tight security. Alcock and Brown lost their radio contact shortly after take-off, when the propeller came off their wing-mounted generator. There was also the little matter of the £10,000 prize (about £500,000 in today's terms). The prize was for the first non-stop crossing of the Atlantic. Down they went into the Derrygimla Bog, having first flown over the nearby village of Clifden and waved to the inhabitants. They had completed the 1,890 miles in fifteen hours, fifty-seven minutes, at an average speed of 118 mph.

Staff from the Marconi company, which ran the first-ever transatlantic radio station on the edge of the bog nearby, were soon sending messages across the world – to the team back in Newfoundland, to the *Daily Mail,* to Brown's fiancée, Kathleen Kennedy, to the Royal Aero Club, and this one to Rolls-Royce:

Congratulations on the performance two Eagle engines which propelled Vickers Vimy safely across the Atlantic. Alcock.

Lord Northcliffe, whose vision had inspired the flight, sent a message from his bed in a London nursing home.

A very hearty welcome to the pioneer of direct Atlantic flight. Your journey … is a typical example of British courage and organising efficiency. Just as in 1913, when I offered the prize, I felt that it would soon be won, so do I surely believe that your wonderful journey is a warning to cable monopolists and others to realise that within the next few years we shall be less dependent on them … I look forward with certainty when London morning newspapers will be selling in New York in the evening.

Others were full of praise for Rolls-Royce's contribution. Winston Churchill said on 20 June 1919:

I do not know what we should most admire in our guests – their audacity, determination, skill, science, their Vickers Vimy aeroplane, their Rolls-Royce engines or their good fortune.

Captain Alcock said in a speech to the Aero Club on 17 June: 'All the credit is due to the machine and particularly to the engines – that is everything.' Three days later his partner, Brown, spoke of 'the wonderful engines'.

Despite Northcliffe's forecast and optimistic headlines in the press, regular flights across the Atlantic did not take place for a number of years. Indeed, apart from two airship flights, it was not until 1927 that the Atlantic was flown again, this time by Charles Lindbergh in the *Spirit of St. Louis,* and it was almost another ten years before regular passenger flights became established. The reasons for the delay were largely to do with safety, the hazards of night-flying and unpredictable weather. As early as 1919, Rolls-Royce engines had proved to be equal to the task in terms of endurance and reliability.

(The subsequent history of Sir John Alcock and Sir Arthur Whitten Brown – both were knighted – was sad. Alcock was killed only six months after their remarkable feat while flying a Vickers Viking to an aeronautical exhibition in Paris. Brown, badly shaken by the loss of his friend – he could not face going to the funeral, although he visited the Science Museum on the anniversary of the flight every year – led an increasingly reclusive life and, heartbroken by the loss of his only son at the Battle of Arnhem in 1944, died in Swansea in 1948 at the comparatively young age of sixty-two.)

Almost immediately after the first transatlantic flight, a Captain Ross Smith and his brother, Keith, took up the challenge and won the prize of £10,000 offered by the Australian Government for the first flight from Britain to Australia (not non-stop!). The Australian Prime Minister, William Hughes, happened to be in Britain visiting wounded Australian servicemen at the time of the Alcock and Brown flight. He was so inspired by their achievement that he cabled his government to request sanction for £10,000 as a prize for the first Australian pilot in a British Empire-built aeroplane to complete the Britain–Australia flight. Again, the aeroplane was a Vickers Vimy and again the engines were Rolls-Royce Eagles. *The Times* was full of praise, writing on 11 December 1919:

The success of these Australian pioneers is a triumph of human and mechanical endurance. The human achievement is in no danger of being overlooked: the mechanical is less evident. The Vickers-Vimy aeroplane has now accomplished the two greatest feats of long-distance flying – the crossing of the Atlantic and the journey to Australia. It has proved itself to be a superb machine, and the utmost recognition is due both to the great firm which has produced it and to the designer of its Rolls-Royce engines. The firm of Vickers need no testimonial. Theirs is among the household names of British engineering achievement. Far less known, beyond a limited circle, is the name of Mr Royce, the designer of the internal combustion engine which bears the names of his partner and himself. Less than a month ago a Special Motoring Correspondent of *The Times* eulogized his work in the designing of motor engines. 'A scientific man,' he called Mr Royce, 'who is incapable of making any change [in design] which has not a scientific basis.' That was a testimonial to the genius of Mr Royce as a designer of motor cars. His work on the aeroplane engine has been as brilliant and as sound – infinite pains allied to an imaginative insight that has the true touch of genius.

'NO MORE CONDORS'

On 11 November 1918, when the Armistice was signed, it was found that it was easier to cease fire than cease production. British industry may have taken a long time to gear up for war production, but by this time it was running at full capacity. Furthermore, in contrast to the mood of autumn 1914 when everyone was saying that the lads would be home by Christmas, in the autumn of 1918 most were expecting the war to continue into 1920 or even 1921. Rolls-Royce continued to manufacture the engines ordered by the Government, but the prospects for further orders seemed dismal, and would depend on the scale of the air force envisaged by Parliament.

The view of the British Government, when peace finally came at the eleventh hour, on the eleventh day, of the eleventh month in 1918, was that the British Empire would not be involved in another major war for at least ten years, and that they could plan their armed forces on that assumption. Massive reductions in military budgets were made immediately, and wartime air defences abolished.

The General Staff have often been accused of short-sightedness in preparations for the Second World War. This is unfair. They knew perfectly well how important bombers and fighters would be, but were expressly forbidden by Government to prepare for such a war.

Nevertheless, the British Government realised that the country must have some sort of air force, and also that a number of aircraft manufacturers would be forced out of business if not given new orders. Partly for this reason of subsidy, and partly to strengthen its hand in international negotiations, the Government set up a Metropolitan Air Force of twenty-three squadrons in 1922. When the Conservatives replaced the Liberals in power later that year, the number was increased to seventeen fighter and thirty-five bomber squadrons, with a total of 598 aircraft.

Under the circumstances, it was not surprising that the Rolls-Royce directors saw the company's future in their motor cars and wanted to return to production of them as quickly as possible.

What effect did the war have on the company as a whole?

Johnson and his fellow directors had been continuously pessimistic about the future prospects for aero engine manufacture, and had spent a great deal of time negotiating with the Government over the value of the investment in plant which, in their view, would be virtually worthless once the war ended. Nevertheless, the war was 'good' for the company, in that the guaranteed war-related orders led to a considerable expansion both in fixed and current assets and, after a profits dip in 1915 and 1916, increased sales thereafter encouraged the issue of a £1-for-£1 bonus share issue at the end of the war.

The company's reputation in the eyes of the public – and the Air Ministry – stood very high, and this position was enhanced by the spectacular success of the transatlantic crossing in 1919. In trying to bring some rationalisation to the production of aero engines, Rolls-Royce were chosen as one of the four manufacturers – the others were Bristol, Napier and Armstrong-Siddeley – to whom the Government was prepared to give aid after the war.

Just as Rolls-Royce faced competition in the motor car business, they also needed to establish their supremacy in the world of aero engines if they were to stay in the aerospace business. To give some idea of the level of competition, between 1909 and the end of the Second World War, nearly 250 basic types of piston aero engine were built, and in their 900 variants they powered nearly 3,000 different types of aircraft.

In the 1920s, Rolls-Royce found themselves head to head in the aero engine field with Napier, their old pre-war rival in the motor car world. In the thirty-second Wilbur Wright Memorial Lecture at the beginning of the Second World War, Roy Fedden said of aero engine development after the First World War:

In Britain, Rolls Royce who had undoubtedly produced the best engines during the war, although retaining their interest in aero-engine development, again concentrated their main efforts on motor cars. Napier, on the other hand, who had also held a leading position in the motor vehicle world before the war, was the one established concern which took the opposite course, and continued to concentrate on aero-engine work. This decision was influenced, no doubt, by the fact that, at just about the time of the Armistice, they had brought their W.12. liquid-cooled 'Lion' engine of 400 h.p. to a successful state of development, and so had the most advanced British engine of the day. Armstrong-Siddeley followed a middle course, and continued with the development of their 14 cylinder two bank radial, concurrently with their motor car work. An exceptional course was taken by the Bristol Company which, although having been concerned only with airframe work, established an aero-engine department to take over the development of the Cosmos Jupiter, which I had had the privilege of initiating with my colleagues at Brazil Strakers during the war. Another factor which influenced the British position was the establishment of the Aircraft Disposal Board with a large stock of engines, which took some years to liquidate, and which undoubtedly had the effect of further depressing interest in new development.

Napier had been given something of a head start by Rolls-Royce in the 1920s, as Claude Johnson had insisted that the company concentrate its efforts on the development and manufacture of motor cars. Johnson was supported in his views by Ernest Claremont, the Chairman, by his own brother, Basil Johnson, and, to an extent, by Royce himself, who was busy on the 20 hp and Silver Ghost replacement. Only grudgingly was Eric Platford, on his return from helping the would-be conquerors of the Atlantic in Newfoundland, allowed to spend modest amounts supporting the engines in service with the RAF, foreign air forces and civil airlines. Further design work on aero engines virtually ceased.

As a result, contribution to Rolls-Royce's progress was confined to over-hauls, leaving the field open for Napier's Lion engine, which had been designed by A.J. Rowledge before he left Napier to join Rolls-Royce in 1921 (as assistant chief engineer to Henry Royce). Rowledge's first job at Rolls-Royce was to redesign the Condor, the result being the Condor III engine. He had been asked to reduce the weight of the engine by 600 lbs. He also changed the epicyclic gear to a spur reduction gear, crossbolted the main bearings and introduced marine-type fork and blade connecting rods in place of master and articulated connecting rods. In many ways, the Condor III was a crucial engine. Many of its features were to be retained in the Kestrel, Buzzard, 'R', Merlin and Griffon, including the four-valve head which Royce had introduced on the Condor.

Rowledge also worked on cars, making a notable contribution to brake design. Four-wheel brakes became increasingly common after the end of the First World War, and Royce felt that some sort of servo assistance was needed to keep pedal pressures sensibly light. His first scheme did not work, but Rowledge produced one that owed something to Hispano Suiza, except that Rowledge's worked forwards *and* backwards. Royce conceded that Rowledge's scheme was right.

By 1927, Napier were employing 1,600 men and producing about fifty aero engines a month. However, by this time the Lion was reaching its zenith and Napier had failed to come up with a replacement. (They had been greatly disappointed when the Air Ministry decided in 1925 to stop funding development of the Cub engine, which Napier had hoped would replace the Lion.) As we have seen, Napier planned to diversify by buying both the Bentley Motor Company and Gloster Aircraft in 1931. However, neither purchase was achieved.

Napier and the Lion were not the only competition. From 1922 until 1926, Armstrong Siddeley were the dominant British manufacturer of air-cooled engines. Their Jaguar engine powered the standard post-war fighters – the Grebe, Flycatcher and Siskin. Until 1926, more Jaguars were sold abroad than any other engine. In that year, the engine was overtaken by the simpler and more powerful Bristol Jupiter, and Armstrong Siddeley, in spite of several attempts to win back their superiority, never regained their pre-eminent position as designers of high-power, air-cooled engines.

There were one or two other competitors. Geoffrey de Havilland initially bought surplus engines from the Aircraft Disposals Company and converted them from eight to four cylinders. He then realised that a specially designed light engine could be a viable proposition. The Government did encourage private flying, even if it was not providing funds for the development of engines. De Havilland's Gipsy engine, designed for the Moth and first produced in 1927, was extremely successful. Alvis was also a competitor, but was moved into the 'shadow factory' scheme under Bristol once re-armament began in earnest in 1935.

In 1925 Air Chief Marshal Trenchard, after consultation with the Air Ministry, made the decision that all future engines for front-line RAF aircraft should have the capability of being manufactured under licence by firms in the motor car industry. The Air Ministry sent Major G.P. Bulman to the various aero engine manufacturers to tell them of this decision. (Bulman was assistant to Lieutenant-Colonel Fell, the Assistant Director of Technical Development (Engines), who later worked for Rolls-Royce.) Nobody disagreed except Rolls-Royce. Basil Johnson (Claude had just died) told Bulman of the Rolls-Royce tradition of not using licensees. Trenchard was upset, and scrawled across Bulman's report, 'No more Condors'. Rolls-Royce were in danger of being excluded from the aero engine business altogether.

THE SCHNEIDER TROPHY

The Schneider Trophy is a vital part of the Rolls-Royce story. Not only did the engines that Rolls-Royce developed for Supermarine in the late 1920s re-establish the company's reputation as the supreme aero engine maker, but also the work carried out by R.J. (Reginald) Mitchell in designing his S5 and S6 seaplanes led directly to his design of the Spitfire, with all its consequences for Rolls-Royce and the country.

Mitchell was born on 20 May 1895 in Stoke-on-Trent. Although born before the first powered flight, he became interested in aeroplanes while still at school. Engineering was his natural calling, and he served his five-year apprenticeship at the locomotive engineering firm of Kerr, Stuart in Stoke, at the same time attending night school and taking classes in engineering drawing, higher mathematics and mechanics. By the time he was twenty-one he was applying for other jobs, and in 1916 was thrilled to be offered a job as personal assistant to Hubert Scott-Paine at the Supermarine Aviation Works in Woolston, Southampton.

The factory had been started in 1912 by Noel Pemberton-Billing, who had become caught up in the new 'flying-machine' craze. He chose the name Supermarine as the opposite of submarine, as he intended to concentrate on aeroplanes that would fly over the sea. Pemberton-Billing lacked the finance to develop the company, and sold his interest to Scott-Paine. As with many such companies, the demands of the First World War attracted Government interest and virtually guaranteed the sale of every aeroplane Supermarine could produce. The company produced the first British flying boat fighter, the Baby.

In 1919 Mitchell was appointed chief designer, and in 1928 – when Supermarine was bought by Vickers – director and chief designer. The 1920s were largely spent by Mitchell designing an aeroplane to win the Schneider Trophy, an international award presented to the nation with the fastest seaplane over a pre-determined, measured course.

The Trophy, mounted on a marble plinth, showed a female figure sculpted in silver and bronze, diving to kiss a cresting wave. It was initially presented in 1913 by Jacques Schneider, the son of a wealthy French armaments manufacturer. Schneider saw the seaplane as the future of air travel over an earth covered with vast areas of water which would provide cheap airports.

The rules of the competition were simple. The contest must take place over water, the contestants' machines must be seaworthy, the entries must be sponsored by a governing body (in Britain's case, the Royal Aero Club), and no country could enter more than three contestants. The winning nation would host the contest in the following year, and three consecutive victories would win the Trophy outright. The length would be about 350 kilometres, flown in a number of laps around a closed circuit.

There were two contests before the outbreak of war in 1914. The first, held in Monaco in April 1913, was won by a Frenchman, Maurice Prevost, in a monoplane flying at an average speed of 45.75 mph and powered by a French Gnome rotary engine. The second, in 1914, again in Monaco, was won by an Englishman, Howard Pixton, flying a Sopwith Schneider biplane fitted with floats. His average speed was 86.78 mph, almost twice that of Prevost.

The First World War meant that there was no further contest until 1919, and that proved to be a shambles owing to bad weather, including fog, in Bournemouth Bay, the venue for the contest. The 1920 and 1921 contests were held in Venice. There were no British entries, and both were won by Italy. In 1922 Supermarine entered a modification of the Sea Lion which they had used in 1919, and in a very close contest in the Bay of Naples, brought the Trophy back to Britain. The year 1923 brought entries from the USA, with Lieutenant Rittenhouse winning the Trophy in a Curtiss-CR3.

Mitchell now realised that only a dramatic new design could compete with the Americans. His solution, the S4 – a monoplane with a wing of cantilever construction – was so expensive that backing from the Air Ministry was required. Unfortunately, the S4 crashed and the Americans retained the Trophy in 1925 (the 1924 contest had been cancelled). The 1926 race was won again by the Italians with no entry from Britain, but Britain won the Trophy back in 1927 with Mitchell's S5, a greatly improved S4 monoplane.

The year 1928 brought a change in the Schneider Trophy rules. It was agreed that the contest should take place every two years, to give countries more time to develop their machines. The next contest, to be held in England, would now take place in 1929, and Mitchell made one significant change in the aeroplane he designed for this contest. Up to this point, all of his Schneider Trophy entries had been powered by Napier Lion engines, but it was felt by this time that this engine had reached the limit of its development. The only other possible engine supplier was Rolls-Royce.

Major Bulman, for most of the inter-war years the Air Ministry official in charge of aero engine development, wrote later of how Rolls-Royce became involved in the Schneider Trophy.

The third and perhaps greatest problem confronting my early months as A.D.R.D.E. (Assistant Director Research and Development for Engines) related to the Schneider Trophy Race due in September 1929 in England. The engine programme had to be settled early in 1928. Since 1927, Italy had continued to advance rapidly in the Air. The Duce was becoming an increasingly truculent leader adding to the temperature and stress of the international field. The Trophy Race would be the most bitter and significant battle between our two countries.

The stalwart and dependable Lion had won the Race in Venice in 1927 in the Supermarine S.5 with its output of 890 HP for 928 lbs weight, tailored down in most of its external dimensions from the standard Service Lion which had for years given yeoman service in the R.A.F. But had it the prospect of producing a much higher output, some hundreds of HP, entailing undoubtedly the introduction of a supercharger, ground so far untrodden by the Napier team? Would it be justifiable to commit the British effort to this one project?

The alternative was to gamble on a completely new comer in the Rolls-Royce development of the Buzzard, recently typetested for service use at 825 HP for 1,460 lbs weight, supercharged, a bigger brother to the Kestrel but far less established. Indeed it had shown a tendency to crack cylinder heads after only short service, as the Japanese must have found with the trial batch of 100 engines they bought [100 Buzzard engines were built, but only 40 went to Japan], but they remained inscrutable in their silence!

The Rolls-Royce engineers had discussed separately with Reggie Mitchell, the Supermarine designer, and myself, the possibilities latent in this engine, given intensive effort for a short life, and were enthusiastic in their hopes. To Mitchell it would mean a considerable re-hash of his S.5 to accommodate the bigger and heavier engine, with its extra cooling and heavier fuel load. To me it meant a desperate gamble to back something virtually untried, entirely contrary to my habit, and to commit the Air Ministry and the nation to a gigantic bet, instead of playing safe by putting all one's money on the well tried faithful Lion.

Mitchell and I met together alone three times over a short period to resolve the problem, and finally mutually agreed that we should back the Rolls project, largely, and for my part wholly, on the faith I had in the Derby team, A.J. Rowledge, the originator years earlier of the Lion, Elliott, long the right hand of Sir Henry Royce, and Hives, the head of the Experimental Shop at Derby. One felt that their sheer determination and guts would give us the best chance.

I reported Mitchell's and my decision to my chief, Sir John Higgins, who immediately asked the Managing Director of R.R. Ltd. to call and settle the deal in principle. Claude Johnson, who had built up the Firm's world wide reputation on Royce's technical brilliance and vision, a man of striking personality, had died in 1926, and his successor [his brother, Basil] it was who came to see Josh and myself, alone. To our utter amazement he begged to be excused from our commission. Racing and all its aspects were things, he said, strictly to be avoided by his firm. Its reputation for sheer quality and perfection must not be smirched by sordid competition of this sort. To participate unwillingly, and quite possibly fail, would be a calamity to the firm with the loss of its prestige, for which the Air Ministry would have to accept grave responsibility. And so on, in dreary defeatism. As I listened to this miserable plea to be 'let off', knowing that the firm's engineers were straining at the leash to go ahead, I uncontrollably blurted out in my fury a single word, unprintable in polite context and essentially masculine. Higgins turned and looked at me for a long second, and then in a steely voice of real Air Marshal calibre said to our guest, 'Mr. ... ... [Johnson], I order your firm to take on this job. We have complete faith in your technical team. The necessary arrangements will be made between our respective staffs. Good afternoon.' As our disconsolate and vanquished visitor closed the door behind him Josh said to me, 'Thank you for summing up the discussion so succinctly,' and gave a huge chuckle as I shot out of his office to telephone the glad tidings to Rowledge in Derby.

To understand the point that Rolls-Royce had reached in their aero engine development when they were approached by Mitchell in 1928, we have to go back to the early 1920s.

Royce had begun work on a new engine, the FX, later known as the Kestrel, in 1924. The Kestrel's 21.24 litre capacity was similar to the Eagle's 20.32 litres, but they differed in other respects. Initially, the engine had dry steel liners, but problems with cooling soon led to the installation of wet liners in direct contact with the coolant. The FX was a V12 like the Eagle, but instead of each cylinder being separate with its own pressed-steel water jacket, the six cylinders on each bank of the engine were enclosed in a single aluminium casting which served as a common water jacket to that bank. Cylinder heads and gas passages were formed integrally with the cylinder castings. A single overhead camshaft carried on each cylinder block operated the valves, the mechanism, completely enclosed, being lubricated by low-pressure oil. The overall result was a very light and rigid engine. Tested as a direct drive unit in development, in production it was offered in geared form. Initially not supercharged, it subsequently became available in both supercharged and non-supercharged form.

Meanwhile, Richard Fairey had designed and built a bomber called the Fairey Fox, and to power it he imported the successful American Schneider Trophy engine, the Curtiss D12, which was later developed into the Curtiss Conqueror. Powered by the D12, his Fairey Fox bomber was faster than any fighter then in service. Fairey took out a licence to build it in Britain. The Government liked the aeroplane but did not want another aero engine manufacturer, and turned to Royce to see whether he could design an engine better than the Curtiss D12. Rolls-Royce brought a D12 to Derby in 1926 to study it, but this was nearly two years after Royce had started work on the Kestrel; he was not influenced by the Curtiss engine, as has sometimes been alleged.

Many different forms of Kestrel were built. As Alec Lumsden put it in his *British Piston Aero-Engines and their Aircraft*, published by Airlife in 1994:

There can have been few, if any families of engines as complex as the Kestrels, of which 4,750 were built. The variants were very numerous and there has been much uncertainty in the past, as to exactly what Kestrel designations implied. Despite this apparent complication, each variant could be identified by observance of a coded string of letters which logically followed the name and saved a lot of time and space.

And the Kestrel was a critical engine in re-establishing Rolls-Royce's position as the premier supplier of aero engines to the RAF. In the 1920s, as an act of deliberate policy, Rolls-Royce had virtually abandoned aero engine development and production, leaving the field clear to its rivals, especially Napier and Bristol. As Major Bulman put it when writing of the RAF Pageant at Hendon in June 1928:

The four main engine firms were fairly well balanced in the service aircraft then in general use; Siddeleys with their Jaguars in fighters (the Siskin and Grebe) with Bristol catching up in the Bulldog and Hawker Woodcock and also in the larger aircraft, the Sidestrand bomber; Napiers with the Lion maintained the heavy stuff with the Vickers Virginia, the Handley Page Hyderabad bombers and the Fairey IIIF, Rolls with the Condor in the Hawker Horsley.

But the Condor and Hawker Horsley were not going to make Rolls-Royce a serious contender. It was the Kestrel that brought Rolls-Royce back in the 1930s. Ultimately, the Merlin made Rolls-Royce world-famous, but the Kestrel was a very important forerunner. As Harold Nockolds wrote:

[T]he fame of the Kestrel does not only rest upon the engines which succeeded it. On its own account it achieved a lasting reputation in the history of aviation, for it was the engine of a classic sequence of R.A.F. machines. It is well to remember that

160

Britain's pilots at the outbreak of the Second World War – especially the fighter pilots – largely owed their fitness for the coming struggle for supremacy in the air to the fact that they had been brought up on the Kestrel breed of aircraft. Their early flying had been done on Hawker Harts and Furies and Fairey Fireflies before those magnificent biplanes were supplanted by Hurricanes and later by Spitfires. But the Kestrel outlived those early first-line fighters, and as the engine of the Miles Master it continued to help in the advanced training of new recruits to the ranks of fighter pilots for some time after the war had started.

Even before the FX was named the Kestrel, Royce had identified the need for a more powerful engine. Using the same basic design as the 'F' engine, the 'H' engine was produced with 70 per cent greater cubic capacity. (Much of the work was done by R.W.H. Bailey, who added extra features such as saddle studs.) It was test run in June 1928, and Royce himself was so pleased with the speed of the development of the 'H' engine that on 13 June 1928 he sent this telegram:

WORMALD, BAILEY, ROYCAR DERBY. EXTREMELY PLEASED WITH EXCELLENT WORK DONE INTRODUCING LARGER AERO ENGINE SO QUICKLY THANKS TO YOUR EFFORTS AND THOSE ASSISTING. ROYCE.

Such open praise from the boss was rare indeed!

This was the point that Rolls-Royce aero engine development had reached when Mitchell approached them to inquire about an engine to challenge for the Schneider Trophy. Royce initially looked at a narrow-angle V16 but decided, with the limited time available, that he had only one option. That was to take the most powerful engine available, the Buzzard (still called the 'H' engine at that stage), and soup it up to create the 'Racing H', or more briefly in due course, simply the 'R' engine.

Rod Banks of the Ethyl Corporation, who had already established himself as one of the country's experts on motoring and aircraft fuel, wrote in his book, *I Kept no Diary*:

Basil Johnson wanted none of it and felt their place remained in the automobile field, despite the success of the firm's aero engines, Hawk, Falcon and Eagle, in the First World War.

But three men who were in favour, E.W. Hives, A.J. Rowledge and A.C. Lovesey, went down to see Royce at his home and head-quarters at West Wittering in October 1928 and found him enthusiastic. It was a bright autumn morning and Royce suggested a stroll along the beach; as they walked he pointed out the local places of interest. But Royce, who walked with a stick, was a semi-invalid, as Montagu Napier had been, and he soon tired. 'Let's find a sheltered spot,' he said, 'and have a talk.'

Seated on the sand dunes against a groyne, Royce sketched the rough outline of a racing engine in the sand with his stick. Each man was asked his opinion in turn, the sand was raked over and adjustments made. The key to the engine was simplicity. 'I invent nothing,' was Royce's philosophy, 'inventors go broke.' Like the Kestrel and the Buzzard the new engine would have only 12 cylinders, against the 18 of the Isotta-Fraschini and the 24 of the Packard. The bore and stroke would be 6″ by 6.6″, and the compression ratio 6:1. The secret of increased power would lie in supercharging.

And, as we have seen, the company had effectively received an order from the Air Ministry to develop an engine capable of winning the Schneider Trophy and putting the upstart Mussolini in his place.

Hives had never been in favour of neglecting the aero engine side of the business, and it was largely through his influence that the engineers Cyril Lovesey, A.A. Rubbra and Ray Dorey had been recruited to work specifically on aero engines. Royce learnt of Basil Johnson's attempts to block development on aero engines when Lieutenant-Colonel Fell, who had joined Rolls-Royce's aero engine marketing operation after a distinguished career at the Air Ministry, inquired about a report he had written for the board. Royce said he had never seen it. Shortly afterwards, Johnson was asked to take early retirement. (He then went to Bentley, and when Rolls-Royce bought Bentley from the Receiver in 1931, Arthur Sidgreaves was forced to say that Rolls-Royce did not want to offer him a job.)

The other element that contributed so much to the performance of the 'R' engine was supercharging. Rowledge had already persuaded Rolls-Royce to take on the expert on supercharging, James Ellor, who had worked at the Royal Aircraft Establishment (RAE). Ellor was being tempted to take his skills to the USA, and the Air Ministry could not match the offer within Civil Service pay scales. To keep Ellor in Britain, it was agreed that Rolls-Royce should make him an offer.

The power of an engine depends on the mass of air and fuel it can consume in a given time, and a supercharger provides a means of getting air through an engine of given size and capacity. Ellor had introduced supercharging into the Kestrel and Buzzard engines, but principally to restore power at altitude. On the 'R' engine, the intent was to increase power at low altitude. His design for this engine included a forward-facing air intake which converted forward airspeed energy into pressure energy, a unique development at that time.

On the fuel side, Rowledge called in Rod Banks, who recalled the tense preparations for the 1929 Schneider contest in his book:

The engine chosen by Rolls as the basis for conversion to racing role was the H, or Buzzard, a 12 cylinder 60° V, a motor of 36.6 litres capacity developing about 825 bhp.

Known as the 'R' engine in racing form, it was strengthened in certain respects and fitted with a large double-sided centrifugal supercharger (to reduce diameter) which increased the sea-level power to 1,850 bhp with the engine operating on 100 per cent benzole. But, during test and endurance running, troubles began to manifest themselves at the hot end, with power fall off, exhaust valve distortion and burning and plug sooting on idling that sometimes prevented the engine being opened up to a full throttle. Rowledge (Rg. as he was known by the Rolls coding of names) asked me to come and help. I had by then joined the Technical Sales Department of the Anglo-American Oil Company.

With only little more than a month to go before the Schneider Contest, I did not have time to do very much; however, by the simple expedient of diluting the benzole with a 'light cut' Rumanian leaded gasoline, it was possible to get the engine through its test satisfactorily and race-ready – the contest being won by Waghorn piloting the Supermarine S6A with the 'R' engine.

The night before the contest provided almost a greater degree of excitement for those directly concerned than the actual affair the next day. A pre-race inspection of the newly-installed race engines revealed some aluminium on the plugs removed from a cylinder in Waghorn's machine. This indicated that the particular piston was probably picking up. According to the Schneider Trophy Contest rules, once the race engines were finally installed they could not be removed; but the Royal Aero Club Contest Committee members at Calshot agreed that components could be removed and replaced *in situ* in the aircraft.

There were some hundreds of personnel from the Rolls Special and Experimental Departments, who had built and tested the engines, in Southampton that evening. They had come to view the event, but were spread all over the town in various hotels and pubs. It took some time to locate and round up the specialists among these skilled people who could remove the cylinder block concerned. Eventually, a team was gathered together under Lovesey, the senior experimental engineer. They worked through the night, removed the cylinder block, changed the offending piston, replaced the block and had the engine running at 8 am.

Waghorn, who won the Contest, was not told until afterwards about the night's happenings.

This account by Banks, though it captures the atmosphere perfectly, contains some errors. The 1929 Trophy was won by Waghorn, not in the Supermarine S6A but in the S6. There were not 'hundreds' of Rolls-Royce personnel in Southampton but a coach-load, there was no such department as the Rolls Special Department and, finally, the block was not 'replaced' (that is, the same one put back) but rather 'changed' for another block.

Jack Warwick (brother-in-law of Hives), a mechanic working on the S6 in Southampton Water, told Dave Piggott (during Piggott's research into Rolls-Royce engines in the inter-war period) that the aircraft had been moored all day for a seaworthiness test and that it was brought into the hangar in the early evening for its pre-race checks. During the evening, Hives left a dinner he was attending with many of the team and asked to look at the plugs. After noticing aluminium specks on them, he conferred with Lovesey. They looked in the B4 cylinder and saw that the piston had seized. They realised that they must change the block, but were not sure if this was allowed under the Trophy rules. They were advised that it was permissible, provided the engine number remained the same. Hives tried to ring the hotel where the team were having dinner, but could not get through, so he drove to the hotel and brought back Coverley, Jack Marsden, Les Buckler and Joe Lowe. While he was doing this, Jack Warwick and Lovesey stripped the engine. After working through the night, the hastily assembled team had the engine ready by 6am.

Prior to this last-minute drama, hundreds of hours of development and testing had been carried out round the clock, much to the irritation of the people of Derby. As well as the 'R' running at full throttle, at the front there was a Kestrel engine driving a blower to create a 400 mph ram effect at the inlet. There was another Kestrel blowing air through giant pipes to cool the sump, and a third one in the yard driving a propeller to blow away the fumes. (This last was important, as Castrol R was a notoriously potent laxative!)

Royce had allowed the design to be handled in Derby though, of course, the design details were still subject to his personal supervision. There were now ten in the aero engine team in Derby, rather than two as in the early 1920s, and they worked day and night. As a result, the engine was completed and tested successfully within three months.

The S6 was similar to the S5, but larger to accommodate the new engine. Fuel consumption was greater, and the floats were redesigned to act as fuel tanks. On its trial run, the pilot, Squadron Leader A.H. Orlebar (Orlie), found he could not get the S6 off the water as, at each attempt, the seaplane swung violently to port due to torque from the propeller. Mitchell solved this problem by transferring most of the fuel to the starboard float. After some hair-raising moments, the S6 won the Trophy for Britain in 1929 and Rolls-Royce, Supermarine and the fuel and oil companies made the most of the favourable publicity. Rolls-Royce were so grateful to Mitchell that they presented him with a Rolls-Royce car.

Britain had now won the Schneider Trophy twice in succession. A third victory in 1931 would win it outright. Unfortunately, the economic depression made it extremely difficult for Vickers – or even the Government for that matter – to provide the £100,000 (about £5 million today) that was felt necessary for Supermarine to build two new aircraft to compete. Philip Snowden, Chancellor of the Exchequer, was a pacifist and saw the Schneider Trophy as fostering what he called 'the pernicious rivalry between nations'.

Furthermore, in very hard times with high unemployment, it was difficult for the Government to help finance a venture that could be described by some as frivolous. In spite of pressure from the Opposition, the press and the Society of British Aircraft Constructors, the Government stood its ground, and the prospects for a British entry looked bleak.

However, out of the blue appeared Lady Houston, the wealthy widow of a shipowner, who offered the Government the money. Prime Minister Ramsay MacDonald accepted it, but no doubt ground his teeth listening to her criticising his Labour Government for reducing Britain to a third-rate power: 'We are not worms to be trampled under the heel of Socialism, but true Britons.' It has been suggested that Lady Houston refused to pay death duties on the death of her husband. Prosecuting and possibly imprisoning such a famous person was not an alluring prospect, and the £100,000 sponsorship may have been a way of saving face all round.

In his book *R.J. Mitchell, Schooldays to Spitfire*, Mitchell's son Gordon writes of Lady Houston:

It has been suggested that without Lady Houston's generous gift which enabled the 1931 race to be held, there might not have been a Spitfire produced in 1936. However, as the S6B was essentially only a modified version of the S6, the major part of the vital experience R.J. gained from the Schneider races, later to be of such value in designing the Spitfire, was in fact obtained in 1927 and 1929 with the S5 and S6.

As Mitchell made modifications to the S6, Rolls-Royce managed to improve the 'R' engine to give an output of 2,350 hp, primarily by making the crankshaft and centrifugal blower run faster, and by increasing the air intake. Their biggest problem was the extra heat produced by the more powerful engine. Somehow they needed to dissipate some 40,000 BTUs of heat per minute. To dissipate this heat from the exhaust valve heads, they introduced sodium-cooled valves. The sodium-cooled valve technology came from the Williams Rich Corporation in the USA; Rolls-Royce therefore had to take out a sub-licence from the Bristol Aircraft Company, because all components had to be manufactured in the competitor nation. The length of the floats was increased, not only to provide more cooling surfaces but also to hold more fuel. Other modifications were made to the intricate oil cooling system.

All parts of the engine needed to be strengthened to take the stress of the higher power output. The engineers set themselves the target of a sixty-minute run at full throttle. As testing continued day and night throughout the spring of 1931, the citizens of Derby protested. Rolls-Royce needed the help of the mayor to appeal to their patriotism at the expense of their sleep. On 12 August, with a month to go, the engine passed the test, running for a full hour at 3,200 rpm and giving 2,350 hp.

Gordon Mitchell knew the debt of gratitude his father felt for Rolls-Royce:

The vital part played by Rolls-Royce, led by their Experimental Manager, Ernest (later Lord) Hives, in the successful outcome of the 1931 race, cannot be over-emphasised and Mitchell was only too ready to acknowledge their outstanding contribution.

When the 1931 contest was won, and the Schneider Trophy had been secured by Britain in perpetuity, there were huge celebrations. The BBC recorded the views and reminiscences of the main participants and contributors. On behalf of Rolls-Royce, A.J. Rowledge said, *inter alia*:

In preparing the engines for the 1929 Contest, we were in many ways at the beginning of the development of this particular engine. In 1931 we had more knowledge and data to enable us to tackle the job but at the same time we had a smaller field for development. The 1931 engine, besides giving more power, was a more efficient engine than its predecessor. As the development of a given engine proceeds the balance of the design improves thus making it more difficult to obtain further improvement, and almost every piece of material in the engine is working at its limit of stress or heat capacity, even for the short life required of such an engine. However, the limit of development has not yet been reached as regards engine construction . . . When taken down and examined after the race, the engine was in particularly good condition. No parts were damaged and the bearings looked almost as new. The engine used for the speed record was equally good.

What were the lasting benefits of the Schneider Trophy? Arthur Rubbra, who joined the Rolls-Royce Experimental Department in 1925, became chief designer in 1940 and technical director in 1954, said of the benefits to engine development of the Schneider Trophy:

I think there are a number of areas where the development of the Merlin was helped by the work done on the R engine, although the target of completion of an hour's run in one piece at full output was rather different from that of completing the official service type test. For this reason, the satisfactory solution of such troubles by this method does not always read across to those met with in service life.

However, there is no doubt that such running at high output for short duration does help considerably in pin-pointing quickly the likely trouble spots and was used extensively and successfully as a general test procedure in the development of the Merlin.

R.J. Mitchell himself produced an article which was published in *Aeronautical Engineering* on 25 December 1929 in which he made it clear that, in his view, information and experience gained in the development of racing aircraft had a profound influence on the design of both civil and military aircraft.

He wrote:

During the last 10 years there has been an almost constant increase in speed in our racing types. To maintain this steady increase very definite progress has been essential year by year. It has been necessary to increase the aerodynamic efficiency and power-to-weight ratios of our machines; to reduce the consumption and frontal area of our engines; to devise new methods of construction; and to develop the use of new materials. The results obtained in the form of speed have been a direct and absolute indication of our progress in aeronautical development.

Arthur Sidgreaves, Managing Director of Rolls-Royce, said after the successful race in 1931:

As a result of the test this year all the main components of these engines have undergone a definite improvement, and in consequence the life of the standard engine in service will be much longer than it would otherwise have been.

From the development point of view the Schneider Trophy Contest is almost an economy because it saves so much time in arriving at certain technical improvements. It is not too much to say that research for the Schneider Trophy Contest over the past two years is what our aero-engine department would otherwise have taken six to ten years to learn . . .

For the last few years Britain's supremacy in the manufacture of aircraft is generally recognised and is due to the experience and knowledge gained in contests such as that for the Schneider Trophy.

And Air Marshall Sir Hugh (later Lord) Dowding, although opposed to such international competitions on both technical and moral grounds, nevertheless appreciated the bringing together of design teams which would otherwise have been difficult in peacetime.

Sir George Edwards, who succeeded Rex Pierson as chief designer at Vickers and rose in the aircraft industry to become Chairman and Managing Director of the British Aircraft Corporation, wrote:

There can be no doubt that the boldness of these designs and the passion for engineering detail which they displayed made a profound impact on aeronautical design and set the scene for the successful generation of British fighters which were so decisive in saving Britain from defeat in later years. If the industry had been limited during these inter-war years to design studies alone and had not been able to translate ideas into hardware by actually building aeroplanes, it is certain that such successful fighters as the Spitfire and the Hurricane would not have emerged.

From Rolls-Royce's point of view, the performance of the 'R' engine in the Schneider Trophy proved to be a turning-point in its progress as an aero engine manufacturer. This is how Alec Harvey-Bailey put it:

To look back a little, although Rolls-Royce had developed an enviable reputation in the aero engine field by 1918 and had subsequently powered the great pioneering flights, including the start of civil aviation, the 1920s saw the Company slip into third place behind Bristol and Napier. At the end of the twenties it was the performance of the R type racing engine which overshadowed the competition, both British and foreign, in the Schneider Trophy races and put Rolls-Royce into serious contention for major RAF contracts.

And to put the final seal on the beneficial publicity from the winning of the Schneider Trophy, Hives was determined that the S6B should achieve a new World Absolute Air Speed Record. Orlebar had achieved it in the S6 after the 1929 contest, attaining a speed of 357 mph. Since then the record had been raised to 379 mph, but the target now was 400 mph. Hives wrote in memos at the time that '400 miles per hour' was a headline maker. The Air Ministry, not interested in such frivolities, wanted the High Speed Flight to hand the Calshot base back to the Flying Boat Squadron. According to Rod Banks:

This caused a furore, but the decision was reversed after Sir Henry Royce interceded on behalf of the High Speed Flight.

Hives asked Banks if more power could be attained by altering the fuel. Certainly there was no time to modify the engine greatly. With Ray Dorey, Banks mixed a high alcohol-content fuel cocktail which gave an extra 250 bhp. The final mix was 60 per cent methanol, 30 per cent benzole and 10 per cent acetone, plus lead. This was fine for performance, but it meant that some modifications to the engine were needed, and it also caused problems with the tanks – the concoction proved to be a good solvent of paint and the sealing compounds. Finally, all was ready and, as Banks put it:

[Flight Lieutenant George Stainforth] then opened the throttle and fairly shot off the lighter for the take-off. On reaching the end of each run on the speed course, he throttled back somewhat on the turn towards the next run and wet fuel vapour was seen coming from the exhausts! But the magic figure was surpassed by 7.5 mph.

Preparing for War

'A REAL KILLER FIGHTER'

THE ARGUMENTS HAVE RAGED back and forth for more than sixty years over Britain's preparedness, or lack of it, for war in 1939. With hindsight it is easy to see that a further war with Germany was inevitable, and indeed the leader of the French Army in the First World War, Marshal Foch, described the Treaty of Versailles as merely a twenty-year armistice, a remarkably accurate prediction. However, the spirit of the 1920s and early 1930s was one of peace and goodwill. There had to be a better way to settle men's differences than by the appalling slaughter that had taken place between 1914 and 1918. It was not only the feeling that there must be a better way that led British Governments of the 1920s and early 1930s to reject the isolated calls for rearmament. There was also a widespread feeling, nurtured by such publications as Maynard Keynes's *The Economic Consequences of the Peace*, that Germany *had* been treated too harshly. And when Hitler began to rant about the injustice of it all, some were inclined to wonder why the Germans scattered around central and eastern Europe should not live under one Government. For example, when the German Army marched into the demilitarised Rhineland in 1936, Lord Lothian said: 'Hitler is doing no more than taking over his own back garden.'

In 1925, the League of Nations, itself formed in 1919 on the initiative of the USA (though Congress vetoed the United States's participation) to

169

prevent further wars, set up a Preparatory Commission to explore the ground for general disarmament. Discussion dragged on for years, until eventually a Disarmament Conference was convened in Geneva in 1932. Proposals were put forward outlawing aerial bombardment and drastically limiting the loaded weight of military aircraft.

In a triumph of hope over experience, the British Government made it clear to the other participating nations that it was declining to authorise the development of new bomber aircraft. The Conference itself dragged on for two years without coming to any conclusions or achieving any result whatsoever.

Perhaps more importantly, British Governments trying to cope with continuing economic difficulties were reluctant to spend the necessary money to rebuild the British Army, Royal Navy and Royal Air Force. The British Empire conferred world-power status, but the small offshore island did not have the economy to sustain it. For Britain's policymakers the nightmare scenario, which eventually came to pass, was war on three fronts – against Germany in Europe, Italy in the Mediterranean and Japan in the Far East. A Naval pact was made with Germany, accepting German rearmament and thereby repudiating the Versailles Treaty. Mussolini was difficult to take seriously, but League of Nations sanctions, following Italy's easy, bullying war in Abyssinia, were blatantly ignored. As for Japan, in spite of its invasion of China, the British Government – so anxious was it to avoid any conflict with Japan – ordered the British Olympic Committee to support Tokyo as the site for the 1940 Games.

The level to which the British aircraft manufacturing industry had been run down is illustrated by the Reports of the Census of Production. In 1934, when rearmament began under the perceived threat of Germany's build-up of air power, fewer than 24,000 people were employed in the whole of the British aircraft industry, and only 1,685 aero engines were produced in that year. Aircraft production in the inter-war period fits into two neat parts: 1919–34, when orders were few and survival was the paramount consideration; and 1934–39, when orders were almost overwhelming and the problem was building up production.

The economic slump of 1920 crushed most aircraft and engine manufacturers, and by 1921 all British civil airlines had stopped flying. They only resumed when the Government began to subsidise them. Sopwith and Airco collapsed, but at least gave birth to new ventures, Hawker and de Havilland. Handley Page only survived because Frederick Handley Page was on the board of the Aircraft Disposals Company. Furthermore, the Government ceased manufacture of its own engines and aircraft at Farnborough. The Royal Aircraft Factory (RAF) became the Royal Aircraft Establishment (RAE), a research and development operation.

However, at this point the Government realised that it would be unwise to allow the industry to collapse completely, and pursued a policy of giving orders to a select group of airframe and aero engine manufacturers. The engine manufacturers chosen were Armstrong Siddeley, Bristol, Napier and Rolls-Royce. Any other companies attempting to produce powerful engines were dissuaded from doing so.

According to P. Fearon, Lecturer in Economic History at the University of Leicester, writing in *British Industry between the Wars*, published by Scolar Press in 1979:

In 1924 C.R. Fairey bought a licence for the American Curtiss D-12 engine, and built round it the Fairey Fox as a private venture aircraft. The Ministry, however, refused to finance the development of the D-12 and instead came to the conclusion that Britain should have a similar engine and asked Rolls-Royce to produce it. [As we shall see, Royce was already developing his 'F' engine by the time the Fox flew with the D-12.] Fairey abandoned, for the time being, attempts at engine production and the Fox was a financial disaster. Fairey returned to the fray again in the early 1930s with a water-cooled V-12 engine built at its own expense. It flew, but the Ministry was not interested and the engine was never adopted for service. The Ministry felt it necessary to have selected aero engine producers for much the same reason as it had a ring of airframe manufacturers. In the immediate post-war period there was a danger that Rolls-Royce would abandon aero engine production as the motor car side of the business was so profitable and surplus aero engines depressed the market. For two years after the Armistice Rolls-Royce were only engine repairers and even when the company was asked to carry on the development of their Condor engine at Government expense, it refused to divert manpower from motor car production. [This is not quite accurate. Rolls-Royce produced some 1,309 aero engines in 1919, 320 in 1920 and 183 in 1921.] The post-war depression altered this situation radically and when the Ministry offered Rolls-Royce a contract for 200 Condor engines, it was accepted.

Meanwhile, Germany, defeated in 1918 and treated like a criminal in the Versailles Treaty, harboured grudges which would not be settled by pious words. Once the country had been further ravaged by the great inflation of 1923 and the hardships of the Depression in the early 1930s, it was ready to listen to a dictator who proposed more radical and forceful solutions to its perceived ills. Although the Treaty of Versailles had imposed strict limits on the number of men under arms, and had forbidden a military air force and navy, by the early 1930s Germany was ignoring these strictures.

Sholto Douglas, who became Commander-in-Chief of Fighter Command during the Second World War and later Marshal of the Royal Air Force, wrote in his book *Years of Command*, published by Collins in 1966:

171

Those of us who had access to the best that our intelligence had to offer could not help but be aware of what was going on in Germany in the build-up of their armed forces. We had known for a long time that the Germans had been sending experienced pilots to Russia to keep up their training in military aviation. The story of the way in which these developments went even further had since been placed freely on record by Adolf Galland, who was to become one of the foremost German fighter pilots of the Second World War. He has spoken of a talk that he had with Hermann Goering in the Spring of 1933. 'The secret training of German pilots in Russia, used as a temporary expedient, must now come to an end', Goering told him. To that Galland added: '. . . we now had the opportunity of training our fighter pilots with the Italian Air Force. In order to avoid international complications for Italy as well as for Germany, the whole affair had to be treated with the greatest possible secrecy and carried out under rigorous camouflage.'

Winston Churchill, former Conservative Chancellor of the Exchequer who had put Britain back on the Gold Standard in the 1920s with such disastrous consequences for Britain's exporters, was by this time in the political wilderness, mainly because of his views on India and other foreign policy issues, but he argued strongly for an expansion of the Royal Air Force. In October 1933 he said to the House:

Germany is already well on her way to become, and must become, incomparably the most heavily armed nation in the world and most completely ready for war . . . We cannot have any anxieties comparable to the anxiety caused by German rearmament.

And in February 1934 he said:

. . . the crash of bombs in London and the cataracts of masonry and fire and smoke will warn us of any inadequacy which has been permitted in our aerial defences.

Intelligence about German activities was brought back by a number of visitors, among them Mutt Summers, the Vickers chief test pilot. Summers had the ear of the Vickers Chairman, Sir Robert McLean, who pressed the Government to sanction the building of a modern fighter aircraft. Unfortunately, allied to the pacifist approach and the reluctance to raise the necessary public expenditure was a widespread belief that 'the bomber will always get through', and that therefore fighters were a waste of time. Fortunately, Air Marshal Sir Hugh Dowding, then Air Member for Supply and Research, did not believe in this theory. He wanted to build a powerful fighter force, which he saw as essential for the defence of the country. In 1930 the Air Ministry issued Specification F. 7/30, a blueprint for the fighter that Dowding thought necessary for the defence of the country.

The specification required a day and night fighter to replace the obsolete fighter then in service with the RAF. Essential requirements were stipulated as:

- low landing speed and short landing run
- maximum speed of 250 mph
- steep initial climb rate for interception
- high manoeuvrability
- good all-round view.

While no shape of air frame was specified, the fighter was to be armed with four Vickers machine guns. Many manufacturers built prototypes in response to Specification F. 7/30, most of them powered by the Rolls-Royce Goshawk engine. However, Sir Robert McLean was very keen that Supermarine should win the contract, and asked Mitchell and his team to proceed with a design suggestion with all possible speed. Their first attempt, the Type 224, powered by a 600 hp Rolls-Royce Goshawk II engine, a derivative of the Kestrel but with evaporative water cooling, was a failure and the Government awarded a contract for the production of the Gloster Gladiator biplane.

In designing Type 224 as a monoplane construction, Mitchell was breaking away from the accepted standard of the time. The classic fighter throughout the world at the beginning of the 1930s was a biplane with either a radial or an inline engine, a fixed undercarriage, an open cockpit and two rifle-calibre machine guns. Its top speed was no more than 200 mph and its range was about 250 miles.

Even as late as 6 July 1935, when King George V received thirty-seven squadrons (consisting of 356 aircraft of the RAF) at Mildenhall and Duxford, every single aeroplane on view was a biplane. In squadron service, the fastest fighter was the Gloster Gauntlet, capable of just over 200 mph and armed, like its 1917–18 predecessors, merely with twin machine guns. Three squadrons were flying the Hawker Fury 1; the rest flew the adolescent Bristol Bulldog. The bomber units were all biplanes, none of which could reach 200 mph.

In the USA the Curtiss and Boeing fighters and in Britain the Bristol Bulldog and Hawker Fury all conformed to standard biplane design. However, various designers were testing monoplanes. The French were looking at parasol designs with the single wing above the fuselage on struts, while the Italians favoured the Warren truss, a system of V-shaped struts. Junkers, the German manufacturer, had produced monoplanes as far back as the First World War. But these were exceptions. The norm was still the biplane.

The British Government tried to persuade Vickers to switch the engine on Type 224 from the Goshawk to the Napier Dagger, but Vickers resisted.

Disillusioned with the Government, McLean became convinced that the specification laid down was not good enough. In a letter to *The Sunday Times* in August 1957 he wrote:

I felt that they [the design team] would do much better by devoting their qualities not to the official experimental fighter but to a real killer fighter. After unfruitful discussions with the Air Ministry, my opposite number in Rolls-Royce, the late A.F. Sidgreaves, and I decided that the two companies together should themselves finance the building of such an aircraft.

The Air Ministry was informed of this decision, and were told that in no circumstances would any technical member of the Air Ministry be consulted or allowed to interfere with the design.

Within a month, on 1 December 1934, the Air Ministry responded to this no-nonsense approach by issuing a contract for £10,000 (about £500,000 today) for the development of the new 'killer' fighter. Rolls-Royce also contributed £7,500. Mitchell now made several radical changes to the design of Type 224. After long discussions with his Canadian aerodynamicist, Beverley Shenstone, he abandoned the straight-winged design for the now famous elliptical configuration. The wing was also made as thin as possible, though near its root it had to be thick enough to take the retractable under-carriage. The cockpit was given a sliding canopy to reduce drag. Most importantly, the steam-cooled Goshawk engine was replaced by the new Rolls-Royce PV12 engine (see below).

Rolls-Royce were as aware as anyone of the need for new fighters with greater power. Virtually every British aircraft was a fabric-covered biplane with so many struts and wires that it was impossible to improve performance by more than a fraction. Cyril Lovesey suggested that the firm should buy the latest and most streamlined monoplane available, and the choice of the German Heinkel HE70 was made. A Kestrel engine was shipped to Rostock, and while it was waiting for the Heinkel to be modified to accommodate it, the Kestrel was used in the maiden flights of two of Germany's most important fighters of the Second World War: the Junkers JU 87 'Stuka' and the Messerschmitt Bf 109. Once in the Heinkel, it showed the potential of monoplanes over biplanes, reaching 260 mph with six people on board.

Sir Henry Royce knew it was vital that, with or without Government help, a new engine should be developed. One of his last decisions, in October 1932, was to authorise the development of a new engine, bigger than the Kestrel but smaller than the Buzzard, and incorporating as much 'R' technology as possible. It was called the PV12 (Private Venture 12-cylinder). This was a courageous decision, because the company's level of output of aero engines had been extremely low in the 1920s, and remained so into the early 1930s. In 1928 Rolls-Royce produced only sixty-seven aero engines out of a total UK output of 539, in 1929 its share was down to thirty-five out of 721, in 1930 it was 122 out of 726, and in both 1931 and 1932 it was still only 315 out of 637 and 738 respectively.

As Gordon Mitchell said in his book:

The decision to fit the Merlin engine [developed from the PV12] into Mitchell's Type 300 fighter was a vital turning point in the development of the Spitfire.

The Kestrel had proved to be a great success in the Hawker Fury, and the Merlin took the concept a stage further. As the following memo from Hives to Sidgreaves on 4 November 1936 makes clear, experience on the Kestrel was invaluable when it came to developing the Merlin.

The following are a few notes which we wish to discuss at the lunch on Friday.

MERLIN POSITION
The Merlin engine, except for the cylinders and valves, has now reached a stage when in spite of the extra power it has a degree of reliability greater than the Kestrel. . . .

At present we have a release for 100 Merlin Fs. Although at the present time we have started on the jigs and tools for the 'G' type cylinders, we must have release for the first Contract of 190 Merlin engines to all be the 'F' type. We cannot possibly deliver any engines with the 'G' type until next April. We are faced with the position in the factory that the Kestrel machine is running out, and we must start on the Merlin engines in order to keep our men together.

When the PV12 was initially built, the 'A' and 'B' Merlins had combined cylinder blocks and crankcases, and a Kestrel-type bathtub head. Single-cylinder testing with a ramphead showed some performance benefits, and the 'C' Merlin was effectively a 'B' Merlin with a ramphead. This engine flew in the prototype Hurricane and Spitfire. The 'C' Merlin also had a separate block, and therefore a two-piece block with a ramphead. The Merlin 'F' retained the two-piece block with ramphead, and went into production as the Merlin I, which was installed in the Fairey Battle.

The ramphead did not give the anticipated performance benefits, and also gave cracking problems. Rolls-Royce recognised that going back to a single, Kestrel-type block would at least be going back to the devil they knew. They reverted to it in the Merlin II, which went into Hurricanes and Spitfires. It was introduced on the Merlin 22, and was standard on all marks of the engine introduced thereafter.

This is what Arthur Rubbra – placed by many alongside Royce, Rowledge and Elliott as one of Rolls-Royce's greatest engineers – said of the early development of the Merlin:

In the early 1930s it became evident that a larger engine than the Kestrel would be required. It was called PV12 with a bore and stroke of 5.4 × 6in, initially giving around 750 hp. It was developed into the 1,000 hp Merlin. In order to provide a more rigid engine crankcase, to allow for higher crankshaft speeds, it was decided to cast the cylinder jacket portion of the cylinder block in one piece with the crankcase and to provide a separate cylinder head with the cylinder liner joint flange clamped between it and the crankcase. This presented quite a foundry problem in maintaining sectional thickness throughout, but this was solved in due course. It was soon discovered, however, on development that a major difficulty was presented because failures in the reciprocating components usually resulted in serious damage to the large crankcase-cum-cylinder jacket casting, this proving an expensive replacement and time-consuming job. Moreover, it was considered that once the separate jacket was bolted to the crankcase the final result, as regards the rigidity of the assembly, was very little different from the one-piece casting and the weight saving achieved by the latter was also small, so the principle of the one-piece crankcase and jacket was abandoned and never raised again. It was, however, used successfully on the V12 engine of the Phantom III motor car.

Elliott carried out a redesign, reverting from the original double helical reduction gear of the PV12 to detachable cylinder blocks and a spur reduction gear. His engine retained the 5.4 inch bore and 6 inch stroke with 1,650 cubic inch (27 litre) capacity. Elliott made a significant change in cylinder design, adopting (after single-cylinder tests) a ramp or semi-penthouse combustion chamber. He had designed this as a two-piece block to try to eliminate the internal coolant leaks to which the Kestrel was prone. The ramphead had shown great promise on single-cylinder tests, and was promoted by a brilliant young graduate, J.D. Pearson, who ultimately became Chairman of the company. But when it was used on the full engine it did not give the anticipated performance, and its asymmetric shape led to cracking in service use. At this point, Hives stepped in and made the decision to revert to a Kestrel-type one-piece block with a single-plane combustion chamber for immediate production, while sanctioning the design of a two-piece block which would eliminate the occasional coolant leakage problem and later facilitate significant power increases.

The initial design idea, as long ago as 1933, had been for an 'upside down' engine, because in this position the wide 'V' of the banks of cylinders would not hamper the pilot's vision, and the exhaust pipes would be below the fuselage, improving the cooling. And indeed, at the end of the First World War Royce had looked at the possibility of designing an inverted Eagle engine. However, both Rolls-Royce and the aircraft manufacturers Hawker and Supermarine quickly decided that the disadvantages of such a design outweighed the advantages, and the concept was abandoned.

According to Harold Nockolds, a mock-up of the 'upside down' engine was made, and was seen on the floor of Rowledge's office by a party of German aeronautical engineers on an official visit to Derby. Nockolds goes on to say:

The Germans evidently thought they had noticed something of supreme significance. There is every reason to believe that the design of the inverted Daimler-Benz engine used in the Messerschmitt 109 and the Junkers engine sprang from this visit to Derby. From their point of view, the inverted engine was desirable because it enabled them to fire the cannon through the airscrew shaft, but this had the serious result of forcing them to mount the supercharger on the side of the engine instead of at the end, a position which necessitated complex piping and which made it difficult to find a suitable place for carburettors. The Germans' later preference for direct fuel injection was attributable to the difficulty of carburettor layout, and not to any objection to carburettors as such.

As we shall see, direct fuel injection gave the Germans a distinct advantage in the dive in the initial stages of the war, until the British modified their carburettors. Whether this surmise by Nockolds is accurate we shall perhaps never know, but as his book was effectively an official history of the company, the Rolls-Royce directors clearly believed it to be the case.

By early 1936, the prototype Spitfire, with the serial number K5054, was ready for its first flight. Sir Robert McLean insisted on the name Spitfire, though others at Supermarine, including Mitchell, were not so keen. The earlier failure, Type 224, had also been called Spitfire. On 5 March, according to Mutt Summers's log book, but almost certainly on 6 March from the evidence of test pilot Jeffrey Quill's record, Mutt Summers took K5054, the Spitfire, on its first test flight.

The aeroplane (F37/34 Type 300) was still unnamed, and was referred to simply as 'the Fighter'. It was unpainted and still in its works finish, with protective treatment on its metal surfaces, and its engine cowlings in natural but unpolished duralumin finish. For the first flight, a special fine pitch wooden propeller was fitted, in order to give higher rpm for take-off and to minimise the effect of torque reaction. Jeffrey Quill, one of the great test pilots of this era, wrote in his book, *Spitfire, A Test Pilot's Story*:

There was a light wind blowing across the aerodrome which meant that Mutt had to take the short run and he taxied towards one of the four large Chance lights which (in those days) were situated round the perimeter, turned into wind and opened the throttle. The aeroplane was airborne after a very short run and climbed away comfortably. Mutt did not retract the under-carriage on that first flight – deliberately, of course – but cruised fairly gently around for some minutes, checked the lowering of the flaps and the slow flying and stalling characteristics, and then brought K5054 in to land. Although he had less room than he would probably have liked, he put the aeroplane down on three points without too much 'float', in which he was certainly aided by the fine pitch setting of the propeller. He taxied towards the hangar and the point where we in the group of Supermarine spectators were standing. This included R.J. Mitchell, Alan Clifton, Beverley Shenstone, Alf Faddy, Ernest Mansbridge, 'Agony' Payn, Stuart Scott-Hall and Ken Scales, the foreman in charge of the aeroplane. There must also have been quite a few other people there but there certainly was not a crowd. It was very much a Supermarine 'family affair'.

When Mutt shut down the engine and everybody crowded round the cockpit, with R.J. foremost, Mutt pulled off his helmet and said firmly, 'I don't want anything touched.' This was destined to become a widely misinterpreted remark. What he meant was that there were no snags which required correction or adjustment before he flew the aircraft again. The remark has crept into folklore implying that the aeroplane was perfect in every respect from the moment of its first flight, an obviously absurd and impracticable idea. After the 15-minute first flight the aircraft was still largely untested and unproven, having done one take-off and one landing. Mutt was far too experienced a hand to make any such sweeping statement at that stage in the game.

However, it was a highly successful and encouraging first flight and Mutt Summers, with his experience of flying a great variety of prototype aircraft, was a highly shrewd judge of an aeroplane. By now I knew him well enough to see that he was obviously elated. Certainly to those of us watching from the ground 'the Fighter' in the air took on a very thoroughbred and elegant appearance, a strong but indefinable characteristic which was to remain with it throughout its long, varied and brilliantly successful life as a fighting aeroplane. Later that afternoon I flew Mutt back to Brooklands in the Falcon and we put the aircraft away and walked across to have a drink in Bob Lambert's well-known and congenial Brooklands Flying Club bar. Mutt was pleased, obviously, to have one more successful first flight tucked under his belt [apart from professional pride, the test pilot who flew a maiden flight received a substantial bonus], and I felt excited about this long, sleek and elegant machine which I knew that soon I would fly. A hundred yards from where Mutt and I were leaning against the bar was the hangar in which was standing K5083, the prototype Hurricane, which had made its first flight in the hands of George Bulman some four months previously.

So the two new fighter aircraft – destined four years later to save our country in time of war – had now both flown in prototype form. Neither was yet anywhere near being a practical fighting machine nor was either yet ordered in quantity by the Royal Air Force, so much work still remained to be done. Ironically perhaps, the very next day, 7 March, Hitler's troops re-entered the demilitarised zone of the Rhineland in direct defiance of the Versailles Treaty.

This is what Harald Penrose, by the mid-1930s a very experienced test pilot, said of his first flight in the Spitfire:

In those days of easy-going biplanes, the highly polished blue-grey Supermarine low-winger was almost intimidating in its very advanced visual experience, and certainly the high wing loading suggested it might be a menace to fly – yet one approached the occasion as always with a sense of detachment, assessed the briefing given by the RAF pilots who had been testing her, and five minutes in the cockpit ensured familiarity with the instruments, the cramped little cabin, and the circumscribed view. The rest was a jumble of new impressions: the sense of tremendous power at a touch of throttle; the rolling gait of the narrow undercarriage as I taxied out; the dropping wing and emphatic swing as the over-coarse fixed-pitch wooden propeller laboriously dragged the fighter into a run faster and longer than any I had previously experienced. The far boundary was hurtling closer. Tentatively I sought to ease her into the air. For a few more seconds she remained earthbound; then the jolting ceased and we were airborne, the nose blotting out the view ahead. For a minute I held the controls quite still and climbed a long flat trajectory which swiftly achieved 2,000 ft. She was extremely sensitive, and that was emphasized when I groped for the hood and closed it. The undercarriage had to be raised by a hand-pump on my right so I changed hands on the stick, but the flight path oscillated with every stroke, for I could not stop my left from moving the control column in unison. That was very disconcerting, but the thuds of the undercarriage legs locking in turn into the wings were reassuring, and it was with relief that I saw their red warning light switch on. Already the Spitfire's formidable personality was becoming part of my consciousness. The thunder and din of its Merlin engine ceased to be recognized as noise and became a subconsciously accepted indication that all was well with the engine. So swiftly were we climbing that I was surprised to find the altimeter already showed 5,000 ft. I levelled off and felt the controls grow firmer with increasing speed; tried a gentle turn, and then steeper. Nothing in it! Relaxed, I looked through the Perspex hood at the broad fields and far vista set like a background stage-drop for a solitary actor.

Suddenly a Gladiator appeared 1,000 ft. above me, offering opportunity of a mock dog-fight with this latest contemporary biplane fighter of the RAF. I drew the stick back in manner long accustomed, unprepared for the lightness of response. A vice clamped my temples, face and muscles sagged, and all was blackness. My pull on the stick relaxed instantly yet returning vision found the Spitfire poised almost vertically and the Gladiator 2,000 ft. below. Ah! If the fighter boys could cope with a machine like this it was going to be an ace, though the undercarriage hand-pumping must be abolished and less sensitive elevators were needed to match the ailerons.

But this flight by Penrose was made after the aircraft had been fully tested. Between Summers's initial flight and 'the Fighter' being sent to Martlesham Heath in Suffolk for its official trials, Jeffrey Quill and George Pickering carried out further test flights and they found that, although 'the Fighter' was a pleasure to fly and its performance seemed exciting, its first measured trials on 27 March showed a rather disappointing maximum true speed of 335 mph at less than 17,000 feet.

Mitchell was aiming at 350 mph, and would not allow the aircraft to go to Martlesham. Rumour had it that the Hurricane, already at Martlesham, was achieving speeds of 325 mph. The Hurricane was designed for ease of production, and if the Spitfire (which would clearly not be as easy to produce) was going to win Air Ministry approval, its performance would have to be significantly better than that of the Hurricane.

Marginal improvements were made, before attention turned to the propeller. It was realised that at the true speed 'the Fighter' was achieving at 18,000 feet, the helical speed of the propeller tips was penetrating well into the compressibility region. A new propeller was designed with modified tip sections, which brought another 13 mph. At 348 mph, Mitchell was prepared to allow his aircraft to go to Martlesham.

On 26 May 1936, Humphrey (later Air Marshal Sir Humphrey) Edwardes Jones tested the Spitfire at Martlesham Heath on behalf of the Air Ministry. On the strength of his report to Sir Wilfrid Freeman, and figures supplied by Supermarine, the Air Ministry placed an order for 310 Spitfires on 3 June. (A contract for 600 Hurricanes from Hawker was signed on the same day.)

Unfortunately, the production of the 310 Spitfires was to prove enormously difficult for Supermarine. Mitchell's Spitfire was revolutionary, and almost every feature called for new and complex manufacturing techniques. The fuselage was to be made in three sections: a tubular case for the engine, a monocoque centre and a detachable aft.

The spars on which the wings were built were made up of tubes that fitted one inside the other. Each tube was different in length so that the spar was thickest where most strength was needed, at the root of the wing, and hollow at the tip. The leading edge of the wing was covered with heavy gauge metal that gave the wing immense strength, while aft of the spar it was clad in aluminium sheeting of a lesser gauge. This gave an ideal combination of lightness and strength.

'ANOTHER WINNER, I THINK'

Alongside the Spitfire in the Battle of Britain was the Hawker Hurricane. Indeed, there were more Hurricanes than Spitfires in Fighter Command at that time. The Spitfire, generally accepted as a more effective fighter, has tended to win more of the accolades but, as Jeffrey Quill pointed out in his book, *Spitfire, A Test Pilot's Story*, the Spitfire was not favoured by the Air Ministry until it had proved itself in battle.

The Sopwith Atlantic was purpose-built in response to
Lord Northcliffe's £10,000 prize for the first non-stop flight
across the Atlantic Ocean. Piloted by Harry Hawker and
Mackenzie-Grieve, it was the first aircraft to leave
Newfoundland, where all of the contestants had
assembled. The aircraft ditched in the sea and the crew
were rescued by the tramp-steamer *Mary*.

The Martinsyde Raymor was also purpose-built. Sadly,
Raynham and Morgan crashed on take-off, due to the failure of
the undercarriage under the weight of the heavy fuel-load
necessary for the crossing. After their mishap, Raynham and
Morgan gallantly donated their field at St. Johns to Alcock and
Brown, whose airfield was not large enough for take-off with a
full transatlantic fuel-load.

The Handley Page Atlantic was based on the V/1500 bomber. Under the control of Admiral Mark Kerr, the aircraft was being prepared sixty miles up the coast from the other contestants. Having suffered radiator problems, the aircraft was not ready to attempt a crossing when Alcock and Brown took off. Once Kerr learnt of Alcock and Brown's success, he decided on a goodwill mission to New York State, in the process of which the aircraft carried the first airmail from Canada to the United States.

Reginald Mitchell, designer of the Supermarine S6, and Henry Royce, who provided its 'R' engine, at Calshot in 1929. Neither Royce nor Mitchell lived to see how vital their last designs were to become to their country – the Merlin engine and the Spitfire fighter.

Recognising the essential strengths of Mitchell's design, Smith [successor to Mitchell at Supermarine] set about the task of expanding its capabilities and performance to the maximum. He recognised and exploited the whole area of advancing technologies within the industry, more especially the potential power growth of the Merlin and Griffon engines, and the advances in aircraft ancillary equipment. 'If Mitchell was born to design the Spitfire,' wrote J.D. Scott, 'Joe Smith was born to defend and develop it.' The verb 'to defend' perhaps needs some explanation. Although much liked by pilots from the outset the Spitfire never found much real favour with the Air Council until it had decisively proved its mettle in battle over Dunkirk. Originally many technical people were suspicious of it, many production advisers in the Air Ministry did not care for it, and the Air Council were outraged during the latter part of 1937 and during 1938 by the delays in production.

On 7 June 1939 a memorandum was sent to the Chief of the Air Staff by the Air Member for Development and Production (AMDP), Sir Wilfrid Freeman, in which he referred to 'orders to be placed now with certain firms whose existing orders will run out early in 1940'. On the subject of Supermarine he wrote: 'Supermarine will run out of their order for Spitfires in February or March 1940 and since it will be impossible to get a new aircraft into production at Supermarine before September 1940 there is certain to be a six-month gap which we will have to fill.

'In order to be able to bridge the gap with as few machines as possible, Supermarine will be told later on to reduce the amount of sub-contracting and get their men onto single shift, so that although Supermarine production is likely towards the end of the present contract to exceed 48 aircraft per month it is hoped that we can reduce the gap production to 30 aircraft a month.'

He went on: 'Vickers are pressing for a more generous release of Spitfires for foreign orders, and it seems to me that provided no releases are made until October, we could go some way to meet them this year and could release aircraft for foreign orders freely after the spring of next year, when the Castle Bromwich factory will be coming into production.' Later in the same memorandum he wrote: 'The type of aircraft that could be put into production at Supermarine after the end of their contract would be Beau-fighter, Gloster Fighter, Lysander or Westland (F. 37/35).'

Clearly, the Air Ministry felt that the initial order for 310 Spitfires might be the total ever made. As we know now, the eventual total was about 23,000.

Part of the reason why many in the Air Ministry and the RAF saw little need for the Spitfire if the Hurricane was going to be much easier to produce, stemmed from the view that the main purpose of such fighters would be to attack bombers. They thought that fighter-to-fighter combat was a relic of the First World War, when aircraft were much slower and could hold each other in their sights long enough for a two-second burst of fire. They viewed both the Spitfire and the Hurricane as bomber destroyers, and the Boulton Paul Defiant was thought of in the same way. As it turned out, the battle over

France and the Battle of Britain showed that all three could cope with bombers, but only the Spitfire and Hurricane could mix it with German fighters. Ultimately, only the Spitfire was a true match for the best of the Luftwaffe.

The Hurricane, on the other hand, was relatively straightforward to produce, and on those grounds alone it was looked on with favour by the Air Ministry. It also had some advantages over the Spitfire. For example, it was a more stable gun platform. Its gunfire converged more effectively since it flew absolutely straight, whereas the Spitfire tended to snake around. It was easier to take off the ground and to land, and it could absorb enormous punishment.

We have already seen how Harry Hawker (with Mackenzie-Grieve) almost made the first transatlantic crossing, and his name lived on through the Hawker Hurricane. Son of a Cornish blacksmith and a Scottish mother, Hawker ran away from school in Australia at the age of twelve and made his way to England. Hooked on the new craze of flying, he hung around Brooklands, where he was eventually hired on a hunch by Tommy Sopwith. By 1912 Hawker had gained his pilot's certificate, and within a year held the British air records for speed, altitude and endurance. Soon he was Sopwith's test pilot, and was contributing ideas as aircraft design developed. In 1919 Hawker achieved popular fame with his attempted transatlantic crossing, but within a year he was out of a job, as Sopwith was forced to put his company into liquidation through lack of orders. Hawker then set up the H.G. Hawker Engineering Company, where he was joined by Sopwith and Sopwith's chauffeur, Fred Sidgrist, as investors.

Within a year, Hawker was killed while testing his Nieuport Goshawk entry at Hendon, four days before the 1921 aerial Derby. But the company survived and in 1923 Sydney (later Sir Sydney) Camm joined as senior draughtsman. Though Camm lacked academic qualifications, Sopwith soon realised that his practical experience gained at Martinsydes between 1912 and 1921 was of great value, and he appointed him chief designer in 1925. It was a brilliant decision. From Camm's drawing board came all of the Hart variants – the Fury, Super Fury, Osprey, Audax and (for South Africa) the Hartebeeste – followed by the Hurricane, Typhoon and Tempest, and the Centaurus-powered Fury and Sea Fury. When the jet age arrived, there came the Sea Hawk, Hunter, Harrier and Hawk.

By the end of the 1920s, Camm was realising that the biplane was reaching the maximum of its fighter potential, and that its performance could not be much improved. (In the air exercises of 1930, no fighter managed to catch his own light bomber, the Hart – powered, of course, by a Rolls-Royce Kestrel.) In the early 1930s, as Reg Mitchell was working on his monoplane ideas at Supermarine, Camm began to work on his idea of a Fury monoplane.

The Air Ministry, still remembering the disintegration of two monoplanes in 1912, was still largely against the type, but Germany's withdrawal from the Disarmament Conference and the League of Nations concentrated at least some minds on the need for faster fighters.

Nevertheless, no Government funding was initially forthcoming, and just as Rolls-Royce were to develop their PV (Private Venture) 12, the Merlin, Hawker were forced to fund development of the monoplane Fury. The Merlin replaced the Goshawk in Camm's design, which necessitated changes, but the steel tubular structure, fabric covering and overall strength which had been a feature of Camm's designs, all remained. New features included a 'greenhouse' built around the pilot because of the anticipated faster speed. Leading and trailing edges of the wings were slightly tapered, and a large radiator was situated under their centre.

The undercarriage was still fixed as in the Fury biplane, and the armament was restricted to four machine guns. Camm moved the radiator eighteen inches aft because the Merlin was heavier than the Goshawk, and this made room for a retractable undercarriage. After discussions with a young squadron leader in the Operational Requirements Branch of the Air Ministry, Ralph Sorley (later Air Marshal Sir Ralph Sorley KCB OBE DSO DFC), who was convinced that monoplane fighters would fly at speeds enabling pilots to hold the target in their sights for no more than two seconds, Camm designed eight guns into his wings.

As the 1930s wore on, the Air Ministry persisted in the view that Bomber Command should have priority over Fighter Command. Prime Minister Baldwin, persuaded by Air Marshals who had fought in the First World War, told the House of Commons in 1932:

I think it is well also for the man in the street to realise that there is no power on earth that can protect him from being bombed. Whatever people may tell him, the bomber will always get through.

In the teeth of all this opposition, Camm presented his mock-up to Air Ministry visitors on 10 January 1935, and on 21 February he sent provisional performance figures to the RAF. The Air Marshals were surprised. The specification called for 275 mph at 15,000 feet. Camm promised 330 mph. When the aircraft returned from its maiden flight and Camm clambered onto the wing, P.W.S. 'George' Bulman, chief test pilot at Hawker Aircraft Limited, said: 'Another winner, I think.' Bulman flew the first prototype, K5083, of what was still known as the 'Interceptor Monoplane' from Brooklands on 6 November 1935. This was the first flight of the Rolls-Royce Merlin engine. Indeed, this Merlin 'C', with its 1,029 bhp and weight of only 1,180 lbs, was essential to achieve such a performance. No two-speed, variable pitch propeller had yet been built for such power, so a conventional Watts-designed, two-blade wooden propeller was fitted.

In February 1936, the prototype was delivered for initial service evaluation to the Aircraft and Armament Experimental Establishment at Martlesham Heath, where it was given high marks for reliability. On 3 June, a contract for the production of 600 was received from the Air Ministry. (The company directors had already approved tooling for 1,000.) On 27 June, the aircraft received a new official name, the Hurricane.

As production proceeded apace and the Hurricane proved much more amenable to volume production than the Spitfire, improvements were made constantly as the aircraft were flown and tested. One of the most significant developments was the replacement of the old fixed pitch, two-bladed wooden propeller, which had a tendency to fly into pieces under stress, by a metal, three-bladed, two pitch propeller made by de Havilland. This enabled the pilot to alter the pitch (or angle) of the blades so that he could use fine (low) pitch for take-off and coarse (high) pitch for greater speeds. This brought greater fuel economy and a better rate of climb.

Meanwhile, Rolls-Royce were experiencing the inevitable difficulties in building up production of a consistently reliable Merlin, as is made clear by Harald Penrose in his book, *British Aviation – The Ominous Skies 1935–39*:

Martlesham reported on the remarkable ease of handling and good control at all speeds down to stall. A top speed of 315 mph at 16,000 feet was established, thus handsomely beating the Air Staff's requirement of 275 mph. 'The only thing which marred the otherwise very satisfactory trials was continued unreliability of the engine,' said Lucas [the test pilot]. 'There were at least three engine changes during the first two weeks due to a variety of defects, the most serious being internal glycol leaks causing rapid loss of coolant, coupled with distortion and ultimate cracking of cylinder heads because of much higher operating temperatures possible with this type of coolant. Soon it was apparent that the engine required a great deal more development before it became sufficiently reliable for Service operation. All this delayed Martlesham tests and the machine's return to Brooklands for development flying and performance measurements. Meanwhile Rolls-Royce decided that the troubles could only be overcome by intensive flight development with re-designed cylinder heads. We learned that Merlin I engines would not be available for production Hurricanes and that the modified Merlin II would not be ready until autumn of 1937, some three months after the first production Hurricane was due off the line. Worse still, we were told that only a bare minimum of engines would be available to keep the prototype flying.'

Major Bulman at the Air Ministry was all too aware of the teething problems in the production of the Merlin.

Initial Merlin production started well after several type tests were run, but after about 100 engines had been made an epidemic of cracks in the walls of the aluminium combined crankcase and cylinder blocks developed. Hives and ourselves had a desperate investigation into the casting procedure but after an agony of indecision for a few days we decided literally to cut the Gordian knot by splitting the one piece casting into three – crankcase and two cylinder blocks! Frantic tests of the new construction were hurried through, and the trouble disappeared. Production with the drastically modified construction restarted, and thanks to the inevitable setbacks in the output of the first Battles, Hurricanes and Spitfires, Rolls were able to regain their substantial lead in Merlin deliveries to meet the aircraft output. But it was a harassing few months, peace mercifully still prevailing!

As with all military aircraft on both sides, the practicalities of how they performed in combat led to constant changes and improvements. On the Hurricane, increased armour to guard the pilot, additional protection for the engine and linatex covers to make the fuel tanks self-sealing were all welcome, but the real drive was to extract greater performance from the engine and greater power for the guns. Although the Hurricane, constructed of wood and fabric stiffened by a metal-tube framework, was a more traditional aircraft than the Spitfire, it proved more resistant to exploding cannon shells than its more glamorous fellow fighter.

The Hawker engine design staff considered alternatives to the Merlin engine, but soon realised that a more powerful version of the Merlin itself would be the ideal solution, since it would mean the least modification to the airframe. It was also the most reliable of the engines on offer, and there was a strong moral obligation for Hawker to use the Merlin, since Rolls-Royce had contributed to the cost of the prototype, K5083. By June 1940, after the retreat from Dunkirk but before the Battle of Britain, Hawker had already produced Hurricanes with Merlin IIs and Merlin IIIs. On 11 June, the famous Hawker test-pilot, Philip Lucas, flew an eight-gun Hurricane 1 fitted with a Merlin XX, the engine developed with Stanley Hooker's super-charger. It gave the Hurricane a top speed of 348 mph. Furthermore, the extra power allowed the aircraft to carry four cannons without significant loss of performance.

Although it was the Spitfire and Hurricane that achieved the greatest success and glory in the Second World War, and for which the Merlin was developed and improved out of all recognition from its earliest configur-ation, the first production order for 200 Merlins was from the Fairey Company for its bomber, the Fairey Battle. The Merlin I was put into production for this aircraft, a single-engined bomber which would carry 1,000 lbs of bombs for 1,000 miles at 200 mph. The engines were rated at 1,020 bhp, an output at the time ahead of any other engine in the world.

THE OTHER ESSENTIALS

The Spitfires and Hurricanes fought the Luftwaffe in the sky but, as we shall see, at the beginning of the Battle of Britain they were outnumbered by three to one. Helping them overcome these odds was their commanders' use of Radar (Radio Detection And Ranging). The British began their experiments with radar in 1935, and although the Germans were ahead by a year, in the practical use of this new science the British excelled themselves. In close co-operation with Dowding, the civil servant Henry (later Sir Henry) Tizard created the radar network that made it possible to anticipate – and therefore have time to get into the position to defeat – the bomber attacks of the Luftwaffe in 1940.

A committee had been set up by the British Government in 1934, under Tizard, to consider possible means of defence against the bomber. Robert (later Sir Robert) Watson-Watt, a slightly overweight scientist at the National Physical Laboratory, was asked to investigate the possibility of a 'death ray'. Watson-Watt and his assistant, Arnold 'Skip' Wilkins, dismissed this idea, since no aircraft would linger in the most intense beam of radio energy that the scientists could produce for long enough to knock out its engine. However, they suggested three areas worthy of investigation: the re-direction of radio-waves to detect aircraft; radio-telephone communication between a ground controller and defending fighters to direct them to the aircraft located; and a coded signal from friendly aircraft to distinguish them from enemy aircraft.

Watson-Watt later received the credit for the development of radar to a usable state, but it was his assistant Wilkins who had recalled how Post Office engineers complained that radio reception was disturbed when aircraft flew close to their receivers. He thought: 'Might not an aircraft's electro-magnetic energy be visually depicted by use of the cathode-ray apparatus?'

This information was considered by the Tizard Committee when it met at the end of January 1935, and on 26 February the first practical test took place. A van containing suitable radio receivers stationed itself in a field about ten miles from the short-wave transmitters of the Daventry broadcasting stations. A pilot flew over a course near the radio station, and the van's instruments detected the aircraft. Such a simple but successful experiment prompted Tizard and Dowding to support Watson-Watt, who took a team to Bawdsey Manor on the Suffolk coast to develop the system further.

By the late 1930s, other nations (including Germany, France, Holland and the USA) had reached a similar state of development, but Germany, antici-pating a short war and rapid peace negotiations with Britain, did not see the necessity for its use in defence, and also failed to appreciate its usefulness in Britain's protection of itself. When the war came, the Luftwaffe never attacked the radar stations in a concerted way. Neither France nor the USA seemed to appreciate radar's military usefulness.

Two factors were essential for the successful use of the early warning system. One was the speed with which the radar information was transmitted, and the other was the continued observation of an enemy aircraft's track and the ability to transmit this information to fighter groups. Major Adolf 'Dolfo' Galland, one of the Luftwaffe's fighter aces, was to say later:

In battle we had to rely on our own eyes. The British fighter pilots could depend on the radar eye, which was far more reliable and had a longer range. When we made contact with the enemy our briefings were already three hours old, the British only as many seconds old – the time it took to assess the latest position by means of radar to the transmission of orders to the force in the air.

'Stuffy' Dowding said:

Where would we have been without RDF [radar] and all that went with it? We could never have maintained the vast number of standing patrols that would have been necessary if we had not had that magic sight.

The other development that was to prove of critical importance in the coming conflict was the variable pitch propeller. On the fighters and bombers of the First World War, the propeller (or airscrew as it was often called in those days) was carved from wood and had a fixed pitch. Even at that stage it was appreciated that a propeller whose pitch could be varied for differing engine speeds would give greater performance. In the second half of 1917, a four-bladed propeller with variable pitch was made and tested at the Royal Aircraft Factory, and in 1918 a two-bladed version was fitted to an SE5. At this time, the variation in pitch was achieved manually by the pilot, but this was clearly not satisfactory and in the mid-1920s Dr. H.S. Hele-Shaw and T.E. Beacham patented a hydraulic device. At the same time, some urgency was given to the development of variable pitch propellers by the increased power generated by supercharged engines. In 1925, tenders for an all-metal variable pitch propeller were invited by the Air Ministry, and in August of that year tests were carried out at RAE Farnborough. Following these tests, a contract for twelve propellers was given to the Gloster Aircraft Company. Two propellers were developed and flown in 1928, one with hollow steel blades fitted to a Rolls-Royce Kestrel engine, and the other with solid duralumin blades to a Bristol Jupiter engine. The pitch range was about twelve degrees.

Hollow blades proved unsatisfactory and, under licence from the Gloster company, Rolls-Royce and Bristol sought to find an alternative. In the meantime, in the USA, the Hamilton Hydraulic Airscrew Company applied for a patent for a two-position propeller in May 1929. By 1934, the Hamilton propeller was in production, and de Havilland acquired a licence from Hamilton.

By 1939, nine out of every ten Mercury and Pegasus engines manufactured by the Bristol Aircraft Company were fitted with de Havilland propellers which were made under licence from Hamilton. At the same time, the German propeller manufacturers had also mastered the design and production of variable pitch propellers.

Roy Fedden, chief engineer of the engine department of the Bristol Aircraft Company (BAC), had become convinced of the need for variable pitch propellers if the new fighters were to achieve their full potential, and he was dismayed by the slowness of development. After trying unsuccessfully to persuade his Bristol board, he was instrumental in persuading de Havilland to take the Hamilton licence. But he was not satisfied with having a competitor as the only producer, and so he went to the Air Ministry. Air Marshal Dowding asked him to produce two propellers to the Hele-Shaw/Beacham design.

Dowding also asked Rolls-Royce to produce some prototypes, and they approached the construction in a different way. While Bristol used a cylinder with radial pins sliding inside the forged steel hub, the Rolls-Royce design used a fixed inner piston carrying an external sliding cylinder which drove the blades by push-pull rods.

But Fedden did not want two versions of the Hele-Shaw to compete with the Hamilton and, in a commercially unconventional and patriotic gesture, he approached his major competitor, Rolls-Royce, inviting Managing Director Arthur Sidgreaves and Ernest Hives to lunch at the Royal Thames Yacht Club. The three reached agreement that a joint venture was necessary and would be successful. At this point, the idea received the blessing of the BAC board and the Air Ministry. On 13 May 1937, Rotol Airscrews Limited was formed. (The name comes from 'RO' of Rolls-Royce and 'TOL' of Bristol, and was apparently the idea of the wife of Bill Stammers, the first general manager.) The prospectus of the new company, based in Gloucester with a nominal capital of £250,000 (perhaps £12.5 million in today's terms), stated:

Although the main production of Rotol Airscrews Ltd. will be of the hydraulically operated type, the electrically operated airscrew will also be made and is a development of the well-known Curtiss-Wright airscrew of the USA, particularly suitable for heavy multi-engined machines as it can be 'feathered'. Initially all propellers will have magnesium blades, but the company will conduct developments with blades of wood and other materials.

The first Rotol propeller was made in the Derby Experimental Department and tested on a Merlin in the original hangar on Sinfin Moor, now the site of Rolls-Royce's main offices. If the variable pitch propeller was a key factor, many have claimed that the Battle of Britain would have been lost but for the use of 100 octane fuel in the Merlins. Indeed, no less a figure than Air Chief Marshal Lord Tedder listed the fuel as one of the three deciding factors in the battle.

By 1937, the British Air Ministry, convinced that 100 octane fuel (developed and tested by the US Army Air Force) could boost the power of aero engines, began importing small quantities and sending them to Rolls-Royce for testing in the Merlin, to Bristol for testing in the Pegasus and to RAE Farnborough for testing in single-cylinder test engines. The Air Ministry was probably influenced by a paper given by Rod Banks (at that time employed by the Ethyl Corporation) to the Royal Aeronautical Society and the Institute of Petroleum on 8 January 1937, in which he said that the RAF should be supplied with engines that could use 100 octane fuel 'even if the supply of such fuel were limited, because the use of high-duty equipment might prove decisive in the early stages of a war'. The Ethyl Corporation carried out continuous research into the effectiveness of various fuels, and Rod Banks made sure that any developments were passed on to the British engine manufacturers.

The first full cargo of 'BAM100' (British Air Ministry 100 octane fuel) was shipped in June 1939 from the Esso refinery in Aruba. The Air Ministry began to stockpile subsequent shipments, while in the meantime the RAF continued to use its standard 87 octane. Most shipments came from Esso and Shell refineries in the USA, but fortunately some came from Aruba and Curacao for, when war was declared on 3 September 1939, the US Congress invoked the Neutrality Act prohibiting the export of strategic materials to belligerent nations.

In the first half of 1940, the RAF transferred all Hurricane and Spitfire squadrons to 100 octane fuel. The effect was described by Bill Gunston in *Rolls-Royce, Aero Engines*:

Instead of being limited to a maximum of 6 lb/sq in boost, pilots could 'go through the gate' to full throttle and 12 lb boost, thus increasing the power of the Merlin II or III from approximately 1,000 hp to 1,310. This 30% power increase made a significant improvement to take-off, rate of climb and maximum speed up to about 9,000 ft, above which boost had to fall away. The new fuel really came into its own on the central-entry blower Merlin XX and 45, which could maintain 12 lb up to fighting altitudes around 20,000 ft. Even so, the difference 100-octane made to the Battle of Britain Merlins was very important, in a closely fought campaign.

The importance of 100/130 fuel was underlined by other factors. The Luftwaffe's standard single-seat fighter, the Bf 109E, was much lighter than either the Hurricane or Spitfire, and it was powered by an engine of 25% greater capacity (2069 cu in compared with the Merlin's 1,649). As there was not much difference in weight between the two engines, it was imperative for Rolls-Royce to develop the Merlin both to tolerate higher manifold pressure for more power at low altitudes and, especially, superior supercharging for greater power at high altitudes. It is a truly amazing fact that Rolls-Royce succeeded on both counts, and kept the Merlin consistently ahead of the larger DB 601 and later DB 605 right to the end of the war. Another factor emphasising the need for 100/130 fuel was that, until the start of the Battle of Britain, large numbers of Hurricanes and Spitfires still had the Merlin II driving crude two-blade wooden fixed-pitch propellers, whereas every Bf 109E had the constant-speed VDM [electrically-actuated propeller pitch control].

THE IMPORTANCE OF HUCKNALL

And if 100 octane fuel and variable pitch propellers were vital elements in perfecting the performance of Britain's fighter aircraft, Rolls-Royce's development of their design testing facilities at Hucknall also made a crucial contribution.

The Rolls-Royce aero engine had been a logical progression from the Silver Ghost car, but whereas the company manufactured chassis and, ultimately, complete cars, it never became an aircraft manufacturer. Others, such as Armstrong Siddeley, Bristol and de Havilland, made both aircraft and aero engines.

There was a big advantage to Rolls-Royce's approach – it could sell to all aircraft manufacturers without worrying that priority be given to its own aircraft. There was also a big disadvantage – there were problems in installing the engines, so that the aircraft customers often had to be shown how to do it. This disadvantage became very apparent with the Eagle and the Falcon, on which the aircraft manufacturers made a poor job of the 'plumbing' (the radiator, piping and so on).

Rolls-Royce came to realise that they had to do more than supply an engine, a handbook and a starting handle. Cyril Lovesey, a private pilot with his own aeroplane, saw the need very clearly. Early attempts to establish a testing operation were hampered by the need to put all resources into developing the 'R' engine for the Schneider Trophy. There was also talk of a national plan to develop a 'centre for speed' somewhere in East Anglia. However, the plan died in the cold blast of the Depression. Nevertheless, some testing was carried out on behalf of Rolls-Royce by the Nottingham Flying Club in the early 1930s.

By the mid-1930s it was clear that the company would have to establish its own facilities. Lovesey took the lead and set up an operation at Hucknall in Nottinghamshire, alongside the RAF. Initially, there was just a hangar to maintain the aircraft, an engineering team (especially skilled on fabrications) and ground test facilities. Lovesey brought the young engineer Ray Dorey over from Derby, and put him in charge of the staff of twenty-five.

Captain Ronnie Shepherd, who had already carried out some testing for the company at the Nottingham Flying Club, was appointed chief test pilot. Their first complement of aircraft in one hangar consisted of a Hawker Hart, a Hawker Fury and a Gloster Gnatsnapper. It was at Hucknall on 12 April 1935 that the PV12 engine flew for the first time, in a Hawker Hart biplane. Most of its first sixty hours in the air were spent on perfecting the cooling system.

Hucknall expanded rapidly during the war, undertaking a great deal of installation work as well as a greatly increased test-flying programme. For example, the Merlin powerplant for the Lancaster bomber was designed and built at Hucknall, as were the prototype installations for the Griffon, Beaufighter and Henley. During the Battle of Britain, a Hurricane repair line was set up.

Ray Dorey organised the Hucknall operation so efficiently that its repair of Hurricane fighters contributed vitally to the number of aircraft capable of flying in the desperate months of August and September 1940. And it was at Hucknall that the Merlin 65 was installed in a Mustang and flown within three months. (North American Aviation, who were also carrying out the conversion, took much longer to complete the operation.) At the same time, in 1942, Hucknall contributed to converting Spitfire Vs to Spitfire IXs, to counter the German Fw 190.

Also stationed at Hucknall was Rolls-Royce's RAF liaison team, which flew regularly to the RAF stations on which Rolls-Royce engines operated, and whose job it was to maintain close contact with the RAF and report to Hives, who listened to them very carefully. Many of the liaison team were Rolls-Royce employees who had flown in the RAFVR or RAuxAF before the war. Some had flown in the Battle of Britain. Alec Harvey-Bailey had reason to be grateful to the liaison team. As he said in *The Merlin in Perspective – the combat years*, written for the Rolls-Royce Heritage Trust:

The Liaison Pilots were helpful in our failure investigation work, particularly when we were in real difficulty, maintaining a two way traffic of communication separate from formal channels. As an example, at the height of the Halifax reduction gear problems Ronnie Harker was able to fly me to 4 Group headquarters at York and to visit some of the worst affected stations including Elvington, Breighton, Rufforth and Holme-on-Spalding Moor in the course of one Saturday. This enabled me to brief the Senior Air Staff Officer, the Group Engineering Officer, station officers and squadron pilots. Aided by Ronnie I was able to put over the problems and the action being taken, and re-establish confidence which had been on the wane. It also enabled us to get Group to press from its end for four bladed propellers which were a quick alleviation to the problem.

THE SHADOW FACTORIES

The developments in radar, variable pitch propellers, 100 octane fuel and Rolls-Royce's development work at Hucknall would all have gone to waste if the Merlin engine and the aircraft in which it was installed had not been produced in vast numbers. It became clear that such numbers of engines and aircraft were not going to be manufactured in time in the existing factories. In March 1934, the Government realised that the Disarmament Conference convened by the League of Nations was a sham (both Germany and Japan had given notice of their intention to quit the League of Nations), and Prime Minister Baldwin announced that Britain was to have parity with the German Air Force. A modest expansion of the RAF was ordered, and most airframe and aero engine manufacturers were able to cope. However, as further expansion schemes were put in place in 1935 and 1936, it became clear that existing facilities would not suffice and that 'shadow factories' would be necessary. The Air Ministry had realised as early as 1929 that expansion would probably necessitate the use of non-aircraft firms, and looked to the motor industry, with its experience of large-scale production, to help solve the problems. The Government financed the building of factories for both Austin and Rootes, to be used for aircraft production.

Hives was happy to co-operate with the Government over shadow factories, but wanted them to realise what was involved. While the shadow factories were being planned and built, the Derby factory was also expanded. Indeed, the Rolls-Royce board showed some reluctance to become involved with other factories, feeling that, suitably expanded, the Derby factory could cope with the increase in demand. Between 1935 and 1939, factory space at the Derby works increased from 803,520 square feet to 1,120,000 square feet.

It was not just a question of reproducing the Derby factory elsewhere. Hives wrote:

The Rolls-Royce factory at Derby had been built and developed around the problem of producing high-class engineering in relatively small quantities with the capacity to change or modify the product quickly. In other words, I should describe the Derby factory as a huge development factory rather than a manufacturing plant. The very structure of the organisation necessitates a large proportion of skilled men who fortunately are available.

As a super aircraft engine development factory there is nothing like it in the world, and therefore in planning for the very big production we want to make sure that Derby is used to the very best advantage. In any big scheme we consider that Derby should be expected to carry all the development work; it should also carry the prototype production over the first two or three hundred engines until all the engineering 'bugs' in the new type of engine have been cleared. It would also have to be responsible for all the inevitable jobs which it is impossible to avoid such as odd spares, changeovers and modifications. This class of work can be done at Derby but upsets the whole scheme of things in a true manufacturing plant.

The production at Crewe has been planned on very different lines to Derby. We are making use of very much more unskilled and semi-skilled labour. There is no doubt we could go further, but we do not wish to have any trouble with labour. Crewe cannot absorb modifications and alterations like the Derby plant. It would be very much more expensive in both tools and delays.

There is no mystery or fundamental difficulty in producing Rolls-Royce engines with unskilled labour. It means a longer time in planning the production, more expense on jigs, tools and fixtures, the co-operation of the machine tool makers, freedom from alterations, and a longer time before production can commence. We could never hope to obtain sufficient skilled men at Crewe if we were using the same ratio as we are at Derby.

It must be appreciated that the Crewe factory was planned to make more use of sub-contractors than we do at Derby. For instance, it has no pattern shop or foundry and no drop forge; it does not produce crankshafts, camshafts, cylinder liners, pistons or gears. We were able to sub-contract these parts successfully to look after the first portion of Crewe but now we have started on the second portion we find that we shall have to produce in that unit a number of parts which were not originally planned for because we have failed to get the necessary numbers from sub-contractors.

If it is decided to go ahead with another factory we recommend that it be located in Scotland, preferably near Glasgow. We have had one of our men up there who had located a suitable site . . . The chief advantage in going to Glasgow is that labour should be available. It should also be available for whatever size it is decided to make the factory. We have definitely decided against recommending any further extensions at Crewe because there is insufficient labour to draw upon, and, so far, insufficient houses . . .

Another advantage of Glasgow is that we are now planning to obtain supplies of steel and forgings from Scottish firms and we feel confident that they will prove satisfactory.

Nevertheless, Hives, convinced since the early 1930s that war with Germany was inevitable, had been a strong advocate of shadow factories, and had written to Lieutenant-Colonel H.A.P. Disney of the Directorate of Aeronautical Production at the Air Ministry on 9 October 1937:

I notice that you have already received a note from Sidgreaves saying that Rolls-Royce are in agreement with the Shadow Scheme. Actually I go further, and I am

193

going to pester you until the shadowing of Rolls-Royce engines is an accomplished fact. I want to assure you that whenever the decision is taken I shall make it my personal job to see that you have our 100 per cent co-operation, and that we go out of our way to make it a success.

The company was to experience long and frustrating delays in bringing its Crewe and Glasgow work forces up to the level of skill required. Moving skilled personnel from Derby also proved difficult, not least in the provision of adequate housing.

Nevertheless, operating in the factory at Glasgow built and run by the Government, Rolls-Royce benefited from lessons learnt in starting up the factory at Crewe. Construction began in June 1939 and the first building was occupied in October, one month after the outbreak of war. Planned output for Glasgow was greater than that for Crewe, and the factory was specifically designed to ensure a smooth flow of production. Machine tools were arranged and set for single-purpose operations and line production. An important distinction between the two shadow factories was that Glasgow was designed to be almost completely independent of sub-contract activity. This aim was successfully achieved. In 1941 Glasgow machined 98 per cent of its production, compared with 51 per cent at Derby and 57 per cent at Crewe. Glasgow also manufactured its own castings, and was equipped with the most modern light-alloy foundry in the country. By the end of September 1940 the whole factory was occupied. With 16,000 employees, it was one of the largest industrial operations in Scotland.

As Ian Lloyd wrote in the second volume of his trilogy on the company, *Rolls-Royce – The Years of Endeavour*:

The Hillington factory was an undertaking of no small magnitude from any point of view. Labour presented one of the most difficult problems and this problem was energetically tackled from the outset. Arrangements were made for the Stow Technical College to train apprentices, a toolroom was established near the site for the training of fitters and eight standard factory units were rented from the Hillington industrial estate to provide a factory in which machines could be put into operation both for training and production as soon as possible. The foundry presented by far the biggest labour problem. This type of work was completely unknown in Scotland and experienced coremakers and dressers were unobtainable elsewhere in the country. It was therefore decided to make the maximum possible use of specially trained female labour and to minimise the demand for highly-skilled labour by employing the most modern mechanised methods of foundry production. Wherever possible all materials were handled mechanically. This in itself necessitated the development of all-metal pattern equipment which was unknown to the pattern-making industry in Scotland. To make this possible local pattern-makers were sent to acquire the techniques employed at Coventry and specially selected men were given a course of training in foundry work at Derby, where the metallurgical and foundry techniques had been developed to an exceptionally high standard.

In this and many other ways the management implemented its promise to the Air Ministry to place the skill and resources of Rolls-Royce at the disposal of the nation. This was done despite the fact that final agreement on the various conditions of the management contract was not reached until the latter part of 1941.

It is all too easy to look back at the two world wars and assume, because Britain was ultimately victorious in both, that everything went smoothly, everyone was 100 per cent behind the war effort, and that factories geared up their production without a hitch to meet the demands of the armed services.

Nothing could be further from the truth. We have already seen how Rolls-Royce had to cope with the sometimes conflicting and competing demands of the Air Board and the RNAS, and how much time was spent wrangling with the Government over plant depreciation and what constituted excess profits during and immediately after the First World War. In producing the engines required in the Second World War, the Rolls-Royce management were faced with appalling bureaucratic delays, and, incredibly, a lack of urgency in some quarters.

The Air Ministry tried to devise a 'programme' which would co-ordinate the production of aircraft with that of engines. Whereas enormous pressure had been placed on Rolls-Royce in the late 1930s, as possible war approached, to produce every engine it could, when war actually came, the 'programme' was cut back! As a result, Hives felt obliged to write to Sir Wilfrid Freeman at the Air Ministry:

The 1941 Air Ministry engine programme calls for far less monthly output than the last six months in 1940. The present programme we are working to is considerably below the programme which was submitted to us in March of this year, and it was on the March programme that the Ford factory was planned. Our estimates show that by the end of 1941 we shall have produced 2,000 more Merlin engines than the latest Air Ministry programme and that by September 1942 we shall be 5,000 over the programme ... We are finding that with a standardised product like the Merlin we are exceeding our estimates for output ... We cannot see how the Ford factory which is to duplicate Glasgow fits into the Rolls-Royce aero production programme.

In response, the Air Ministry tried to persuade R.H. Coverley, in charge of the Rotol factory, to become a Director of Engine Production at the Ministry. Needless to say, Hives was horrified by the prospect of losing such a key man (Coverley had been Hives's manager of manufacturing in the Experimental Department before the war), and said to Freeman:

It is difficult for us to understand what the duties of a DEP entail. If we go by our experience the only discussions we have are on engine programmes which do not mean anything because they are altered every few weeks. We have given up worrying about the programmes, and we have accepted that our problem is to produce as many engines as possible and to watch the aircraft constructors' output to see that we are making the right type of engine.

However, Freeman was insistent that Coverley should join the Ministry as Director of Engine Production. He indicated that though Rolls-Royce might produce all the engines required of them, others were unlikely to do so:

I do not think I am giving away any secret when I say that the cumulative deficiency of Bristol engines by the end of 1941 will exceed 2,500.

Another factor contributing to the slower build-up of both engine and aircraft output in the early months of 1940 was the concentration of management in organising sub-contract programmes which would take time to yield results. As anyone involved in the production of sophisticated pieces of engineering knows, output cannot be turned on, off and on again like a tap. As it happened, many people were not too alarmed in these early months of the war, when nothing much seemed to be happening. Such complacency was very soon shattered when Hitler's Blitzkrieg began in May 1940.

At Rolls-Royce there was no complacency, merely extreme frustration at the incompetence of the local authorities in both Crewe and Glasgow in providing the housing necessary for the company to build up its labour force. Crewe Council had promised to build 1,000 houses by the end of 1938, but by February 1939 had only given one contract for a hundred. In May 1939, Hives was so incensed that he threatened to move the whole plant unless something was done. As late as October 1939, T.S. Haldenby was telling the Rt. Hon. Sir Kingsley Wood of the Air Ministry that there was little point in opening up the second part of the factory because there was no accommodation for the 2,500 employees who would work there. There were wrangles between the Council and private builders, who were hampered by restrictions and fearful of the escalating costs of materials. In the end, the Air Ministry was forced to step in and make sure adequate housing was built. In the meantime, billeting was imposed on both Crewe householders and the new employees.

There was a similar situation in Glasgow, and again Rolls-Royce were forced to threaten that they would abandon the operation. Hives, immensely frustrated by the delays and excuses, said:

Please do not refer me to another government department or point out that there is a shortage of building materials. You would be surprised if you knew all the shortages that we have to contend with and overcome.

As late as 12 January 1940, Hives felt compelled to write to Sir Kingsley Wood at the Air Ministry:

I understand that you will shortly be receiving a letter from the Lord Provost of Glasgow, Mr. Dollan, on the question of houses in the Glasgow district, and especially in connection with the new Rolls-Royce factory at Hillington.

When the site for the factory was chosen it was on the understanding that schemes were in hand to build a large number of houses in the vicinity of the Works. What has happened is that the factory has gone ahead at an accelerated rate, and the building of houses has stopped altogether.

We have had various meetings with all the local authorities, representatives of the Air Ministry, the Commissioner for Special Areas, and the Department of Health for Scotland, but so far – although there is unanimous agreement to the fact that there are no vacant houses in Glasgow and that there is no possibility of obtaining any houses unless they are built – no decision has been taken.

We anticipate obtaining approximately 90% of the labour in the district, but approximately 10% will hold key positions and we require approximately 1,500 houses.

I am pleased to say that the factory is making very good progress. We have over 1,200 people working for Rolls-Royce at the Hillington factory. We have already started producing a small number of parts for Merlin engines. We have obtained agreement from the Unions to use a very high proportion of female labour, a large number of whom are already being trained.

Where we are going to be stuck is on the housing problem. We have had several cases where key men have been transferred to Glasgow but would not stop, solely on account of not being able to find a house and with no prospect of finding a house.

Lord Provost Dollan knows the position quite well, and I trust that when you receive his proposals some action will be taken.

In retrospect, in view of the desperate situation faced by the country, and considering how close Hitler's forces came to invading, it seems incredible that production of vital war components – and they do not come much more vital than Merlin engines for Spitfires and Hurricanes – should have been held up by strikes. In 1940, production was held up at Crewe by a strike that was called when girls were assigned to capstan lathes previously operated by boys. The union claimed that 'skilled labour' had been displaced. Management stood firm and the men concerned returned to work on 19 April, ten days after German forces invaded Denmark and Norway, and only three weeks before they invaded Belgium, Holland and Luxembourg.

Again, the situation in Glasgow was just as bad, if not worse. Hives, in response to complaints about quality and scrap rates, said to Major Bulman of the Air Ministry:

We must expect that we shall get criticism in the management of any factory. But any criticism we get from outside cannot possibly approach the criticism we level against ourselves. The district is seething with communists, and strikes and threats of strikes occur the whole time.

William J. (Bill) Miller was put in charge of the operational side of the Glasgow factory, and he too was critical of some of his work force. He wrote later:

During the first six months of operation at Hillington we took on and trained the machine-operators required for production, but as nearly all fit males had already been called up for war service, only those men who were unfit for the army, or were conscientious objectors, were available for employment. Unfortunately, a large number of the conscientious objectors were Communists and many of them managed, by hook or by crook, to become shop-stewards – with militant attitudes. Many of the shop steward committees were inclined to encourage strike action for the most trivial of reasons. Also, most Clydeside factories called for their machines to be operated only by time-served men, and most of the machines we were using were considered to be skilled-type machines. Because of this, we had to negotiate a special 'relaxation' agreement to allow us to use unskilled labour for both operating and even setting these machines. We were finally successful in getting the sought-after agreement from the unions – but for the duration of the war only.

We have to feel a certain sympathy for the grumbles of the work force. The hours were punishing, as is made clear by Miller:

After some months at Hillington, with many periods being spent by the employees in underground shelters when the air-raid sirens sounded, absenteeism began to rise considerably due to the workers suffering from physical and mental fatigue, and in a bid to try and resolve the problem we reduced the working hours slightly – i.e. to eighty-two hours a week – by means of arranging one half-Sunday a month as holiday for the work-force.

In spite of all these problems, the first complete engine came out of the Glasgow factory in November 1940, and even before then, Crewe and Derby output had benefited from parts supplied from Glasgow. By June 1941 the target of 200 engines per month was reached, and by March 1942 output exceeded 400 per month.

CHAPTER EIGHT

'THE WHOLE STORY IS ENGINES, MERLIN ENGINES'

'VERY WELL, ALONE'
'ENGINE DEVELOPMENT LED THE WAY'
THE SUPERCHARGER
AMERICAN MERLINS
TILLY SCHILLING
THE GRIFFON

'VERY WELL, ALONE'

THE ORIGINAL CONTRACT FOR 310 Spitfires called for delivery to begin on 12 October 1937 and to be completed by March 1939, but by April 1939 only 150 had been delivered. The Air Ministry was outraged, effectively accusing Sir Robert McLean of keeping production within Supermarine and failing to use sub-contractors early enough.

The problems of finding sufficiently skilled labour and efficient sub-contractors were not confined to Supermarine. Rolls-Royce were suffering similar difficulties, as is clear from a report by Hives written in October 1937:

People doing sub-contract work have such a choice of work that they will only take on profitable and easy jobs. When they are months behind-hand for the delivery, if we attempt to take any strong measures we are told to take the work away . . . The condition of labour is very difficult and we are losing skilled machinists continuously and we are not able to replace them . . . There is no skilled labour unemployed.

At the same time, Hives was commercially minded, and he kept a close eye on how Spitfire production was progressing so that Rolls-Royce did not produce engines that would sit around waiting to be purchased. As he reported to his directors:

We think we should be given a lot of credit for the 'timing' of the Merlin production. Although we were bullied and threatened for deliveries 18 months ago, we kept an intelligent eye on the Aircraft Production and timed the Merlin Production so that there would not be a stack of engines piled up in some stores which could have been better and more up to date engines if more time was spent on them.

The Aircraft Constructor cannot deceive us with any optimistic promises. We can make a very accurate estimate of when engines are required, and the fact that we have never kept a machine waiting proves this.

And Hives found, as so many other industrialists have found before and since, that Government departments are notorious for both vacillating over decisions and changing their minds. In his report of 5 December 1938, he said:

Records will prove that Rolls-Royce Limited have always kept their promises to the Air Ministry on deliveries of engines to programme. These records date back to 1915.

The original engine programme for 1938 was for 1,375 Merlin engines plus spares and repairs. At the end of May the programme was reviewed and the output was increased to 1,575 Merlins. At the present time we are approximately 100 engines ahead of programme, and we anticipate that the output of Merlin engines for this year will be approximately 1,700.

Providing a reasonable time is given from the instructions to proceed to the delivery dates, we have no anxiety whatever in producing more and more engines. We feel, however, that our job would be easier if the Air Ministry took us into their confidence and told us of their projected programmes.

Foreign Office Intelligence had changed its mind about Germany's preparedness for war. Original calculations suggested a date sometime in 1942, but in 1936 fresh information indicated that the Germans might be ready as early as January 1939. This was one of the reasons for the rapid signing of contracts for Hurricanes and Spitfires before either had been fully tested. The anger of the Air Ministry might well have been better directed at those who had allowed Britain's aircraft manufacturers to be starved of Government contracts through the 1920s and early 1930s.

As we now know, Germany did not invade Poland in January 1939 but at the end of August that year, and the anticipated war was declared on 3 September. By that date, 308 of the 310 Spitfires had been built and tested. What we do not know, and never will, is whether Prime Minister Neville Chamberlain was being Machiavellian when he negotiated with Hitler at Munich in September 1938, knowing full well that Britain was not prepared for war. Historians have disagreed ever since about Chamberlain's motives. For example, A.J.P. Taylor, Britain's populist historian of the 1960s and 70s, wrote in the *Oxford History of England*, published in 1965:

The clearest lesson to be drawn from the crisis over Czechoslovakia was that Great Britain should be more heavily armed, whether for negotiation or for war. Chamberlain, a persistent advocate of rearmament, emphasized this lesson strongly and gave Hitler some excuse for complaining that Chamberlain was as insincere in appeasement as Hitler himself was accused of being.

On the other hand, Peter Clarke, Professor of Modern British History at Cambridge, argues in his *Hope and Glory, Britain 1900–1990* (a volume in the *Penguin History of Britain* series) that:

The cynical idea that he was buying time at Munich, put around by some later apologists, had no part in Chamberlain's thinking.

Sholto Douglas, by this time Assistant Chief of the Air Staff, made it quite clear that he was extremely concerned about the possibility of war with Germany in 1938. He wrote later:

By the summer of 1938 I was among those who became very alarmed over our unpreparedness should we be forced to go to war with Germany in the immediate future: an apprehension that was universal among the senior officers of the Air Staff.

Denis Richards has produced records of the comparability of the two air forces:

In September 1938 to oppose the Germans' long-range striking force of some one thousand two hundred modern bombers, Fighter Command could muster, including all reserves, only ninety three of the new eight-gun fighters. All the remainder of its six hundred and sixty six aircraft were the outdated biplanes. No Spitfires were yet in the line; and the Hurricanes, being without heating for their guns could not fight above 15,000 feet, even in summer.

Sholto Douglas submitted a written report on the RAF's unpreparedness to the Chief of the Air Staff, Cyril Newall, who duly passed it to the Secretary of State for Air. Douglas wrote later:

After a great deal of discussion, [Sir Kingsley] Wood placed these views of the Air Staff before the Prime Minister and the Cabinet; and it was with this vital information in mind that Chamberlain had to conduct himself in the tortuous negotiations that ended in Munich.

Whatever the truth of his intentions, Chamberlain effectively gave Czecho-slovakia to the Germans. Jan Masaryk, the Czech minister in London, said to Lord Halifax, the British Foreign Secretary:

If you have sacrificed my nation to preserve the peace of the world I will be the first to applaud you. But if not, God help your soul.

Chamberlain had bought another year for Britain, and for Britain's factories to turn out the weapons of war. It is generally accepted that the Battle of Britain came within a whisker of being lost, and that this would have left the way open for a German invasion. Certainly, 'Stuffy' Dowding had no doubts about the wisdom of Chamberlain's deal with Hitler, saying: 'It was a very good thing that he did act in that way.'

It was not only the combat aircraft situation that improved so dramatically. (In September 1938 the RAF could muster six efficient squadrons, whereas a year later it had twenty-six.) Radar cover, so critical when war came, was also extended. From coverage of only the Thames estuary at the time of the Munich crisis, it was in operation from Orkney to the Isle of Wight a year later.

Whether or not Chamberlain had deliberately bought time, that precious commodity was well used in Britain (and, as was learnt later, in Germany too) to manufacture military equipment. In the case of the Spitfire and Hurricane, the breathing space was vital. By the end of 1938, Supermarine had produced forty-eight Spitfires, and by March 1939, 130. Thereafter there was a dip, due partly to a shortage of embodiment loan items (essential items of equipment which were the responsibility of Government), and partly to the amount of help given by Supermarine to the Nuffield shadow factory in Castle Bromwich, where they were finding that the production of aeroplanes was very different from that of mass-production cars. However, the original contract was completed by September 1939.

Prime Minister Chamberlain made his fateful address to the nation on BBC radio on 3 September 1939, concluding:

This morning the British Ambassador in Berlin handed the German Government a final Note stating that, unless we heard from them by eleven o'clock that they were prepared at once to withdraw their troops from Poland, a state of war would exist between us...

... I have to tell you now that no such undertaking has been received and that consequently this country is at war with Germany.

Few people in Britain can have expected after this announcement that for the next six months their lives would continue virtually unchanged. This was the period that became known later as the 'phoney war', during which both sides limbered up for conflict.

The phoney war came to an end in spring 1940, when Britain sent troops to aid the Finns fighting a border war with the Soviet Union, by this time

Germany's ally following the Molotov–Ribbentrop Pact. The idea was to land British troops at Narvik in the Arctic region of Norway and then move them across Sweden to Finland. The War Cabinet gave its approval for this expedition in early March, but the Finns then sued for peace. Left in an embarrassing position, Prime Minister Chamberlain blustered: 'Hitler has missed the bus.'

Hitler, surmising that the British force might still be sent to Scandinavia to try to protect the northern route into the Atlantic, invaded both Denmark and Norway in early April. Although the British troops captured Narvik in the north and Namsos and Åndalsnes in southern Norway, the Germans soon forced them to evacuate, and Chamberlain was forced to explain the shambles to an angry House of Commons. As Peter Hennessy put it in his *Never Again: Britain 1945–51*, published by Jonathan Cape in 1992:

The deployment of British forces in Norway . . . was chaotic in conception, confused in execution and humiliating in its outcome.

A two-day debate took place in the Commons on 7 and 8 May 1940, at the end of which the Colonial Secretary, Leo Amery, turned on Chamberlain and used the words that Oliver Cromwell had spoken to the Long Parliament:

You have sat here too long for any good you have been doing. Depart, I say, and let us have done with you. In the name of God, go!

And Chamberlain went, to be replaced by Winston Churchill, Lord of the Admiralty again, just as he had been at the beginning of the First World War. Churchill feared the call had come too late, but he was going to fight. He said to the House of Commons on 13 May in perhaps his most memorable and most quoted speech:

I would say to the House, as I said to those who have joined this Government: I have nothing to offer but blood, toil, tears and sweat.

We have before us an ordeal of the most grievous kind. We have before us many, many long months of struggle and of suffering. You ask what is our policy? I will say: it is to wage war, by sea, land and air, with all our might and with all the strength God can give us; to wage war against a monstrous tyranny, never surpassed in the dark, lamentable catalogue of human crime. That is our policy.

You ask, what is our aim? I can answer in one word: it is victory, victory at all costs, victory in spite of all terror, victory, however long and hard the road may be; for without victory there is no survival.

They were powerful words designed to put resolution into his listeners, and that resolution would soon be tested. Three days earlier, on 10 May 1940,

German aircraft had flown over France and the Low Countries, bombing air bases and attacking aircraft both on the ground and in the air. The Dutch and Belgian Air Forces were virtually destroyed in the first hours of the attacks, and many of the 275 day fighters and seventy bombers available to the French Air Force were destroyed on the ground.

Whereas the French aircraft industry had been the world leader when the First World War broke out, in the 1920s and 30s it had stagnated, and both performance and production capacity had been neglected. In September 1939 the front-line strength of the French Air Force consisted of only 600 fighters, 170 bombers and 360 reconnaissance aircraft. The fighters were outclassed by the Messerschmitt Bf 109.

On the ground, France had come to live with the delusion that the Maginot Line protected them from invasion by the old enemy, Germany. Alsace and Lorraine had been lost to the Germans in the Franco-Prussian War of 1870, but regained in 1918. Now it looked as though it would be necessary to defend them again. Alsace was fairly easily defended, the River Rhine providing a natural barrier. To defend Lorraine, the minister of pensions, André Maginot, a hero from the Great War, forced through the financial provision necessary to build the line of fortifications that came to bear his name. However, this left the Ardennes to the south and the border with Belgium to the north.

The French general staff defended this situation by saying that the forests of the Ardennes were impenetrable by a large modern army and that the French Army would prevent any flanking movement through Belgium, as had occurred in 1914. In May and June 1940, neither the Ardennes nor the French Army proved capable of holding up Hitler's Panzer divisions for long. While the Maginot Line was taken from behind, General Gamelin, aged sixty-seven and a former aide to Marshal Joffre in 1914, wrote to the Prime Minister, Reynard:

We need tanks of course but you cannot hope to achieve a real breakthrough with tanks . . . As to the air, it will not play the part you expect . . . it will be a flash in the pan.

Many of the British aircraft in France, such as the Fairey Battles, were outdated and no match for the Luftwaffe. At least there were six squadrons with ninety-six Hurricanes, which *were* a match for the Luftwaffe, and desperate appeals were made for more. However, Dowding, charged with the defence of Britain, did his utmost to keep them there. He requested a personal interview with the Cabinet, and on 15 May showed Prime Minister Churchill, the new Air Minister, Sir Archibald Sinclair, the new Minister of Aircraft Production, Lord Beaverbrook, and Sir Cyril Newall, Chief of Air

Staff, a graph of the Hurricane losses since Hitler's invasion of France. It proved that if losses continued at the current rate there would be virtually none left to defend Britain if the battle for France was lost. As increasing entreaties came from Reynard, a compromise was reached. Further Hurricane squadrons were committed, but they had to return to England each night.

The attacks on Belgian, Dutch and French airfields had been followed by the dropping of parachutists at key installations and by the invasion of German Panzer divisions. By the end of May, Belgium and Holland had been overrun, the French were in full retreat and the British Expeditionary Force, with about 50,000 French troops, were pinned down on the beaches of Dunkirk. Thanks to heroic efforts by the Navy, supported bravely by hundreds of small privately owned sailing craft and a flotilla of Thames pleasure steamers and motor launches, the majority of troops embarked safely and were ferried to England. (It was calculated that a total of 338,226 British and Allied troops were taken off the beaches.) A postscript was given at the end of the nine o'clock news on the BBC Home Service by the famous author, J.B. Priestley:

We've known them and laughed at them, these fussy little steamers, all our lives. We have called them 'the shilling sicks'. We have watched them load and unload their crowds of holiday passengers – the gents full of high spirits and bottled beer, the ladies eating pork pies, the children sticky with peppermint rock. Sometimes they only went as far as the next seaside resort. But the boldest of them might manage a Channel crossing, to let everyone have a glimpse of Boulogne . . . They seemed to belong to the same ridiculous holiday world as pierrots and piers, sand castles, ham-and-egg teas, palmists, automatic machines, and crowded sweating promenades.

But they were called out of that world – and, let it be noted – they were called out in good time and good order. Yes, these *Brighton Belles* and *Brighton Queens* left that innocent foolish world of theirs – to sail into the inferno, to defy bombs, shells, magnetic mines, torpedoes, machine-gun fire – to rescue our soldiers. And our great-grandchildren, when they learn how we began this war by snatching glory out of defeat, and then swept on to victory, may also learn how the little holiday steamers made an excursion to hell and came back glorious.

It was a high point for British morale, which was going to need every boost it could get over the coming months and years.

During June 1940, the Panzer divisions pressed on towards Paris, and on 22 June the French signed an armistice in the same railway wagon in which the German generals had accepted defeat in 1918. As newly installed Prime Minister Winston Churchill said: 'The Battle for France is over, the Battle of Britain is about to begin.'

By the time of the French surrender, the RAF had lost 959 aircraft in the battle for France and another sixty-six in Norway, 509 of them fighters. At this point there were only 331 Hurricanes and Spitfires available to defend Britain, supported by 150 outdated fighters – Blenheims, Defiants and Gladiators.

Every day was vital now. The fifty-two fighter squadrons that the RAF had believed was the minimum necessary for the defence of the country had been reduced to thirty-two by the battles and losses in France. Seven of the thirty-two were still equipped with Blenheims, Gladiators and Defiants. Fortunately, the Germans themselves wanted to recover from their losses, and took until early August to prepare themselves for the onslaught on Britain. As John Keegan makes clear in his book, *The Second World War*, the Luftwaffe's commanders were concerned at what Hitler expected them to achieve when, on 16 July 1940, he issued his Führer Directive (No. 16) on *Preparations for a landing operation against England*. The Luftwaffe was instructed to 'prevent all air attacks', engage 'approaching naval vessels' and 'destroy coastal defences . . . break the initial resistance of the enemy land forces and annihilate reserves behind the front'. In other words, the preconditions for victory were to be achieved before the Army and Navy had even been committed. The six-week breathing space while the Germans prepared for invasion allowed the RAF to build up its fighter force to sixty squadrons of 654 aircraft, forty-nine of the squadrons (565 aircraft) consisting of Hurricanes and Spitfires.

Lord Beaverbrook, now Minister of Aircraft Production, had applied his bullying, ruthless, but extremely effective personality to increasing the rate of aircraft production. He accepted no excuses from either management or the trades unions, and received the full support of the union-sponsored Members of Parliament who were now Cabinet Ministers such as Ernest Bevin and Aneurin Bevan.

There had been some disagreement over exactly how much credit Lord Beaverbrook should receive for stepping up Spitfire production in time for the Battle of Britain. Alex Henshaw, test pilot on the spot at Castle Bromwich, was obviously close to these events, but could scarcely be said to be closeted in the corridors of power. He wrote:

Strange as it may seem today, the Spitfire was not accepted with alacrity. No one would doubt its speed and handling qualities but many doubted its armament potentiality and harboured grave doubts about the feasibility of mass producing such an advanced aircraft. This ominous doubt was reinforced to some extent by the huge Nuffield factory at Castle Bromwich, specifically built to turn out fighters and bombers on a prodigious scale [William Morris, created Baron Nuffield in 1938, had built up his very successful Morris Motors Ltd. between the wars, and had been an obvious candidate to operate a shadow factory]. The frustrating problems and difficulties encountered at this factory, in spite of modern equipment and a vast workforce, seemed insuperable. It all came to a crisis point when France collapsed and the mighty German blitz swept us to the Channel ports.

Our backs were now to the wall – we needed weapons of every description but most of all we needed fighter aircraft.

One can only speculate upon what might have happened had Nuffield remained in charge of this vital source of supply. It was fortuitous that the dynamic, ruthless and astute Lord Beaverbrook came into power at this time as Minister of Aircraft Production. Ruthless he may have been, but it is very doubtful whether anyone else was really alive to the situation that faced us or had the ability and guts to handle an industry under such conditions.

Aware that the very survival of the Free World could depend only upon our own efforts and with the War daily taking a more depressing and ominous turn, heads had to roll and Beaverbrook was certainly the man to chop them off.

He trapped Nuffield into a situation where his resignation was irrevocable. He then called in Supermarines, the only aircraft Company which could possibly alleviate what was rapidly becoming a national scandal.

From the time I had arrived in Southampton in November 1939 until May the following year, the Nuffield progress with the Spitfire Mk II was pitiful. Therefore, when Supermarine were handed this headless giant on a plate, it represented a somewhat frightening challenge of immense proportions. It did not help matters when feelings between the two organisations became strained and not exactly harmonious.

There is no doubt in my mind that but for the intervention of Lord Beaverbrook and the handing over of the Nuffield factory administration to Vickers-Armstrongs and the Supermarine organisation, many of whom were sent up to Castle Bromwich, we might well have been invaded before a single aircraft had flown from the factory.

On the other hand, Sholto Douglas, about to take over from Dowding as Commander in Chief, Fighter Command, disagreed strongly when Prime Minister Churchill recorded in a minute to the Secretary of State for Air on 3 June 1940: 'Lord Beaverbrook has made a surprising improvement in the supply of aeroplanes, and in clearing up the muddle and scandal of the Aircraft Production branch.' Douglas thought it another example of Churchill's 'genius for self-deception' and grossly unfair to Wilfrid Freeman, who had taken over from Dowding as Air Member for Research and Development at the Air Ministry on 1 April 1936. In Douglas's view, Freeman had achieved miracles in these four years, bringing the Spitfire and Hurricane to the point of readiness for battle, setting up the radar network which was to prove so vital to Britain's survival, and laying down the plans for the four-engined bombers.

John (later Air Chief Marshal Sir John) Slessor agreed with Douglas. In his capacity as Director of Plans, Air Ministry from 1937 until 1941, he was in a position to observe Freeman's contribution closely. He said later:

The original responsibility for the Battle of Britain Fighters was not Freeman's – they were already decided on before he came into the Air Ministry. The original Shadow factory scheme – based on the motor-car industry – was also initiated before his time. But the development and production of the HURRICANE and SPITFIRE were his responsibility. He presided over the whole tremendous expansion of orders for all types from 1936 to the middle of 1940. He sponsored the great extensions of the 'Shadow' factories, and the creation of a vast reserve of manufacturing capacity. And he developed to the utmost the design resources of what were known as the 'family' firms.

But there were many developments of vital importance during the years of 1936 to 1939 for which the responsibility and the credit lay with Freeman. Hundred octane fuel – the Variable Pitch propellor [*sic*] – the air rocket, for instance. And, above all, the initiation of the four-engined bomber policy. I well remember, as Director of Plans, the excitement and interest of discussing with him, his proposals for the first production orders of those aircraft, which were destined to have such a tremendous influence on the outcome of the war.

And Slessor added:

A man who was in a better position than most people to know – Lord Hives of Rolls-Royce – has written to me – 'it was the expansion which was carried out under Wilfrid's direction in 1937/39 which enabled the Battle of Britain to be won. Without that foresight and imagination, no efforts in 1940 would have yielded any results.'

Furthermore, asked Douglas, how could Beaverbrook make such a dramatic improvement when he had only been appointed three weeks earlier? Major Bulman, promoted by Freeman in October 1938 to oversee all engine and propeller production for the Air Ministry, wrote of Beaverbrook's contribution:

Lord Beaverbrook's name will always be associated with the tremendous explosion in aeronautical production which followed his appointment as the M.A.P. Much indeed was owed to his dynamism and readiness at any time to tear up any previous agreement or understanding which seemed to him to get in his way in grabbing every priority or potential source of material like an impish pirate with complete disregard for any resultant side effects. Some credit may also be accorded to the Air Ministry team he had inherited (and hadn't already figuratively executed!) who by a super effort sweated to maintain the fundamental machinery of production they had built up during the preceding years, often concealing from their Master some aspects of it, lest he trampled on them.

In calm retrospect one can only conjecture how much the build-up of output following Dunkirk would have occurred without his unique personality. How much was due to the summation of effort by every man and woman in the Industry in the face of the menace of Hitler, working often till they dropped from sheer exhaustion, achieving unknowingly their Finest Hour, with that unity of purpose and self sacrifice which only War can inspire in the Nation? All the tools had been laid down in the years before, producing a rapidly accelerating output, further escalated by the hearts of ordinary men and women inspired by Winston Churchill's magical broadcasts and the direness of the cataclysm erupting during 1940. Rome was not built in a day; or by the genius of one man.

The answer probably lies somewhere in between these opposing views of Beaverbrook's contribution. He undoubtedly did step up aircraft production, but not by 3 June 1940.

Whatever other people's view of Beaverbrook, Rolls-Royce, and especially Hives, responded well to a man who, in modern parlance, 'cut out the crap'; or, as Commander Stephen King-Hall (who had done so much to alert everyone to the Nazi threat during the 1930s) put it more delicately, 'raised the voltage at the Ministry of Aircraft Production'.

On 22 June 1940, just after the evacuation from Dunkirk, when invasion was moving from the realm of possibility to probability, Beaverbrook wrote a letter to Hives giving him enormous power, and showing the level of trust which Hives engendered.

I appoint you Chairman of a Committee of one required to deal with Rolls-Royce properties in the case of enemy attack. You have complete authority and discretion in the organisation of Rolls-Royce output on such terms and conditions as you desire. Your authority will also extend to all sub-contractors of Rolls-Royce whose works may be subjected to enemy attack.

However, Beaverbrook's fondness for precipitate action did cause some concern in Derby. On 28 May 1940, his Ministry telephoned instructions to Rolls-Royce that a complete set of Merlin and Griffon drawings should be prepared in order that they could be shipped immediately, with key drawings from other firms, to the United States. The drawings were collected and sailed on a warship to Canada, where they were delivered to M.W. Wilson, President of the Royal Bank of Canada. Beaverbrook telegraphed Wilson:

Please go to Washington and deliver the Rolls-Royce and Handley Page plans to the President forthwith, intimating that you are handing them over upon my official authority and instructions with a view to their immediate use for the production of aircraft engines and frames. The rights of Rolls-Royce and Handley Page can be left for subsequent determination and adjustment between the two countries.

The Chairman, Lord Herbert Scott, was extremely concerned at this high-handed action by Beaverbrook.

> Such action would place our shareholders in an impossible position . . . Knowing something about Beaverbrook's methods he would be unscrupulous to gain a point considered to be in our national interest. If, for instance, he could barter Merlins with the United States, for, say, ships, guns, munitions etc, he would not hesitate to do so without any reference to ourselves or regard to our shareholders.

Scott had been a director of Rolls-Royce Limited since 1906, and had already witnessed Beaverbrook's methods when Beaverbrook bought Charles Rolls's shares after his death in 1910. Managing Director Arthur Sidgreaves was more sanguine:

> By the time America can produce any Merlins, the engine as a type will be out of date here. Quite frankly our feeling (I think we can include Hives) is that if their having the drawings would enable us to win the war we would willingly give them without any claim. If we lose the war it certainly won't matter about the drawings.

Sidgreaves will almost certainly have been party to Churchill's attempts to persuade the USA to back Britain's war effort. A study given to the War Cabinet in May 1940 under the title, 'British Strategy in a Certain Eventuality', said, according to Hancock and Gowing in their book, *British War Economy*, that 'they ruled out submission but saw no chance of final victory unless full economic support was forthcoming from the United States'.

Rolls-Royce had looked at the possibility of having Merlins made in the USA before the outbreak of war, as is made clear in this memo to Sidgreaves from Hives on 12 October 1938:

> We have had from time to time various enquiries as to whether we would contemplate granting a licence to manufacture our aero-engines in America. They have come from finance people and some from aircraft constructors . . . I suggest it is very important that the licence should only be given to some organisation that has already established an engineering background.
>
> You will remember when the Pratt & Whitney people came into the engine business they had previously been machine tool manufacturers and as a result had the right mentality and have made a great success. [This respect for Pratt & Whitney was significant for Rolls-Royce's handling of the US market in the immediate post-war period.]

The following month, Sidgreaves sent a memo to Hives about another possible licensee who was interested – Packard. He wrote:

This of course sounds pretty good as we know that Packard's are a reliable engineering firm to whom we could entrust the job.

At the same time, Hives wanted Beaverbrook to be aware of the enormity of the task of ensuring that Merlin engines produced in another country over 3,000 miles away were up to the standard required. He consequently wrote to Beaverbrook on 8 July 1940:

The three Rolls-Royce Engineers whom you have agreed should go to the USA in order to assist in the production of Rolls-Royce engines or parts have now received the official information that they will be enrolled on the Ministry of Aircraft Production Staff in the USA, working in conjunction with Rolls-Royce.

When Mr. Sidgreaves and I see you on Wednesday afternoon, we are very anxious to clear up the question of how you expect them to operate. We are positive that any project for producing Rolls-Royce engines or parts in the USA can only be successful with the full co-operation and experience of Rolls-Royce help. THE FACT THAT MERLIN DRAWINGS HAVE BEEN SENT TO THE USA DOES NOT MEAN THAT THEY ARE IN A POSITION TO PRODUCE MERLIN ENGINES [author's capitals].

Hives subsequently went on to list a number of questions in an attempt to make Beaverbrook appreciate the scale of the task.

Meanwhile, opposing the 654 aircraft in Fighter Command were 1,971 German aircraft, including 594 of their best fighter, the Messerschmitt Bf 109E. Emil ('Willi') Messerschmitt, the son of a Frankfurt wine merchant, had been born three years after Mitchell and, like him, became a passionate air enthusiast during his childhood. His early design work was on gliders, and he designed one or two not very successful aircraft before turning his attention to a fighter in the early 1930s. As we have seen, in one of those strange quirks of history, the prototype of his Bf 109, precursor to the famous Bf 109E, was powered by an imported Rolls-Royce Kestrel engine (as was the Junkers JU 87, the Stuka). This engine was soon replaced by the German Jumo 210D, and when the Bf 109E was developed in 1938, it was fitted with the Daimler-Benz 601A engine, which generated 400 extra horsepower for its extra 400 lbs of weight.

During July 1940 the Germans attacked convoys in the English Channel and British ports, but they knew that to complete a successful invasion it was necessary to gain command of the skies, and therefore it was the RAF and its bases of operation that they had to destroy. During the early part of August the Luftwaffe began to attack British airfields. Goering, making light of the protests of other Luftwaffe commanders over the difficulties, told them:

The Führer has ordered me to crush Britain with my Luftwaffe. By means of hard blows I plan to have this enemy, who has already suffered a crushing moral defeat, down on his knees in the nearest future, so that an occupation of the island by our troops can proceed without any risk!

On 15 August, the Luftwaffe launched its main attack on what was code-named Adlertag (Eagle Day). It was not a great success. The Germans lost seventy-five aircraft, but the British lost thirty in the air and another twenty-four on the ground. In his book, *A Short History of Air Power*, James Stokesbury tells the story of the next few days:

This fighting went on for three more days, with losses too heavy to bear on both sides. Fighter Command won its only Victoria Cross on August 16, when Lieutenant J.B. Nicholson stayed in his burning Hurricane to shoot down a Messerschmitt. The highly touted and much feared JU 87 Stuka proved such an easy mark for the British fighters that it was withdrawn from the battle, and by August 18 the Germans had to pause for breath.

No one could tell how he was doing. By accepting pilots' claims, the Germans thought they should already have destroyed the British, yet obviously they were still there. Every time the Luftwaffe flew a raid, there were a handful of Hurricanes or a pair of Spitfires coming down out of the sun to meet them.

The last week of August and the first week of September proved the crucial period for the RAF. In those two weeks the Germans finally got their priorities correct and went after the whole structure of Fighter Command – the radar stations, the airfields, the control mechanisms. They also increased the number of free-fighter sweeps, and, by unremitting pressure, they began to win. Some of the radar went out, a couple of the most forward airfields were untenable and, most important of all, pilot attrition was wearing down the fighter strength. Dowding was scrounging pilots from Coastal Command, the Fleet Air Arm, any place he could get them. The British were feeding in Polish and Czech refugee pilots who could barely understand English commands over the radio, and by September 7 they were palpably losing. In two weeks they lost 264 fighters, and though many of their pilots parachuted or crash-landed on their own territory and lived to fight again, many did not. They went to sea, they were burned, shot or invalided, and their places had to be taken by younger, less experienced, and more vulnerable fliers. The attrition rate was just as bad for the Germans, worse, in fact, as they were fighting over enemy territory, but there were more Germans to get through. [This may not be completely accurate. The way the Luftwaffe drove its pilots – demanding more missions and sending them up while still recovering from wounds – suggests that it was as short of pilots as the RAF.] In a war of attrition the side that can stay longer wins. The Germans were now winning. Dowding believed that three more weeks would destroy his command, thereby opening England to invasion. The Germans were collecting barges along the coast.

212

On September 7 Goering threw victory away. Believing the exaggerated claims of his pilots, steadfastly misunderstanding the nature of his enemy, and indeed of air war, he decided the British were already finished. He thought Fighter Command was a broken reed; the battle was won. On September 7 he ordered the *coup de grace* for England. The army and the navy were all but ready to go; moon and tide would be right from September 8 through September 10. The British had put out an invasion warning, and on the afternoon of September 7, more than a thousand aircraft took off from bases across the Channel, formed up in massive units, and droned out towards England.

Park [later Air Chief Marshal Sir Keith Park, he commanded the vital No. 11 Fighter Group during the Battle of Britain] and his 11 Group watched them come with grim determination. They knew it was all over; the thin blue line was fraying out into invisibility. Waiting for their last best shot, they watched for the Germans to break up and head for the airfields and factories; while they did, the huge armada droned stolidly on, disdaining targets in the flat green countryside below. Incredulously, almost too late to do anything to stop it, the British realized the Germans were heading straight for London itself.

While Park called in every fighter he could find, the Germans bombed the London docks and the East End. Immense fires piled up into the sky, to last all night and be seen a hundred miles away. Hermann Goering, whose pilots sometimes unkindly called him 'Nero' in reference to his pretensions and pomposity [and possibly his addiction to drugs], stood on the cliffs at Calais and warmed himself with the glow of London burning. His cup ran over. He did not know he had just lost his war.

Goering may have made a fatal mistake in attacking London instead of continuing to destroy the airfields, but critical battles are won and lost for a variety of reasons. The Spitfires and Hurricanes, flown by their indomitable pilots, and positioned and preserved by intelligent and resourceful leaders, had withstood the might of the Luftwaffe, which at that time outnumbered them three to one. Both aeroplanes were powered by Rolls-Royce Merlin engines. What was the verdict of those that flew them?

An expert judgement came from Jeffrey Quill, of whom Sir George Edwards OM said: 'Jeffrey Quill was one of the most articulate test pilots I ever encountered . . . and to him goes much of the credit for turning Mitchell's brilliant concept into a great fighting machine.' In his book, *Spitfire, A Test Pilot's Story*, published by John Murray in 1983, Quill wrote:

At the end of it all I felt a very friendly disposition towards the new Merlin engine. It started for me a process of confidence in that remarkable piece of machinery which was to grow ever stronger as my hours in the air with it increased and as progressively I demanded more and more from it in the way of continuous running at full power in the course of rigorous performance testing. I learned to be meticulous in the matter of

213

correct engine handling at all times and although I never hesitated to run it to the absolute limit of its capabilities I was careful never to exceed those limits except when unavoidable. In return the Merlin hardly ever let me down and such total power failures as I experienced – and over the years inevitably there were many – were due as often as not to extraneous causes rather than to anything fundamental to the engine. The Merlin really was the pilot's friend.

Duncan Smith, later Group Captain W.G. Duncan Smith DSO DFC, said of the Spitfire and Merlin:

611 Squadron were equipped with MK 1 Spitfires, some with pump-handle operated landing gear and others with recently modified gear which was hydraulic operated. The engines were Rolls-Royce Merlin IIs rated at 1,050 hp [Smith is understating the performance. By the time of the Battle of Britain, 100 octane fuel was being used and the performance was 1,250–1,300 hp]. The aircraft was a joy to fly and its armament of eight Brownings and splendid handling qualities gave me a confidence in the Spitfire that stayed with me through operational experiences spanning eleven different Marks. One has, of course, to include the various types of Rolls-Royce engines that powered Spitfires over a period of many years. Reliable to an extent that was fantastically excellent, never did I ever think I would be let down by engine or airframe. One could stretch both to the very edge of disaster and yet feel fully confident in the operating ability of both.

Wing Commander Stanford Tuck, one of the heroes of the Battle of Britain, described the Spitfire as 'thirty feet of wicked beauty . . . with practically no relation to any of the aircraft I'd flown previously'. Group Captain Douglas Bader, who lost both his legs in a flying stunt in the early 1930s and was allowed back into the RAF when war broke out, described the Spitfire as behaving like 'a highly strung thoroughbred'.

'ENGINE DEVELOPMENT LED THE WAY'

The development of the Spitfire from the Mark I of 1938 through to the Seafire FMK 47 which was twice as heavy, whose maximum horsepower was more than double, whose maximum speed was 90 mph greater, whose maximum rate of climb was almost double and whose range was almost three times as far, would not have been possible without the parallel development of its engines, the Merlin and the Griffon. Indeed, as Jeffrey Quill pointed out, 'to a large extent it was engine development and power growth that led the way'. Not only was the power of the Merlin increased from 1,000 bhp in 1936 to over 2,000 bhp in 1944, the band of heights at which the power was available nearly doubled from 16,000 to 30,000 feet, which was of considerable tactical significance.

The Spitfire in the form of the Seafire became a Naval carrier-borne fighter and also a long-range, unarmed, high-speed, high-altitude photographic reconnaissance aeroplane. But the Spitfire was at its best as a fighter, and this meant that its pilots were looking for more speed, higher rates of climb, better manoeuvrability, more firepower, greater range and endurance. It was nearly always more power, or the same power at a greater height, from the Rolls-Royce engines that would lead to a new mark of Spitfire which would then be able to incorporate heavier armaments, fly further, faster and higher and therefore enjoy a greater role capability.

There were many different models, from Spitfire I in the later 1930s through to the Spitfire XIX of 1945 and the 21, 22 and 24 of the post-war years. However, the leaps forward in performance all came about through the improved performance of the Merlin and, latterly, the Griffon. Indeed, in a memo to Sir Wilfrid Freeman on 8 November 1942, Hives complained about both the lack of improvement in the Spitfire itself and the constant search for a dramatically new aircraft that would transform the war:

We started the war with two very good fighters – the Spitfire and the Hurricane – and the progress which has been made up-to-date is that we are now left with only one – the Spitfire. It is fortunate that the Spitfire has the fundamentals of an ideal fighting machine. We do not think a better fighter can be produced and in quantities before 1944. We should like to see this recognised and accepted, and, having been accepted, there should be a steady development on the aircraft side comparable with what we are planning for the engine.

There are one or two obvious faults on the Spitfire which ought to be and could be improved if there was the will and the desire to do it, and not this craving to produce something different. The manufacturing finish of the Spitfire is bad. This is shown up by the variation from machine to machine in performance, and the controls. We do not think it is sufficient to improve the paintwork, although this is the last thing we should want to stop, but given a continuity of production we should expect the aircraft to be manufactured to a higher quality.

The controls on the Spitfire compare very unfavourably with either the Fw 190 or the Mustang. As we increase the performance of the machine, these faults show up to a greater degree, but the controls can be and should be improved.

Earlier, at the beginning of 1940, the RAF knew that more power was needed at altitude. Rolls-Royce felt that they could achieve this, but the drawback was a loss of power at sea-level. The solution was the Merlin XX with Hooker's supercharger, which gave power at altitude and also maintained it at lower altitudes through a second gear on the supercharger. Early in 1940, both Hawker and Supermarine were looking at ways of installing the Merlin XX in the Hurricane and the Spitfire. Hawker were able to accommodate the extra length of the Merlin XX, and Hurricanes with this new engine saw action at the end of the Battle of Britain. Supermarine found it more difficult, and decided that the Merlin XX should be fitted into the new Spitfire III. Unfortunately, the development and production of this airframe had to take second place to the priority of producing Spitfire Is and IIs.

By the winter of 1940, it was becoming clear that the Messerschmitt Bf 109 was beginning to outpace the Spitfire Is and IIs. The improved Spitfire III with the Merlin XX would not be available for the anticipated spring offensive of the Luftwaffe. Just before Christmas 1940, Hives met Henry Tizard and Sholto Douglas at the Aircraft and Armament Evaluation Establishment at Boscombe Down, and suggested that Rolls-Royce should fit into the Spitfire a Merlin RM5S, a Merlin III fitted with Stanley Hooker's new central-entry supercharger but without the two-speed drive. The significance of leaving out the two-speed drive was that the original length of the engine was retained, but the engine still gave enhanced power at fighting altitudes. Furthermore, Hives undertook to carry out the first fifty conversions at Hucknall. This stop-gap Spitfire became the famous Mark V with the Merlin 45, ultimately the Spitfire with the highest production run.

As development work continued around the clock to achieve greater speed and performance, it was heartening for Hives to receive letters of appreciation from the front line. Air Marshal Dawson, in charge of RAF engineering in North Africa, wrote from Headquarters, Royal Air Force, Cairo on 7 June 1941:

I thought this message would interest you, and might be the sort of thing you would like to display in the works.

I was talking to-day to the Squadron Commander of an Australian Fighter Squadron which has been using Hurricanes in the Western Desert. I asked him about my old friend the 12 lb boost. He said: 'You can't blow up a Rolls-Royce engine. I would fly behind a Merlin anywhere.'

This sort of feeling after the struggle they have had in the Western Desert is something to be remembered. I thought you would like to have the message.

And again on 23 February 1942:

You will like to know that the Merlins have given surprisingly little trouble considering the appalling conditions under which they run. The requirement for an engine out here is that it must stand up to sand in the intake; however efficient the air cleaners may be, sand gets through and it is quite impossible to clean them adequately in the desert.

The Merlin XXs have been particularly successful, so far – touch wood – no trouble at all. The engines are good, the aeroplanes are good, the worst feature is the installation. There seems to be no clear appreciation of overseas conditions and what is necessary in order to ensure success. Tomahawks were lucky because they had a top air intake and a downdraught carburettor placed so that little sand seemed to get in; this does not always apply: on the Bostons, although there is a downdraught carburettor and a top intake, sand goes straight in picked up by the airscrews and also spraying off the nosewheel.

The best position for the intake appears to be as near the airscrew disc as possible and close to the hub, but it is quite clear to us here that these things have not been properly considered in design and production in sufficient time. Bostons and Baltimores all have to have the intakes moved here and filters fitted. The very 'fine' lubrication condition in the R.2600 won't stand up to desert sand: we have to fit up special scraper rings in order to prevent the engines becoming unserviceable due to heavy oil consumption in a very short time.

Incidentally, in order to be economical and because supplies cannot be maintained, we rebuild Merlins with reground piston rings and are chromium plating the cylinder barrels and regrinding and lapping.

This sand is a great problem here. The Germans use a filter intake with a special by-pass shutter which they can open when they are in the air. It is a good scheme; we should have done it earlier on.

The pressure for improved performance was always present. In August 1941, Air Marshal Sholto Douglas, by now Commander in Chief, Fighter Command, submitted a memorandum to the Chief of the Air Staff marked 'Most Secret'. It expressed grave concern about whether Fighter Command, equipped with Spitfire Mark Vs, would be able to maintain parity with the Luftwaffe by the spring of 1942. It noted that the Spitfire was already inferior to the Messerschmitt 109F in speed and climb at heights above 31,000 feet. While the Air Ministry chiefs were considering this memorandum during the autumn of 1941, increasing numbers of Focke-Wulf 190s were appearing. This aircraft was proving itself more manoeuvrable and heavily armed than even the versatile Bf 109F. By this time, there were plenty of people, including rival manufacturers, claiming that the Spitfire was past it.

Hives warned that the only way to *guarantee* having a better aeroplane a year in the future was to improve on what you had *now*. Both Hives and Lovesey were aware of the possible improvements that could be made to engines, but they also knew that they would take time to develop and manufacture. The Luftwaffe had to be tackled today, tomorrow and the day after that, not some time next year. He was not sure where he had read it, but Hives was fond of quoting the line: 'The better is the enemy of the good.' Lovesey talked of 'infiltrating' modifications into production. Both he and Hives were only too aware of the enhanced performance of the Bf 109F – Bill Lappin, through his work in liaising with the RAF, would have kept them fully informed.

The Merlin 60 had been conceived as a high-altitude engine for the Wellington bomber, effectively a replacement for the Hercules. The engine ran for the first time in the spring of 1941, and Hives and Lovesey felt it would be an ideal engine, with suitable changes to the supercharger gearing to optimise power at the required altitudes for a fighter, to install in the Spitfire. Lovesey instructed Hucknall to install this modified Merlin 60, called the Merlin 61, into a Spitfire V airframe. This became the Spitfire IX. Its performance was a revelation, and another aircraft was converted and sent to Boscombe Down for evaluation by the RAF.

'Knocking' of the Merlin had started as early as 1937, as we can see from a report written by Hives on 16 December that year, in which he said:

We consider that it is in the interests of the Air Ministry as well as Rolls-Royce Limited, that the statement which has been made that the Merlin engine is out-of-date should be contradicted.

The Merlin engine has only just started its useful life, and unless the whole of the experience of all makes of aero engines is to be disregarded, the Merlin should have a useful life of five or six years. [With development, its useful life proved to be much longer than five or six years!] Look in any direction you like and it can be proved that more improvements on aero engines have come from development rather than design . . .

. . . We do not think it is realised sufficiently <u>that the Merlin engine is the most powerful engine in production in the world today</u>. [This comment followed a report from Major Bulman at the Air Ministry, after his visit to Germany, stating that air-cooled engines were going to be more powerful than the Merlin.]

Hives continued:

If we are going to be judged on what it is assumed the output from the German engines might be some day, then it must naturally follow that these should be compared with our projected Merlin powers.

And on 16 October, just after what later became known as The Battle of Britain, a battle in which the Merlin had surely proved itself as much as the Hurricane and Spitfire, Sidgreaves felt obliged to send a report to Lord Beaverbrook complaining about the loose talk in the press praising 'wonderful new fighter aircraft which the RAF possess':

<u>MINISTER OF AIRCRAFT PRODUCTION</u>
There is only one object in writing this report, and that is with the idea of helping the Minister of Aircraft Production in his most difficult job and tremendous responsibility.

The reason we claim that we may help you is that there is no other aero engine firm in this country which has had the same experience as Rolls-Royce. We are the only firm designing and producing aero engines in this country to-day who were producing their engines during the last war, and we contributed considerably to the success of the R.F.C. and the R.N.A.S. The Bristol Engine Company did not exist at that time, although Mr. Fedden was employed by Brazil Strakers, who were subcontractors of Rolls-Royce. Napiers attempted to produce aero engines, but their contribution was practically nil. Armstrong-Siddeley made a large number of engines, but they were not designed by them.

During our 25 years' experience of producing aero engines we have watched the rise and fall of Air Ministers, and the coming and going of senior R.A.F. Officers, and our long experience has enabled us to formulate a correction factor for the Civil Service.

Consistently every few years we have been faced with some wonderful new engine, which was the last word in performance and efficiency, and that it was only a matter of time before Rolls-Royce would be out of business. There have been times when we have been so impressed with the information that we have believed it ourselves, but fortunately we have never believed it to the extent of dropping the substance and chasing the shadow. It has been embarrassing at times because some of the senior technical officials at the Air Ministry have backed these projects to an extent far beyond what was justified and proved by subsequent results.

Our anxiety at the present time, which is the most dangerous and critical in our history, is whether experience is being overlooked. We read in the press about the wonderful new fighter aircraft which the R.A.F. possess. It gives one the impression that the Spitfires and Hurricanes are already out of date. It may be necessary to publish these things, but there is always the danger that if a thing is said often enough, even people who know better accept it as a fact. The fighter pilots, who know very little of what is going on technically, will get the impression that they are being sent into the air with an out-of-date machine.

We know the position as regards fighter aircraft, and it is positively certain that the only machines we shall have to fight the Germans with in 1941 are the Hurricanes and Spitfires. The fact that we may have a few Westland fighters and Beaufighters and other odds and ends will provide just a mere irritation; the basis of the fighters for 1941 is positively Hurricanes and Spitfires. If this is accepted, which it must be, then every effort should be made to ensure that those Hurricanes and Spitfires are as good as we know how to make them. We are not at all satisfied that this is being done, in fact we are certain that it is not.

Sir Wilfrid Freeman appreciated the significance of Hives's (and therefore Rolls-Royce's) single-mindedness in concentrating on producing Merlins. They wrote to each other frequently and frankly, and met occasionally, even though according to Air Ministry rules this was not allowed. Freeman deeply admired Hives, and credited him with giving the Spitfire a qualitative superiority over enemy fighters. He was to say of Hives in 1944:

That man Hives is the best man I have come across for many a year. God knows where the RAF would have been without him. He cares for nothing except the defeat of Germany and he does all his work to that end, living a life of unending labour.

Following the introduction of the Focke-Wulf 190, a crash programme was put in hand to convert the Spitfire Vc to the Merlin 61 engine which, as we have seen, had been developed by Rolls-Royce following their work on engines for the high-altitude Wellington. The conversion meant a substantial modification to the cooling system, which involved the fitting of an additional external radiator under the starboard wing, as well as a new and larger oil cooler unit and the fitting of an intercooler radiator in the port duct. In turn, this necessitated considerable modification to the pipe runs. New engine cowlings and a four-bladed Rotol propeller were also required. Eventually the Spitfire IX emerged, a highly successful variant, of which 5,665 were built. When it was introduced it gave a great boost to morale. As Jeffrey Quill said:

The great thing about the appearance of the MKIX at that juncture was that it was extremely difficult for the German pilots to distinguish a MKIX from a MKV in the air. Therefore every Spitfire in the sky soon became potentially a MKIX to the German pilots. This had a marked effect upon their confidence and thus upon the level of their aggressive tactics.

However, the British feeling of superiority was soon brought down to earth with a bump when, on 23 June 1942, a German pilot, disorientated after a battle with Spitfires over the Channel, landed his Fw 190 at Pembrey in South Wales. The aircraft, undamaged, was quickly despatched to RAE at Farnborough, where tests were carried out in a trial against the Spitfire Mark IX. These trials showed that the edge the Spitfire held over the Fw 190 was much narrower than had been thought. Indeed, between 15,000 and 23,000 feet the rate of climb of the Fw 190 was faster. Its lateral manoeuvrability was also noted, and it was acknowledged that the Focke-Wulf was superior to the Spitfire generally at low altitudes.

Shortly afterwards, on 14 July, the new Minister of Aircraft Production, Colonel Llewellyn, made a statement in the House of Commons implying that the British fighter aircraft were superior to their German counterparts in all respects. This statement led to the Chief of the Air Staff complaining to Sir Archibald Sinclair, the Secretary of State for Air, that the Minister's statement was inaccurate, and that in the very important height band of

15,000–25,000 feet the Spitfire Mark IX's rate of climb was inferior to that of the Fw 190. Moreover, most of the Spitfires in Fighter Command were Mark Vs, which were considerably inferior to the Fw 190. These exchanges soon brought demands on Rolls-Royce for even greater performance from the Merlin 61. In the short term, the company was able to produce an increase in allowable manifold pressure for combat from plus 12 lb to plus 15 lb, with the hope that 18 lb would soon be achieved. In the longer term, it resulted in the re-scheduling of both the low and high blower gear ratios, which brought better performance at the low and medium altitudes at the expense of the higher altitudes. Thus the 15,000–25,000 feet gap was filled. This new engine – the Merlin 66 – was in production by early 1943, and was fitted into the Spitfire Mark IX. Alan ('Al') Deere, one of the most successful fighter pilots of the war, wrote later:

The Spitfire MKIX attained its best performance at 21,000 feet, or at roughly the same altitude as did the Focke-Wulf 190. At this height it was approximately 30 mph faster, was better in the climb and vastly more manoeuvrable. As an all-round fighter, the Spitfire IX was supreme, undoubtedly the best Mark of Spitfire produced, despite later and more powerful versions.

Group Captain (later Air Vice-Marshal) Johnnie Johnson agreed with Deere.

We flew hard during those summer months of 1943 and scored some decisive successes against the Luftwaffe. Our Spitfire IXs were superior to both the Focke-Wulf 190 and the latest Messerschmitt product, the 109G.

The Merlin was initially designed to power air defence fighters, but it was also used in the Fairey Battle day bomber and in the Armstrong Whitworth Whitley IV and V heavy bombers, as well as in the Vickers-Armstrong Welling-ton II and the four-engine Handley Page Halifax. Some 1,650 Whitleys, 440 Wellingtons and 3,000 Halifaxes were produced. The Halifax was the third of the trio that made up the bulk of Bomber Command's aircraft, alongside the Stirling and the Lancaster. Like the Lancaster, it was originally designed as a two-engine aircraft but was subsequently modified to take four engines. The Lancaster, originally called the Avro Manchester III, was renamed after the failure of the Avro Manchester with its Vulture engines.

In his book, *The Avro Lancaster*, published by Aston Publications, Francis Mason goes into great detail about the development of the Manchester and its replacement by the Lancaster. His conclusion is that pressure for a new bomber forced the pace too hard, both for the airframe and the engine manufacturer. The origin of the Rolls-Royce Vulture was the search for a high-powered engine with more potential than the Buzzard. In the mid-1930s,

Rowledge developed an engine which was essentially one Kestrel above another, one upside down, and both using the same crankshaft. The first prototype ran in September 1937, the second in January 1938 and the third in May 1938. Following lessons learnt, a prototype Vulture II, with a two-speed supercharger, ran in September 1938.

Testing continued into 1939 and, in the light of experience with the Merlin and other engines, major modifications were made to Vulture I so that Vulture II appeared not only with an improved supercharger, but also with a down-draught carburettor, a modified ignition set-up, and a number of other improvements. It passed its type-test quite quickly and went into production. However, it soon ran into problems.

The first was that one half of the split cooling system could airlock and the coolant flow into two cylinder blocks could cease, with subsequent piston seizure. Once the mechanism was established, the cure, a balancing bleed between the two coolant pumps, was not difficult. The second problem was more serious and more difficult: bearing and con-rod failures. The con-rod arrangement was that there was one master con-rod with a full-size big-end on the crank-pin. The other three pistons had con-rods which had a grudgeon pin at each end, one in the piston and the other in a similar bearing in the master rod big-end. Originally it was thought that the problem lay in the master rod big-end, but deeper investigation indicated that the two halves of the crankcase had been moving relative to each other. In the X formation, each half crankcase carries half of each main bearing; this meant that the movement affected the main bearings, and through them the big-ends. The problem was cured by fitting one-inch diameter steel dowels in each crankcase end panel to ensure positive location of the two halves with each other.

The Vulture V with these various modifications was a very satisfactory engine, even at ratings higher than the Vulture II. There were some continuing difficulties, but these were allied to the installation rather than the engine. The Manchester suffered from design faults on the airframe, and it was soon realised that the wingspan would need to be increased and extra tail-fins added. The Vulture engine was prone to two sorts of failure. First, it tended to throw con-rods, either through lack of oil or because of the mechanical loads on the big-ends at maximum rpm. Second, it overheated and the Glycol coolant caught fire. This was not the fault of the Vulture engine itself, but rather of the installation, designed by Avro. The cowling was too close to the engine, and did not allow sufficient ventilation.

However, the damage had been done. The Manchester had already built up a bad reputation from which it would be difficult to recover, and Avro were now looking into the four Merlin engine idea. However, the Napier Sabre had reached the stage at which it could be a relatively easy replacement for the Vulture in this and other possible applications. It was therefore logical to drop the Vulture so that Rolls-Royce could concentrate on the Griffon, for which there was no ready replacement.

A.A. Rubbra, closely involved in the development of the Vulture, wrote later about the engine's problems:

A serious trouble arose on the first production engines due to main bearing failures which were eventually traced to the top and bottom halves of the main bearings being built out-of-line. The bolting together of the two crankcase halves was achieved by what were known as cross-bolts which were positioned normal to the cylinder facing in order to deal directly with the explosion loadings arising from the cylinder blocks. These bolts being slightly staggered fore and aft to clear one another where they cross on the split line. Although a step was provided in the joint face between the halves of the crankcase to align them, this was not sufficient to prevent transverse slight relative movement applied at 45 degrees through the joint face and dependent on the order of tightening of bolts. The condition was slightly improved by imposing a rigid tightening order but was finally cured by the provision of cylindrical dowels, in the form of 'cheeses', which were large enough in diameter to allow the cross-bolts to pass through them; this also provided for location of the dowel endwise. With this modification no further main bearing trouble was experienced.

One item of interest was the burning out of certain cylinder blocks as a result of the breakdown in the coolant circulation. The Vulture had two coolant pumps in parallel, with the result that one pump could get a complete breakdown in flow due to cavitation at its inlet, whilst the other pump maintained full flow. This effect was investigated by making the two pumps in a transparent material and the solution was to balance the inlet pressures to the two pumps by introducing a balance pipe.

Unfortunately in service as the engine of the Manchester bomber a number of connecting rod bolt failures occurred. As a result several aircraft were lost, causing a crisis in Bomber Command. It was this problem and the decision to use 4 Merlins instead of 2 Vultures, leading to the highly successful Lancaster, that caused the Vulture to be stopped, as the great power potential of the Merlin was then being appreciated.

Ronnie Harker, one of Rolls-Royce's liaison test pilots, remembered that although the Vulture problems were overcome, it was not before a number of Manchesters were lost, and he witnessed the loss of the test aircraft. It should be noted that a number of the crashes were not caused by the failure of the Vulture engine.

For example, on its first flight from Ringwood to Boscombe Down, the crew switched on the reserve instead of the main fuel tank and the fuel ran out. At Boscombe Down itself, the piston failed because the wrong spark plugs had been fitted. These were bought by a Government agency and fitting them was not the responsibility of Rolls-Royce engineers. Another crash at Woodford was the result of bearing failures. Furthermore, the weight of the Manchester kept increasing, and Rolls-Royce increased the power of the Vulture accordingly, but in the end the aircraft was too heavy to fly on one engine. This meant that any trouble with one engine would mean a crash landing.

Harker wrote later in his book, *The Engines were Rolls-Royce*:

I happened to have flown over to Ternhill Aerodrome where I was giving a talk to the pilots of the fighter conversion unit. I was standing on the aerodrome talking to Squadron Leader Gerry Edge who, incidentally, was to become godfather to my second daughter! He was a good friend of mine and I had joined his 605 Squadron at the end of the Battle of Britain, where it was operating from Croydon. It had been the first squadron equipped with the Hurricane Mark II. Group Captain Teddy Donaldson, who was the station commander, was also with us.

We saw a Manchester approaching the aerodrome with one engine on fire. The pilot, Reg Curlew, one of our test pilots, and very experienced on large multi-engined aircraft, seemed to be well in control; he was making a downwind approach with enough height, so it seemed, to be able at least to turn and land across-wind. He must have thought he could get round into wind, so he continued the circuit before turning into wind for the final approach. Alas, he undershot and landed just short of the aerodrome in a field which had some large trees in it. He hit one of these and a wing was pulled off, rupturing the fuel tank; there was an explosion and the whole aeroplane went up in flames. We rushed to the spot in the group captain's car only to find a mass of flames; the two flight observers had managed to crawl out of the rear door and were not badly burned but there was no sign of Reg Curlew. Gerry Edge and Teddy Donaldson, amidst the exploding ammunition, did get into the aircraft by the rear door for a few moments. Gerry Edge said he saw the pilot still in his seat but crushed against the control column and obviously either dead or unconscious. One of the tyres then burst, the aircraft settled down and another tank burst so Gerry made a hurried retreat, getting out just in the nick of time before the whole thing became one mass of flames.

Major Bulman, a key figure at the Air Ministry, recalled that after this crash

Air Marshal Tedder and Sir Wilfrid Freeman went to Avros just after this prototype had spun in, and Dobbie Dobson the irrepressible [Sir Roy Dobson, managing director of A.V. Roe Ltd.], with a model Manchester in his hand, said none of them were happy with results to date and that Rolls-Royce seemed lukewarm about the Vultures. Whereupon he slipped off the model's wing and replaced it with another mounting four Merlins. Hence the Lancaster which was destined to become the best British bomber of the war. No doubt Hives had warning of this vital change in talks with Dobbie, and may even have inspired the thought in Dobbie's mercurial brain.

Dave Piggott has no doubt that Hives would have suggested that the Vulture be replaced by the Merlin. He pointed out that Rolls-Royce were looking for a replacement for the Vulture as early as 1937. The Vulture was Kestrel technology, and the company was developing a more modern 2,000 hp, 24-cylinder X engine known as PV24. However, as war became more and more likely, Hives stopped development work on it so that resources could be concentrated on the Merlin and Griffon. In spite of all Hives's efforts to persuade Dobson to replace two Vultures with four Merlins, he needed the help of Sir Wilfrid Freeman to clinch the argument. This was made clear in a letter written by Hives to Sir John Slessor in the 1950s, after Slessor had given an address on Battle of Britain Day in which he praised the contribution of Freeman. After acknowledging Freeman's help with the development of the Merlin, and in persuading Ford to produce them in Manchester, he added:

One of the particular projects where he actually, in spite of all our efforts, had to give a final push was to make the Lancaster with 4 Merlins instead of with 2 Vultures.

The Lancaster, with its four Merlin XX or 22 engines, or Packard Merlin 28, 38, 24 and 224 engines, gradually became the dominant force in Bomber Command, and turned out to be their success of the war. Serving from January 1942, it dropped just over 60 per cent of Bomber Command's entire bomb tonnage in the war. Some 4,000 of the 7,300 Lancasters built were lost, mainly in action, while nine of the thirty-two Victoria Crosses awarded to air crews went to Lancaster crews. Air Chief Marshal 'Bomber' Harris called the Lancaster 'a shining sword in the hands of Bomber Command'.

As well as powering Spitfires, Hurricanes and Lancasters, the Merlin was also fitted into other wartime aircraft. The Mosquito, designed by Bishop and Clarkson of de Havilland, was a wooden-airframed aircraft designed as a bomber with the performance of a fighter. It could fly at high altitudes and was therefore virtually invulnerable to anti-aircraft fire. It was also difficult to intercept, and these two factors made it very popular with the RAF. Flying at high altitudes, it was a natural for the Merlin XX and its derivatives. Early Mosquitoes were powered by single-stage Merlin 20 series engines, while later models were fitted with two-stage Merlin 60s and 70s. Mosquitoes built in Canada were powered by Packard-built Merlins, and the last production variants of the Mosquito, the Marks 34, 35 and 36, were fitted with the Merlin 113 and 114 engines which delivered 1,430 bhp at 27,250 feet, with a boost pressure of plus 18 lb. Over 7,700 Mosquitoes were built.

Ronnie Harker described the Mosquito as 'a most versatile aeroplane and a mix of bombs, guns, rockets and long-range fuel tanks' which could be fitted according to the task in hand. (He could have added cameras, used for PR purposes, and flares, used in Pathfinder sorties.) He wrote later:

They even flew to neutral Sweden to pick up ball bearings which, for a time, were in very short supply in England. For the latter operation they were painted in British Overseas Airways Corporation colours and were flown by airline pilots, even a passenger being sometimes carried in a bomb bay! At times, the Mosquitoes were intercepted by Focke-Wulf 190s but they were able to outpace them; none were lost.

Add to these the 23,000 Spitfires and 14,500 Hurricanes, and we can see that the demand for Merlin engines was heavy and constant. Derby alone could not cope, and the shadow factories at Crewe and Glasgow were also working around the clock. At the same time, a new factory in Manchester was built and run by the Ford Motor Company to manufacture Merlins, while the Packard Motor Company in Detroit and the Continental Motors Corporation in Muskegan also made them under licence from the US Government who, as we have seen, were given the drawings by Beaverbrook.

This was how Harald Penrose recorded the Ford developments in his book, *British Aviation – The Ominous Skies 1935–39*:

Despite Sidgreaves' antipathy to shadow factories, Sir Wilfrid Freeman insisted that Fords of Dagenham, with their enormous resources, must contribute to Merlin production, and A.R. Smith, their managing director under the chairmanship of Lord Perry, agreed that 400 a month was feasible. Said Major Bulman: 'Smith was a great man in every sense, and realized that his team must steep themselves in all the know-how of building aero engines as distinct from Ford cars. With the complete support of Hives, he therefore sent ninety of his best men to Derby for training and they were there for nine months. The Ford estimate of production cost was £5 million [£250 million in today's terms], and it was Freeman's view that the matter was so urgent that he side-stepped the usual approval of the ACCS and sent me to the Treasury to get the necessary authority, and incredible though it seems, I received it within five minutes due to the perception of our administrative Civil Servants of those days. Smith decided to build an entirely new factory at Trafford Park, outside Manchester, compromising on the true Ford method of production in order to begin delivery in June 1940 rather than his initially estimated two and a half years. The result was a machine shop containing single-purpose tools tailored to the Merlin's design, though less capable of being switched to different engines, fundamentally far more productive of Merlins than the Rolls-Royce line, and making a cheaper engine of no less superb quality.'

Initially, Ford in Manchester experienced severe problems. Stanley Hooker remembered that a number of Ford engineers came to Derby to familiarise themselves with the drawings and methods of manufacture. This was how Hooker put it in his book, *Not much of an Engineer*:

One day their Chief Engineer appeared in Lovesey's office, which I was then sharing, and said, 'you know we can't make the Merlin to these drawings'.

I replied loftily, 'I suppose that is because the drawing tolerances are too difficult for you, and you can't achieve the accuracy'.

'On the contrary', he replied, 'the tolerances are far too wide for us. We make motor cars far more accurately than this. Every part on our car engines has to be interchangeable with the same part on any other engine, and hence all parts have to be made with extreme accuracy, far closer than you use. That is the only way we can achieve mass production.'

Lovesey joined in, 'well, what do you propose now?'

The reply was that Ford would have to redraw all of the Merlin drawings to their own standards, and this they did. It took a year or so, but was an enormous success, because, once the great Ford factory at Manchester started production, Merlins came out like shelling peas at the rate of 400 a week. And very good engines they were too, yet never have I seen mention of this massive contribution which the British Ford company made to the build-up of our air forces.

The total production of Merlins and Packard-built Merlins was 168,040. Derby built 32,377, Crewe 26,065, Glasgow 23,647, Ford Manchester 30,428 and Packard Detroit and Continental Muskegan 55,523. What should be remembered in noting these production figures is that Derby not only had to provide the engineers to advise the other plants, it also bore the brunt of developing and manufacturing every new type of Merlin at Derby itself, often coping with much shorter runs of an engine type than the other plants. And the expansion of its production was staggering. In the first year of the war, about 2,000 were produced. By 1943 the Derby, Crewe and Glasgow factories were producing at the rate of 18,000 a year. On top of this, Ford were making 200 engines a week in Manchester and Packard 258 a week in the USA. The 100,000th engine was delivered on 29 March 1944, and by 8 May 1945, when victory in Europe was declared, over 150,000 Merlins had been produced.

THE SUPERCHARGER

In improving the performance of the Merlin engine – and therefore the performance of the Spitfires and Hurricanes – the supercharger was vital. We have already seen how the expert of the 1920s, Jimmy Ellor, was brought to Derby from the Royal Aircraft Establishment at Farnborough in late 1927 (with their blessing, it should be said). The man who developed the supercharger further in the late 1930s was Dr. Stanley G. Hooker, later to become a key, if slightly controversial, figure within Rolls-Royce. His description of a supercharger in his book, *Not much of an Engineer*, published by Airlife in 1984, is much better than anything I could achieve:

Briefly, a centrifugal supercharger consists of a rotor carrying a number of equally spaced radial vanes. In the case of the Merlin supercharger, which I was examining, the rotor was 10.25 in (260 mm) in diameter and had 16 vanes. It was driven by the engine through a step-up gear, and revolved at 28,000 rpm. The air entered at the centre of the rotor, moved out radially under the centrifugal force, and was flung off the rim into a stationary 12-vaned diffuser, the object of which was to convert the velocity of the air into the pressure which forced greater masses of air into the cylinders of the engine. If one thinks of the cylinders and pistons of an engine as the heart which converts the force of the burning air and petrol mixture into mechanical power by the downward motion of the piston, then the supercharger is the lungs of the engine, and by its efficiency controls the power output.

Clearly, the efficiency of the supercharger depends upon the efficiency of its component parts – the rotor and the diffuser – and to get the best results the maximum efficiency of the rotor must be made to coincide with the maximum efficiency of the diffuser. I found, by mathematical analysis and much to my surprise, that this happy coincidence did not occur on the Merlin supercharger, and that changes to both the rotor and diffuser were necessary. I even computed that the efficiency of the supercharger would improve from the existing 65 per cent to a new level of 75 per cent by such changes, but could it be true? How could the great Rolls-Royce firm have missed this?

Conscious that he might have made a mistake, Hooker checked and re-checked his calculations. He then sent a report to A.G. Elliott, who said that he would send it on to the accepted expert, Jimmy Ellor. After a number of days, Ellor arrived in Hooker's office with the report in his hand, and said: 'Did you write this?' Hooker replied nervously that he had. 'Well done, jolly good stuff,' said Ellor. 'From now on you are in charge of supercharger development.'

Hooker began to make improvements which were incorporated into what became the Merlin XX and 45 for Spitfires and the Merlin XX for Hurricanes, Mosquitoes and Lancasters. As Hooker put it:

For me the impossible had come to pass. I had changed an engine designed by the great Henry Royce himself.

Although Hooker was to receive most of the credit for the supercharger which gave the Merlin its vital extra performance, it is very important not to forget the contribution made by Jimmy Ellor. And Hooker himself acknowledged this contribution, writing:

This work is a continuation and amplification of that begun under the direction of Mr. J.E. Ellor.

The Merlin XX, first produced in July 1940, and the Merlin 45, first produced in January 1941, increased the full-throttle altitude of the engine from 16,000 feet with the Merlin III to over 19,000 feet with the Merlin 45.

But development did not stop there. Everyone knew that the Germans would be constantly improving the performance of their engines and aircraft. The British must try to outguess them and stay ahead. And it was not only by refinements to the supercharger that the power of the Merlin could be improved. Fuel quality was also important. As Hooker pointed out:

There was another vital reason for keeping the boost pressure constant at a pre-determined value, and this was the need to prevent the engine detonating. The ideal situation is that the charge of fuel and air should burn smoothly in the cylinders. If too much charge is forced in by too high a boost pressure from the supercharger, then detonation can begin and, instead of burning smoothly, the charge literally explodes, and causes shockwaves, like those at the nose of bullets, to bounce around inside the cylinders. These waves are of such intensity that serious mechanical damage can be caused to the cylinder head and pistons, which for lightness are made of aluminium, and thus can be relatively easily damaged.

The onset of detonation can be controlled by the octane value of the fuel, which in 1939 was limited to 87. Just before the Battle of Britain, small amounts of 100-octane fuel became available from the USA and this enabled us to open the throttle further on the Merlin and, in fact, to obtain nearly 2,000 hp without detonation. Thus, the 100-octane fuel made a crucial contribution to the performance of the Spitfire and Hurricane in that battle, as did the work of Lovesey, Rubbra, and their teams, which enabled the Merlin to withstand double its design power for short periods without mechanical failure.

To obtain the increased power, the pilot had to override the boost control which was normally limiting him to 1,000 hp. To do this, he had to pull a knob in the cockpit, and break the seal on it. So we always knew when he had done it! But in the Battle of Britain, 1,000 ft of extra altitude or 5 mph in speed could mean the difference between shooting down the enemy or being shot down by him, such was the equality between the performances of the Bf 109 and our fighters.

Thus, with the advent of 100-octane fuel, we were for the time being released from the nightmares of detonation. We could concentrate on improving the mechanical integrity of the Merlin to withstand higher power, which was Lovesey's job, and improving the performance of the supercharger so that the power could be increased and also maintained to higher and higher altitudes, which was my job.

The next big leap forward in performance stemmed from development work carried out by Hooker and his team on behalf of the Air Ministry. Rex Pierson, the chief designer at Vickers, had designed a capsule which fitted into the nose of the Wellington bomber in which the pilot and the bomb-aimer could sit. Pierson's idea was to pressurise the capsule so that the aircraft could fly above 30,000 feet. The Wellington's standard engine was a Bristol Hercules sleeve-valve radial. To boost its power to get the Wellington above 30,000 feet, Bristol had decided to fit an exhaust-driven turbosupercharger, similar to the ones being used by the Americans on their air-cooled engines. The Air Ministry considered this Wellington project so important that they wanted Rolls-Royce to turbocharge a Merlin as insurance.

Barnes Wallis, later to become immortalised by his 'bouncing bomb' (used successfully in the Dam Busters raid on the Mohne and Eder dams in Germany on the night of 16–17 May 1943), had been working at Vickers as a designer, and had convinced Beaverbrook of the possibility and efficacy of flying bombers at high altitude. Beaverbrook became determined to equip the RAF with such a weapon, and on 9 January 1941 he wrote to Vickers:

High-altitude bombers are to be developed intensively. I wish you to undertake this work. The Wellington V is to be fully developed with Hercules and Merlin engines. The Merlin is to take preference.

As Hooker pointed out, this was not going to be easy. Ray Dorey and Harry Pearson had already carried out a great deal of work at Hucknall on the Spitfire and Hurricane, taking the exhaust from the Merlin and ejecting it backwards through very short exhaust pipes where it acted as a means of jet propulsion equivalent to about an extra 150 hp. With an exhaust-driven turbocharger, that effect would be lost. Hooker argued that to raise the necessary power the full-throttle height of the Merlin should be raised from 16,000 to 30,000 feet by putting two superchargers in series at the back of the engine, driven by the same gears already fitted to the standard Merlin.

However, there was a snag to this suggestion. Because of the high compression of the charge, the temperature would soar and the old problem of detonation would return. The solution was to add an extra liquid-cooled 'intercooler', which would cool the charge to 100 degrees C before it entered the cylinders. Desk-top calculations showed that by this method the power of the Merlin at 30,000 feet could be doubled from 500 to 1,000 hp. All that they had to do was determine the size of the two superchargers. Within months, after experiments with both the Merlin and Vulture superchargers, and with help on the intercooler from the RAE, Rolls-Royce had an engine ready for testing. It worked well on the test-bed, and shortly afterwards two engines were installed in a Wellington at Hucknall. On its first flight, the Wellington reached 29,750 feet – clearly the experiment had worked.

But Hives was not satisfied with that, and asked: 'What would happen if we put it in the Spitfire?' It was an obvious idea, though it does not appear to have occurred to anyone else. It would, however, require considerable modification to the aircraft, because this engine was nine inches longer than the standard Merlin. The whole of the nose, including the engine mounting and controls, would have to be re-designed. A new four-blade propeller would be needed to convert the power into thrust, and an extra radiator under the wing would be needed to dissipate the heat in the coolant that cooled the charge. However, all this was achieved, and in 1941 a Spitfire flew with this Merlin 61 engine, reaching a height of 40,000 feet.

This was the prototype of the famous Spitfire IX. The new Merlin 61 had increased its fighting altitude by 10,000 feet and its top speed by 70 mph, and it arrived in the sky just in time to do battle with the Focke-Wulf 190. Hooker related in his book that Harry (later to become Air Marshal Sir Harry) Broadhurst, one of the country's leading fighter pilots, told him that he had seen the look of astonishment on a German pilot's face as he climbed past him in a Spitfire IX.

Ironically, the Wellington bomber with the pressurised cabin never went into service, but the new Merlin went into mass-production and was fitted into Spitfires, P-51 Mustangs and Mosquitoes. It proved outstandingly successful in the Mustang, which in Hooker's words 'was the only aircraft that really challenged the supreme performance of the Spitfire'.

AMERICAN MERLINS

The reputation of the Merlin and the performance of the Hurricane and Spitfire had prompted the French Government in early 1939 to put pressure on French aircraft manufacturers to consider buying the Merlin engine. Monsieur Dollfuss, Managing Director of Fordair, the French subsidiary of the American Ford Company, was asked to negotiate with Rolls-Royce for a licence to manufacture the Merlin. Negotiations began in March 1939 and the Air Ministry became involved, as did the Ford headquarters at Dearborn in the USA. A number of Ford personnel from both France and the USA visited Derby. Most of the information went back to Dearborn, where the parent company had taken charge of the whole project.

The two Rolls-Royce representatives at the Fordair plant in Bordeaux, Willis and Buxton, reported to Derby:

This Company in the past, in the production of Ford cars, have had all the construction and organising work done for them by the American parent concern, who have prepared all designs of highly specialised plant and tools and have managed the planning and starting of plant here, leaving only the maintenance work to be done by themselves, with the result that the organisation here do not appear to know how to start on their own initiative without outside help to start the plant for them.

Hives had always been extremely sceptical that negotiations with the French Ford company would ever come to anything, as is made clear by his letter to Air Marshal Sir Wilfrid Freeman at the Air Ministry on 25 September 1939:

Replying to your letter of September 22nd, I quite agree with your letter to Mr. Dollfuss. I think we are in a better position to tell you the facts about the French Ford factory than even Mr. Dollfuss.

The engineer whom we have appointed to operate for us in the U.S.A. has given us all the particulars of the position as the job stands out there.

My own views are that the French Ford Co. are just playing with the job; in fact, I even doubt their honesty of purpose. The impression I have is that they have been given huge orders by the French Air Ministry for Ford trucks, and they certainly have not the capacity to tackle the Merlin job unless it operates as an entirely separate division.

One of our men is leaving for France to-morrow, and he is to have an interview with Mr. Dollfuss and also with M. Guy la Chambre.

For your own information, attached herewith is copy of the minutes of a meeting we had in Derby on this subject.

The promises which the French Ford Co. made to the French Air Ministry to produce Merlin engine parts and engines were just ridiculous. It either meant they were thoroughly dishonest or that they had not grasped in any way the job they had undertaken.

I will certainly keep you posted as regards the position of the French factory, but do not expect that much help will be coming from that source until we have straightened them out.

I should like you to treat the contents of this letter as confidential.

In spite of Hives's view of the French Ford operation, when it came to producing Merlin engines in the USA, Sidgreaves for one felt that Ford would be the most appropriate company. And Henry Ford, in spite of his pacifist leanings, declared on 28 May 1940, as Hitler's Panzer divisions thundered west into France, that the Ford Motor Company stood ready to 'swing into a production of a thousand airplanes of standard design a day'. However, his former employee, William Knudsen, by this time President of General Motors, had just been appointed Commissioner for Industrial Production by President Roosevelt, and Knudsen wanted Ford to produce aircraft engines, not aircraft. With the British Purchasing Commission anxious to find a US manufacturer to produce 6,000 Merlin engines, Knudsen proposed to Henry Ford's son, Edsel, that Ford should take on this job. According to Robert Lacey in his book on Ford, Henry agreed and Edsel publicly announced the project. On 20 June, the New York *Herald Tribune* reported that Lord Beaverbrook had given Ford an order for 6,000 engines.

Beaverbrook also announced the deal in London. For some reason, this irked Henry Ford, and Knudsen received a call from Edsel that they would not, after all, be making the engines. Knudsen regarded the deal as so important that he flew out to Detroit to talk to Henry Ford in person. Ford agreed to make the engines, provided the order was channelled through the US Government, but he would not make them directly for a belligerent nation (interesting sentiment from someone who had employed armed police to break strikes in his factories, and even stranger since Ford companies in both Britain and Germany were producing armaments for their respective host countries!). Knudsen, in attempting to persuade Ford, told him that he had mentioned the proposed deal to President Roosevelt, and that the President was very pleased about it. Ford was not a fan of Roosevelt, and that killed the deal. Edsel announced that Ford would not be manufacturing the Merlin engine in the USA, and, as a result, not in France either, though as we have seen, Ford in the UK produced them in great numbers.

Maurice Olley, who had done so much for Rolls-Royce in the USA in the 1920s, and who had gone to General Motors when the Springfield plant was closed, was now asked by Hives to represent Rolls-Royce in the USA for the duration of the war. General Motors agreed to release him, and on 21 June 1940 Olley called on Knudsen at his home to discuss the situation with him. By this time, it was clear that Ford would not be making the Merlin. Fortunately, negotiations had been carried on concurrently with the Packard Company by the British Purchasing Commission and the Defence Finance Corporation, and on 27 and 28 June, Packard executives called on Ford to collect the Merlin drawings. As we have already seen, Packard had approached Rolls-Royce before the war with a view to manufacturing Rolls-Royce aero engines under licence. They were happy to accept an initial order for 9,000 engines, 6,000 for the British Government and 3,000 for the US Government. The two governments also took an option to purchase a further 10,000 engines.

The US Air Corps were initially resistant to the idea of using Merlin engines. They were happy with their existing engines, and wanted to avoid the duplication of spares and the complication of servicing a different engine. However, when they tried out first a Derby Merlin and then a Packard Merlin at their test establishment at Wright Field, they changed their mind. The Wright Field engineers said that it was the first time an engine had gone through their test procedures without giving any trouble, and also the first engine that achieved its predicted altitude performance.

It soon became clear that expertise would be required from Derby, though Rolls-Royce could hardly spare such people. With some reluctance, they seconded Lieutenant-Colonel T.B. Barrington, by this time chief designer of the Aero Division, Jimmy Ellor, the supercharger expert and by then chief experimental engineer, and J.M. Reid, a production engineer, to the Government, who sent them to the USA. Sidgreaves said:

Although this is a direct contract from the British Government to the Packard Company and therefore Rolls-Royce carry no responsibility for the placing or execution of the contract, it is inevitable that the success of the undertaking will depend on Rolls-Royce and it is certain we shall be blamed for any failure or difficulties which may arise.

Major Bulman wrote of the Packard production of Merlins:

The Packard Merlin was virtually interchangeable in detail with the home product except in the supercharger drive which was of Packard design. These American Merlins were of immense help to us in the War from 1940 on [actually 1941], as was the aircraft, named Mustang for the R.A.F. purposes, which became a formidable weapon, augmenting and at times exceeding the performance of the Spitfire against the German fighters. It was so liked by the U.S.A.A.F. that they collared a large proportion of the deliveries, having previously regarded this British intrusion into American aviation with some scorn if not derision!

For inter-Government reasons largely, all correspondence between Rolls-Royce and Packhards [sic] passed through my office, and there were never lacking several cables a day to be transmitted with top priority and in code, which became quite a nightmare at times.

The pressure on the three Derby men was immense, and it is significant that Barrington [actually in July 1943] and Jimmy Ellor died soon after the war, far before their time. John Reid retained his native accent, and when I remarked on this following his return home, he grinned and said 'Aye but they are all talking broad Lancashire now out there.' It was the devotion of men like these on which British aero engines was sustained, though for most of them their very names have long been forgotten.

With the help of the Rolls-Royce experts, Packard were producing their first engines within a year of the signature of the contract on 3 September 1940. The limitation on the build-up of production was, as was the case at the Glasgow factory, the output of gears. An early hold-up was caused by the sensible decision to stick with all the British threads for reasons of inter-changeability. British threads were dated by then, so it was difficult to get thread cutting or rolling equipment for these peculiar threads, especially in wartime and with everyone in the UK overstretched. Nevertheless, by April 1942 production had reached 510 engines per month, and in 1943 averaged 1,024 engines per month. In 1944 it nearly reached 2,000 a month, with a total for that year of 23,619 engines.

Packard supplied Merlin engines to the RAF, which were used in Lancasters, Mosquitoes and Spitfires. Their early engines, Merlin 28s, were similar to the Merlin XX, but had a two-piece block designed in the USA. The Packard Merlin 38s were equivalent to Merlin 22s, and used the Rolls-Royce-designed two-piece cylinder block.

On the Dam Busters raid, the Lancasters used Packard-built Merlin 28s. Packard Merlins for the US Air Force used the designation V1650, with slash numbers to denote the mark. The RAF Mustangs were fitted with V1650-3 or V1650-7 engines. These were two-stage engines, as opposed to the single-stage Merlin 28s.

The major difference between the Rolls-Royce and Packard two-stage Merlins was the supercharger drive. While the former used the Farman drive, the Packard used epicyclic gearing. The single-stage engines were essentially the same. For convenience, Packard used magnetos manufactured in the USA, and carburettors made by Bendix (also in the USA).

Packard made a total of 55,523 Merlins for the RAF and the USAAF. The two-stage Merlin built by Packard also replaced the Allison V1710 in the North American Mustang. The Mustang was first specified and ordered by the British Purchasing Commission in the USA in 1940, when it was seeking to find a fighter to add to the Hurricanes and Spitfires in Britain's offensive and defensive armoury. It was produced in less than four months, and was delivered with an Allison V1710 engine. This low-altitude rated engine did not allow the Mustang's aerodynamic features to be fully exploited, and the aircraft was initially only given close-support duties, while the Spitfire remained the RAF's premier fighter.

However, on 29 April 1942, Wing Commander Ian Campbell-Orde, commanding officer of the Air Fighting Development Unit (AFDU) at Duxford, rang Ronnie Harker, the Rolls-Royce service-liaison pilot, and asked him if he would like to come and try this new aeroplane from the USA which, in his opinion, was the best to come from that country so far. This was how Harker remembered it when he wrote his book, *Rolls-Royce from the Wings*, published by Oxford Illustrated Press in 1976:

The General took me to the aeroplane and showed me all around it, explaining as he did so some of the history of how the specification had originated. As I flew the Mustang, I felt that it had a number of desirable features which the current fighters lacked. I was particularly impressed by its large fuel capacity of 269 gallons on internal tanks. This was three times as much as the Spitfire. I also liked the six .5 heavy machine-guns mounted close inboard in the wings, the light and effective aileron control which gave a high rate of roll and perhaps most important of all, its low drag which gave it a very noticeable increase in top speed over both British and German contemporary fighters.

With the low full throttle height of the Allison engine its overall performance was adequate for Army operation and reconnaissance duties at low altitude. However, one saw immediately the possibility of the Mustang as an air-superiority and long-range penetration fighter – if only it could be fitted with our latest two-speed, two-stage supercharged Merlin. If this was successful, it could be the answer to both the Me 109 and the Focke-Wulf 190, thus providing certain qualities that the Spitfire lacked. I discussed this proposal with The General after my flight, and we agreed to put it up as a serious proposition.

On returning to Hucknall, I asked Witold Challier, our Polish performance expert, to estimate what the Mustang would do when fitted with a Merlin 61. He reported that there would be a greatly improved rate of climb and an increase of some 40 mph in top speed at 25,000 feet and above. This estimate, together with the fact that her tank capacity would give her longer range meant that the Mustang, when fitted with the Merlin, would be superior to any other fighter at that time.

Harker experienced difficulties in persuading the powers-that-be, but with the support of Ray Dorey he eventually convinced Hives. According to Harker, Hives said: 'If you really believe that it will do as you say and be superior to the Focke-Wulf 190, then we must do it.'

Hives telephoned Sir Wilfrid Freeman, Vice Chief of the Air Staff, and discussions began between Rolls-Royce and the Air Ministry. The drawback to installing the new Merlin 61 (which had been Harker's recommendation) was the fact that the Ministry wanted every Merlin 61 available to go into Spitfires to counter the new Fw 190.

To an extent, Rolls-Royce were in sympathy with this view, as is made clear in this memo from his assistant, Bill Lappin, to Hives on 14 May 1942, after a meeting at the Ministry:

Re: Mustang
At a meeting yesterday on a very high level, it was suggested to the Minister that the LX1 should be tried in the above machine, so you may hear about this, but if not you could put it on your list of points for next meeting with CDR.

I feel myself that it might pay a very good dividend, if it can be done quickly, to install the Merlin XX in this machine.

Discussions ranged back and forth, but soon tests took place, both at Hucknall and in the USA. In the USA, the proponents of installing the Merlin 61 into the Mustang found an important ally in Major Thomas (Tommy) Hitchcock, a former fighter ace of the First World War who became Assistant Air Attaché at the American Embassy in London. At the end of 1942, he gave a briefing to the Assistant Chief of Staff for Intelligence in Washington, saying, *inter alia*:

This fighter business in Europe is a little bit like the women's dress business . . . the question of styles and fashions keeps changing all the time. When I went back to London about seven months ago, the English Fighter Command wouldn't look at anything that wouldn't fly at 28,000 to 30,000 feet and have plenty of speed. Since then the Focke Wulf has come into active participation on the Western Front; and now all the talk you hear is about greater climb and additional acceleration. This is because the Focke Wulf had those capabilities to a very great degree.

The whole story of the English fighter planes is more a story of engines than it is of the planes themselves. When you talk about engines, you get practically down to the Rolls engine – that is the Rolls Merlin engine. It started out at about 850 hp with a critical altitude of around 15,000 feet.

Now, when I first went over there, I was rather surprised to run into a report that the Mustang, which is our P-51, was 35 miles an hour faster than the Spitfire V at around 15,000 feet. At 25,000 feet it went a few miles an hour faster and was pulling 290 less hp. That indicated there must be something aerodynamically good about the Mustang. Dr. E.P. Warner, prominent aeronautical engineer in this country, came over to England and made considerable studies as to the aerodynamic quality of the fighter planes. He reduced it to co-efficient drag. The Mustang had a very low co-efficient drag as compared to the Spitfire and that is why it goes faster. It had the lowest co-efficient of drag of any plane in that theatre; and the English gave it a very good report and became very enthusiastic about it.

They said, 'Now, if we can put a high altitude engine in this plane we will have the answer to a maiden's prayer.' So they put a Merlin 61 engine in it; and they have got us to put one into it in this country. Originally they were going to put in the 61 that peaked at 30,000 feet. Then because the Focke Wulf peaks at 21,000 feet (and because the Spitfire is lighter than the Mustang) they decided the thing to do was to let the Spitfires have the high cover, and try and make the Mustang a fighter against the Focke Wulf. They took the Merlin 61 engine and put a different blower ratio on it so as to get the critical altitude at 21,000 feet, and this is the plane which gives about 426 miles an hour at 21,000 feet. Their original thought was to bring it up higher with the 61 version that peaked at 30,000 feet.

The white hope of the English, in order to combat the Fw-190, and particularly the Focke Wulf with the fully rated engine (which they are probably up against now), is by putting the Merlin 61 into the Mustang. They believe that will be the best fighting plane for the next year or two; and their preliminary tests indicate they are right.

Mark Arnold-Foster wrote in *The World at War*:

If they were to bomb by day over Europe, what the Americans needed was a long-range fighter. They had reached the same point of frustration that the Luftwaffe had reached at the end of the Battle of Britain. The bombers. The Allies, unlike the

Germans, found a solution. It was the North American P-51B Mustang fighter, powered by the Rolls-Royce engine. The Mustang was probably the most remarkable combat aeroplane produced during World War Two. It represented the ultimate development of the highly stressed internal combustion piston-engined aeroplane.

The Mustang with the Merlin outperformed, as Harker had promised Hives it would, both the Messerschmitt 109 and the Focke-Wulf 190. In a memo to Sir Wilfrid Freeman on 8 November 1942, Hives wrote:

The results in the air fitted with the Merlin engine confirm that with the same power the Mustang is 20/25 mph faster than the Spitfire. We appreciated the inherent qualities as soon as one of our test pilots flew one at Duxford in May last, and realised its possibilities.

We do not look upon the Mustang as a replacement Spitfire, we look upon it as a replacement Hurricane . . . We can anticipate that Fighter Command might choose the Mustang in preference to the Spitfire unless something is done to overcome the obvious faults which we have mentioned (poor quality manufacture and finish).

Eventually, more than 12,000 Merlins were built for the Mustang.

After the US Eighth Air Force lost a number of bombers on a disastrous raid on Schweinfurt, it ordered substantial numbers of the Merlin-powered P-51B Mustang. In *A Short History of Air Power*, James Stokesbury wrote:

Deliverance of another sort was at hand, however, in the appearance of the North American P-51 Mustang, a happy marriage of an American airframe designed for a British purchasing mission and the great Merlin engine. The Mustang's conception went all the way back to 1940, but the first American combat group to fly them did not get to Britain until November 1943, which gives some idea of the lead time necessary to create the whole air-force system. On December 1, Mustangs flew their first long-range escort mission, nearly 500 miles to Kiel and back. That was just the beginning. By March 1944, the Mustangs, the bombers' 'little friends', escorted Flying Fortresses and Liberators all the way to Berlin, 1,100 miles. No longer were German fighters free to make their killing passes at the hard-pressed formations of plodding heavy bombers. Allied fighters over Berlin meant air supremacy, fulfilling Trenchard's old dictum that command of the air begins at the enemy's aerodromes. The few Germans knowledgeable about air war knew they had lost when they saw Mustangs over the heart of the Reich. The corner was turned at last.

This was the verdict of Sholto Douglas:

The Mustang after it had been built with our Merlin engines which were built under licence in the United States, became one of the finest and most versatile of all the fighters that were produced during the Second World War.

TILLY SCHILLING

The Merlin engine justifiably achieved an enviable reputation but, as with all mechanical devices, it suffered its share of problems. There were very few on single-engine installations or on the Lancaster whose powerplants were carried well forward of the wing. The biggest problems arose on the Halifax and Mosquito. The Halifax suffered no fewer than ninety-five gear reduction failures in a period of six months. The powerplant was set close to the wing and well above the leading edge, causing a great deal of disturbed airflow around the propellers. The three-blade propellers meant considerable vibration for the engine, and a change to four-blade propellers was tried. It brought some improvement.

Ronnie Harker, in his liaison role, heard of any complaints from the front line. He recalled that, during the Battle of Britain and for some time after, there were a number of big-end failures. Sometimes these caused a fire, leading to a forced landing or even the abandoning of the aircraft. Cyril Lovesey, in charge of engine development, tried everything he knew on the test beds, but could not establish the cause. Harker tried in the air with a flight that included 167 slow rolls and twelve vertical dives, but still could not replicate the failure. The problem was finally solved by a Wing Commander Boyd at the Aircraft and Armament Experimental Establishment at Boscombe Down. He took an aircraft up to 30,000 feet, rolled it on its back, thus losing oil pressure, over-revved to 3,600 rpm and, with a slight negative 'G' force all the way down, held this condition. This meant that the engine was exceeding maximum rpm for at least thirty seconds while starved of oil, and therefore air was getting to the bearings instead of oil.

Hives took a very close interest in any complaints coming back from both the test pilots and those in combat action. Perhaps the most intractable problem they faced was what became known as the 'skewgear failure'. Alex Henshaw describes it in detail in his book, *Sigh for a Merlin*. Suffice it here to say that there were several failures, and as Henshaw put it:

These skewgear failures were more disturbing because there was no warning of any kind and they often occurred after a machine had been climbed, dived at full throttle, tested and probably had several landings and adjustments.

Finally, on 18 July 1942, Henshaw suffered a nearly fatal crash in the Black Country, virtually demolishing a house. As a result, tremendous pressure was brought to bear from Hives to find the cause of the trouble. Alec Harvey-Bailey, in charge of defect investigation on the Merlin and Griffon during the war, remembered that both engine testing and failure investigation were treated with great respect:

At the start of a new factory or new engine type, all engines were endurance tested, stripped and rebuilt for final test. As engine conditions permitted this was eased until only a sample of engines were stripped, the remainder being endurance final tested and, if satisfactory, despatched. This system was no formality. One would find very senior people on the inspection lines seeing for themselves. At that time a number of features, such as reduction gear tip correction and tooth alignment, was determined almost entirely by bedding patterns. Bearings, pistons and rings, and joint conditions would be looked at critically and, if warnings were present of impending trouble, action would be initiated. Later in the War, Production Proof Tests were introduced when sample engines from the line would be subjected to the last 25 hours of the type test and then examined with the object of seeing troubles that might not show on normal non-easement engines. If one reads this in context with the failure investigation activity and the monitoring of repair engine condition, and recognising the short timescales involved, it will be seen that there was an effective system for handling the situation.

As Derby built pilot quantities of major new types, various parameters including final performance limits and such things as piston profiles, ring gaps and other features would be established on production, not without some lively and competitive arguments with other interested parties.

To help Alec Harvey-Bailey further, Rolls-Royce's liaison pilots, such as Ronnie Harker and Athol McIntyre, visited squadrons and brought home broken bits in their Spitfires and Mustangs. And indeed it was Alec's father, R.W.H. Bailey, whom Hives put in charge of the skewgear failure inquiry. When the problem was finally solved, Alex Henshaw remembers that Hives telephoned him personally to say that the solution had been found.

By January 1941, with the Battle of Britain successfully won, the RAF began sorties over Northern France, and complaints started to come back from the Spitfire pilots (because of their greater speed, Spitfires were used rather than Hurricanes) that the improved Me 109F and the Focke-Wulf 190 were outperforming the Spitfire. Sholto Douglas wrote later:

In the introduction of new aircraft with improved performance it was still, as always, a see-saw, with first one side and then the other gaining the upper hand. With our improved Spitfires we had caught up with the Me 109F. The struggle had remained on a fairly equal footing until towards the latter part of the summer of 1941; and then we were caught flat-footed. My pilots reported seeing over Amiens a new type of radial-engined fighter. It was in the course of one of the Circus operations, and there were some particularly experienced pilots flying in the wings from Kenley, Tangmere and Northolt. Our intelligence people ridiculed the idea. But what the pilots reported was correct: they were seeing for the first time the Focke-Wulf 190.

One other problem with the early Merlins was the limitation imposed by the float-type carburettors. A rapid dive would cause the engine to cut because the float chamber was flooded. The Messerschmitt 109E did not suffer the same problem, as its Daimler-Benz 601A engine did not have a carburettor – it used a direct-injection fuel system instead. The German pilots soon appreciated the opportunity, and could escape Hurricanes and Spitfires on their tail by going into a steep dive. If they attempted to follow, the British aircraft would splutter and misfire, the propeller would go into fine pitch which slowed the dive even more, and when the engine picked up again it would overspeed violently. Even if the British rolled into the dive, they still lost ground.

The problem was partially solved by an ingenious engineer at the RAE at Farnborough, Miss Tilly Schilling. She developed a washer with a small calibrated hole to place in the fuel supply line, the small hole passing just enough fuel for full power at sea level under negative 'G' conditions. Pilots, perhaps better known for straightforwardness than subtlety, referred to the device as 'Miss Schilling's orifice', and it was installed throughout Fighter Command by March 1941.

Gordon Dawson, who worked under Harry Cantrill in the Testing Department (largely on developing the Griffon engine), remembered that it was learnt pretty quickly after the Schilling solution that the Americans had found a complete cure for the problem with the Bendix pressure diaphragm carburettor, but it took some time to secure supplies. In the meantime, both Rolls-Royce and the SU carburettor company, in conjunction with the RAE at Farnborough, developed anti-'G' versions of the Merlin carburettor. Both worked well, but were replaced by the Bendix carburettor when it became available.

THE GRIFFON

The first reference to the engine which became the Griffon was in a memo from Royce dated 22 August 1930, in which he requested that an 'H' (Buzzard) engine be built with a double helical reduction gear, which would give quieter running. This engine became known as the Modified 'H' engine. There was little progress during 1931, because of the concentration on the Schneider Trophy. The first time the Griffon name was applied was on a design scheme, DES 1618, dated 30 January 1932. The first run of Griffon Serial No. 1 was on 6 January 1933, and the last run of this engine was in 1934. The programme was abandoned in the spring of 1936 as priority was given to the Merlin. Initially, the Merlin also had double helical reduction gears, but when it suffered failures it moved on to straight spur gears, as did the Griffon.

At the beginning of 1939 Hives, already appreciating the need for a more powerful Merlin, ordered the development of a new Griffon to be inter-changeable with the Merlin; thereafter the Griffon of the early 1930s was referred to as the 'old' Griffon. The new Griffon was called Griffon I, and ran for the first time on 30 November 1939. However, it was clear by then that it was too heavy, and a weight-saving project was put in hand. Harry Cantrill, who had joined Rolls-Royce from Armstrong Siddeley, and his team took 200 lbs off the weight of the engine. This lighter engine became the Griffon II (the Griffon I, of which only three were built, was abandoned). The Griffon II first ran on 26 June 1940, but suffered a number of problems, including torsional vibration of the crankshaft. This was corrected by changing the firing order and by altering the mounting system from back and middle to back and front. This modified Griffon was called the Griffon IIB, and first ran in December 1940.

The Griffon IIB performed well from the start, undergoing its type test and going into production with remarkably little further development. An inten-sive programme then started for more power and higher rated altitude, with a range of different specifications to suit various applications. The latter was simplified by the new auxiliary gearbox carrying many of the accessories which in the case of the Merlin had been engine-mounted. This avoided the need for many engine modifications. The first actual engine modification, implemented shortly after production started, was the switch to the Bendix injection carburettor to cure the negative 'G' problem (before the Merlin).

Following the experience with the Merlin, a two-stage supercharged version came quickly, and in two years boost went up from plus 12 lb per square inch to plus 25 lb per square inch, power from 1,700 hp to 2,300 hp, and FS rated altitude from 14,500 feet to 26,000 feet. Meanwhile, develop-ment was proceeding, and the major decision here was to continue with the forward cam and magneto drives but to revert to rear crank drive for the supercharger. Important innovations were the end oil-feed crankshaft (which made the main and big-end bearings much less vulnerable) and an external drive for a gearbox which carried all the auxiliaries and freed the engine from the multiple drives for these. It also had an improved supercharger and an updraught carburettor with a number of other detailed improvements. As the higher grades of fuel became available in service, the engine was able to use the boost they permitted. The addition of water-methanol injection on top of the plus 25 lb boost gave a take-off rating of about 2,500 hp. The heavy programme went through with a few problems, which were solved, and the engine was very successful in service.

By late 1939, both the Air Ministry and Supermarine were showing interest in the possibility of the Griffon being installed in the Spitfire. Sir Wilfrid Freeman's interest was significant, because earlier in 1939 he had been discussing the idea of turning Supermarine over to production of the Beaufighter. Opinion at Supermarine itself was that every possible power increase should be squeezed from the Merlin, but that eventually it would be superseded by the Griffon. At Derby, Hives was heard to refer to it as 'the second power string for the Spitfire'. Joe Smith at Supermarine said, 'A good big 'un will always beat a good little 'un', and he wanted the Griffon tested in a Spitfire as soon as possible.

During the summer and autumn of 1940, other more pressing events delayed any testing of the Griffon, and it was not until 27 November 1941 that Jeffrey Quill made a test flight in a Mark III airframe fitted with a Griffon engine, the RG 2SM. This aircraft was designated the Mark IV. This is what Quill wrote about it later:

The main differences, insofar as they affected the pilot, were: because the Griffon engine rotated the opposite way to the Merlin, it caused the aeroplane to swing right-handed instead of left-handed on the take-off; there was somewhat less ground clearance, resulting in a slight reduction in propeller diameter; the power available for take-off was much greater; and the engine RPM were lower than in the Merlin.

All this meant that the throttle needed to be handled judiciously on take-off but, once in the air, the aeroplane had a great feeling of power about it; it seemed the airborne equivalent of a very powerful sports car and was great fun to fly. Changes of trim with changes of power were much more in evidence, both directionally and longitudinally, and the aeroplane sheared about a bit during tight manoeuvres and simulated dog-fights. I realised at once that we should have to correct its directional characteristics and probably its longitudinal stability also, both of which, in due time we achieved. Indeed, DP845 eventually went through many phases of development, remaining in our flight development unit throughout and I, and others, flew in it a great deal; it became one of our favourite aeroplanes.

However, by the end of 1941, the two-stage supercharger with intercooler system was being fitted to the Merlin, and the single-stage Griffon had been leapfrogged. As a result, the Mark IV had no production future, but the practicality of fitting a Griffon into a Spitfire had been proved. There was every reason to think that whatever supercharger technology was applied to the Merlin, could also be applied to the Griffon.

Further developments to build a new Spitfire with a big two-stage Griffon were put in hand, but in the meantime Jeffrey Quill showed what could be done in a Spitfire with a single-stage Griffon – 'by then almost my favourite aircraft with its spectacular rate of climb "off the deck" and very good low-level performance', as he put it. In July 1942, Quill was asked to race this Spitfire against an Fw 190 and a Typhoon in front of some VIPs at Farnborough. He wrote about the day later:

On reflection the general scheme became clear. The Spitfire was to be a sort of datum pacemaker – 'Mr Average Contemporary Fighter' – and its job would be to come in last, the real excitement of the proceedings being by how much it would be beaten by the Fw 190 and the Typhoon, and which of these two bright stars would beat the other and by how much. Outside on the tarmac at Worthy Down stood the inoffensive-looking but highly potent DP845. Nobody had said what sort of Spitfire I should bring. Just a Spitfire. I rang up Joe Smith. 'Joe', I said, 'about this thing at Farnborough. I reckon if I take DP845 I will beat the pair of them. Will that upset any applecarts?' 'You bet it will', he said. 'Take it.'

At Farnborough I parked DP845 as inconspicuously as I could and walked into Willy Wilson's office. Kenneth Seth-Smith of Hawkers had arrived with his Typhoon, and we discussed the plan.

We would all three take off together and fly to a point westwards of the aerodrome at Odiham. We would then head back towards Farnborough in open line abreast at a moderate cruising speed at 1,000 ft, Willy Wilson in the centre with the Fw 190 and Seth-Smith and myself on each side. At a signal from Willy we would all open up simultaneously to full power and head for the finishing line at Farnborough where the assembled VIPs would be waiting.

All went according to plan until, when we were about half-way between Odiham and Farnborough and going flat out, I was beginning to overhaul Fw 190 and Typhoon. Suddenly I saw sparks and black smoke coming from the Fw 190's exhaust and at that moment Willy also saw it and throttled back his BMW engine and I shot past him and never saw him again. I was also easily leaving the Typhoon behind and the eventual finishing order was, first the Spitfire, second the Typhoon, third the Fw 190.

This was precisely the opposite result to that expected or indeed intended. It certainly put the cat among the pigeons, and among the VIPs. When I taxied in, everybody crowded round the DP845, as the message sank in that it was the Griffon Spitfire which had handsomely beaten what were then supposed to be the two fastest fighters in service. The sensation was considerable.

Although the engine ended with a long list of Mark numbers, there were only five production applications – Firefly, Spitfire, Seafire, Barracuda and Shackleton – and only the first two of these initially. There was in addition a considerable range of prototypes: Beaufighter, Hawker Henley, Tempest and Fury, Seagull, Martin Baker MB5, Blackburn B54, Spiteful and Seafang. Although useful as prototype testbeds, these were replaced in service by gas turbine-engined aircraft.

The Griffon 100/120 series was the ultimate version intended for the Spitfire 21, Spiteful, Seafire 46 and Seafang, most of which were prototypes. All of these had three-speed, two-stage superchargers, and some had contra-rotating propellers.

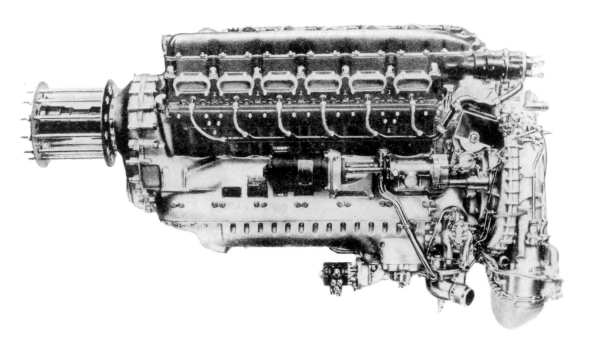

The Merlin evolved from Rolls-Royce's PV12 (Private Venture)
engine, launched by Royce just before he died.
The development process proved difficult. The first
engines to go into service incorporated the
ramphead cylinder block, and were known as Merlin Is.

The Merlin engine was launched on three new aircraft types:
the Fairey Battle bomber (ABOVE), the Hawker Hurricane
(OPPOSITE TOP) and the Supermarine Spitfire (OPPOSITE BOTTOM).
The aircraft shown here are the prototypes, towards all
of which Rolls-Royce contributed financially in order to secure
the selection of the Merlin.

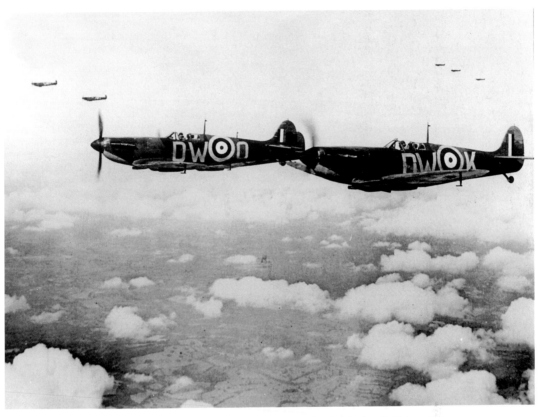

This photograph is one of the few available of Spitfires in action
during the Battle of Britain.

OPPOSITE TOP: No. 65 'East India' Squadron flying its Spitfire
F1s in formation just before the outbreak of war in 1939. The
nearest aircraft was piloted by Flt. Lt. Stanford Tuck, later to
distinguish himself in the Battle of Britain, as did Flying Officer
Kingcome, seen flying FZ 0.

OPPOSITE BOTTOM: By the time the Battle of Britain began in
August 1940, the RAF's Hurricanes and Spitfires were powered
by Merlin IIIs. As the battle progressed into autumn, a number
of Spitfires were fitted with the Merlin XII, which gave
enhanced altitude performance. Later in the battle, the
Hurricane II appeared, powered by the Merlin XX with its
improved supercharger intake design and two-speed
supercharger drive.

A Heinkel III attacks a Spitfire.

The Rolls-Royce work force toiled twelve hours a day for seven
days, followed by twelve hours a night for six nights,
with one day off every two weeks. To maintain the pace as
dawn approached, the workers sang together.

The Merlin 45 series incorporated the much-improved single-stage supercharger with central entry introduced by Dr. Stanley Hooker. It was known on the shop floor as 'the baby's bum'. Whereas Hawker introduced the Merlin XX series – which incorporated the new supercharger and a two-speed drive – in the Hurricane II late in the Battle of Britain, Supermarine were unwilling to accept the XX, which was some two inches longer. Instead, the new supercharger was incorporated on the single-speed engine, and powered the Spitfire V. This gave a major improvement in performance.

OPPOSITE TOP: This painting by Roddy Lovesey, son of Cyril Lovesey (who was in charge of Merlin development throughout the war), depicts Pilot Officer Denis (later Air Marshal Sir Denis) Crowley-Milling shooting down his first enemy aircraft over Essex on 30 August 1940, after taking off in a Hurricane from Duxford with 242 Squadron.

OPPOSITE BOTTOM: Thanks to the installation of radar, Britain's commanders received some warning of impending attack. Nevertheless, every second counted.

Spitfire VB with Merlin 45 series engine.

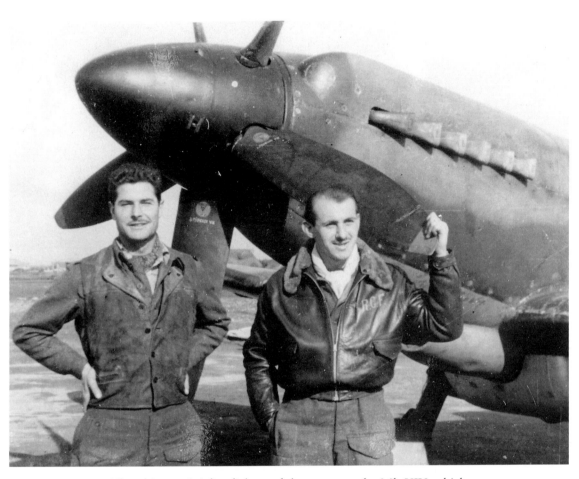

The ultimate Spitfire fighter of the war was the Mk XIV, which adapted the two-stage, two-speed intercooled Griffon 60 series engine to the Mk VIII airframe. Driving the efficient Rotol five-bladed propeller, it was more than a match for the Bf 109 and Fw 190 at any altitude, and in fact was the first Allied fighter to shoot down an Me 262 jet fighter. The photograph shows pilots of 350 (Belgian) Squadron, RAF, Roberto Muls and Robert François, with one of their Mk XIVs in the Low Countries in the spring of 1945. Among the aircraft they flew was the Mk XIV bought by Rolls-Royce in 1949.

Throughout the war, the Spitfire was developed to counter improvements in the enemy aircraft it faced. A first key improvement was the Spitfire V with its Merlin 45 series engine. Altitude performance was then dramatically improved with the creation of the Spitfire VIII with its two-stage, two-speed intercooled Merlin 60 series engine. This more than matched the new Focke-Wulf Fw 190 at medium to high altitude, but the Fw 190 was appearing in large numbers. Spitfire Vs were converted or completed with the Merlin 60 series, thus creating the Mk IX, of which far more were built than the definitive Mk VIII. However, the Fw 190 could still outfly all but the Hawker Typhoon at low level in 1942, and the RAF was concerned about the latter's reliability. In consequence, a hundred Spitfire V airframes were modified to accept the single-stage Griffon. This created the Spitfire XII. An early encounter occurred when 91 Squadron caught 190s trying a low-level evening raid on Folkestone. The squadron shot down five of the fourteen intruders.

TOP: The de Havilland Mosquito was perhaps the most versatile aircraft available to the RAF during the war, serving as a bomber, fighter (especially at night), pathfinder, and even as a transport aircraft of material and personnel from neutral Sweden. This photograph shows Ivor (later Air Marshal Sir Ivor) Broom with his navigator, also called Broom (Tommy). Inevitably, they were known as the broomsticks (see crossed broomsticks on nose).

BOTTOM: This photograph shows Mosquitoes taking off on a night raid. Such was their speed that the squadron said: 'Berlin and back and in the bar before it closes.' This also gave the option of flying two missions in a night.

The Avro Lancaster was the RAF's most successful bomber of
the war. It evolved from the Manchester, powered by two
Rolls-Royce Vulture engines. When Hives sidelined the Vulture,
he offered four Merlins to replace it, and transformed the
aircraft. As with the Wellington and the Halifax, variants of the
Lancaster were also powered by air-cooled radial
Bristol engines.

As the war progressed, the two-stage took over from the single-stage Griffon and led the development effort. The last Griffons to be produced were the 37 for the Barracuda and, after further improvements, the 57 and 58 for the Avro Shackleton. The Griffon 58 was cleared originally in 1946 for the Shackleton prototype, but stayed in production until 1955; one was redelivered to the RAF, after a major overhaul at the Glasgow factory, as late as 1986.

The Griffon remained in service in the Shackleton until 1991, operating on a daily basis at nearly 2,500 hp at take-off and with a life of 2,000 hours. This was the same power achieved in 1931 by its forebear, the 'R' engine, with the same bore and stroke but with a life of only one hour, a fine example of the progress of detailed mechanical development over a period of sixty years.

There are those who believe that it was the Griffon that ultimately made the Spitfire the outstanding fighter of the war. And it was not just performance that endeared it to the RAF. The service personnel reported that it had the best test record of any engine they handled, with a higher percentage of Griffons reaching their overhaul time limit without mechanical problems than any other type of engine.

CHAPTER NINE

HOLDING IT ALL TOGETHER

'THE DOOR IS ALWAYS OPEN'
KEEPING THE TEAM TOGETHER
PLANNING FOR A NEW ERA
'MORE POWER THAN THE MERLIN'

'THE DOOR IS ALWAYS OPEN'

BECAUSE SO MANY DETAILED, technical books have been written on Rolls-Royce engines, it is easy to lose sight of the company itself, its ethos, conditions and vision of the future. Fortunately, perhaps because Rolls-Royce was, and still is, such an inspirational company to work in, a number of people who enjoyed distinguished careers with the company have written about their experiences, and we can learn a great deal from them.

One was Dr. (later Sir) Stanley Hooker, who joined the company in January 1938 at the age of thirty, after being tempted away from his position as Senior Scientific Officer at the Admiralty Research Laboratory. His interviews and first days bore an uncanny resemblance to the situation that R.W.H. Bailey had experienced twenty-five years earlier, and which we read about in chapter two.

Hooker initially received a letter from an old Oxford University friend, Dr. Frederick Llewellyn Smith (later to run the Motor Car Division at Crewe and, ultimately, the Oil Engine Division at Shrewsbury as well, but at that time in the Engineering Department at Derby).

Hooker went for an interview with Colonel Barrington, chief designer, and while waiting met Arthur Rubbra, already the assistant chief designer. Hooker remembered being shocked that such a young man could hold such a senior position:

I expected Rolls-Royce engineers to be grizzled men with beards and at least 50 years old.

After lunch at the Midland Hotel at Derby Station, 'with its frightful exterior and very comfortable interior', Hooker was sent back to London with what he described as a 'don't call us, we'll call you' farewell. Hooker may not have known it, but this was the usual response to interviewees.

However, two months later he was summoned to see the general manager, Ernest Hives. On his desk were copies of Hooker's published works. Hives asked him, 'What's a Karman Vortex Street?' After Hooker had tried to explain, Hives said, 'You're not much of an engineer, are you?'

Hives said that it didn't matter. The place was full of engineers, and it was Hooker's mathematical ability that Rolls-Royce were interested in. 'When can you start?', asked Hives. This was all too abrupt for Hooker, who wanted to know what he would be expected to do, and for how much.

Hives asked, 'Whom do you work for now?' Hooker told him, and Hives immediately ordered his secretary to get Charles Wright at the Admiralty on the telephone. 'I have a man called Hooker here, who says that he works for you, and who wants a job with us,' said Hives. After he put the telephone down, he said to Hooker: 'He says that you are a dirty dog to leave him after he has just promoted you, but he recommends you and says that we can have you.'

Hooker was aghast at this treatment, but was won over by Hives's charm and by the acceptance of his request to be paid £1,000 a year, about 18% more than he was earning at the Admiralty. (It probably equates to £50,000 in today's terms, and was certainly a very good salary for a thirty year old in 1938.) Hooker remembered that Hives went on to talk to him about the great store of knowledge of mechanical engineering built up in the company, thanks to Sir Henry Royce's insistence on perfection. He also talked about the firm's manufacturing skills, and their loyal work force with its father-to-son tradition. He emphasised his own involvement with the shop-floor, saying:

This door is always open to our men. Only the other day a fitter came in and said, 'Our Bill is leaving school on Friday', so I said, 'You had better send him round to see us on Monday, and we will see what we can do with him'.

As we have already seen, Hives felt that some of the company's thinking and techniques had not kept pace with the changing times, and he said to Hooker:

I am no mathematician or scientist, but I have a feeling that we are going to need such people in the future. We need a more technical and analytical approach to some of our engineering problems, and I am going to look to men like you to give us that lead.

Hooker recalled that he left the office elated. He joined Rolls-Royce in January 1938, but as with Bailey, his first few days were a great disappointment to him. Indeed, on his first day he could hardly believe that his interview with Hives had taken place. This is how he recalled it in his book, *Not much of an Engineer*:

It was a damp, cold day in January 1938 when I garaged my car at the junction with the Osmaston Road and began to walk up Nightingale Road towards the great Rolls-Royce works in Derby.

The dreariness on the left, interspersed with the odd conversation to a general grocer's or tobacconist, and on the right a small open lot used as a works car park, matched the foreboding in my mind. Not a soul was in sight, nor was there any noise, because the workshops were set back from the road behind the front facade of offices.

With each step I took, my heart sank further. Why had I left my comfortable and interesting job in the Scientific Research Department of the Admiralty? And what was I going to do in the formidable Rolls-Royce company, which represented the very pinnacle of engineering excellence?

I was no engineer. I had been trained in Applied Mathematics, so how could I hope to compete with, or even to help, the semi-Godlike engineers with which, I was convinced, Rolls-Royce must be stocked – doubtless trained by the legendary Sir Henry Royce himself?

The apprehension grew as I approached the main entrance on my right. It stood back a few yards from the pavement, with an oval drive in and out in front. At the door stood a very smart uniformed commissionaire. I approached him with caution.

'Yes, Sir, you will find Mr. Elliott's office in the next block. Take the next gate on the right, and then the entrance to the Engineering Offices is on your left.'

I found my way easily enough, and stumbled along the corridor until I reached the office marked A.G. Elliott, Chief Engineer. I knocked and was told to enter. It was not a large office, and very sparsely furnished. Mr. Elliott sat at his desk, back to the windows and facing the door. In the further corner sat his personal assistant, A. Lidsey.

Elliott clearly had not the foggiest idea who I was, and had forgotten that he was to interview me. He spoke very quietly and enquired about my business. I explained that I was the new man joining the firm, by name Hooker. He smiled as the memory came back and said, 'Of course, welcome to Rolls-Royce. We have prepared an office for you, and Mr. Lidsey will show you to it.'

The interview was over that quickly, and it was not at all what I had expected. Lidsey led me around the corridor, and at a junction he opened a door, and said 'This is your office, cheerio'. The walls were painted metal for the first four feet from the floor, and frosted glass above. It was about eight feet square and contained a desk, a chair, an empty bookcase and a telephone, and nothing more. I sank bewildered into the hard chair and gazed at the nothingness of the wall.

248

All around me there was a hive of industry. I could hear telephones ringing, the clacking of typewriters, and the hum of conversation. Mostly offices were much larger open spaces with similar dividing walls, but housing groups of men working with intense concentration. A very large area was clearly devoted to design, and full of towering drawing-boards.

Later I learned that rumour and curiosity was rife about the new so-called 'mathematical whizz kid' who had been granted the rare privilege of a private office. At the time I was just ignored, completely.

And so the day wore slowly on. I had anticipated that I would have been put into the charge of some awe-inspiring engineer, who would have allocated me some simple tasks while instructing me in the mysteries of the super aero engines that Rolls-Royce was designing and producing. But it was not so. I, who had never seen an aero engine at close range, and who only had a schoolboy's knowledge of its inside, did not even know the names of the engines Rolls-Royce was producing.

At 5.00 pm there was a general exodus, and I departed with the rest, thoroughly dispirited at the emptiness of my first day. However, after my evening meal, I cheered up a bit when it occurred to me that the only possible explanation must be that the powers that be were still debating my ultimate fate, and had not yet reached any conclusion about the job I was to do.

But nothing happened, and after a number of days Hooker decided that he had better go and explore. After a time, he came across someone whose job it was to test superchargers. Hooker realised that he was now in an area where his knowledge and experience could be used, and at last he could do some useful work. He found out later that this apparent neglect of him by the senior management had been deliberate. Hives did not want to have him diverted into routine activity, but to find his way about and then concentrate on what he knew best. We have already seen Hooker's great contribution to the development of the supercharger, which was so important in enhancing the performance of the Merlin.

KEEPING THE TEAM TOGETHER

In the production of successful aero engines, two essentials have to come together: design and production. Rolls-Royce were a complete, virtually integrated company – they designed, developed and produced their engines. Whereas in Royce's day design had been paramount, in Hives's day development and production moved to the fore. How did the Design Department cope with the demands of war?

Even before Royce died, A.G. Elliott moved back to Derby, taking Charles Jenner with him. When Royce died in 1933, Elliott had established himself in Derby, and the others were forced to slot in as best they could. By the mid-1930s, Rolls-Royce were recruiting from English and Scottish universities with the best engineering departments by making known to their Vice-Chancellors and Principals the company's need for engineering graduates. This policy brought in a number of graduates who later became well known in the industry. A number of other more mature recruitments were made in the late 1930s, including: Dr. Stanley Hooker, the aerodynamicist whose contributions to supercharger development we have noted above; Dr. A.A. Griffith from RAE Farnborough, who had been developing ideas on gas turbines; and Harry Cantrill from Armstrong Siddeley, who contributed enormously to the development of the Griffon.

The Engineering Division set-up reached its wartime level in 1939, and continued thereafter with remarkably few organisational changes until 1946. When war was declared in 1939, all of the staff departments were removed from Derby. The Chassis Division relocated itself at Clan Foundry in Belper; the Advanced Project Design, Doc Griffith and Model Making were put into Duffield Bank House; and Design, Detail Drawing and Technical Functions were housed in cottages and various other places in Belper, including the swimming baths.

The Engineering Division was in three main departments: Design Offices, Workshops, and Experimental. The shops and design arrangements were pretty conventional, but both had to introduce increasing amounts of gas turbine work during the second half of the war. The Experimental Department was somewhat different. It had nine different sections, including two separate engine test departments. It was a loose organisation with loose lines of command. The section heads knew very well the various programme objectives, but their detailed programmes had to be kept flexible because a failure on test or a sudden new switch of prototype requirement could alter the priorities in a number of sections. This, of course, also affected the shop and design programmes, but to a lesser extent. There were hiccups, but these were always overcome by dedication and hard work, and they began to decrease after 1943, when the total pressure on the programme lessened as the centre of gravity of the fever-pitch Engineering Department switched to Barnoldswick and the development of the gas turbine engine.

There were two main cores to the experimental work: performance and durability. The performance work was centred on supercharger development. The principal facility here was a supercharger test rig, on which designs could be tested away from the engine. This was supported by a single-cylinder test section, a carburettor section and a performance section.

Those involved in the design, development and manufacture of aero engines were working flat-out against a nearly impossible timetable. Most who had been involved on the car side were switched over to the manufacture of aero engines, but there were those, especially in the Car Design

Department, who continued to work under W.A. Robotham on other products, and also to prepare for car production after the war.

It was assumed that total sales would be about 1,500 cars annually, and for this to be profitable it would be essential that all models should have as many components in common as possible, and that 'bought out' components should be used wherever possible (providing quality was not sacrificed), in order to take advantage of the economies of mass production.

The Managing Director, Arthur Sidgreaves, reported to his fellow directors in October 1939:

It is quite clear that the days of what may be described as the Silver Ghost mentality have gone and there will have to be an entirely fresh outlook not only on design, manufacturing and production methods, but also on sales methods.

Hives had already expressed his view that an entirely separate factory for car production would be desirable, if only to get away from the traditional production methods at Derby. Once Crewe had been picked as the home for the shadow factory, Hives named it as a possible post-war site for car production.

And Lord Herbert Scott, who had joined Rolls-Royce as a director as long ago as 1906, and was now Chairman, wrote to Sidgreaves in November 1939:

It might be well to consider whether the original programme of one model which made the name of Rolls-Royce world famous would not be a sound proposition to revert to for the initial stages of post-war production. Such a plan commends itself to me because it would give breathing space for our sales and those concerned to discover the reaction the war had produced on the motor-car market due to taxation and other causes.

In Derby, car production, albeit on a diminishing scale, continued right up to the outbreak of war, and the whole technical staff remained in place working on new models. However, when war finally arrived, the entire Derby factory was required for aero engine work, and everything to do with cars – whether it was experimental cars, tools and fixtures or production patterns – had to move out and find accommodation elsewhere. A number of tools and patterns deteriorated to the point of uselessness, as some of the storage places found were damp and unheated. At least Robotham managed to complete two full sets of drawings of the planned post-war cars, and Hives found time to arrange with the Admiralty to have one set shipped to Canada (later followed by two complete cars). Robotham deposited the other set in the strong-room of a bank in Ashby-de-la-Zouch, a small town about twelve miles from Derby.

Robotham was desperate to keep his design team together and employed, but all suitable accommodation in Belper was commandeered by the Aero Engine Division, who naturally had priority. It was assumed that the Derby factory would be a prime target for the Luftwaffe, and Hives therefore evacuated all technical staff, mainly to Belper but also to the surrounding villages (although Hives himself remained in his office throughout the war).

The Car Division's eventual salvation was described graphically by Robotham:

Things were beginning to look a little desperate when I heard of a disused iron foundry situated on the southern outskirts of Belper, just north of the little village of Milford. I lost no time in following up this lead.

Clan Foundry, as it was called, could scarcely have had a less prepossessing exterior or interior, and the sight of its gaunt outline was calculated to strike a chill into the stoutest heart. It was depressing, it was derelict, it was disintegrating. The building consisted of tarred corrugated-iron and was built on a slag heap. A small wooden office was situated alongside the main structure next to the road. This had obviously once been painted green, but smoke from the foundry on the opposite side of the road and from its own antiquated boilerhouse had converted the green to a mottled grey.

At the foot of the slag heap ran the main railway line to Manchester, alongside the River Derwent. As the trains thundered past it seemed more likely that eventually the vibration would precipitate the ramshackle building and the rubble on which it was perched into the flowing stream.

The inside of the foundry had a dirt floor, and in the many places where corrosion had got the better of the tar the roof leaked. The covered space available had an area about the size of two tennis courts. The place was obviously infested with rats, and masses of willow herb stalks carrying feathery heads crowded the slopes of the dump.

The senior members of the motor car design staff who were asked to work in these unpromising surroundings were Charles Jenner and Ivan Evernden, both of whom, as we have seen, had worked with Royce at West Wittering. John Draper was responsible for the drawing office personnel and Fred Hardy led the development team. Harold Whyman, who had been in charge of the experimental garage before the war, was made responsible for making the foundry habitable. He succeeded, though some time was wasted initially in building slit trenches in the field nearby. (Clearly someone thought that Hitler was concerned about the future of Britain's luxury cars!)

Finding accommodation was one priority, now solved. Another was to find worthwhile work. The aero engine design team did not need any help, so it was a relief when it was suggested that Robotham's team might help on a 40 mm aircraft cannon being designed by Spirito Mario Viale (a designer who came to Rolls-Royce from Italy via Armstrong Siddeley) at the Drawing

Office at his home on Burton Road, Littleover. Viale employed his own design team, but Robotham's team were able to help on the mountings. This kept them occupied, and they were also involved in repairing Peregrines, Kestrels and Merlins, but Hives decided that the manufacture of guns was best left to Vickers, Bofors and Oerlikon, and the project was abandoned.

Hives had initially taken up the challenge of making the gun at a Ministry of Supply meeting, at which he had been shocked by the complacency of Vickers, who said it would take five years to develop the required 40 mm gun. Hives said: 'Rolls-Royce don't know anything about guns but we'll do it in twelve months.'

The gun was developed, but was superseded by air-to-ground rockets. Nevertheless, a number were manufactured by the British United Shoe Machinery Company in Leicester, as the Two Pounder Quick Fire for the Royal Navy.

By the autumn of 1940, Robotham was becoming desperate again. It was then that he made contact with an old school friend, Henry (later Sir Henry) Spurrier, a senior executive at the truck maker, Leyland. The result was an agreement to pool the design teams of Leyland and the Rolls-Royce Motor Car Division to offer help to improve the reliability and fire-power of the tanks currently being used by the Army. Leyland were already producing the Centaur tank, which was fitted with a Liberty engine and whose design dated from the First World War. Spurrier was occupied with converting his factories from truck to tank production, and it was agreed that Rolls-Royce would analyse the defects in the tanks the Army were using.

Three designers from Leyland – John McHugh, Cyril Meynell and Bill Dennison – moved to Belper and joined Charlie Jenner, Ivan Evernden and Bill Allen. They worked in an office set up by Robotham in a squash court which he had built before the war in the garden of his house in Duffield, Park Leys. (Alan Swinden, who worked with Charlie Jenner in this squash court before becoming Hives's personal assistant, remembered it as being exceedingly cold; the stove gave off heat above waist level only, so that throughout the winter they all worked with hot heads but cold feet.) Initial investigation into the British tank situation showed that their armament and reliability were unsatisfactory, but it was too late to start work on a new tank. It would be necessary to take the tank currently in use with the greatest potential, and modify it to achieve reliability and durability.

A new engine was essential, and the Crusader (the Centaur and Cavalier were slight variations of this tank) was chosen as the tank to modify, since its engine compartment would accommodate a Rolls-Royce power unit. Its hull was also large enough to mount a turret which would take a larger gun than the hopelessly inadequate two-pounder currently in use. But modifying an aero engine to replace the Liberty engine (also originally an aero engine) presented some fearsome problems, not the least of which would be converting it to run on pool petrol as opposed to high octane fuel.

The Liberty engine could be crudely described as an American rehash of Royce's Eagle, created with mass-production in mind. Indeed, Rolls-Royce had lent Maurice Olley to help with its design. The engine was a fine piece of production engineering, but was not fully developed. Hives was surprised that the British would want to produce it again.

The choice lay between the Kestrel and the Merlin. The Kestrel was 25 per cent smaller, and thus easier to fit into the space. But there were disadvantages too. On the low grade fuel available, the Kestrel would only develop about 475 bhp, and this would not provide sufficient performance in a 30-ton tank. Also, there were no plans at Derby to produce Kestrels, since all production was concentrated on the Merlin. It had to be the Merlin, therefore, and the first task was to design an unsupercharged version. This modified engine was called the Meteor. The next task was to see what bhp it would achieve on pool petrol. Then the engine had to be fitted into the Crusader, and the effect of its increased power on the suspension, steering, brakes, clutch and transmission would have to be assessed.

There were no manufacturing facilities at Clan Foundry, and so when the drawings were finished they were rushed off to Leyland in an experimental car, for the pieces to be made. Once made, they were taken to Crewe and put onto the test-benches there, as Derby had no spare capacity. On test, the engine developed the predicted (and hoped-for) 600 bhp on pool petrol. Within five months of starting the project, on 6 April 1941, the first Crusader with the Meteor engine installed was despatched to Aldershot for ground tests.

At this point, Leyland, concerned about the effect that the extra power of the Meteor was having on other parts of the Crusader, withdrew from the joint project and reverted to manufacturing Liberty engines. Robotham, in desperation, turned to Hives, who said: 'Well, we'll have to make the blighters ourselves.'

Lord Beaverbrook, appreciating Rolls-Royce quality, was also applying pressure on Hives for 'tanks, tanks and more tanks!'. Hives told Beaverbrook that he already had his hands full producing Merlins for aircraft, and if Beaverbrook wanted Rolls-Royce to produce modified Merlins for tanks, then Rolls-Royce would want £1 million (£50 million in today's terms) to their credit, and 'no interference!'.

This prompted a telegram from Beaverbrook which said:

Hives, Rolls-Royce, Derby.
The British Government has given you an open credit of one million pounds. This is a certificate of character and reputation without precedent or equal.

Beaverbrook

On 29 July 1941, Hives accepted an order for 1,000 Meteor engines, promising delivery of the first engine in six months. But Clan Foundry still had to solve the cooling problem which had so alarmed Leyland. Robotham gave the credit to

Fred Hardy, our chief development engineer at Belper . . . for originating the design which finally solved our problems. It was an outstanding piece of engineering and the results speak for themselves. In the final installation, the 600 bhp Meteor was better cooled than the 330 bhp Liberty. At the same time, the hp required to drive the fans was reduced from 60 to 32 and simultaneously, even after taking up 16 gallons of petrol space with the air cleaners, the fuel carried was increased by 14 per cent over the Liberty installation. The saving in fan hp meant that the Meteor hp to the tracks or useable hp was almost exactly double that of the Liberty.

Robotham may have given the credit to Hardy, one of his old experimental team, but it was Ivan Evernden, formerly of Royce's design team, who received an MBE for his work on the cooling system of the Cromwell, as the Meteor-powered Crusader became known. And it was not only on cooling that a great deal of development work was carried out. The team also made great progress on transmission, tracks and suspension, and even on crew accommodation and ammunition storage.

The team that progressed the Meteor towards production after Robotham was seconded to the Ministry of Supply in London as Chief Engineer, Tanks, was led by Alec McWilliams, and included A.H. 'Flap' Fletcher, J. Ray Thompson and Alec's brother, Eddie McWilliams. Although they were at Belper, finance came from the Government via Rolls-Royce, Hillington, Glasgow.

The Meteor-engined Cromwell tank manufactured by Birmingham Railway Carriage and Wagon went into action for the first time when the Allies invaded France in June 1944. Many travelled nearly 4,000 miles in the eleven months before victory was achieved in Europe on 8 May 1945. In September 1944, Major General C.L. Verney, Commander of the Seventh Armoured Division, wrote to the War Office:

I feel that I must write you a short note to tell you how superb the Cromwell tank has been during our recent activities, and I hope that you will pass on the gist of this letter to the various people responsible for the production of this magnificent machine.

PLANNING FOR A NEW ERA

From 1939 until perhaps the middle of 1942, everyone in Great Britain was concentrating on survival and the avoidance of defeat. In retrospect, some would argue that the Allies' cause was won from the moment the Japanese attacked Pearl Harbour in December 1941 and brought the world's greatest industrial power into the conflict. However, it did not seem that way in the early months of 1942. The Japanese were rampant. On 23 January they landed in New Guinea and the Solomon Islands, on 15 February they accepted the surrender of Singapore and on 9 March that of Java. As late as June 1942, the German Army captured Tobruk in North Africa.

However, on 2 July Montgomery defeated Rommel at El Alamein, and by the autumn Rommel was in full retreat in North Africa. On 16 July the RAF made its first *daylight* raid on the Ruhr. In the Far East, the Americans fought the Japanese in the Battle of Midway. Losses on both sides were heavy, but for the Japanese Midway was effectively a defeat. As Martin Gilbert wrote in Volume Two of his *A History of the Twentieth Century*:

Four Japanese aircraft carriers and eighty-six warships were en route to Midway from Japan, together with 5,000 soldiers on board twelve troop transports. It was the largest Japanese task force ever assembled. Four sustained American aircraft attacks against the invasion fleet failed to hit their targets, and sixty-five American aircraft were shot down. The fifth American attack, on the morning of June 5, sank three of the four Japanese aircraft carriers. The fourth carrier was destroyed that afternoon. Three of the carriers sunk had been among the five that had taken part in the attack on Pearl Harbour six months earlier.

A Japanese cruiser, the Mikuma, was also sunk. In all, the Japanese lost 332 aircraft and 3,500 men. American losses were one carrier – the Yorktown – fatally damaged, 150 aircraft destroyed and 307 men killed. The Battle of Midway was not only a defeat for Japan; like the Battle of the Coral Sea a month earlier it was also a defeat in the arm of warfare that Japan had chosen for conquest: air power.

In September 1942 the German advance into Russia stalled at Stalingrad and, as the vicious Russian winter set in, the Red Army began to push the German Armies back. On 18 January 1943 the siege of Leningrad was raised, and on 31 January the remnants of the German Army at Stalingrad surrendered.

Neither the German nor the Japanese forces were going to give up easily and, as we know, the war dragged on in Europe until May 1945 and in the Far East until August 1945. Nevertheless, by 1943 it was possible to foresee the end and that victory would be attained. In December 1943 Churchill met Stalin and Roosevelt in Teheran to discuss the post-war political and economic geography of the world. By this time, planning for peace became necessary for the directors of every large company as well, and Rolls-Royce were no exception.

Rolls-Royce would surely be justified in feeling that any planning for civil aviation after the war would include them as the prime supplier of engines.

Hives must have been bemused, to put it mildly, to receive a letter from Lord Beaverbrook on 30 September 1943 which said:

Questions arise in my office concerning civil aviation now and after the war.

It has been said in the House of Commons that engines now turned out by Rolls-Royce and other engineering firms will not be suitable for civil aircraft when the war is over.

Would you see me here on your next visit to town and explain to me the whole situation? Besides, I am longing to see you again.

The last sentence indicates that Beaverbrook was as puzzled as he expected Hives to be. Presumably, some people were suggesting that Merlin engines, admirably suited to the high performance for short periods necessary in a fighter aircraft would not be appropriate for the longer flights necessary in civil airline operations. The obvious flaws in this thinking were as follows.

- Who was producing engines that had proved themselves in civil operations?
- Were the engineers at Rolls-Royce who had produced the high-performance engine incapable of designing a reliable engine for long, steady performance flights?

Furthermore, hundreds of Merlin-powered bombers were flying to Berlin, Hamburg and Cologne night after night. Lancasters were also flying across the Atlantic, while Mosquitoes were flying to Sweden to bring back ball and roller bearings as well as escaped prisoners of war. These were all effectively airline operations.

A committee had been set up under Lord Brabazon of Tara, the Minister of Aircraft Production and a very distinguished pioneer motorist and aviator, to look into the future of civil aviation after the war. (You will remember that Lord Brabazon, as Moore-Brabazon, had been a close friend of C.S. Rolls at Cambridge and in their ballooning days. After Rolls's death in the accident at the Bournemouth show in 1910, Moore-Brabazon had given up flying in protest at the encouragement of flying stunts.) For some reason, Brabazon seemed to think that military engines such as the Merlin and the Griffon would not be suitable for civil use. After a meeting with Sir Wilfrid Freeman on 1 September 1943, Elliott reported to Hives.

Suitability for Civil Requirements
The Brabazon Committee say military engines not suitable for civil requirements, and that it is necessary to start again. These appear to be more the personal views of Lord Brabazon.

Rolls-Royce entirely disagree with this. Our War time engines will completely satisfy full civil requirements and cannot be improved upon except possibly in respect to slight increase of compression ratio and non-pressure cooling.

Freeman was clearly not in agreement with Brabazon, but nevertheless saw the necessity of providing proof that Rolls-Royce's engines could provide the steady reliability that would be required by civil airlines. Elliott reported:

Experimental Civil Flying
(a) Sir Wilfrid Freeman is arranging for T.C.A. [Trans Canada Airlines] to have two more Lancasters from this side, if possible.
(b) He will consider the suggestion for B.O.A.C. [British Overseas Airways Corporation] to have a Lancaster for the Swedish route.

Engine Ratings for Reliability and Endurability
Rolls-Royce have fixed up tentative ratings for Merlin and Griffon, and are proposing to run engine and power plant tests based on an endurability period of 700 hours.

The debate over whether liquid-cooled or air-cooled engines were more reliable continued to rage. Elliott reported:

Liquid Cooling Versus Air Cooling
Rolls-Royce say liquid cooling offers advantages for civil work of greater engine reliability, better performance, lower drag. The liquid cooled system can be self-contained in detachable power plants and absolutely reliable.

Sir Wilfrid Freeman expressed preference for liquid cooling and said that he thought such a power plant could be made to establish the same reputation for reliability as Rolls-Royce motorcars.

Hives wrote to Brabazon on 13 October 1943:

I feel that the Rolls-Royce company and its achievements have been ignored in the plans now being prepared for post-war civil aviation. We know that several orders have been placed for transport machines, not a single one of which is specified for Rolls-Royce engines; neither have we seen the specifications or been invited to submit our proposals.

I am not suggesting that you or your Committee are responsible for this position, but we are certainly not content to accept the present position. We would have claimed that anyone thinking or planning a long-term policy of civil aviation for this country would have accepted that Rolls-Royce engines were essential, and that a minimum of 50% of the British civil machines should be fitted with Rolls-Royce engines.

No-one can dispute Rolls-Royce have established themselves as the number one aero engine firm in the world. It has not been achieved by accident; it is because we are the best equipped technically.

One could almost believe that the greater the contribution a firm has made in the war effort, and the more successful it has been, the less likely it is to receive any consideration for civil aviation.

I do not think it is worth while going over the technical arguments of air versus liquid cooling . . . It is a very good thing for the nation that Rolls-Royce did not fail or falter in their faith in liquid-cooled engines. For years we listened to the criticisms from all quarters, especially from the USA, that the liquid-cooled engine was finished, and yet, in whichever situation we look where British aviation is leading, those aeroplanes are fitted with Rolls-Royce engines.

The idea that Rolls-Royce can make a super-efficient engine and are not capable of producing an engine for civil work is unthinkable.

In the Imperial Airways days we disagreed with their policy. They certainly had their air-cooled engines, and there never was a civil line with a more lamentable record for engine failures.

And if Hives was concerned that Rolls-Royce might miss out in the British civil air market after the war, he was also worried about the possible lack of control over all the Merlin engines produced by Packard during the war, and what might happen if they were dumped on the market. He wrote to the new Minister of Aircraft Production, the Rt. Hon. Sir Stafford Cripps, on 4 November 1943:

Merlin engines are, as you know, now being manufactured in America in large and ever increasing quantities, and we are concerned as to what may happen at the termination of hostilities.

The Americans themselves have become very enthusiastic about our engines, are building up to a programme of some 1,000 a week, and are also making strenuous efforts to see that all the latest improvements are incorporated as quickly as possible . . . Visitors from the Packard Motor Company and Continental Motors are becoming numerous, all of which inevitably results in disclosure of our latest developments and technique . . .

We are not raising here any question in regard to design rights as, after discussion with Contracts Dept at Harrogate in February 1941, it was considered best to leave this until after the war . . .

We consider it is a matter of the greatest importance to this Company, and even to the British Government, that the manufacture of our products in America or elsewhere after the war be controllable, and that we are in a favourable position to negotiate terms should either of the firms now manufacturing wish to continue to do so in the future . . .

At the end of the war the American Government is likely to have large numbers of Merlin engines for disposal, and we would appreciate your assurance that these engines cannot be 'dumped' in various parts of the world.

Hives's concerns about Packard were fully justified. Indeed, he was deeply shocked to receive a letter from Sir Wilfrid Freeman, written on 17 October 1944, warning him that the export of Merlin engines could contravene the terms of the lease-lend agreement.

Freeman wrote:

A point has occurred to me in connection with Pearson's forthcoming trip to U.S.A., and the proposal to fit Rolls-Royce engines into DC4s ordered by the Australian National Airways.

The overall lease-lend and mutual aid agreement which we are now negotiating with America is likely to contain a clause forbidding us to export goods 'identical' with those which we are now receiving on lease-lend.

The exact meaning of this clause, and in particular to the word 'identical', has not yet been determined, but I think it certain that some such provision will go into the final agreement.

The bearing of this on your present project is obvious: so long as we are receiving aircraft engines from Packards on lease-lend, we will not be entitled to export them commercially.

I do not know whether your plans relate to a period a good many months ahead or to the immediate future. If, however, the engines are to be sent out within a short while, you will see that it might cause us serious embarrassment, and we may even have to put a veto on the transaction.

Hives responded immediately, telling Freeman that Rolls-Royce were working on an order to supply engines and powerplants to Canada, that J.D. Pearson was meeting the Australians with a view to supplying them, and that TWA had expressed interest in the Griffon.

He wrote:

It would be untenable for any restrictions to be put on our export of Rolls-Royce engines for use in civil transport, due to lease-lend agreements. In effect it would mean that because of our success with the Merlin engine, in which the U.S.A.A.F. have shared, we should be singled out as the one aero engine firm in the world to be penalised under lease-lend. We cannot believe that this could be put forward as a serious proposition.

A month later he wrote to Freeman again, pointing out how justified were his concerns.

If you do not already know you will be interested to hear that Arthur Nutt, who was President of the Curtiss-Wright Corporation, and has been with them for 28 years, has now joined Packard.

One would read into this that it is Packard's intention to carry on with aircraft engines after the war. As we have always generously provided Packard's with complete information of what we are doing, and to a great extent what we are also thinking, it will be interesting to see whether the total reward for our efforts is that we have established a powerful competitor!

Even this would be nothing new, because Fedden's entry into the aero engine business and likewise Bristol's, was the direct result of their being sub-contractors to Rolls-Royce during the last war 1914/18.

And his fears that the Americans would become a competitor in export markets were realised when, towards the end of the war, the US Government began to sell Mustang fighters to other friendly governments. On 17 April 1945, Sidgreaves wrote to Cripps reminding him of Hives's letter of November 1943, and pointing out that the US Government had sold 50 Mustangs to the Swedish Government:

This, I am sure you will realise, raises a very important question of the American Government being allowed to export and sell Merlin engines made in America under an arrangement which was purely to meet war-time requirements. It is a definite loss of possible export business to us and to the country.

He went on to point out that Rolls-Royce had been negotiating with the Swedish Government themselves, and would now probably lose the business. He also reminded Cripps that neither the US nor the British Government had been very interested in the Mustang until, on Rolls-Royce's initiative, it had been fitted with a Merlin engine.

I mention this point because it indicates that in trying to do everything possible to win the war we are going to suffer in consequence.

Sidgreaves continued his letter by reminding Cripps that it was now eighteen months since the company had first raised the matter with the British Government concerning the danger of US Government sales of Merlin engines after the war.

He concluded:

At the same time we also raised the question of the licence interchange agreement being brought into effect and thus limiting American manufacture to the war period. I am sorry to say that your people have not been successful to date in achieving this object either.

Whether Rolls-Royce were going to receive co-operation from the Government or not, the board still had to make preparations for the inevitable disruption to its activities that peace would bring. And the Government would certainly be interested to know what Rolls-Royce's plans were, if only because it wanted to avoid the mistakes made after the First World War, when hundreds of thousands of demobilised soldiers were thrown on to a jobs market which could not absorb them. In November 1943 the Chairman, Lord Herbert Scott, wrote to Sidgreaves, Hives and Captain Eric Smith, Chairman of the National Provincial Bank and a non-executive director of Rolls-Royce, laying out the choices that the board would need to consider.

It was clear that the company would not be able to survive on producing aero engines, and that the motor car business would need to be revived. Should aero engines and cars be produced in one factory? Definitely not, was the view of Hives and Sidgreaves. Derby had been modernised to produce aero engines and should continue to do so. Cars, then, should be made at either Crewe or Glasgow, but both the factories and the machinery in them were owned by the Government, and as there would be many Government factories coming on to the market, there might be a more suitable location. Perhaps a new company structure would be sensible, comprising a holding company overseeing two subsidiaries, one producing aero engines and the other motor cars, each with its own board of directors.

Hives, for one, advocated retaining a strong commitment to the aero engine business.

Our first problem will be the liquidation of over 30,000 employees and, in addition, absorbing those who were called up in the fighting forces, whom we must take back.

We should dismiss from our minds that the manufacture of motor-cars is going to be an answer to this problem. The Directors are fully aware of the state of our motor-car business before the war, and one thing that we can say for certain is that the cost of producing the same motor-car will be considerably higher. Consideration would have to be given to this problem before we accepted any orders for cars.

Interestingly, he also said:

We also want to forget that civil aviation is likely to help us to any extent.

Hives was a man of vision, and would almost certainly have seen the potential in civil aviation. He would have meant that in the short term, civil aviation would not help. J.D. Pearson worked hard to convince Hives that, in the long term, civil would be bigger and more lucrative than military aviation.

Hives was concerned that the Government, in allocating engine orders, would be inclined to favour Bristol and Napier if they felt that Rolls-Royce's primary interest was motor cars, as it had been in the 1920s. And Hives knew that Rolls-Royce's neglect of the aero engine market after the First World War had allowed others to catch up. He concluded:

Looking at the position to-day, therefore, I recommend that our policy is that we should stick to the aero business at all costs and carry on energetically with the development of a motor-car programme which can prove to be a profitable business.

It should also be remembered that a considerable expense will have to be incurred in new plant, machinery, and jigs and tools. There have been no replacements to Rolls-Royce plant since the beginning of the war, and the depreciation has been very heavy, so we may have to look forward to an expenditure of approximately one million pounds, if we are to enter a competitive market with our products.

I have every confidence that we can build up an extremely profitable motor-car business. We have a complete measure of the ability and talent possessed by Morris, Fords, Standards, Leylands, Rovers and Austins. Rolls-Royce possess more talent in all departments than those firms have, but we can never hope to build up a profitable motor-car business until we dismiss from our minds entirely what I call the Phantom III outlook.

'MORE POWER THAN THE MERLIN'

Nothing after the Battle of Britain in the summer and autumn of 1940 was quite as dramatic but, as we know, Britain came perilously close to losing the war, which dragged on for another five years. Merlin-powered aircraft continued their front-line involvement throughout the world for the whole of those five years.

As we have seen, Hives's policy was to concentrate on improving the Merlin and Griffon engines and, more importantly, to make sure that they were produced in ever-increasing numbers. At the same time, Rolls-Royce were working on other engines. In the 1930s, development work had begun on the Peregrine, the Exe and the Vulture. However, the priority given to the Merlin and Griffon meant that development on these other engines was either slowed down or placed on a back-burner. As early as August 1940, Hives wrote to Wilfrid Freeman saying that he wanted to stop work on the Peregrine, Exe and Vulture so that all the company's efforts could be concentrated on the Merlin and Griffon.

The Peregrine, effectively an updated Kestrel, had entered the war as the engine for the Westland Whirlwind. In some ways, it could be described as more technically advanced than the Merlin at that stage, but the Merlin was the engine in the key fighters – the Hurricane and Spitfire – and the Peregrine was dropped, though not immediately. As Freeman said, it must continue to power the Whirlwind.

Similarly, the Exe, an air-cooled engine and a competitor to the Merlin, became a casualty of priorities.

As we have seen, there had been a continuous debate over whether air-cooled engines were more effective than liquid-cooled engines, and it could have been one of the reasons that the Brabazon Committee was appearing to favour other engine manufacturers ahead of Rolls-Royce when considering engines for civilian use after the war. It is probable that Hives saw the air-cooled Exe, and its successors, the Pennine and Snowdon, as an insurance against the failure of the gas turbine. By this time, however, Hives was becoming certain that gas turbines were the future. This note, written by him on 17 November 1942, shows that he had only gradually become convinced of their importance:

Some time ago I made up my mind to write to the Minister and point out that a lot of effort was being wasted on jets, and that they would never do any good for this war. I started with a definite anti-jet outlook. As a result of the investigation, I have been converted to a turbine enthusiast! and have come to the conclusion that our development and research work in connection with jets should be extended.

In early 1945, Air Marshal Ralph Sorley, by then Controller of Research and Development at the Air Ministry, wrote to Hives:

Develop the Pennine engine to give a take-off power of 2,800 horse-power, with a possibility of achieving 3,200 BHP with improved quality fuel. This engine is already under consideration for military aircraft and its application for civil use should constantly be borne in mind.

The Vulture continued for a time, again at Freeman's insistence, as the engine for the Manchester bomber, but as we have seen, it too would eventually give way to the Merlin.

In his notes for a discussion with Sir Wilfrid Freeman on 17 November 1942, Hives wrote of the Vulture:

The biggest decision Rolls-Royce have made during the war was the scrapping of the 2,000 HP Vulture engine, after four years' work. Some unkind people might suggest that the Vulture engine was not a good engine, but there are quite a number in service today which are giving excellent results, and there is no shadow of doubt that if we had continued it would have been the best 2,000 HP engine in existence today.

The reason we scrapped the Vulture was that after full consideration we decided that it was not the engine that was required for this war. If we had carried on with the Vulture, the Merlin development would inevitably have suffered. We would go so far as to say this would have resulted in a grave national disaster.

Another engine, the Eagle, was developed in response to Freeman's request in May 1942 that Rolls-Royce produce an engine bigger than the Merlin. Freeman was probably becoming frustrated by continuing problems with Napier's Sabre, which was used in the Tempest 5 and Typhoon. These were effective low-level fighters, but poor performers at altitude because of their lack of a really efficient supercharger.

The Eagle was essentially a scaled-up Sabre with Rolls-Royce engineering skills built into it. A 46-litre, sleeve-valved engine, it was theoretically a better and more economical engine than the Merlin with its poppet valves, except that sleeve valves were more likely to seize under high boost. Fifteen development Eagle engines and fifteen production engines were built. The Eagle's only service was in the Naval fighter, the Wyvern, in which it was eventually replaced by the Armstrong Siddeley Python propjet. The Eagle kept its supporters virtually to the end of the war. In the same letter, written on 28 February 1945, in which Sorley had encouraged Hives to develop the Pennine further, he also wrote:

Develop the Eagle to give a take-off power of 3,000/3,300 BHP, and to as near 4,000 BHP as possible with improved quality fuel. This engine is basically better suited to fighters than to bombers or civil types, but nevertheless, its suitability as a civil type, if de-rated, should not be disregarded.

Another engine under development at Rolls-Royce during the war was the Crecy, or the P1 as it was known in its early years. The P1 was a two-stroke, sleeve-valve and supercharged engine, and the hope was that it would give a much better power-to-weight ratio than any four-stroke engine in production or under development. The chief development engineer of the P1 development team was Richard Thomas. Writing many years later, Geoff Wilde (who from 1940 until 1943 was responsible for experimental and development work on the centrifugal superchargers for the Merlin, Griffon, Peregrine, Vulture, Exe, P1 (Crecy) and Eagle) said of Thomas:

[He] was often seen walking in a carefree manner in his plus-fours between the P1 development office and the single-cylinder test beds. I once asked him how the engine was performing and what power was being produced. The answer he gave was 'the engine will give more power than the Merlin and even if made of cast-iron will have a higher power-to-weight ratio than the Merlin'. One could not take him seriously.

By the end of 1942 the development of the P1 engine was lagging. Hives, growing impatient, transferred supervision to Hooker and Lovesey, and gave them three months to make an appraisal. The engine's Achilles' heel was inadequate piston cooling. As Wilde said:

This was no surprise to anyone because if you try to produce a given power from a piston and cylinder twice as often as in a four-stroke engine it is hardly surprising to find that the piston gets hotter!

Hooker and Lovesey recommended termination of the P1 development, and Hives accepted their verdict. Wilde also agreed with the decision:

Apart from the fundamental power limitations of the P1 engine, it came too late to be seriously considered for installation in any aircraft. It has been claimed that had jet propulsion not arrived, the P1 engine would have been the next engine to follow the Merlin. I cannot see any substantial evidence for this view.

Whatever the Crecy's potential, it was never to be realised. Along with the Exe, Peregrine, Vulture, Eagle, Pennine and Snowdon, development was abandoned (no Snowdon engine was ever built; it never got beyond the stage of a 'paper' engine). On 2 July 1945 the Hooker/Lovesey memorandum was circulated, recommending that further work on the two-stroke engine be dropped. It was clear that the main reason was the exciting new gas turbine.

... There are no aeroplane committments [sic] for this engine as is the case with the four-stroke engine projects, nor are we sufficiently far advanced with the development to approach aircraft designers.

For this type of engine to have sufficiently attractive advantages over the four-stroke it must function in conjunction with the turbine; it then has the merit of developing high powers on 100 octane fuel for a given piston displacement at low fuel consumption up to 90% of its maximum power.

This engine has actually demonstrated the possibility of surpassing the four-stroke in power, consumption and heat rejected to coolant. Nevertheless, turbine projects have developed so rapidly as to show even greater possibilities can be attained with more economic development effort.

As far as operational characteristics go, it is in the turbine engine class in that it is a full throttle engine and functions at high cruising powers. It has not, however, the advantages possessed by the turbine engine as regards weight and power for size.

And on 18 July, Hives wrote to Sorley at the Air Ministry:

Owing to pressure of work on I.C.T.s [Internal Combustion Turbines], we have reviewed our engine programme and we have come to the conclusion that we should like to be relieved of any further work on the Crecy engine.

The Crecy is the only engine in our programme on which we are not committed to an aircraft constructor. It is inevitably suffering at the present time owing to higher priority work, and there is no possibility of us being able to put the effort on to it.

As you are aware, on the I.C.T. we have five different new engines, all of them committed to aircraft and which are required urgently. These are – the Derwent, the Nene, the Clyde, the Dart, and the further one for Petter's machine which so far has not been named.

We have now mentioned the gas turbine aero engine – the 'jet' – a number of times, and this will be investigated more thoroughly in the companion volume to this book on Rolls-Royce. However, the background must be covered here, because its influence became increasingly important during the war, as Hives and others realised its significance for the future.

Chapter Ten

'The turbine engines have arrived'

OVER-OPTIMISTIC ASSUMPTIONS

The story of the modern jet engine begins in the 1920s, when two men, both working for the Government, quite independently put forward ideas for propulsion by a means different from the reciprocating engine. In 1926, Dr. A.A. Griffith of the Royal Aircraft Establishment's Engines Experimental Department published a paper, *An Aerodynamic Theory of Turbine Design*, which proposed the use of a single-shaft turbine engine with multi-stage axial compressor as a means of driving a propeller through a reduction gear. The paper and its supporting test work were reviewed by the Engines sub-committee of the Aeronautical Research Committee (ARC) in April 1930. The committee concluded that:

At the present state of knowledge the superiority of the gas turbine over the reciprocating engine cannot be predicted.

As a result, the RAE did not fund further investigation into this development until 1936.

Meanwhile, in 1928, an RAF officer, Frank Whittle, had also written a paper, *Future Developments in Aircraft Design*. He envisaged aircraft flying at speeds of 500 mph, at a time when the fastest RAF fighter could not reach 200 mph, but felt it would be necessary for the aircraft to fly at great heights where the air was rare. At this stage, he was not sure about the means of propulsion, although he was already considering rockets and gas turbines driving propellers. A year later, in October 1929, Whittle suddenly realised that the gas turbine could be *substituted* for the piston engine because the exhaust would propel the aircraft, rendering the propeller unnecessary. As John Golley put it in his book, *Whittle, the true story*, published by Airlife in 1987:

He realised that this change would require the compressor to have a much higher pressure ratio than the one he had visualised for his piston engine scheme. But once this idea had taken shape, he found it extraordinary that he had taken so long to arrive at a scheme which seemed so very obvious and was disarmingly simple.

At this point, thanks to a friend at RAF Wittering, Pat 'Johnny' Johnson, and his station commandant, Group Captain Baldwin, Whittle was sent to the Air Ministry to see W.L. Tweedie, a technical officer in the Directorate of Engine Development. He also saw A.A. Griffith in the Air Ministry's South Kensington laboratory.

History has tended to condemn Griffith for his attitude to Whittle's ideas. For example, Golley is fiercely critical. However, we must remember that Golley wrote his book in collaboration with Whittle and Bill Gunston (an acknowledged expert on aero engines) in the mid-1990s, and obviously recorded faithfully Whittle's memories of these meetings. He was not able to interview either Tweedie or Griffith, since they were both dead. According to Golley (and therefore presumably Whittle), the meetings with Tweedie and Griffith were not likely to encourage Whittle in his endeavours:

Tweedie told him [Whittle] bluntly that the Air Ministry's attitude towards the practicability of the gas turbine was coloured by a highly unfavourable report written a few years previously.

In spite of this, Tweedie took Whittle to meet Griffith, who, after listening to Whittle, told him that his 'assumptions were over-optimistic and that there was at least one important mistake in the calculations'. At this point, Golley, presumably with the agreement of Sir Frank Whittle, is extremely critical of Griffith:

Griffith was a highly qualified scientist with a growing reputation in the academic world. He certainly had the knowledge to do a quick design study of Whittle's turbojet proposals. Had he done so with intellectual honesty he would inevitably have come to the conclusion that, with easily foreseeable improvements in materials and component efficiencies, a revolutionary (in every sense of the word) aircraft propulsion engine was at last within reach.

Speeds of 500 mph would be attainable at heights up to and above 40,000 ft. Though the fuel consumption might seem somewhat excessive, this would be largely compensated by the very low power plant weight. Griffith should have recognised that here was an engine of very low weight, not limited to high-grade petrol as fuel, of great simplicity and vibration free and, above all, capable of operation at heights and speeds entirely out of reach of the piston engine/propeller combination.

He was at that time far more qualified than Whittle to point out ways in which the gas turbine as a high-speed aircraft power plant was a much more favourable proposition than a stationary gas turbine for shaft power at sea level. This was by virtue of the very favourable effect of very low air temperatures at great height, the high efficiency of that part of the compression due to ram effect at high forward speeds, and so on. Yet, seemingly, this intellectual giant failed entirely to do what he should have done. Not only then but eight years later when, after Whittle's first engine had run, Griffith wrote a report damning the project with faint praise.

It is not as though Griffith shared the view of most of the engineering world that the gas turbine was not a practical proposition, and that there had been many failures to prove it. On the contrary, Griffith himself was advocating the development of gas turbines, but driving propellers.

It was a few years before Griffith succeeded in getting Ministry support for his own proposals. One cannot say for sure that, had he given a favourable report on Whittle's jet engine, this would have resulted in Ministry backing. Whittle's proposals being far simpler than his own, it is very likely that modest sums needed to initiate the development would have been forthcoming.

Why then did Griffith, and therefore the Ministry, damn the project? Sheer incompetence, despite his reputation and qualifications? Professional jealousy? Intellectual jealousy? Or a combination of these things? We shall never know!

Whittle admitted that Griffith had been right in pointing out the mistake, and did his calculations again. He told Golley:

I discovered another important mistake which largely had the effect of neutralising the first one, and so I was happy to find that my conclusions were not so very wrong after all. Nevertheless, I can well imagine that my first error may have done much to prevent the scheme from being as carefully considered as it otherwise might have been.

Shortly after his visit to London, Whittle received a letter from the Air Ministry saying that his scheme was a form of gas turbine, and therefore impractical, because the materials capable of withstanding the combination of high stresses and high temperatures necessary for a gas turbine engine to be efficient, did not then exist. Unsure what to do next, Whittle, encouraged by Johnson, filed a Provisional Specification for a patent on 16 January 1930.

Correctly, Whittle notified the Air Ministry, who did not express any official interest and, as a result, Whittle's invention was not put on the secret list. It meant that, when the patent was granted in October 1932, it was published throughout the world. Almost incredibly, when the date for renewal of his patent arrived in January 1935, Whittle allowed it to lapse. He said later: 'I had lost hope of the successful development of the turbojet engine by January 1935.'

There was also the matter of the £5 fee, and by this time Whittle was married with two small sons, one of whom had recently been ill. Then, £5, perhaps £250 today, would have seemed a lot of money.

POWER JETS LIMITED

Not long after Whittle had declined to renew his turbojet patent, he received this letter from an old Cranwell colleague, Rolf Dudley Williams, who had retired from the RAF through ill health.

This is just a hurried note to tell you that I have just met a man who is quite a big noise in an engineering concern and to whom I mentioned your invention of an aeroplane, sans propeller as it were, and who is very interested. You told me some time ago that Armstrong's had or were taking it up, and if they have broken down or you don't like them, he would I think like to handle it. I wonder if you will write and let me know. My address is:

C/o General Enterprises Ltd, Callard House,
Regent Street, W.1.

Do give this your earnest consideration and even if you can't do anything about the above you might have something else that is good.

Please give my regards to your wife. If you like to ring me up at the above address my number is Regent 2934, and I shall be there on Tuesday at 12 o'clock.

Shortly afterwards, Williams and another former RAF pilot, J.C.B. Tinling, visited Whittle in Trumpington, Cambridge (the RAF had paid for Whittle to take a Mechanical Sciences degree), and told him that they would pay to take out further patents and provide the expenses necessary to raise the £50,000 which they felt would be needed to develop a complete jet-propelled aeroplane. Although £50,000 does not sound much today, in 1935 it was the equivalent of £2.5 million, and although the Depression of the early 1930s was past its worst, it was certainly not an economic boom period. Williams and Tinling (later known affectionately by the Whittle children as Uncle Willie and Uncle Con), in return for a quarter share of the commercial rights, would act as Whittle's agents.

Whittle was concerned about them approaching anyone associated with the aircraft industry, as he was convinced that his ideas would be 'stolen' and that their patent protection would be worthless because they did not have the funds to fight for them in court. As it turned out, the man who took things to the next stage, M.L. Bramson, was heavily involved in the aircraft industry, but Whittle's suspicions were allayed when he met Bramson, a pilot and an engineer, with whom Whittle struck up an instant rapport. Bramson suggested an approach, not to an aircraft manufacturer, but to a financial institution in the City, O.T. Falk & Partners. (Falk sat on the board of a number of investment trusts with the redoubtable Maynard Keynes.) O.T. Falk obviously also liked Bramson, and they asked him to prepare a formal report on the feasibility of Whittle's idea.

The report was favourable, and an agreement between Falk & Partners and Whittle and his associates was drawn up. As Whittle was still a serving officer in the RAF, this agreement needed Air Ministry approval. This was eventually granted, subject to a number of amendments, including the condition that the President of the Air Council (the Secretary of State for Air) become one of the parties of the agreement. This became known as the Four-Party Agreement, the four parties being the President of the Air Council, O.T. Falk & Partners, Williams and Tinling, and Whittle. It was dated 27 January 1936. The company was to be called Power Jets Limited.

Whittle, realising that his turbojet project might now see the light of day, began to think about a possible manufacturer. In view of his family connection with Coventry and his frequent visits to the home of his parents-in-law, he hoped to find one in the Midlands area. He had already had some conversations with British Thomson-Houston (BTH), based in Rugby, about ten miles from Coventry, and he approached them again. Ironically, in view of later developments, BTH expressed some concern over a possible conflict of interest, because they were doing some work for Rolls-Royce on exhaust-driven superchargers. BTH seemed to overcome their concern, and agreed to manufacture an engine for Power Jets on a cost-plus basis, and on the condition that if it went into full production they would manufacture the first hundred, provided their price was not more than 7.5 per cent more than the cheapest competitor.

Throughout 1936 and in the early months of 1937, Whittle struggled to organise the necessary co-operation between the various suppliers in order to build a prototype engine. Finally, on 12 April 1937, the engine was run. Whittle recorded the event in his diary:

Pilot jet successfully ignited at 2,000 r.p.m., speed raised to 2,000 r.p.m. by motor. I requested a further raising of speed to 2,500 r.p.m. and during this process I opened valve 'B' and the unit suddenly ran away. Probably started at about 2,300 and using only about 5 h.p. starting power . . . noted that return pipe from jet was overheating badly. Flame tube red hot at inner radius; combustion very bad . . .

Further testing was carried on through April, but as Whittle himself recorded later:

By the end of April it was very clear that we still have a long way to go on the combustion problem, and that the compressor was well below its design efficiency.

Further modifications were tried during the summer months, but in August 1937 testing stopped, partly because BTH requested Power Jets to find another site. The chief engineer, H.N. Sporborg, felt that testing in the open works was too dangerous. Shortage of money was a constant problem, and a loss of confidence by Falk & Partners aggravated the situation. In December 1937, Whittle made a discovery which was to have a dramatic influence on the development process. This concerned turbine blade design. He said later:

There had been a number of technical controversies before this, but usually discussion had led to a satisfactory compromise. There had been no argument about the turbine blade design, because I had assumed that the B.T-H engineers were far more competent in such matters than I was, and so I had left it entirely to them.

At this point, it is necessary to be a little technical to explain the nature of the controversy.

Everybody has seen the vortex or whirlpool which often forms when water runs out of a bath or wash-basin and most people will have noticed that the water spins more rapidly as it spirals towards the centre. Also that as the water goes towards the centre it goes 'downhill' i.e. the velocity increases as the pressure decreases. In an ideal vortex of this kind the product of the whirl velocity and radial distance from the centre remains constant. This is the characteristic of a free circular vortex. The pressure rise from the inside to the outside is caused by the centrifugal force of the whirling fluid.

I had taken it for granted that the flow of hot gases or steam from a ring of turbine nozzle blades would have the characteristics of a vortex and had supposed that steam turbine engineers designed accordingly.

I discovered that there was a fundamental difference of view on this point early in December, 1937.

My diary for the 4th December recorded:

'Am roped into a heated argument which is going on between Collingham, Cheshire, Randles [W.A. Randles was the engineer immediately responsible to Collingham for work on the Power Jets contract] and one of Cheshire's colleagues. The position is that the new nozzle and blade design involves an end thrust on the bearing of 1,500 lb as against the original 180 lb. Collingham and I say that the bearing could not possibly stand this and the net result is that Cheshire is instructed to return to an impulse section.'

I was a very puzzled man when I left the meeting to which this entry referred, and so spent a few days revising my turbine theory and trying to account for so large a difference in end thrust for two designs of turbine blades intended for the same job. I could not reconcile the figures at all, and so set about trying to find out what the engineers in the blade design office had done without betraying what, I supposed, was my own ignorance. I found the answer when I casually asked Cheshire one morning what their figure was for the pressure difference from the inside to the outside of the annular ring of gases leaving the nozzle ring. He was very surprised by the question and told me that they assumed that the pressure was constant. I pointed out that according to me, in the case of our engine at least, there was a very considerable difference of pressure due to centrifugal force. I showed him my calculations and conclusions. Cheshire was rapidly 'converted' and inferred, much to my surprise, that I had made a fundamental discovery in turbine design.

According to my theory, the change of angle or 'twist' from root to tip of the turbine blades ought to be twice as great as that provided in the B.T-H design. Also it led to a quite different result for the end thrust on the bearing. Indeed, according to me the end thrust was negligibly small.

It may seem a very strange thing that specialists on turbine design had overlooked a phenomenon which I had more or less taken for granted. I heard somebody once define a practical man as 'one who puts into practice the errors of his forefathers'. This blade business was a good example of it and of how, if habits of thought become deeply rooted, errors may persist from generation to generation. Turbines had slowly evolved from the primitive form in which a few steam jets (often four only) spaced evenly, impinged on the blades or 'buckets' of a single wheel. In such cases it had been reasonable to assume that the velocity and pressure in the blast from each jet was uniform and to design the blades accordingly. It had seemingly occurred to no one that as jets were made more numerous and placed closer together until 'full peripheral' admission was achieved, there would be a fundamental change in the nature of the flow.

Randles also was quickly converted to my view and said that there was no doubt that it was a matter of fundamental importance, and, as far as he knew, quite a new concept in turbine engineering. Apart from Cheshire and Randles, however, my theories met with the strongest opposition and a certain amount of resentment. This last was understandable. No one who has been a specialist in some particular field for years is likely to feel pleased when some young 'amateur' tells him that he has been wrong from the start.

Whittle insisted that BTH made the blades at the angles specified by him, and caused further resentment by taking out a patent that protected his vortex discovery.

Development work continued through 1938 into 1939, but Whittle struggled to show concrete results to appease the investors on the one hand and the RAF on the other. By February 1939 the pressure on Whittle was becoming intense, and he was told by the Deputy Director of Scientific Research that he would have difficulty in securing the retention of Whittle's appointment. Whittle said later:

This was, perhaps, the most critical moment in the whole history of the development. Had the Air Ministry lost interest in the job, it would almost certainly have meant closing down altogether. Any suggestion of delay at that time would have resulted in the withdrawal of all official support. I was forced into a policy of more haste, less speed.

Fortunately, progress thereafter was more rapid, and by June 1939 test runs of the engine were beginning to look promising. Whittle said:

On 23 June we reached a speed of 14,700 rpm; the next day we went to 15,700 and then on the 26th we ran up to 16,000. We did several runs up to this speed on succeeding days and on one of these occasions – 30 June – DSR [Director of Scientific Research] was present.

This day was critical, since Dr. Pye, the DSR, became completely converted to the project, believing that Whittle now had the basis for an engine. An important turning point in terms of the attitude of the Air Ministry had been reached in the spring of 1937, when a colleague of Dr. Griffith, Hayne Constant, had made the case again for developing the gas turbine to the Engines sub-committee of the ARC. By this time, the committee was chaired by Sir Henry Tizard, and it recommended

[t]hat the Air Ministry should take up the development of the Internal Combustion Turbine as a matter of urgency and make all possible arrangements for its production at the earliest possible moment.

Dr. Pye agreed that the Air Ministry should buy the experimental engine, but still leave it with Power Jets for continuing experimentation. For Power Jets, there was now the added bonus that the Ministry would pay for spares and modifications. Whittle recalled:

I had the curious experience of having DSR enthusing on all the advantages of the engine; very light weight; no vibration; could run on any fuel; – the lot. His manner of doing so was almost as though he was talking to a sceptic. I was tactful enough not to point out that he was preaching to the first of all the converts. It was a measure of the degree to which Pye was carried away by his enthusiasm.

As a result of this Air Ministry conversion, a great deal more support was forthcoming, not only in financial terms but also in personnel, and by the end of 1939 a considerable team had assembled at Power Jets. One of them was Reg Voysey, who recalled later:

My time with Power Jets was the happiest and most exciting period of my life. Intellectual honesty pervaded throughout, and there was a streak of nobility in the characters involved because they didn't need to be mean. People sorted themselves into age groups rather than rank. They comprised the early twenties, thirties and a few forties, who were all on Christian-name terms amongst themselves.

I addressed Whittle as Squadron Leader Whittle, and my seniors as Mr. Whyte, Mr. Tinling and so on. Williams was the man who called everybody by their Christian name, and instigated the practice. He was a light-hearted, somewhat flippant character, extremely good with people and a sound thinker who, even then, had political ambitions. [In 1951 he became Conservative Member of Parliament for Exeter, and was PPS to the Secretary of State for War in 1958 and PPS to the Minister of Agriculture 1960–64; he became Sir Rolf Dudley-Williams in 1964.] Tinling, his partner, was much more serious and a man of unfailing integrity. They seemed an odd pair and yet they worked well together and had a lot in common, especially the noble RAF code which, like Whittle, they clung to.

Whyte had lectured in physics, and had a mystical interest in the subject which was one of the oddities of his character. He was about 5ft 9in tall, with good shoulders and a full chest making him appear biggish. His fleshy face betrayed a vague sandy colour under the skin, and he had brown eyes and golden-brown hair flecked with a few specks of grey. Always dressed in a well-cut suit, he wore gold-rimmed glasses and my impression of him during my first interview was that he was a bit tricky, because he tried to catch me out. There was an intellectual coldness about Whyte and, as time went on, I began to realise that while Whittle wanted cash flow to develop the project, Whyte was primarily concerned with getting the best deal.

In those days I regarded anybody of thirty or more as being old, and W/Cdr 'Daddy' Lees was in that category. He was a big, genial man with pale blue eyes and a typical RAF moustache. There was a father/son relationship between him and Whittle which had developed ever since Whittle was an apprentice at Cranwell and Daddy Lees was one of his instructors. Lees always spoke good sense and was quite selfless, almost priest-like – in the best sense.

Leslie Cheshire, on loan from BTH, was one of the older men in the team. He was slightly built and had a wrinkled face and a small head, which I found most disconcerting bearing in mind all the brains he had in it. He was easy to get on with, a gentle man and, in his way, a quiet rebel who served as a chopping block for many of Whittle's ideas.

The thing I most remember about Frank Whittle at that time was his total absorption in what he was doing – a total concentration which impinged itself on the

TOP: Packard in the USA built Merlin engines in huge numbers, with technical support from Rolls-Royce, for both the British and US Governments. This Packard Merlin was built to accept American accessories. It will be noted that the propeller shaft differs from the normal standard.

BOTTOM: Dr. Stanley Hooker was recruited by Hives in 1938, and his brilliance as a mathematician lay behind the improvements in supercharging which doubled the power of the Merlin between the outbreak of war and D-Day. He was posted as chief engineer to take over Rover's work on Whittle's jet engine at Barnoldswick early in 1943. A year later, the RAF received its first operational jet powered by the Welland engine developed there.

Although the Mustang first flew with a Merlin engine at Hucknall, the installation adopted for production was that of North American Aviation. It preserved the clean lines and advanced radiator developed for the Allison engine, and thus optimised performance with the Merlin. The most numerous variant was the P-5ID; the aircraft shown is an evolution towards that variant.

OPPOSITE: The P-51 Mustang was built by North American Aviation after the British Purchasing Commission in the USA requested that they build the Curtiss P40 under licence. North American responded that they could produce something better and quicker, and this proposal was accepted. The outcome was the P-51 Mustang. When the Mustang arrived in England, Rolls-Royce test pilot Ronnie Harker was invited by the RAF to fly it at Duxford. He was most impressed by its performance, powered by an Allison V1710. However, he realised that the latest 60 series Merlin engine would give even greater performance, particularly at medium and high altitudes. His report led to a race between Rolls-Royce at Hucknall and NAA in Los Angeles to see which could fly a Mustang with a Merlin first, so that its performance could be demonstrated to the RAF. These photographs, taken in October 1942, show the first Merlin-powered Mustang to fly, Hucknall's Mustang X, serial no. AL975-G. (The -G signified that it should have an armed guard at all times when on the ground.)

The Griffon was of 37-litre capacity, the same as the Buzzard and 'R' engine, and although this was ten litres more than the Merlin, frontal area was only increased from 7.5 sq. ft. to 7.9 sq. ft. Originally designed as a low-altitude engine for the Fleet Air Arm, it also came to be installed in the Spitfire. Early marks of Griffon, the 3 and 4 as illustrated, powered the Spitfire XII and equated to the Merlin XX series in having a single-stage supercharger with two-speed drive.

The Merlin engine came close to serving in all four elements
during the war – in the air, on land, at sea and under the sea.
This photograph shows a motor torpedo boat powered by a
Merlin in the early stages of the war.

The Crecy, originally known as the P1, was a two-stroke, sleeve-valve and supercharged engine. It was hoped that it would give a much better power-to-weight ratio than any four-stroke engine in production or under development during the Second World War. However, its Achilles' heel was inadequate piston cooling. As Geoff Wilde said: 'If you try to produce a given power from a piston and cylinder twice as often as in a four-stroke engine it is hardly surprising to find that the piston gets hotter!' Hives asked Hooker and Lovesey to appraise the situation, and when they recommended termination of the development, he accepted their verdict.

Lord Hives, created First Baron of Duffield in 1950 in
recognition of his outstanding service to both
Rolls-Royce and his country. (The photograph was taken
by Karsh of Ottawa.)

Acknowledged father of the jet engine, Frank Whittle
struggled for many years to win Government support. His
progress with the gas turbine convinced Hives that the future of
Rolls-Royce lay with this new form of propulsion. This
photograph was taken in November 1944 on a visit to
Barnoldswick, where Rolls-Royce were developing their jet engine.

A.A. Griffith, a boffin recruited by Hives in June 1939 to
continue development on his axial compressor units. Hives
instructed him to 'go on thinking'.

This photograph is of a painting by Roddy Lovesey
commissioned as a gift to Sir Frank Whittle by Rolls-Royce. It
depicts the very first run of his WU engine at the BTH
factory in Rugby on 12 April 1937, and was presented on the
50th anniversary of the occasion.

OPPOSITE TOP: Frank Whittle's first engine, which was
installed in the Gloster E.28/39 for its historic maiden flight on
15 May 1941.

OPPOSITE BOTTOM: The Gloster E.28/39, Britain's first jet aircraft,
which flew with Whittle's W.1 engine on 15 May 1941.

TOP: When Rolls-Royce took over the work of the Rover
company on the jet engine at Barnoldswick, great progress
had already been made with the Whittle type
W.2/B23. Dr. Stanley Hooker and his team put the weight of
Rolls-Royce's resources behind the project and, within
the year, the engine entered service with the RAF
when 616 Squadron received their Gloster Meteor fighters.

BOTTOM: Gloster Meteors of 616 Squadron, which became
the first Allied unit to receive jet aircraft in 1944. Based at RAF
Manston in Kent, they were used principally for destroying
V.I flying bombs.

atmosphere surrounding him. It was very hard for anybody to evaluate him, because he was a many-sided person who had a charming naiveté. He trusted people, and believed that everybody was motivated by a common good. I had the utmost respect for him as a leader and, of course, for his genius.

In January 1940 the team was visited by two very influential figures, Air Vice-Marshal Tedder (later Marshal of the RAF, Lord Tedder), at that time Director-General of Research and Development, and Sir Henry Tizard, Chairman of the Aeronautical Research Committee. Tizard said: 'A demonstration which does not break down in my presence is a production job.'

Power Jets were thus assured of further Air Ministry support, but in the meantime relations with BTH deteriorated further, and Whittle came to the conclusion that a new sub-contractor would be better.

Some officials at the Ministry had also come to the conclusion that it was time to place the whole project in the hands of an established aero engine manufacturer. W.L. Tweedie of the Department of Scientific Research favoured Armstrong Siddeley, whose subsidiary, the Gloster Aircraft Company, had already discussed with Whittle the possibilities of their manufacturing the aeroplane for Whittle's engine. In spite of the reservations of both Whittle himself (who was nervous of being involved with an aero engine manufacturer) and some of the Gloster board, the Gloster Company developed an aircraft suitable for Whittle's engine.

By coincidence, one of the Power Jets directors, Tinling, knew Maurice Wilks, chief engineer of the Rover Car Company, as their wives were friendly. Whittle met both Maurice Wilks and his brother Spencer, the Managing Director, and following much negotiation, sometimes fraught, both Rover and BTH were given contracts by the Air Ministry to work on the production of the Whittle engine.

The resignation of Neville Chamberlain and the appointment of Winston Churchill as Prime Minister brought further Government support for Whittle's project. Initially, however, the crisis in Europe as Hitler's Panzer divisions swept all before them led to a short-term break in the development programme. On 20 May 1940, telegrams were received by Power Jets, Rover and BTH stating that all non-priority work was to stop so that companies could concentrate completely on production of parts vital for the immediate war effort.

Fortunately, priority for the project was restored three weeks later, but in Whittle's view the lost momentum took several months to be regained. More constructively, the Ministry of Aircraft Production (MAP) was formed, with Lord Beaverbrook in charge. After interviewing Whittle for three minutes, Beaverbrook made sure that further resources were placed at Power Jets' command, and that the production of the Gloster/Whittle E.28/39, Britain's first jet aircraft, continued unchecked. By the autumn of 1940, a small industry was developing.

In October, the decision was taken to press on with production of the twin-engined F.9/40 jet fighter. Production of eighty airframes and 160 engines per month was planned, which would mean not only a sharp step-up in activity for those involved, but also that there would be no spare engines.

The staff of Power Jets itself increased by fifty-three during November and December, and the initial participants – Power Jets, Gloster, BTH, Rover and Vauxhall – were now joined by others in advancing the project. Lucas worked on combustion development, while Ransome & Marles and the National Physical Laboratory began some bearing tests. The Ricardo Engineering Company (who, as we have seen, had long been close to Rolls-Royce) and Firth Vickers researched the possibilities of finding improved materials for turbine blade and combustion chamber parts. The Royal Aircraft Establishment was also helping, notably by carrying out wind-tunnel tests for Gloster.

By April 1941 the Gloster/Whittle E.28/39 was ready, and it was decided to try out both aeroplane and engine in taxiing trials. On 7 April, Whittle and the BTH engineer, L.J. Cheshire, went down to Gloster's airfield at Brockworth. The next day, Gloster's chief test pilot, Gerry Sayer, not only taxied the aeroplane but also took it off the ground three times and flew for 200–300 yards. His notes afterwards said:

The engine is very smooth indeed, and no vibration was observed in the pilot's cockpit.

The throttle control, however, is too coarse, a large increase in engine revolutions being obtained with very little forward movement of the throttle lever . . . the engine ran very well indeed throughout the taxiing trials.

The first proper flight took place at Cranwell (deemed to be safer and more secure than Brockworth) at 7.35pm on 15 May 1941. It lasted seventeen minutes, and Whittle recalled:

I was very tense not so much because of any fears about the engine but because this was a machine making its first flight. I think I would have felt the same if it had been an aeroplane with a conventional power plant . . . I do not remember, but I am told that, shortly after take-off, someone slapped me on the back and said, 'Frank, it flies!' and that my curt response in the tension of the moment was: 'Well, that was what it was bloody well designed to do, wasn't it?'

Whittle wrote in his book, *Jet, the story of a pioneer*, published by Frederick Muller in 1953:

Sayer was in position at about 7.40 pm. He ran the engine up to 16,500 rpm against the brakes. He then released the brakes and the aeroplane quickly gathered speed and lifted smoothly from the runway after a run of about 600 yards. It continued to the west in a flat climb for several miles and disappeared from view behind cloud banks. For several minutes we could only hear the smooth roar of the engine. Then it came into sight again as it made a wide circuit preparatory to landing. As Sayer came in it was obvious he had complete confidence in the aeroplane. He approached in a series of gliding turns as though he had flown the machine for hundreds of hours. Those of us who were pilots knew that he felt completely at home. He made a perfect landing at the far end of the runway and came to a stop somewhere short of where we were standing . . . He taxied towards us, stopped, and gave us a 'thumbs up' sign. We, of course, rushed to shake him warmly by the hand.

There was only one person from the Ministry of Aircraft Production present, but news soon reached the powers-that-be in London, and a large delegation led by the Secretary of State for Air, Sir Archibald Sinclair, arrived on 21 May for a demonstration. John Golley describes the scene very well:

Gerry Sayer brought gasps from the uninitiated onlookers with a high-speed run downwind, when the strange whistling roar of the propellerless engine riveted their attention as they watched the E.28 pulling up into a steep climbing turn and shoot skywards. The absence of a propeller was a source of amazement, and few of those privileged to see Sayer could have had any doubts that they had witnessed the beginning of a new chapter in aviation history.

   . . . One of two officers watching the E.28 take off was heard to ask, 'How the hell does that thing work?' His companion replied, 'Oh, it's easy, old boy, it just sucks itself along like a Hoover' [Whittle himself said that it 'sucks itself along like a bloody great vacuum cleaner!']. Dan Walker of Power Jets was amused to hear one officer – not knowing that Walker was one of the engineers intimately concerned – assure everybody in his immediate vicinity that the power plant was a Rolls-Royce Merlin engine driving a small four-bladed propeller inside the fuselage. He stated positively that he had seen it!

As well as Sir Archibald Sinclair (later Lord Thurso), several other VIPs came to see the demonstration flight, including Geoffrey de Havilland and his son, Roxbee Cox (later Lord Kings Norton), Patrick (later Sir Patrick) Hennessey, the deputy for the Minister of Aircraft Production, and Air Vice-Marshal Linnell, Controller of Research and Development. Also there were the Wilks brothers from Rover, as well as Williams and Tinling, who saw the aeroplane fly for the first time.

   Having been slow to believe in Whittle's project in the 1930s, the Ministry now swung to the opposite extreme and, at a meeting presided over by

Tizard, decided that a production target should be set for 1,200 engines and 500 aircraft, the first to be available in June 1942. It was hoped that the 500 aircraft would have been manufactured by the spring of 1943. However, Whittle knew that there were still many technical problems to be ironed out (the engines had been suffering from 'surging', an intermittent reverse flow in the compressor), and he wrote to Tizard on 27 May 1941 requesting the maximum possible support for further development effort.

Everything now turns on getting the test bench results and we have not got them yet, and we shall not succeed in getting them in time unless the effort is as intense as I have indicated above. I feel confident that the job can be done in the end, but that is not enough, it has to be within the next two or three months, and nothing that Rover's or the BTH or anybody else tries to do, starting virtually from scratch, can really affect the development within that time.

What is required is concentration of effort on those features of the W.2B which are in doubt, rather than the frittering away of energy on the design and making of alternative structure, gearboxes, fuel systems etc, etc, such as is going on in the BTH and the Rover Co, all of which will be a costly waste if nobody succeeds in making a turbine which will do its job.

We know the gearbox works, we know the fuel system works, we can feel fairly confident of the combustion chambers and blower, but there is grave doubt about the turbine end at present, and by far the greater part of the total effort should be directed to solving that problem. The BTH can help immensely, by making a series of alternative wheels for several W.2Bs (to Power Jets' drawings), otherwise made by the Rover Co, with the assistance of the Coventry Gauge and Tool Co.

Failing this, it is my duty to say that I cannot guarantee success before the end of the year.

It became clear that Rover were carrying out their own development work, rather than just making the engines.

'SEND THE DRAWINGS TO DERBY'

Rolls-Royce would have been aware of developments in the Internal Combustion Turbine (ICT) field, and on 1 June 1939 they recruited A.A. Griffith and gave him the facilities to continue developing his axial compressor units. Hives instructed him to 'go on thinking', and Griffith proposed the most advanced of his concepts from the RAE – a contra-rotating engine, the CR1, with a fourteen-stage high-pressure system and six-stage low-pressure ducted fans. He was still critical of Whittle's system.

While encouraging Griffith, Hives also made contact with Whittle, whom he had met at Power Jets' factory in 1940 at the instigation of Stanley

Hooker. As we have seen, Hooker had been recruited to Rolls-Royce just before the war and made an enormous contribution on the Merlin super-charger. Hooker had already been to see Whittle, and reported to Hives that Whittle's engine was producing 1,000 lbs of thrust, the same as a Merlin in a Spitfire at 350 mph. This news soon brought Hives to the Power Jets factory in Lutterworth, where he was shown round by Whittle. Whittle remembered Hives saying, 'I don't see many engines. What's holding you up?' Whittle explained the problems in having certain components made, whereupon Hives said: 'Send us the drawings to Derby, and we will make them for you.'

In 1994, Whittle recounted to Sir Ralph Robins, the Chairman of Rolls-Royce plc, that he also emphasised to Hives the simplicity of his engine. Hives thought about this and replied: 'We'll soon design the bloody simplicity out of it!'

Within a short time, Rolls-Royce were making turbine blades, gearcases and other components for Power Jets. For some reason, perhaps sensing their integrity, Whittle felt comfortable with Rolls-Royce, while he felt threatened by the likes of Rover and Armstrong Siddeley. Whittle recalled:

This was based on our respect for their outstanding engineering ability, particularly in the field in which we were engaged. I believe that this respect was mutual.

By the spring of 1941 Rolls-Royce were deeply involved, and on 28 May 1941, shortly after the first flights of the Gloster/Whittle E.28/39, Hives wrote to Hennessey at the MAP:

We had a very successful meeting on Sunday afternoon at the Rover factory where we met the Wilks brothers and Thomas. I took with me our superintendent who looks after the production of all experimental pieces. It was agreed provisionally which parts we should undertake, and another meeting has been arranged for Friday when we hope to bring back the drawings, and get on with the job.

I also arranged with Wilks that I would send our Mr. Rowledge, Dr. Griffith and Dr. Hooker to the factory at Clitheroe where it was hoped they would see one of the engines stripped . . . Any suggestions which we have to offer will in no way interfere with the production of the parts for Rovers, and we have agreed that in order to cover the finance and contract position, we will act as sub-contractors to Rovers on the production of pieces. We are expecting in six to eight weeks' time to have our own machine running.

During the summer of 1941, a Gas Turbine Collaboration Committee was formed. The idea probably came from Hives. Whittle certainly thought so, writing in his book: 'I understand that the original suggestion for this committee was made by Hives.' And this view was supported by a letter to

Hives from Roxbee Cox at the MAP on 21 August 1941, which said, *inter alia*:

I do not expect that there will be any obstacle to the constitution of a committee for pooling our gas turbine facilities and experiences but it will take me a few days to make sure of everyone's co-operation.

The Committee was duly formed, and on 3 October 1941 Air Marshal Linnell wrote to all participants, including Rolls-Royce:

As you are aware gas turbine development is now going forward in various organisations and along several different lines, and it is clearly desirable, to ensure economy in our efforts to produce power units of this new kind as quickly and efficiently as possible, that all parties concerned should collaborate.

To encourage and guide collaboration, it has been decided to form a committee under the chairmanship of Dr. Roxbee Cox on which all the firms engaged on gas turbine projects will be represented.

Rolls-Royce helped Whittle with his 'surging' problems, building a test rig with a 2,000 hp Vulture piston engine with a step-up gear made by putting two Merlin propeller reduction gears in series and driving them backwards to achieve the 16,500 rpm required by Whittle's W.2 compressor.

On 12 January 1942, Hives wrote to Whittle inviting him to Derby to discuss a proposal that Rolls-Royce should build a version of his engine. As we have seen, Hives had already recruited A.A. Griffith (who had moved from the Air Ministry research laboratory to the RAE in Farnborough). However, Griffith's axial flow ideas were proving difficult to convert into a practical engine, and Hives liked the simplicity of Whittle's engine. Griffith, in a memo to Hives on 15 June 1939, had effectively debunked the very basis of the Whittle engine:

The basic problem to be solved is that of obtaining a sufficiently low fuel consumption. For this purpose the prime necessity is a turbo-blower of high overall efficiency, a figure of at least 70 per cent being desirable. The present type of turbo-blower used for exhaust supercharging, comprising a single-stage impulse turbine and a single-stage centrifugal blower, is not capable of reaching this figure since both components have relatively low efficiencies at the required pressure ratios.

Griffith had failed to see that speed and light weight were acceptable counter-balances for the poor propulsive efficiency of a pure jet, and that a simple layout with poor fuel consumption was therefore tolerable. Nevertheless, Hives was still keeping his options open on Griffith's developments, as is made clear by a letter he wrote to Dr. Pye at the Ministry of Aircraft Production on 25 March 1941:

I shall be grateful for any help or advice you can give me on the following –

Dr. Griffith, when he was at the RAE, took out a patent in 1929 for the contra-flow supercharger. This patent was, and still is, on the secret list. As you are aware, we have now decided to go ahead with an ICT (Internal Combustion Turbine) using the contra-flow system. The scheme is well in hand, and certain of the details are being issued to the shops.

As we are putting a considerable amount of technical skill into this development, we naturally would like the patent position clarified.

It was agreed that Power Jets would be the main contractor on Whittle's engine, and that Rolls-Royce would be the sub-contractor. On 30 January 1942, Hives visited Power Jets and, having made the point that he wanted Rolls-Royce to be in the forefront of jet engine manufacture, said that more than technical collaboration would be necessary. In the short term, however, not much happened except that the MAP gave Power Jets a contract for the design and development of six engines, and Power Jets immediately placed sub-contracts with Rolls-Royce.

Much of 1942 seems to have been spent struggling with attempted solutions to mechanical problems. It was clear early in the year that Rover were wondering how they could extricate themselves. Spencer Wilks was finding it very difficult to work with Whittle, and early in February 1942 he put forward a proposal to Hives whereby Rover and Rolls-Royce could collaborate. Hives wrote to him on 11 February:

I have discussed with Mr. Sidgreaves the proposition you put forward last Saturday.

The decision we have arrived at is that it would be impossible to take advantage of your offer. As I pointed out to you, in agreement with MAP and Power Jets Ltd., we are producing a Whittle turbine to Rolls-Royce designs, and we have undertaken the development work. In connection with this project, we have agreed to act as sub-contractors to Power Jets Ltd. I am sure you will appreciate the impossible position which would arise if we have any link-up with the Rover Company.

For his part, Whittle was becoming frustrated by Rover's lack of progress. Only the day before Hives wrote to Wilks, Whittle had also written to Rover:

We can summarise our views by saying that experimenting cannot go on indefinitely before a decision is made on the first production model, and in the meantime, if we have the correct picture of the situation, the mechanical side is being seriously neglected.

Despite the many difficulties during 1942, Hives became more and more convinced that gas turbines were the future for the aircraft industry. He realised that Whittle's W.2B engine worked, because Rolls-Royce were testing it at Hucknall, as is clear from this letter from Ray Dorey to Flight Lieutenant W.E.P. Johnson at Power Jets, written on 14 April 1942:

Wellington Test Bed (W.2B into Wellington)
We had a small discussion with DRD after you left the other day, and provisionally fixed for a Wellington II to be sent to us for this job.

As Whittle made further progress on his W.2/500 engine, he suggested to Hives that Rolls-Royce should take over production, as Power Jets were clearly not in a position to do so. Hives and Sidgreaves visited Power Jets on 8 October, and Hives did so again on 4 December.

At this latter meeting, Hives told Whittle that he and Sidgreaves had discussed Whittle's suggestion with Sir Wilfrid Freeman, by this time Chief Executive of the MAP, and Air Marshal Linnell himself. Hives summarised Rolls-Royce's position, which was that the company was definitely entering the aircraft gas turbine field, they were interested in Power Jets' W.2/500 and would like to undertake the production, and because of their own commitment to Merlin production, Rolls-Royce would require extra facilities to produce the W.2/500.

Power Jets' willingness for Rolls-Royce to take over production is set out clearly in a letter from Tinling to Hives on 16 November 1942.

The W.2/500 is nearing the stage of readiness for production . . . We are of the opinion, against the background of some knowledge of other firms, that your Company is the best able to produce this engine as it should be, and among the few with whom we would feel entirely happy to collaborate.

The MAP called a meeting for 11 December, having received this letter from Hives dated 17 November:

As you are aware, we started work on Turbines when we engaged Dr. Griffith from the R.A.E. in April, 1939.
    We still think the Rolls-Royce contra-flow turbine is the best in existence, except that we cannot get it to work!

As we have seen, Hives had been concerned that the effort which should have been directed exclusively towards winning the Second World War was being wasted on jets. However, he had now become what he referred to as 'a turbine enthusiast':

Apart from our own contra-flow turbine, we have designed, and shall have running by the end of this month, a Whittle type turbine. Our approach to the Whittle turbine was that we set out to design a turbine with a modest output, but one which we hoped would run and continue to run. Our turbine will be the heaviest and biggest, and relatively give less thrust, than any of the others, but we shall be disappointed if it does not run reliably, and for sufficiently long periods for us to learn something about it, and we can then proceed to open up the throttles, in short, to follow the usual Rolls-Royce practice on development. We are fortunate inasmuch as we work in the most friendly way with Whittle. We have a great admiration for his ability. We are also equally friendly with the Rover Company. We have shown our friendship in a practical way by producing in our Experimental Department quantities of difficult pieces, both for Power Jets and Rovers.

We have been approached by Whittle to undertake the production of the W-500. To do this we should require extra facilities. We are confident of one thing, however, that jets are never going to make any real progress until some well-established firm [obviously Rolls-Royce] becomes the parent or big brother, to get a move on.

A comparison of the rate of the U.S. development and ours shows us up badly. It is already time that some of the various jet projects were brought together, and the researches pooled.

Some decision should be taken as regards the Power Jets factory at Whetstone. I was astonished at the size of it, and the emptiness of it, when I visited it a short time ago.

This was how Whittle recalled the meeting with the MAP:

During most of the talk I was seated, while Sir Wilfrid paced back and forth speaking forcefully and rather abruptly, emphasising his remarks with vigorous arm movements. Air Marshal Linnell sat at one side of the room and said very little.

Freeman opened by saying that every jet engine up to then was either a flop or likely to be. Three years had passed and there was little to show for it. When I protested that this was not a true representation of the facts, he admitted that he might be exaggerating slightly. He then concentrated on the W.2B situation – he laid great emphasis on what he described as the failure of the W.2B and inferred that I was primarily to blame. I said I refused to accept the blame, and that on the contrary I had repeatedly protested against the course of events which had led to the situation as it then was. Here was the state of affairs I had long foreseen. Though I had been deprived of any effective control of the development of the W.2B long before, I was blamed for the results of a policy which had failed.

Freeman said that his first impulse, when he took up his new post, was to close down the whole job. After this he had felt that the best thing would be to bring all the different firms together into one organisation, which he implied would be dominated by Rolls-Royce. Though he had been dissuaded from so sweeping a step, he had nevertheless made up his mind to bring together the resources of Rolls-Royce, Rover and Power Jets under the primary control of Rolls-Royce.

The Rover management would cease to have anything more to do with the job. Though he did not say so explicitly, I gathered that Power Jets would cease to have an independent existence. At this point he stopped in his peregrinations and asked, abruptly, 'Well what do you think of it?' I felt I had to gain time so I replied that I had not really grasped what he was proposing, so he went over more or less the same ground once more.

He seemed to be antagonistic to the Board of Directors of Power Jets: he admitted that Williams and Tinling had done a good job of work in initiating the venture, but thought that they had ceased to have any useful function. He went so far as to say he would have them called up. I gathered that he proposed to include Johnson amongst those he intended to call up. I protested vigorously, and said that all the people he had referred to were still doing very important work. Williams and Tinling had done far more than initiate the venture – amongst other things they were mainly responsible for the expansion which had taken place, and in particular for the bringing into being of the Whetstone factory.

Once more he stopped and asked me what I thought about it all, so again I stalled by saying that I had not clearly grasped what he had in mind. I was almost sure that what he really meant was that Power Jets was to be handed over to Rolls-Royce, lock, stock, and barrel, but that he could not bring himself to put it quite as bluntly as that. So once more he stalked up and down embroidering the theme.

I told him that any proposal which disturbed the Power Jets' team as an entity would be disastrous. He replied that what he had in mind did not involve the disbanding of the team. He went on to argue that a firm like Rolls-Royce with their vast resources could obviously do much better than a small organisation like Power Jets. I asked him whether the record of the past year supported his point. I pointed out that no one had equalled, let alone beaten, the Power Jets' record in the time of manufacture of the W.2/500 or in test-running results after completion of manufacture.

He made it clear that he had quite definitely decided to transfer Barnoldswick and Clitheroe to Rolls-Royce management. He remarked that he had yet to break the news to the Wilks brothers. I said that at least was a feature in his proposals which had my full approval.

On 21 December, Hives wrote to Sir Wilfrid Freeman:

I thought you would be interested to know that I had a talk with Wilks yesterday. He raises no objection to Rolls-Royce taking over the management of the I.C.T. from Rovers; in fact, he thinks it is a very wise move. I propose meeting him up at Clitheroe next week, and to go over the job, and afterwards submit to you a programme of how we think it should be carried out. Now that we have Wilks' support on the policy, it gives us time to work out the details.

We can discuss this further when we visit the MAP for our usual monthly meeting on Tuesday, the 29th.

Hives and Stanley Hooker met Spencer Wilks for dinner the following week. Hives asked Wilks: 'Why are you playing around with the jet engine? It's not your business, you grub about on the ground, and I hear from Hooker that things are going from bad to worse with Whittle.' Wilks replied: 'We can't get on with the fellow at all, and I would like to be shot of the whole business.' Then Hives said: 'I'll tell you what I'll do. You give us this jet job, and I'll give you our tank engine factory in Nottingham.' And that was it. The deal was done. Now the professionalism of Rolls-Royce swung into action. As Hooker put it:

Instead of small teams working in holes in the corner, in one stroke, nearly 2,000 men and women, and massive manufacturing facilities, were focussed on the task of getting the W.2B engine mechanically reliable and ready for RAF service. The knowledge that Rolls-Royce had taken over, and the personal pressure that Hives was able to apply to all the ancillary suppliers, galvanised everybody into top gear. And, I am glad to say, Frank Whittle was delighted. From then on, he generously gave us every possible assistance.

But Hives was not happy with one aspect of the agreement tentatively reached at the MAP. At the side of one of the points set out by Roxbee Cox in a letter to Hives on 15 December 1942, he marked two heavy pencil lines. He was happy with the other points relating to the production of the engine (except that he wanted Rover's W.2B rather than Power Jets' W2/500 to be in the hands of Rolls-Royce, and the existing Rover facilities at Barnoldswick to be used). But he was not happy with the following:

Research on and development of centrifugal type units to be in the hands of Power Jets at Whetstone and Lutterworth.

If gas turbine engines were Rolls-Royce's future, Hives wanted control of development as well as production. Indeed, in a memo of 28 December 1942, Hives made his determination on this point perfectly clear.

The first responsibility we shall assume is the technical responsibility, and in addition, to decide on what types and numbers of turbines should be manufactured.

He was magnanimous about Rover's efforts:

We do not blame Rover for lack of success on the turbine project; we have every sympathy with their difficulties. Broadly speaking, there has been too much slide rule and not enough hardware.

Nor was he planning many changes at Barnoldswick:

Our intention is to bring back our Works Engineer, John Reid, from Packards, and put him in charge. Now that Packard has produced nearly 8,000 engines Reid can be spared, and he wishes to return. We also expect to put one man in on the development side [Stanley Hooker]. Apart from that we shall be disappointed if we cannot use the Rover organisation as it is.

On 24 January 1943, Hives wrote to Sir Wilfrid Freeman:

I thought you would like to know the present position that we have arrived at in taking over the Rover ICT project . . . We are gradually assuming complete responsibility for this organisation, and so far we have achieved it without losing any of the good-will of the people who have been working on the job.

'IN OPERATION AGAINST THE ENEMY'

On 7 January 1944, the RAF and the USAAF released a joint statement about the new 'Jet', and Whittle and his family soon found themselves almost overwhelmed by the media. Air Marshal Sorley at the Ministry of Aircraft Production was not amused, writing to all the companies involved in jet work:

As you know a joint statement by the RAF and the USAAF has been released to the BBC and to the Press to the effect that jet propelled fighter aircraft have successfully passed experimental tests and soon will be in production.

In view of this release I think it is more likely that many people will assume that the strictest security arrangements which have in the past governed jet aircraft have to some extent been relaxed. This is not the case of course and it is absolutely imperative that your staff and workpeople who, in the course of their work, come into contact with this type of aircraft, should appreciate that the utmost secrecy still obtains.

The release was couched in the broadest terms. Except so far as is necessary in the course of their work, I should be glad if you would warn those concerned that in no circumstances whatever should any reference be made to this type of aircraft and engine other than the details which have already been made public.

In May 1944 the first Meteor Is, powered by Rolls-Royce Wellands (the production version of the W.2B), were delivered to the RAF. Wing Commander H.J. Wilson had put together a unit known as CRD Flight under the auspices of the RAE at Farnborough, and by June 1944 this Flight had been equipped with six Meteors. Within a few weeks these aircraft were transferred to 616 Squadron at Manston, and they began operations against Germany's latest weapon, the V.I flying bomb, on 27 July 1944.

The Minister of Supply, Stafford Cripps, was able to write to Rolls-Royce on 16 August 1944, requesting that a message be posted on the notice-boards at Barnoldswick:

TO THE STAFF AND WORKERS AT MESSRS ROLLS-ROYCE, BARNOLDSWICK

I can now tell you confidentially – please do not repeat it outside the factory – that your engines are in operation against the enemy. My heartiest congratulations to everyone whose work has contributed to this fine result. This is only a beginning and we want all the spares and additional engines that you can make for us as soon as possible. I know I can rely on you all to do your best.

However, gas turbine-powered aircraft saw little action in the war. As the *News Chronicle* wrote in July 1945:

They [the Meteors] operated over the Channel outside the gun and balloon belts. Against such difficult and fast targets as the flying bombs the Meteors had considerable success.

In the meantime the German jet-propelled fighters and fighter bombers were appearing in increasing numbers over the battlefields in Holland and Germany. These were the single-jet Messerschmitt 163 [in fact, it was rocket powered] and the twin-jet Messerschmitt 262 and the Arado 234. The German pilots relied mainly on their high speed for their protection against interception by our fighters. Only the Tempests and one of the later marks of Spitfire had a hope of dealing with the German jets. [The *News Chronicle* was being very patriotic. The American P-51 Mustang, admittedly powered by the Rolls-Royce Merlin, was also capable of, and indeed succeeded in, shooting down Me 262s.]

Air Marshal Sir Arthur Coningham, commanding the RAF, Second Tactical Air Force, became more and more anxious to match the British jet against the German jet. It became increasingly obvious that only a jet could be set to match a jet; but no one had practical experience of air fighting at speeds in excess of 500 mph.

During the closing months of the war in Europe the Meteors were sent across the Channel. For a while they were stationed near Brussels until the pilots familiarised themselves with the conditions. Later the Meteor unit was moved forward into Holland and finally into Germany. During this period the operations of the Luftwaffe declined until they reached vanishing point. The Meteor pilots waited in vain for the chance to show what they could do.

'WE'LL SOON DESIGN THE SIMPLICITY OUT OF IT'

We must wait until the next book in this story of Rolls-Royce (due to be published by Icon Books in March 2001) to see how the company exploited the gas turbine engine to the full, both in the military and civil markets, and how it rebuilt its luxury car business, while also using its skills, knowledge and experience in the diesel engine field and the marine, conventional, and nuclear power, industries. Suffice it to conclude here that Hives had appreciated that the gas turbine engine was the future, and once he had persuaded everyone that the war would be won by concentrating on developing (and producing in vast numbers) the Merlin and Griffon engines, the Rolls-Royce design and development resources would be turned towards making the gas turbine a practical proposition.

Hives was convinced, but of course he could not sell gas turbine engines unless he could convince everyone else, otherwise the necessary aircraft would not be ordered, designed and produced.

On 15 November 1944 he wrote to his old friend, Sir Wilfrid Freeman.

Our own view is that it is certain we shall finish the war with an entirely obsolete Air Force. I know this is the last thing you would like to see, having been responsible for maintaining the technical superiority of the RAF for so many years.

The turbine engines have arrived! Our recent success with the B-41 emphasises that on the engine side the efficiency and performance has been well demonstrated. The Service experience with jet engines in the F.9/40 shows that they can be made as reliable as present conventional engines.

There is no mystery about turbine engines: they allow one to crowd much more equivalent horse-power into a very much lighter power plant. For instance, the B-41 in a modern fighter is equivalent to a piston engine of 7,000 HP.

All we can see as regards aircraft for these new type engines is a small amount of planning on fighters, but there is no sense of urgency at the back of it. The urgency all appears to be concentrated on the Brabazon type of civil machines.

It is unfortunate that the timing of the introduction of turbines should coincide with the demand for civil aircraft, but we consider the RAF should have preference.

On jet engines there is very little invention: the fact that we could design, produce, manufacture and demonstrate the full performance on the B-41 in 6 months confirms this point.

You know better than I do how long it will take to replace the various RAF machines with modern types – the first thing to face up to is that the present machines are already obsolete, and that the Air Ministry, and the Cabinet, and the Nation should face up to it.

The Germans are already ahead of us on the practical use of jet machines. As regards the technical details of their engines, we should say that they are not as good as we can provide; but on the other hand, their development is handicapped because of the best materials not being available to them.

When Hives had said to Whittle in 1940, 'We'll soon design the simplicity out of it!', it was not entirely a joke. Hives knew that if the jet engine was too simple, anyone could make it and Rolls-Royce would not be able to exploit their design and engineering skills to the full. In June 1945, Hives told his board:

The very fact that we have been able to design an entirely new jet engine, put it on the test bed for the first time and complete a 100 hours test without looking inside it indicates that as regards jet engines they are relatively simple to design and produce, and as soon as things become simple then one must expect keen competition. Generally we rely on making difficult products where it does not pay people to compete. Fortunately the tendency on jet engines will be for them to become more complicated and therefore more difficult, which is more in our line of business.

On 7 May 1945 Field Marshal Jodl, on behalf of the Wehrmacht, and Lieutenant General Bedell Smith, on behalf of the British and American forces, with French and Russian officers as witnesses, signed the German surrender document in Rheims. There followed a similar ceremony in Berlin between the Germans and the Russians, and on 8 May all hostilities ceased. The longest, most destructive war in modern history had ended, at least in Europe. The war against Japan was to continue for another three months.

The relief was enormous, but the future daunting. Throughout Europe the spectre was one of famine. It was estimated that even a year after the end of the war, over 100 million people in Europe were surviving on 1,500 calories a day or less. People trying to lose weight live on such rations, not growing children or those doing heavy physical labour. And even this meagre level could not be maintained. In 1946 the British and American occupation zones cut the daily ration to 900–1,000 calories. The loss of a ration book meant starvation. And, as winter approached, lack of fuel meant many faced death through hypothermia.

Industry and, above all, transport were virtually paralysed. The Ruhr coal industry was producing 25,000 tons a day compared with 400,000 before the war, but even if there had been plentiful supplies, there was no method of transport. Some 740 out of 958 important bridges in the British and American zones had been destroyed. There was only one usable bridge, at Nijmegen, across the Rhine, and only one, in Hamburg, across the Elbe. Railway transport in Germany was scarcely functioning, and in France only 35 per cent was operational. Europe had fought itself to a standstill, and was close to complete collapse.

Britain, of course, had not been invaded. Nevertheless, she had been severely weakened. She had sold a third of her overseas assets, and consequently her income from overseas investment was severely diminished. She had incurred large debts, and sterling was undermined. The Merchant Navy was only 75 per cent of its pre-war size, and only 2 per cent of British industry was producing for export. Dependent on imports for two-thirds of her food and the bulk of her raw materials, Britain's situation, even as a victor nation, seemed about as bleak as that of the vanquished.

And yet there was great hope for a better future. Everyone had fought in the war or endured its privations because they had no choice, but many also felt that they were fighting a just war, not only to defeat evil regimes led by dictators, but also to create a better way of doing things, even in the so-called democracies. As a result, and to the surprise of many, in the General Election of July 1945 the British electorate voted out the war hero, Winston Churchill, and his Conservative party – the 'Guilty Men', as Michael Foot dubbed them – and opted for the Labour Party with its fair-shares-for-all philosophy.

How hope coped with reality, and how Rolls-Royce coped with both, we shall see in the next book.

SHORT BIOGRAPHIES

Many people served Rolls-Royce, and it is not possible to give them full credit in the book without breaking the flow of the text. This section of short biographies gives the background and main achievements of those who played a considerable part in building on the foundations laid by Royce, Rolls, Johnson, Claremont and Hives.

Again, I am most grateful to Mike Evans for his contribution to the compiling of these biographies.

It should be noted that all employees on this list were known by their 'references', addressed as such both in writing and face-to-face, referred to by reference and even *thought of* by reference. First names were very rarely used.

J.E. ALDRED

The name Aldred is inextricable from the story of the American-built Rolls-Royce. In the last two years of the First World War, the company had established a small but strong team in the US, which sought to get Eagle aero engines produced there. Soon after the war ended, Claude Johnson instructed the solicitor, Kenneth Mackenzie, to explore possibilities for establishing a suitable plant and financial backing to manufacture cars in America. This he did, together with M. Olley and G. Bagnall, who also remained there from the Eagle initiative. Johnson's motivation was to form a major insurance against the economic and political disasters that he feared would prejudice Rolls-Royce's future car production in the UK. In this he was perhaps to prove too far-sighted, since the political damage he foresaw was not inflicted until car production was resumed after the Second World War.

Mackenzie's first interview was with Duke, the tobacco magnate who was thought to own a large block of Rolls-Royce shares; he had advised on aero engine production. Duke advised again: 'A consideration which is contrary to our manu-facturing in the United States is the fact that, in the eyes of at least some customers, the Rolls-Royce car has an inflated value simply because it is made in England.' Duke estimated this at some 3 to 10 per cent of the value of the car.

Duke's advice should have been heeded. Instead, Johnson pressed ahead with his vision of an American Rolls-Royce company, committed to manufacturing Derby designs but for sale only in North America, controlled by Derby but financed by American money. Duke again should have been heeded when he said that Rolls-Royce Limited should raise the money and set up an American subsidiary. Instead, matters proceeded in accordance with Johnson's vision and it was at this stage that J.E. Aldred & Co., an entrepreneurial finance house of the old school, entered the frame. From the flotation of Rolls-Royce of America Inc. in 1919 to its sad end during America's Depression, Aldred was key to the financing of the enterprise. His commitment throughout was beyond question, and the failure of the venture really lay in Derby's lack of desire to understand the difference between the American market and others it served, coupled with the uneasy relationship between American financiers who did not want to become car men, and Rolls-Royce car men in England who did not want to risk becoming international financiers. The Depression simply served to kill a dying enterprise.

Some 70 years on, Silver Ghosts and New Phantoms built at Springfield, Mass. under the technical control of Olley are greatly prized for their qualities and for the excellence of their coachwork.

NURSE ETHEL AUBIN

Nurse Aubin was recruited following Henry Royce's first serious illness in 1911. Mrs. Royce was fearful of illness in any form, and it was clear that she would not be able to face dressing Royce's wounds. It had been equally clear to Claremont and Johnson that part of Royce's over-work problem reflected frustration at the lack of certain home comforts. They knew that Mrs. Royce would not travel overseas; the home at Le Canadel, although it took Royce away from his wife, allowed Nurse Aubin to move in. Her professional care and concern for the well-being of Royce ensured his ability to live and work for a further 22 years. Royce left his estate in part to his wife and in part to Nurse Aubin, but it is significant that he left his ashes in the care of the latter. Nurse Aubin later married Royce's solicitor, Tildesley, but the marriage was short-lived after she found that he was not altogether heterosexual. Nurse Aubin survived into the 1960s.

R.W.H. BAILEY (By)

Already experienced in automotive design, notably of pioneering front-wheel-drive vehicles, R.W.H. Bailey joined Rolls-Royce in 1910, initially on design. In 1912, he worked for a period on Royce's design team before becoming chief technical production engineer. His prime task over many years was to translate the designs of Royce's distant team and those of A.J. Rowledge and his staff in Derby into comprehensive manufacturing instructions. Additionally, he scaled the Eagle down to produce the Falcon, and the Kestrel up to produce the Buzzard. He was deeply involved in the design of the 'R' engine. He also produced the design for the PV12. Based on a scaling of the PVG, it became the forerunner of the Merlin. In 1937 Hives appointed 'By' (as he was known) chief engineer of the newly formed Chassis Division. Work on a new rationalised range of cars was well advanced when, on the outbreak of war, Hives asked him to return to aero work. He made a major contribution to the Merlin on production, serviceability and the codification of modification and repair procedures. He retired when the war ended in 1945 at the age of 68. (There has been considerable debate as to when R.W.H. Bailey began to refer to himself as R.W. Harvey-Bailey. We have decided to stick with R.W.H. Bailey.)

LT. COL. TIMOTHY B. BARRINGTON (Bn)

Colonel Barrington joined Rolls-Royce as head of the Derby design office after serving with the Aeronautical Inspection Directorate during the First World War. He left when it came to light that he had told the Air Ministry that Rolls-Royce were not interested in aero engine work for the future. This was in 1921, and he was replaced by A.J. Rowledge. Before returning to run the Derby aero design team once more in 1934, he had worked with Bentley until its bankruptcy, and latterly with Fedden on Bristol aero engines. Barrington's preliminary studies for a two-row air-cooled radial led Fedden to conclude that it would be difficult providing valve gear to operate four valves per cylinder. It was this that led Fedden to turn to the sleeve valve. When the Second World War came, Barrington was seconded, along with Ellor and Reid, to the Ministry of Aircraft Production. They were posted to America, where they helped Packard produce the Merlin. Barrington died there.

T.E. BELLRINGER (Br)

Joined Rolls-Royce in 1911. Works manager, London Repair Depot, between the wars.

ARTHUR BIDDULPH

Night superintendent at the Derby Works when war broke out in 1914. When Johnson declared that the market for the luxury car must be considered as dead, Biddulph saw that there was an opportunity in manufacturing armaments. He immediately began to fill the factory with orders for shells, flechettes and other work for the armed forces.

ARTHUR HARRY BRIGGS

Wealthy worsted manufacturer from Bradford in Yorkshire, and enthusiastic owner of an early four-cylinder 20 hp. Proposed that Rolls-Royce Limited be formed, and saved the first public share flotation in December 1906. Without his financial support, the company would have failed in its first year.

LES BUCKLER (LB)

When R.H. Coverley left Experimental in 1937, he was succeeded by Horace Percy Smith – HPS – who inherited a first-class team, including experts such as Les Buckler, who had been technical assistant to both, and Les Say (LFS). Les Buckler came from the right background (his father Josiah, known as 'Si', had been one of the first members of the Experimental team on chassis work) and was a great practical joker to boot! Buckler joined the company in 1922 as an apprentice under Platford, but later moved to Experimental. Later, he became one of the trio (with Joe Lowe and Jack Marsden) who performed the block and piston change on Waghorn's Schneider Trophy-winning Supermarine S6 on the night before the contest in 1929. In 1942, he took charge of Meteor tank engine production at Bobbers Mill in Nottingham. Early in 1943, Rolls-Royce began to take over the work of Rover on the Whittle gas turbine at Barnoldswick and Clitheroe. Much has been written of the outstanding achievements of Dr. Stanley Hooker (as chief engineer sent from Derby) and his team of Rover and Rolls-Royce personnel. Far less has been written on the posting of Les Buckler as works manager (supported by Les Say and others) by Derby to cut metal at Barnoldswick. Hives himself commented that with Rover there had been too much slide-rule and too little hardware. Buckler changed all that, and his work had as much to do with the acceleration of the pace of development as did the arrival of Hooker. When Hives moved the centre of gravity of jet engine work to Derby after the war, Buckler initially became manager of Barnoldswick, returning later to Derby as head of Experimental following the tragic death of Horace Percy Smith. Two years later he became assistant general manager, Manufacturing, Derby Factories and in 1958 he became general manager, Manufacturing, Derby Factories. Ultimately he became a director on the Aero Engine Division board. He was quiet, highly approachable, focused and capable.

CHARLES CAROLIN (CC)

Carolin was a designer who worked for a time on Royce's personal team at West Wittering. He left the company in 1921. His specialisation had been General Arrangement drawings.

ERNEST CASWELL

Ernest Caswell managed the Rolls-Royce motor car service centre set up in New York some years before the formation of Rolls-Royce of America Inc., which followed the First World War. His sister Florence was secretary to the Hon. C.S. Rolls, and to Claude Johnson for a time after Rolls's death. She then worked with Henry Royce at Le Canadel. She left to become companion to Lady Llangattock – Rolls's mother – after she had lost her husband and all three sons.

WITOLD W.O. CHALLIER (Chr)

Born in Poland in 1904, Challier graduated in mechanical and aeronautical engineering at the Technical University of Warsaw. By the outbreak of war in 1939, he headed Poland's equivalent of the Royal Aircraft Establishment – the Aircraft and Equipment Division of the Technical Institute for Aeronautics. When Poland fell, he found his way to Britain and joined the Rolls-Royce team at Hucknall in January 1941 as a performance expert. He was to remain for nearly 30 years, specialising in performance prediction and analysis of aircraft and their engines.

Among Challier's early tasks was the analysis of the performance of the P-51 Mustang fighter and prediction of the improvement to be gained from fitting a Merlin 61. So competent was his work that his reputation extended beyond the company. It was said that Sidney Camm, chief designer of Hawker, would telephone Challier to seek advice. In 1949 he was appointed chief project engineer, transferring to Derby in 1955. He retired in 1970.

R.H. ('Bob') COVERLEY (RHC)

Coverley was a long-serving member of the Experimental Department under E.W. Hives, and was already shop superintendent by the early 1920s. In this role, he was in charge of the manufacture and assembly of experimental components for motor cars and aero engines. When Hives was appointed general manager of Rolls-Royce, production was split. Coverley became production manager, Car Division, and H.J. Swift production manager, Aero Division. Coverley's report on car production costs underscored the vital need to replace existing models with the intended Rationalised Range. At the beginning of 1940, initially (it was stated) on a temporary basis, Coverley became 'controller' – a title of his own making – of the propeller manufacturer Rotol, set up on Roy Fedden's suggestion by Rolls-Royce (RO) and Bristol (TOL) in mid-1937. He was placed over the head of Stammers, the general manager, and ruled over the organisation with dynamism. On precisely what basis he did this is unclear. Beaverbrook, newly appointed Minister for Aircraft Production, wrote to Coverley in June 1940: 'I confirm that I have appointed you to the post of Director of the Production of Aero Engines and Airscrews.' Coverley had no option but to accept, but gained agreement that two days a week would remain free so that he could manage Rotol. A month later, Beaverbrook wrote again: 'I have decided that I must ask you to undertake full-time duties as Advisor to me on the Production of Aero Engines, severing your connection with Rotol.' Coverley declared to colleagues that he intended to pay periodic visits to Rotol, and so maintain effective supervision unostentatiously. He seems to have succeeded. The company responded to his strong leadership to great effect throughout the war, but he resigned in December 1945 through differences over future policy. Coverley was capable and knew the value of his men, but would not pay a rise to anyone who lacked the courage to ask. He enjoyed bullying some of his subordinates, albeit in a humorous manner. On the positive side, he developed many outstanding subordinates this way.

WILLIAM M. COWEN (C)

A senior member of the London motor car sales team at Conduit Street from the early days, rising to sales and general manager in 1928.

MAJOR LEN W. COX (Cx)

A senior member of the London motor car sales team at Conduit Street, having joined C.S. Rolls & Co. in 1905. He rose to become chief of sales. He survived well into his nineties, sailing almost daily, single-handed, at sea from his West Country home.

JAMES GORDON ('Jock') DAWSON CBE (JGD)

Joined Rolls-Royce in October 1938. After six months in the Electrical Laboratory, he worked as an assistant tester in the Experimental test-beds. Sent to Sinfin (now Moor Lane) in 1940 to run the new test-beds being built, which eventually handled all new piston engines and the first gas turbines. Went to Shell Research in 1946, becoming chief engineer of Thornton Research Centre. In 1955 he joined Perkins Diesel as chief engineer and later technical director. Moved to the Dowty Group as director of Dowty Hydraulics in 1966, and in 1969 took over the Zenith Group as Managing Director, becoming Chairman in 1977. He was President of the Institution of Mechanical Engineers in 1979–80.

BERNARD INCLEDON DAY (Da)

Bernard Day was the leading designer behind the Sheffield Simplex car which, at one stage, was among the few that challenged the Silver Ghost. He was recruited in 1913 to work in the Derby-based Design Office, and during the First World War headed the Royal Airship Design Office (RADO) at the Derby works, designing and building swivelling propeller drive assemblies for both propelling and steering airships. At the end of the war, he was in charge of the Motor Car Design Office in Derby, which launched the first proposals for the post-war cars. In 1921, with several of his assistants, he was posted to Royce's personal design staff at West Wittering, specialising in chassis, suspension, steering, axle and brake design. He transferred to Derby after Royce died, and became chief designer of the Chassis Division when it was formed in 1937. During the Second World War he transferred to aero work, initially concentrating on propeller reduction gear design. In 1940 he became assistant chief designer, and later personal technical assistant to A.G. Elliott, the chief engineer. A gentleman – both liked and respected – he retired in 1945, remaining in Derby, where he died in 1956.

JOHN DE LOOZE (D)

Joined Royce in 1893, becoming company secretary of F.H. Royce & Co. Ltd. in the following year, of Royce Ltd. in 1899, and Rolls-Royce Limited in 1906. Dour and feared by many, he was extremely hard-working. A key figure in the success of Rolls-Royce, he retired in 1943 after 50 years' service, and died in Derby in 1953.

FRANK DODD (Dd)

Dodd joined Rolls-Royce in Derby in 1917 and served his time as a fitter. On completing his apprenticeship, he became Henry Royce's personal driver and remained so until Royce died in 1933. He then became a test driver, gaining foreman status in 1936. Three years later, he transferred to the Chassis Division at Clan Foundry, being promoted to quality engineer at Crewe when car production commenced there after the Second World War. In this role, Car Test came under him. He was the last of Royce's team to survive, finally passing away in 1999.

RAY N. DOREY (Dor)

Dorey joined E.W. Hives in the Experimental Department from Bristol University in 1927. In charge of testing the 'R' engine for the 1929 Schneider Trophy, he subsequently became installation engineer, liaising with aircraft constructors on engine installations. Appointed manager of Flight Test at Hucknall in 1935, he succeeded A.C. Lovesey who had established the facility a few months earlier. In 1937, Hives – now general manager – had decided that Hucknall would design complete powerplants for Rolls-Royce engines, including low-drag evaporative cooling. When the Second World War came, Dorey organised liaison flights to RAF squadrons in addition to test flying, and after the Dunkirk evacuation he set up a repair line on Hurricanes. This was followed by the first conversions of Spitfire Is to Spitfire Vs, and later of the Mark Vs to the Mark IX. In October 1942, Dorey – by then general manager – got the first Merlin-powered conversion of the Mustang flying. In the same year, he installed and test-flew a Whittle W.2B jet engine in the tail of a Wellington bomber. Throughout, Hucknall performed superbly with Dorey and his buccaneering enthusiasm at the helm.

In 1947, Dorey was brought back to Derby by E.W. Hives and placed in charge of Nene, Reheat, Tay and Dart engine development. From being king of his own castle, he found himself in unfamiliar circumstances in which one or two colleagues were less than helpful. He became dispirited and nearly joined Avro in Canada in 1951. Hives offered Dorey the choice of Managing Director at Rolls-Royce Canada, which was to build 900 Nene engines for the RCAF, or general manager of the Motor Car Division at Crewe. Dorey chose Crewe. He was greatly involved in the production of the Silver Cloud and Bentley S series of motor cars from 1955 on, including the introduction of the V8 engine in 1959.

Dorey was instrumental in creating Mulliner Park Ward Limited, and in setting up aero engine nozzle guide vane manufacture at Crewe, as well as production of Continental engines for light aircraft. His biggest challenge was the launch of the Rolls-Royce Silver Shadow and Bentley Series T, with their monocoque construction and advanced technical specifications. His final years at Crewe were not happy ones. Sir Denning Pearson sent Geoff Fawn to Crewe, and set him and Dorey up as joint

Assistant Managing Directors in 1966. Fawn's aggressive nature led Dorey to take early retirement at the age of 61 in 1968. He died in 1977.

JOHN DRAPER

Draper was a draughtsman, and became manager of the Chassis Division Drawing Office when E.W. Hives split car and aero work in 1937. When war broke out in 1939 and all technical staff were dispersed from Derby, most found themselves in Belper. For a while, however, more than one Design or Drawing Office operated from the domestic residence of a senior official. In the case of Draper, the move was to W.A. Robotham's home at Park Leys, Duffield, and in particular to his squash court. At first there was little to do, as the Chassis Division had not found a useful job for the duration. Office staff thus put on overalls and stripped crashed Merlin engines to find parts to keep the RAF flying. Returning to the squash court, apart from the fact that heating in winter was a problem (hot heads and frozen feet), Draper, as Robotham recalled, managed the 'Dilemma of Draughtsman'. He added that Drawing Office staff were traditionally temperamental, and yet with Draper's good humour and forceful personality, the office ran smoothly. The squash court became the source of the 'PL' schemes, this prefix standing for Park Leys. Draper stayed with Robotham after the war, but sadly died before the Oil Engine Division moved to Shrewsbury in the late 1950s.

ALBERT G. ELLIOTT (E)

One of the first recruits from Napier, Elliott joined Rolls-Royce in 1912. He had studied engineering at Northampton College, London University, before gaining early motor car experience with Napier. A gifted designer whose work was elegant, he became Royce's principal design assistant before the First World War, working both in the south of England and the south of France. When Royce's end drew near, Elliott returned to Derby to ensure a place in the hierarchy. In 1937, Hives appointed him chief engineer of the newly formed Aero Engine Division, and later he rose to become chief engineer of Rolls-Royce. He was appointed a director in 1945, and then joint Managing Director with E.W. Hives in 1951. In 1954, he became Executive Vice Chairman to Lord Hives, in which capacity he retired at the end of 1955. Referred to by some as 'foxy', he remained on the board of Rotol into the 1960s.

JAMES E. ELLOR (Lr, pronounced Ell-ar)

When Rolls-Royce first added mechanically driven superchargers to the Eagle XVI and FX in the mid-1920s, A.A. Rubbra was given the task of development testing both in Derby and at RAE, Farnborough. It soon became evident that the country's leading expert was 'Jimmy' Ellor at RAE. His expertise was widely known, and there were attempts to recruit him to work in America. Restricted to Civil Service pay scales, the Government had little flexibility, and in order to retain his expertise in the United Kingdom it was suggested to Rolls-Royce that they recruit him.

Ellor joined Rolls-Royce in late 1927, bringing an understanding of aerodynamics to the company for the first time. Apart from his work in supercharging the Kestrel and Buzzard engines, he did outstanding work on the 'R' engine for the Schneider Trophy, and this was to the subsequent benefit of the Peregrine, the Vulture and, in particular, the Merlin. Ellor rose to be chief experimental engineer and was posted, together with Colonel Barrington and J.M. Reid, to Packard in 1940. There his contribution to the production of the Merlin was recognised as beyond measure. Ellor returned to Derby in 1944 in his previous role. He died in 1951.

J. LEE EVANS (JLe)

Joined Rolls-Royce in 1909 as an assistant car tester. In 1912, he was posted to Barkers, the coachbuilders, as the resident Rolls-Royce tester. After testing armoured cars in the early part of the Great War, he transferred to aero work, visiting aircraft firms and aerodromes on engine installation and testing problems. He also went to France, visiting squadrons equipped with the Eagle-powered FE 2d fighter. In 1920, he returned to London in the Final Test Department. For a period in the Second World War, he liaised between Hythe Road in London and Derby on Merlin repairs and salvage. Became manager of the Lillie Hall Test Department in Fulham (Rolls's original workshops in 1902) when it re-opened after the war, responsible for the final test of all custom-built cars. He retired in the early months of 1953.

H. IVAN F. EVERNDEN (Ev)

Having been called up while finishing an engineering degree at King's College, London in 1916, Evernden failed his medical and was directed to Rolls-Royce as a draughtsman. His initial work was on tooling to produce the Madsen Automatic Rifle for which Rolls-Royce had taken a licence, but this was followed by designing under B.I. Day in the Airship Drawing Office. Early in 1921, he was posted to West Wittering to work with Henry Royce. There he became the specialist in styling, coachwork concepts, exhaust systems, body mountings and liaison with the coachbuilders. He was one of Royce's favourites and, in later years, remarked that he was one of the few who not only admired but also liked Royce. His 1930s concepts included Continental coachwork and the scheme that led to the Bentley Flying Spur in post-war years. Evernden succeeded Day as chief designer of the Chassis Division team during the Second World War, and was awarded the MBE for his design work on the installation and cooling of the Meteor engine in the Cromwell tank. Evernden stayed with the cars after the war as chief project engineer, and retired from Crewe in 1961. It was said that his mannerisms were such that to meet him was to meet Henry Royce himself.

DONALD EYRE (DE)

Joined the staff of R.W.H. Bailey as a draughtsman in 1920. He was posted to West Wittering in 1928 as an engine draughtsman, and also worked at Le Canadel. Eyre was small in stature and cheeky by nature, and Royce had a soft spot for him – an exchange of witticisms between the two was not unknown. Eyre was also an accomplished sketcher and watercolourist. He was encouraged in this and was even asked by Royce to help him develop his own painting abilities. Eyre returned to Derby before Royce died, and in the late 1930s was appointed designer to Dr. Griffith. At Duffield Bank House and in post-war years at The Old Hall, Littleover, Eyre turned Griffith's concepts into drawings which communicated with great clarity.

Lt. Col. L.F.R. FELL (F)

Fell, like Royce and Bentley, served his apprenticeship with the Great Northern Railway. When war broke out in 1914, he joined the Royal Flying Corps and, in 1915, was posted to the Engine Repair Station at Pont de l'Arche in France, which ultimately he commanded. In 1919, he returned to London and became the first Assistant Director of Technical Development for Engines at the newly formed Air Ministry. While there, *inter alia*, he suggested to Rolls-Royce that they re-design the Condor (the first task given to Rowledge on joining the company in 1921). In 1927, Fell joined the staff of Rolls-Royce in their Conduit Street offices in London, and wrote a report on the state of the aero engine industry. It never got through to Henry Royce, a fact that emerged subsequently in conversation. Its interception was attributed to Basil Johnson, who shortly thereafter retired on grounds of ill health. In 1934, Fell left to become chief engineer of Armstrong Siddeley, remaining there until he was succeeded by S.S. Tressilian upon rejoining Rolls-Royce in 1938. Fell became chief of powerplant design (based after the outbreak of war in Belper; in 1944 the team was moved to Hucknall), and afterwards worked in aero sales and headed Public Relations. An enthusiast for rail traction, his last working years were spent running Fell Developments, a concern that adapted the Rolls-Royce 'C' range oil engines to automatic transmission for self-propelled local passenger service rolling stock.

EDWARD GOULDING (LORD WARGRAVE)

Goulding joined the board as a nominee of Sir Max Aitken, later to become Lord Beaverbrook, when Aitken acquired a substantial number of shares in Rolls-Royce from the estate of Charles Rolls in 1911. Even after Aitken lost interest in trying to manipulate Rolls-Royce in 1913, Goulding remained, becoming Chairman in 1921. He was succeeded in 1936 by Lord Herbert Scott.

DR. ALAN ARNOLD GRIFFITH (Gr)

Griffith took a first in mechanical engineering at Liverpool University in 1914, following that with a Master's Degree in 1917 and a Doctorate there in 1921. In 1915 he was accepted by the Royal Aircraft Factory as a trainee, before joining the Physics and Instrument Department in the following year, where he held a number of posts before being appointed senior scientific officer in 1920. It was during this period, in 1917, that Griffith co-authored a paper with G.I. Taylor which earned him the nickname 'Bubble Griffith'. It was a fundamental contribution to the understanding of torsional stress.

Griffith remained a senior scientific officer at RAE until 1928, and it was in 1926 that he wrote his classic paper, 'An Aerodynamic Theory of Turbine Design'. In it, he foresaw the advantages in employing an axial gas turbine engine rather than a piston engine to drive a propeller; he also foresaw the way in which to develop efficient multi-stage axial gas turbine engines. As a result of the paper, the Aeronautical Research Committee supported small-scale experimentation with a single-stage axial compressor and single-stage axial turbine. Work was completed in 1928, and it confirmed the correctness of Griffith's theory, the high efficiencies obtained showing him to be the true originator of the multi-stage axial engine.

Following this, Griffith became principal scientific officer in charge of the Air Ministry Laboratory in South Kensington. There, in 1928 and 1929, he evolved the contraflow principle for gas turbine design. In 1931 he returned to the Royal Aircraft Establishment to take charge of engine research, but it was not until 1938, when he became head of the Engine Department, that the decision was made to build an experimental contraflow compressor. It was built by Armstrong Siddeley in 1939.

Early in 1939, Griffith was invited by E.W. Hives to join Rolls-Royce as a research engineer, with the mandate to 'go on thinking'. A full account of his achievements in the gas turbine era does not belong in this volume, but the Avon engine can be attributed to him, as can Britain's leadership in the field of jet-borne vertical/short take-off and landing, exemplified by the Harrier and its Rolls-Royce Pegasus engine. It all resulted from a Griffith memo headed 'Thistledown Landing'.

Strangely, Griffith did not propose the turbojet engine. Pilot Officer Frank Whittle did that, and in 1929 he found opportunity to explain his proposals to the Air Ministry. W.L. Tweedie of the Directorate of Engine Development explained the official negative view of gas turbines, yet took him to see Griffith at South Kensington. Griffith was anything but supportive, describing Whittle's assumptions as over-optimistic and finding fault with his calculations. Some have accused Griffith of lack of intellectual honesty, others of 'not invented here' reactions. It may be true that Griffith's response delayed the development of the gas turbine, but his reason was almost certainly his pursuit of perfectionist solutions. His long-standing colleague at RAE, Hayne Constant, said of him: 'I think that his work on the gas turbine was typical of his approach to engineering. He was never a man for whom half measures or pragmatic solutions based on empiricism had any attraction.'

Griffith retired in June 1960, continuing his work as a consultant to Rolls-Royce until his death in late 1962.

TOMMY S. HALDENBY (Hy)

Haldenby joined Royce Ltd. at Cooke Street on 27 September 1900 as an apprentice. His wages were 5s (25p) for a 54-hour working week, with an annual increment of 2s (10p). These hours were the minimum; he often worked from normal start time on Friday morning non-stop until lunchtime on Saturday. As an apprentice still in 1903, Tommy Haldenby shared much of the testing of Royce's first petrol engine with Eric

Platford. In 1907, Haldenby was made manager of Lillie Hall, C.S. Rolls & Co.'s London repair depot, when it was absorbed by Rolls-Royce. He remained there until 1913, when he jointly established the Experimental Department with E.W. Hives. Then, shortly after A. Wormald became general manager, Haldenby became assistant general manager, later rising to general manager. In this role, he headed Plant and Equipment, and spearheaded the massive task of factory expansion in the Second World War, notably at Crewe and Hillington. His last task was the establishment of the Rolls-Royce Canada premises near Montreal in the early 1950s, by which time he was a consultant to Lord Hives on plant and buildings. He retired in November 1952.

CAPTAIN W. ('Billy') HALLAM (Hm)

Manager of the Repair Department in Derby, he was undisputed ruler of his domain. Captain Hallam had only one arm, as a result of injury in the First World War.

P.V.C. ('Vic') HALLIWELL

Following the Schneider Trophy victory of 1929, Sir Henry Segrave decided that two 'R' engines might do better than a single Napier Lion in his attempts to raise the world water speed record. The Air Ministry released two engines, and Lord Wakefield of Castrol fame commissioned a new boat, *Miss England II*. In June 1930, the boat was taken to Windermere. Segrave chose Michael Willcocks as his riding mechanic, and Rolls-Royce sent Vic Halliwell and Stan Orme. Halliwell was in charge of all the Experimental test beds in Derby, and rode in *Miss England* to monitor engine cooling and other parameters. On Friday 13 June 1930, Segrave established a new world record in his first two runs, but in attempting a third run, the boat came to grief. Willcocks escaped with light injuries. Segrave died soon after being rescued and taken ashore, but Halliwell was not found for two days. It is said that when retrieved from the water he was still grasping his notes. A well-liked and capable man, he was greatly missed in Derby. Lord Wakefield erected his gravestone at Portishead, and Castrol did not forget – fifty years later, Halliwell's grave was refurbished by them in tribute to his memory.

FRED HARDY

Brother of Bill Hardy, Fred was also on the car side. He headed the development team of the Chassis Division through the Second World War at Clan Foundry in Belper. W.A. Robotham said of him that he looked the personification of a technician, with his prominent forehead, receding hair and horn-rimmed spectacles. His un-expectedly deep bass laugh revealed an otherwise well-concealed sense of humour. His right-hand man was one of the Bastow brothers, Geoff, persuaded by Robotham to leave Vauxhall and join Rolls-Royce. The latter said he had never met two more competent engineers in the automotive field – and praise from Robotham did not come easily!

Fred Hardy mainly concentrated on the cooling system and transmission of the Cromwell tank, while Geoff Bastow specialised on its suspension. It was recalled that, despite his academic appearance, Hardy drove 30-ton tanks over the Derbyshire moors at frightening speeds. He also incurred the displeasure of the county surveyor, as his driving caused the tank tracks to pluck the cats-eyes from the centre of the Milford Road and toss them over the wall into the River Derwent.

W.G. ('Bill') HARDY (Hdy)

Hardy first worked for the Clement Talbot motor car company in London before joining the Royal Naval Air Service in the First World War. There he served in what became the Aeronautical Inspection Directorate, latterly being posted with Rolls-Royce in Derby. On demobilisation, he returned to Talbot but was taken on by Rolls-Royce in 1919 as a designer on chassis work under B.I. Day in Derby. He moved to West Wittering when the Camacha studio became available in 1921. He specialised in brakes, gears, gearboxes and propshaft designs, continuing this work in Derby after Royce's death. On the outbreak of the Second World War he transferred to the aero side, working for about a year on the Vulture reduction gear. He then joined the main aero engine design office, taking over the Crankcase and Stress Sections in Belper. In 1943, he was appointed assistant chief designer of Aero Engine Development. After the war, he became chief designer of the Motor Car Division at Crewe, commuting daily from his home just north of Derby. His last major achievement was the design, largely created under him by Jack Phillips, of the V8 motor car engine which was to remain in production until the turn of the millennium. He retired in 1956 and moved back to West Wittering, where he had worked with Henry Royce so many years earlier.

RONNIE W. HARKER (Hkr)

Ronnie Harker joined Rolls-Royce as a premium apprentice in 1925, at about the same time as his brother Edmund, but had to leave at the end of his training because of the general recession. With his father's encouragement he joined flying clubs, and was gaining pilot skills when recalled to Rolls-Royce on aero engine development. In time, this led to liaison with airframe manufacturers, whose aircraft he would fly to assess engine performance.

Rolls-Royce began its own flight testing early in the 1930s at Tollerton airfield near Nottingham, engaging the services of Captain Shepherd, the local flying club instructor. As the operation began to grow, Harker became a company test pilot – the first, in fact, as Captain Shepherd had not yet been recruited as chief test pilot. Harker first flew in his new role in November 1934, piloting a Gloster Gnatsnapper. He also joined 504 Special Reserve Squadron at nearby Hucknall to augment his income.

Early in 1935 Rolls-Royce set up its own flight test establishment at Hucknall, and from then until 1939 Harker's test flying was shared with Captain Shepherd and Harvey Heyworth. The outbreak of war saw Harker posted to his squadron as a Flight Lieutenant on Hurricanes, but he was recalled to test-flying duties just before the Battle of Britain in 1940. Harker became one of a number of pilots who not only flew on test, but also liaised closely with the many Rolls-Royce-powered operational squadrons. It was during this period that Wing Commander Campbell-Orde, in command of the Air Fighting Development Unit at Duxford, invited Harker to fly the newly arrived North American P-51 Mustang. On 30 April 1942 he did so, and was so impressed that he urged E.W. Hives to re-engine the Mustang with the two-stage, two-speed 60 series Merlin. His proposal was taken up, and as a result the Mustang became a legend on both sides of the Atlantic, and indeed much further afield.

In 1947 Harker ended his test-flying days and became aero export manager, based at the Conduit Street office in London. He also took on Bill Lappin's military and industrial liaison roles when the latter retired. Finally, he became military aviation adviser in 1957, a role he performed until his retirement in 1971. He then formed his own aviation consultancy company to continue his interest in aviation, before finally retiring to New Zealand, where he died shortly after enjoying his ninetieth birthday in 1999. He had last put a Mustang through its paces at the age of eighty-eight.

ALEC H. HARVEY-BAILEY (AHB)

Alec was the son of R.W.H. Bailey, and joined Rolls-Royce shortly before the Second World War. After a period on the most advanced models of the Rationalised Range of cars, he headed defect investigation on the Merlin and Griffon through the war years. Subsequently he set up Rolls-Royce Australia Pty., before running Aero Service in Derby. From there he moved to become chief quality engineer on aero engines and then production director in the Aero Engine Division. Latterly, he served in Miami and New York to support the RB211 when launched in America. He then moved to Beirut when the engine entered service in the area. His final major post was as Managing Director of the Arab British Engine Company in Cairo, before returning for a brief period to Derby as an assistant director, personnel. After retiring, he wrote many books on the history of Rolls-Royce.

Dr. (Later Sir) STANLEY G. HOOKER (SGH)

A gifted mathematician from his schooldays, Hooker took an Honours Degree in the subject at Imperial College, London. While there, he became interested in aerodynamics, which he studied further at Oxford, gaining his Doctorate in 1935. His first employment outside the academic world was with Woolwich Arsenal, on anti-aircraft rockets. By then, his abilities had already been recognised by one of E.W. Hives's most gifted young engineers, Dr. Fred Llewellyn Smith, and this led to an interview with Hives. It was on this occasion that Hives remarked that Hooker was 'not much of an engineer'. Hooker was offered employment, and joined Rolls-Royce in January 1938.

Towards the end of 1937, Rolls-Royce had begun a systematic programme of supercharger development in order to carry Ellor's work forward in terms of efficiency levels. Much of this became Hooker's responsibility. Rapid improvements were achieved on the Merlin, first with the central entry supercharger and subsequently with the two-stage intercooled unit. By 1944 the Merlin's power had doubled, and so too had the altitude at which the engine could still give 1,000 hp. Hooker also contributed significantly to the mathematical understanding and prediction of aircraft and engine performance at altitude.

Rolls-Royce first took an active interest in jet propulsion in 1938, when a gas turbine design office was formed. Although work centred on Dr. Griffith and his concepts for axial engines, Hooker kept a close eye on the progress of Frank Whittle, who had chosen the centrifugal compressor. By 1940 Rolls-Royce was making parts to help Whittle, and that was followed by a Whittle-type demonstrator designed and built in Derby. At the end of 1942, recognising the progress being made on Whittle's engine by the Rover company – and the impasse that had developed between Rover and Whittle – Hives swapped the Rolls-Royce Meteor tank engine (an unsupercharged Merlin) for Rover's factories at Barnoldswick and Clitheroe. Hooker was posted there at the beginning of 1943, and in April he became chief engineer. Parallel postings strengthened the machining and assembly capability. Under Hooker's leadership, the Whittle W.2B became the first jet engine to enter service with the Allies, as the Welland in the Meteors of 616 Squadron in 1944. The Derwent and Nene followed, along with the Clyde, and by the end of the war Hooker and his team had given Rolls-Royce the world lead in gas turbine aero engines.

In 1948 Hooker became impatient in his ambitions, in addition to which Hives suspected that lack of progress on the Avon axial jet might be due to Hooker's known enthusiasm for the centrifugal. Hooker left the company and joined the rival aero engine manufacturer, Bristol. There he led the Proteus propjet through difficult development problems. He also contributed greatly to the growth of the Olympus engine, both for the Vulcan and TSR2 military aircraft, and for Concorde as the Olympus 593. His greatest concept, however, was the Pegasus vectored thrust engine which powers Harriers to this day. In 1966 Rolls-Royce acquired Bristol Siddeley, and – in consequence – Hooker. He retired four years later, disappointed never to have become technical director of Rolls-Royce. Shortly afterwards, he was recalled to lead a team of fellow-retirees in seeing the RB211 through the most critical period in its development history. He did so as technical director, and it was the crowning achievement of his life's work, for which he received a knighthood in 1974. He lived to see the RB211 become a great success, and just witnessed the launch of his autobiography before his death in 1984. Hooker was a big man in every respect, possessed of an enormous intellect and yet with a boyish personality. Throughout his life, he inspired all who knew or worked for him. Despite the 'falling out', Hooker never lost his respect and affection for Hives, and that feeling was mutual.

CHARLES L. JENNER (Jnr)

Recruited in 1911 from Phoenix Motors Ltd., Jenner was one of the small group of the best designers in the country attracted into Rolls-Royce. He joined Royce's personal design team at West Wittering in 1918, and was the leading engine designer. Earlier, he had worked under R.W.H. Bailey at the Pilgrims Way Motor Company, and it was Bailey who both recruited him into Rolls-Royce and ensured his posting to

Royce's personal staff. Jenner did much of the work on the 20 hp engine and its derivatives (including the Bentley applications), and on the Phantom engines. When the Chassis Division was formed in 1937, he worked under B.I. Day and led the design of the 'B' range of rationalised petrol engines which, post-war, powered both Rolls-Royce and Bentley cars, as well as the wheeled fighting vehicles of the British Army. His major achievement in the Second World War, by then working under H.I.F. Evernden, was the evolution of the Meteor tank engine from the Merlin. Post-war, he returned to motor car engine and diesel engine design, finally being appointed car engine project designer in 1951.

BASIL JOHNSON (BJ)

Brother of Claude Johnson, Basil was recruited to absorb some of the former's workload, and when Claude died in 1926, Basil succeeded him as Managing Director. Basil lacked his older brother's courage and imagination, and on more than one occasion he attempted to protect the reputation of the motor cars by avoidance of risks on the aero engine side. In 1929, he took early retirement on health grounds, allegedly at the invitation of Henry Royce.

WILLOUGHBY ('Bill') LAPPIN (Lp)

Described on his retirement as 'the salesman who never sold an engine', Lappin was a great ambassador for Rolls-Royce. He was born in Northern Ireland and served in the First World War in armoured cars with the Royal Naval Air Service in the German colonies in Africa and Egypt, before joining Rolls-Royce at the Conduit Street office in London in 1917. Not unusually for the company, he had no grandiose title – indeed, at its most imposing it was 'personal assistant' to E.W. Hives – yet few have enjoyed the freedom to communicate with other organisations that was his. His daily dealings were with the leaders of the aviation industry, the pilots and the inner sanctum of the Air Ministry. Lappin had great faith in Rolls-Royce and its products, and worked tirelessly to ensure that customers received the product and service they expected. During the Second World War he was very close to Air Staff, and enjoyed a special relationship with its Assistant Chief, Sir Wilfrid Freeman.

Lappin was possibly the best salesman Rolls-Royce ever had. He worked until he was seventy, retiring in 1958 when he was succeeded by Ronnie Harker. An Air Marshal once said of him, 'he worked for the RAF and was paid by Rolls-Royce'. Lappin lived to the age of eighty-six, dying in 1974.

A.J. ('Arthur') LIDSEY (Lid)

Lidsey joined Rolls-Royce in 1920. Together with W.A. Robotham and A.C. Lovesey, he made up the team of development technical assistants reporting to E.W. Hives, manager of the Experimental Department in the 1920s. He tested many cars from the prototype 20 hp onwards, and on occasions shared the wheel with Hives himself. A well-known picture shows Lidsey at the wheel of the experimental sports Phantom I, 16 EX, at the top of No. 1 yard at Nightingale Road. The car had been parked there to try to interest HRH The Prince of Wales in purchasing it, to add to his fleet of three 20 hp Rolls-Royces. This event took place in February 1928.

Before Sir Henry Royce died, and sensing that the end was not far distant, A.G. Elliott left West Wittering to establish a power base in Derby in the early 1930s. He took Lidsey on as his personal assistant, and as his control of engineering activity deepened, Lidsey provided the necessary administration. Initially, this covered both car and aero design work, but the formation of separate Divisions in 1937 saw Elliott appointed chief engineer on the aero side. Dr. S.G. Hooker records in his book, *Not much of an Engineer*, that it was Lidsey who shared Elliott's office and who was asked by Elliott to escort Hooker to his office on his first day.

In the post-war era, Lidsey did much to establish and oversee the processes of recruitment, training and placement of qualified engineers in Derby. He also did a great deal of work in creating albums containing details of the company's aero engine projects from the Eagle onwards, including photographs and brief project histories. These prove invaluable to the present day.

For the first half of its existence, Rolls-Royce was a comparatively small and close-knit community. In Lidsey's case, apart from working so closely with Hives and Elliott, marrying A. Wormald's daughter drew him into the fabric of families which were the founding dynasty of the company. And, like so many others, when he retired in the 1950s, at least one member of his family was just beginning as the next generation at Rolls-Royce.

Dr. FREDERICK ('Fred' or 'Doc') LLEWELLYN SMITH (LS)

Born in 1909, 'Doc' Llewellyn Smith took his Master's Degree in Engineering at Manchester University in 1930, and followed this with a D.Phil at Balliol College, Oxford. In 1933 he joined Rolls-Royce as a technical assistant on aero engines in the Experimental Department under E.W. Hives. A year later, he transferred to work on the development of experimental cars in the same department; it was during this period that he wrote to Dr. S.G. Hooker, who had also been doing his doctorate at Oxford, inviting him to consider joining Rolls-Royce. This initiative was followed through by E.W. Hives, with the result that Hooker did so.

On the outbreak of war, Llewellyn Smith was transferred to Crewe and later to Glasgow to work on the technical aspects of expanding Merlin engine production and the logistics of production support. He was a senior member of the team at Hillington when the war came to an end in Europe and the Government ordered its factory manager there, Harold Morris, to run the workforce down from 26,000 to 15,000. Morris promptly left, whereupon Hives announced that Llewellyn Smith would run Hillington until the war was won in the Pacific; thereafter, he would transfer to Crewe and re-establish car production as general manager.

Once the war was over, Llewellyn Smith duly moved to Crewe and established a manufacturing organisation there, as well as marketing and customer services functions. He put the Bentley VI, then the Silver Wraith, Silver Dawn and Phantom

IV into production, these having emerged from the rationalised range under the leadership latterly of W.A. Robotham at Clan Foundry, Belper.

In 1947 Llewellyn Smith was appointed to the board of Rolls-Royce Limited, and when Divisional boards with financial accountability were formally instituted in 1954 for the Motor Car and Aero Engine Divisions, he became Managing Director of the former. The Oil Engine Division was created in 1956 under W.A. Robotham, but when the latter retired prematurely in 1963, Llewellyn Smith became Chairman of the Oil Engine Division as well. In 1967 he relinquished his position as Managing Director of the Motor Car Division, soon being succeeded by G. Fawn rather than his other Assistant Managing Director, R.N. Dorey. He remained, however, as Chairman of the Motor Car Division, as well as of the Oil Engine Division. The objective was a broadening of responsibilities, soon to come in the form of his appointment as group executive of Rolls-Royce and President of Rolls-Royce Holdings Canada Limited.

'Doc' Smith was a shy man who tended to manage from the sanctum of his office. He was, however, extremely competent and straightforward, and a man of great natural courtesy. As we have seen, he ran two of the company's Divisions, while Jim Pearson ran the third and largest, the Aero Engine Division. It was often said that Lord Hives saw these two men as the key contenders to succeed him, and that perhaps was the mark of 'Doc''s stature.

A. CYRIL LOVESEY (Lov)

After serving as an observer/air gunner in the Royal Flying Corps – latterly Royal Air Force – in the First World War, Lovesey took a BSc at Bristol University. He joined the Rolls-Royce Experimental Department under E.W. Hives in 1923, and initially worked on both motor cars and aero engines. When the 'R' engine was developed for the Schneider Trophy, Lovesey was 'the man on the spot' with the High Speed Flight at Calshot in both 1929 and 1931. He also subsequently supported Sir Malcolm Campbell in his land speed record runs with *Bluebird* in America.

Lovesey believed strongly that it was not enough to test aero engines solely on the bench, as the whole installation in the aircraft had to be right as well. His efforts led to the establishment of flight testing, and for a while he was flight development engineer at Hucknall. In the late 1930s, he returned to Derby to work with J.E. Ellor in developing the Merlin. Just before the Battle of Britain, Lovesey was put in charge of Merlin development. His contribution to the engine, in doubling its power while improving reliability and at the same time extending service life, was enormous.

After the war, he undertook the difficult task of making the Merlin serve in civil roles as well as it had in combat. In parallel, Rolls-Royce had launched the AJ65, which became the Avon jet engine, at Barnoldswick. It proved difficult to develop and was moved by E.W. Hives to Derby in 1947. Lovesey was put in charge of development. By 1949, it was flying at the Farnborough air show, where it was said that Lovesey 'had breathed on it'. It entered squadron service in the Canberra in 1951.

In 1957, Lovesey became chief engineer (aircraft engines) and subsequently deputy director of engineering and a member of the Aero Engine Division board. He retired in 1964, but continued to serve as a consultant, particularly on problems with the

RB211 in the early 1970s. He died in 1976. Lovesey was a quiet and modest man. A good listener and a brilliant development engineer, he was never driven by ambition, and did much to help young people get established in their careers. He was greatly liked and held in universal respect.

JOE LOWE

Rolls-Royce in Derby has an enviable record of industrial relations, due in large measure to the understanding of A. Wormald, who was works manager and a director from the time of Royce's major illnesses. All works Trades Unions interface with the management through a works committee and convener, and Joe Lowe was the second of these, succeeding George Oliver when he became an MP. When the failed piston was discovered in the 'R' engine in Waghorn's Supermarine S6 on the night before the 1929 Schneider Trophy contest, a cylinder block and piston change became necessary. This was allowable under the rules, whereas an engine change was not. Lowe was among the employees who had taken holiday to watch the event at Calshot. He was pulled from bed and spent the night acting as crane man for the cylinder block change, still in his pyjamas. On the next day, Britain won the contest. To this day, there have only been seven conveners in Derby, and Lowe's work that night epitomised their commitment to the success of Rolls-Royce.

BOB LYONS

Rolls-Royce provided support for the attempts at the first direct transatlantic flight. As the man in charge of Aero Test and Service, Eric Platford headed the team in Newfoundland, and Bob Lyons was his choice to support Alcock and Brown's Vimy. Red-haired and very much a lone wolf, this Mancunian did not mix with the others.

Fred Green, a cheerful, easy-going Nottingham thirty-year-old, supported the Sopwith Atlantic. Bob Smith, a dry-humoured young Derby man, was instructed to support the Martinsyde Raymor and George Clark, quiet, studious and reserved, was placed with the Handley Page operation. Lyons left the company in 1922, Fred Green died in 1935, Bob Smith retired in the 1950s and George Clark worked as a service engineer late into the 1950s.

R.L. ('Monty') MARMONT (M)

When A.G. Elliott married Royce's secretary, Miss Gray, he incurred Royce's displeasure and was only allowed a Saturday morning off for his honeymoon. Perhaps for this reason, and no doubt influenced by Nurse Aubin, Miss Gray was succeeded by a male secretary. Monty Marmont typed memoranda, ran errands, liaised between the two design offices at West Wittering, and did the many things necessary to support a design group working in such isolation. He also had duties relating to Royce's farm there.

JACK MARSDEN

With Les Buckler and the help of Joe Lowe on crane, Marsden changed the cylinder block and piston on Waghorn's 'R' engine in the S6 on the night before the 1929 Schneider Trophy victory. Led by Coverley, there had been some serious drinking and celebrating going on at the Crown Hotel, Southampton, with the result that few of the Rolls-Royce contingent were sober. Marsden, Buckler and Lowe did not drink, and it was for this reason that they found themselves contributing to history in such a unique manner.

ALEXANDER CHARLES ('Alec') McWILLIAMS (McW)

Born in 1910, Alec McWilliams grew up just around the corner from the Nightingale Road factory in Derby. His father being a neighbour of many of the leading figures in Rolls-Royce, Alec and his brother Eddie were raised in an environment which spoke of little else. Despite this, when Alec left school, he took up the study of art. A year on, however, he decided that his continued studies would be too big a burden for his parents, so he joined Rolls-Royce. E.W. Hives, no less, arranged for Alec McWilliams to be admitted to a craft apprenticeship, despite officially being a year too old. In due course, he became the first trade apprentice to be given day-release to pursue higher qualifications. By the later 1930s, he was responsible for the novel task of machining the newly introduced hypoid gears for motor car back axles.

When war came, W.A. Robotham's Chassis Division developed the Meteor tank engine version of the Merlin, and the task of putting this into production was given to McWilliams. This he did with a young and competent team working from a disused mill in Belper, yet on the charge of the Government Imprest Account operated through the Scottish factories. It was this exercise that triggered the famed telegram from Lord Beaverbrook giving E.W. Hives open credit of £1 million (£50 million in today's terms) as a 'certificate of character . . . without precedent or equal'.

In early 1943, Hives made the equally famous swap with the Wilks brothers of Rover, whereby Rolls-Royce acquired the 'jet job' at Barnoldswick and Clitheroe in exchange for production of the Meteor engine. While Rolls-Royce engineers – notably Stan Hooker – moved north immediately, Rover took some time to get a hand on their new task. In the meantime, McWilliams and his team continued to manage the process.

By 1944, the first jet engine order for the Welland had been completed at Barnoldswick, and the task of manufacturing the Derwent I lay ahead. Hives had taken the view from the outset that Barnoldswick was the right size for development work, but not for production. Somewhere else was needed, and away from Merlin and Griffon production. Newcastle-under-Lyme provided the location, and McWilliams and his team the management.

Many more senior tasks followed (and not just in Derby) on aero engine production, before McWilliams became a director of the Aero Engine Division in the late 1960s. Then he ran the whole of component manufacturing as 'Alec in', with Alec Harvey-Bailey, a director of Engine Build and Test, as 'Alec out'. The events after

February 1971 were kind to neither – particularly McWilliams, whose career ended then – or so it seemed at the time. But he came back and set up the Rolls-Royce manufacturing facility in Miami some years later.

All who had the privilege of knowing McWilliams held him in the highest regard. He died shortly before Christmas 1996. Early in that year, he had returned to his early love of painting, producing a work in oils depicting a Cromwell tank with Winston Churchill shortly before D-Day. Its engine – unseen – had been put into production more than half a century earlier by this courteous and capable artist-turned-engineer.

EDDIE McWILLIAMS (EMc)

Brother of Alec, Eddie McWilliams was also capable, and rose to manufacturing management status in the 1950s. He was in charge of production control in Derby, responsible for factory loading, progress and parts delivery performance.

WILLIAM J. ('Bill') MILLER (MR)

Miller took his degree in engineering at Edinburgh immediately after the First World War, then joined Daimler as a post-graduate apprentice. He soon became superintendent of car test, and then chief inspector when Daimler, Lanchester and BSA combined. When the Managing Director retired, the successor from BSA displaced the top team and Miller found himself out of work. He rejoined as works manager when the latter was appointed to a similar position at Humber/Hillman. He was to be part of the Air Ministry's 'shadow factory' scheme, and to that end was appointed chief inspector of car and aero factories. In 1936 he joined de Havilland at the invitation of another of the old Daimler team, Lawrence Pomeroy – again as chief inspector. While there, a neighbour told him of the intended shadow factory at Hillington, Glasgow, which was to make the Merlin. He wrote to E.W. Hives in Derby.

Hives appointed Miller chief quality engineer of Hillington, a task he performed with distinction. At the end of the war, however, instructions were issued to encourage all employees to try to get their pre-war employers to take them back. Between VE Day and VJ Day, the workforce was reduced from 26,000 to 15,000. As a result, the Government-appointed manager, Harold Morris, left. He was replaced by Dr. F. Llewellyn Smith, pending the latter's move to Crewe to re-establish motor car production. Miller was to be his deputy at Hillington. In due course, Llewellyn Smith moved to Crewe and John Reid succeeded him on his return from working with Packard in America. Reid did not see any chance of Hillington surviving, and asked Hives for a move. Late in 1945 he became general manager of Rotol, in succession to Bill Stammers.

When Reid left, Miller succeeded him as general manager – with orders to dismiss the remaining 15,000 employees and close the plant. It was a Government directive that all shadow factories were to be shut, unless the companies who had operated them had a post-war requirement to take them over. Miller fought long and hard against the closure, making the case to the Ministry that the sale of Merlin-powered aircraft to air forces around the world after the war would generate spares and overhaul business. Orders were duly placed on Rolls-Royce, and as a result 4,200 jobs were saved, and six factory blocks retained at Hillington. In April 1947 the shadow factory passed to Rolls-Royce management, with Miller as its general manager.

From that point on, Miller handled expansion in Scotland to meet the requirement for Avon engines at the time of the Korean War. He acquired Blantyre, Larkhall and Cardonald, but even that did not suffice. In 1951 the new factory at East Kilbride was begun, and it opened in November 1953. Miller retired in 1964 with the distinction not only of having saved the Rolls-Royce presence in Scotland, but also of having led its growth and success.

J.A. MOON

Moon and Cockshutt were responsible for the jig and tool design functions in the early Derby years and, at times, were castigated by Royce. Questioned in one of Royce's memos in 'The Bible' (the book containing Royce's memoranda on the Eagle aero engine), Moon was able to demonstrate that the inference of error had been proved wrong, and that Royce had agreed this. In consequence, pp. 199–200 were cut from all copies of 'The Bible'.

PERCY NORTHEY (Pn)

Joined C.S. Rolls & Co. as a demonstration driver in 1905, and drove a four-cylinder 20 hp into second place in the first-ever Isle of Man Tourist Trophy (TT) race in that year. Accepted in society circles, and sometimes known as 'Percy-vere' Northey.

MAURICE OLLEY (Oy)

Joined Rolls-Royce initially as a jig and tool designer in 1912. When the First World War came, Henry Royce designed his first aero engine – the Eagle – and in this task he was supported by two men: Maurice Olley and Albert Elliott. In line with his contract, Olley went to America during the war to study sheet metal pressing. He joined Claude Johnson there in all the work to get the Eagle manufactured in the States, and was at one stage seconded to help America design their Liberty engine. After the war, Olley served with distinction as chief engineer of Rolls-Royce of America Inc. in Springfield. When Rolls-Royce car production stopped in the Depression in 1930, no posts were available in Derby, so Olley joined the Chevrolet Division of General Motors. There he was responsible for the introduction of the now universal independent front suspension in 1934. In 1937, Hives invited him to return as chief engineer of the Chassis Division, but he felt unable to leave GM until he had sorted out Vauxhall cars. When war came, he was granted leave by GM to help get Merlin engine production under way in the States. Among the greatest, most inspiring and humorous engineers of the 20th century, he was GM's gain and Rolls-Royce's loss. His last project before retirement in 1957 from the Paramount

Engineering Company, attached to the Chevrolet Division of GM, was the Corvette sports car.

J. STAN ORME (JSO)

Orme joined Rolls-Royce in the days of the Eagle engine, on which he was a fitter. He was one of the team that tested the 'R' engine in Derby and worked on them at Calshot in 1929.

In 1930, he was sent to Windermere with Vic Halliwell to support Sir Henry Segrave in his attempt at the world water speed record. Segrave established a new record in two runs on 13 June, but on the third run *Miss England II* crashed. Segrave and Halliwell were killed. Orme had worked hard on the boat's 'R' engines and, the loss of his boss apart, was tired. E.W. Hives rang him and asked him to visit Halliwell's parents at Portishead in Somerset to offer the company's sympathies in person. Any second thoughts Orme might have entertained disappeared when Hives said he wanted Orme to do so not just for Rolls-Royce, but to 'do it for me'. Orme did – and in those days the drive from Bowness to Portishead was not an easy one. In his later working years he was manager of Rolls-Royce Sinfin A site in Derby, and had as his deputy Charlie Conway. They retired in the early 1960s.

HARRY PEARSON (Prsn)

Pearson took a first in physics at Oxford in 1935, after which he worked for British Celanese and Standard Telephones and Cables before joining Rolls-Royce at Hucknall in 1940. There he did sterling work on piston aero engine exhaust systems, both in the suppression of visible flames for night operations and in developing ejector exhaust stubs. These turned exhaust gases from the cylinders into thrust, augmenting that from the propeller. Exhaust thrust became significant at higher altitudes.

When Dr. Hooker moved to Barnoldswick to head the work that Rover had been doing on the Whittle engine early in 1943, Pearson followed him, along with a number of the company's best young engineers. There he worked on the performance of the Welland, Derwent and Nene, and then on the Clyde and Avon. In 1946 he returned to Derby, some two years ahead of the main move of Barnoldswick activity to Derby. The post he was given was that of chief performance engineer. Three years later he became chief research engineer. In due course the roles were combined, and in 1960 Pearson was appointed a director of the Aero Engine Division. He was the focal point within Rolls-Royce in the complex calculation of optimum bypass ratio for fan jets, which, as it happens, the company got wrong.

In 1964, a step change took place in his career when he was appointed director of personnel and administration for the Aero Engine Division. Then, following the merger with Bristol Siddeley in 1967, he became company adviser, engineering methods, with the huge task of rationalising the different engineering systems of Derby and Bristol. Here, not only differences in method and organisation needed addressing, but also problems of a cultural nature.

Following the events of February 1971 and the return of Dr. Hooker as technical director, Pearson was appointed assistant technical director. With the efforts of other 'seniors' such as A.A. Rubbra and A.C. Lovesey, the RB211 development programme was rescued, and by the following year the TriStar entered airline service. Pearson retired in 1976.

J.D. ('Jim', later Sir Denning) PEARSON (Psn)

Pearson was a Whitworth Scholar when he joined the Derby Design Office in 1932, shortly before Royce's death. One of Royce's design team, Don Eyre, was working in Derby at the time, and told his wife that a young man had just taken the drawing board next to his. 'He will go right to the top', he told her. Eyre was proved right. Strangely, Pearson first came to the fore in the late 1930s as the proponent of the ramp cylinder head. Whatever its thermodynamic advantages, it failed because of its propensity to crack due to asymmetric expansion. When Hillington opened, he was posted there to run the Technical Department, in due course becoming chief technical production engineer. As such, he became closely associated with the Packard Merlin which TransCanada Airlines were using in the Lancastrian on the transatlantic route. This contact continued when TCA and the RCAF ordered the Canadair-built DC4 powered by the Merlin, with the result that Pearson was posted to Canada where he set up the Rolls-Royce Technical Office in Montreal. He was convinced that the company should major in commercial aero engines, and he persuaded Hives that this should be the strategic intent.

Pearson returned to Derby as general manager, Sales and Service, on the aero side and was given a seat on the board in 1949. In 1954 he became Managing Director of the newly-formed Aero Engine Division, and in 1957, on the retirement of Lord Hives, Chief Executive and Deputy Chairman of Rolls-Royce, as well as Managing Director of the Aero Division.

In the early 1960s he succeeded Lord Kindersley as Chairman and continued as Chief Executive, but he appointed David Huddie Managing Director of the Aero Division. Just as Pearson had possessed the courage to launch the Spey as a private venture engine in the recession of 1960, he and Huddie knew that the launch of the RB211 would prove fundamental to the long-term future of Rolls-Royce. The cost of the exercise brought their careers to a premature end in 1970, and saw the company placed in receivership in the following year. The correctness of Pearson's long-term vision was ultimately proved by the success of the RB211 and Trent families of engine.

G. ERIC PLATFORD (Ep)

Together with Tommy Haldenby, also an apprentice at the time, Eric Platford did much of the testing of the first Royce two-cylinder 10 hp prototype engine in 1903. He shared in the driving of the Silver Ghost on the 15,000 mile run, drove Silver Rogue in the 1908 Scottish Trial, and came third in the 1913 Spanish Grand Prix.

As chief tester he covered motor cars and aero engines, and was in charge of the engine preparation in Newfoundland for the direct transatlantic flight contestants in 1919. Liked by everyone, his early death in 1938 caused great sadness in Derby. Ernest Hives vowed that no one would ever bear the title 'chief tester' again.

S.F. ('Sammy') POTTINGER (SFP)

Joined Rolls-Royce as a designer in 1914 and worked at West Wittering under Elliott for a time from 1918 onwards. Returned to Derby as senior designer under A.J. Rowledge in the Engine Design Office. Pottinger drew the first design scheme for an engine to bear the name 'Merlin' – a project which called for an inverted V12. Earlier in the same year, 1932, Pottinger had designed the PV G – the first aero engine to have integral crankcase and cylinder blocks. Of Kestrel size, it was later scaled up in R.W.H. Bailey's department to become the PV12, direct forerunner of the Merlin.

JOHN M. REID (JRd)

At the time of writing, the early career of Reid remains a mystery. He first came to prominence when Packard set out to build the Merlin in 1940. Rolls-Royce had been in discussion with Packard over a possible Merlin licence in the late 1930s, but action was precipitated in 1940 when Lord Beaverbrook was appointed Minister for Aircraft Production. He granted a licence for the Merlin engine on behalf of the British Government to the US Government. Rolls-Royce was not consulted, but there was a war to be won, and the company immediately gave every support to the exercise. Colonel Barrington for design, J.E. Ellor for development and J.M. Reid for production were seconded to the Ministry of Aircraft Production, to act as resident engineers at the Packard plant. Packard, in turn, seconded Ralph B. Hayne to Derby as their liaison man.

The Rolls-Royce team gave their all to the task. However, as Packard got the Merlin into full-scale production, it became possible for Hives to think of fresh challenges for Reid. There remains on file a note from Hives inviting Reid to return as general manager of a fresh but unnamed undertaking in the north of England. Its timing suggests Barnoldswick and Clitheroe, which were indeed named 'the Northern Factories', but for reasons unknown Reid did not return until 1945, and then it was to the Hillington shadow factory.

Between VE and VJ Day, Hillington was run down from 26,000 employees to 15,000. The Government manager of the plant who had been there throughout the war, Harold Morris, left. Hives sent the message that Llewellyn Smith would be in charge, with W.J. Miller as his deputy, until the former moved to the Crewe factory to establish post-war motor car production. It was when Llewellyn Smith departed for Crewe that John Reid succeeded him. However, Reid judged the chances of Hillington's survival as slim, since all shadow factories were being shut down by the Government, except in the instances where companies which had managed them saw an ongoing need for them. Hives accepted Reid's request for transfer, and put his

317

deputy Miller in charge, with orders to close the plant. Reid transferred to Rotol, where he succeeded W. Stammers as general manager, a title that regained its full meaning on the departure of R.H. Coverley. Reid retired in 1951.

W. ARTHUR ROBOTHAM (Rm)

Son of a Derbyshire 'county class' family, Robotham joined Rolls-Royce (following service as an officer in the Royal Artillery) as a premium apprentice in 1919, and in 1923 became technical assistant to Ernest Hives in the Experimental Department, where he specialised in car development. Along with Hives and Bailey, he was responsible for the launch of the Derby Bentley, and contributed to the success of Eddie Hall in the Ulster TT (Tourist Trophy) races of 1934–36. When Hives established the Chassis Division in 1937, he made Robotham chief assistant to R.W.H. Bailey. When war came, Robotham succeeded Bailey and developed the Meteor tank engine variant of the Merlin. The power of this engine caused failures in the Cromwell tank, which led to Robotham's team being given technical responsibility for the tank as well as the engine. As war progressed, he was seconded to the Ministry of Supply under Lord Beaverbrook as chief engineer of tank design. Post-war, he secured the standardisation of the Rolls-Royce 'B' range of petrol engines to power the British Army's wheeled fighting vehicles, and launched the 'C' range of diesel engines. The Oil Engine Division was created to market and manufacture these, with Robotham as Managing Director. He was also appointed to the main board.

Robotham was not an easy man to work for. It was said that you either loved him or hated him, but that with him you always knew where you were going – even if you knew it was the wrong direction. He retired, after forty-four years' service, in 1963 to pursue other engineering interests, in part because he did not think Rolls-Royce was large enough to compete with American manufacturers in commercial gas turbine aero engines. The launch of the Spey caused the dissension – and the Spey ultimately proved him wrong. Sometimes known by his workforce as 'Rumpty'.

GEOFFREY ROWE

Rowe was Sir Max Aitken's other nominee to the board of Rolls-Royce during the latter's period as a major shareholder. As with Goulding, Rowe remained a director after Aitken disposed of his holdings in 1913.

ARTHUR J. ROWLEDGE (Rg)

Following the First World War, a chief designer was sought for Henry Royce, to be based in Derby. Roy Fedden declined, Mark Birkigt was delighted to be invited but also declined when he found that the offer greatly strengthened his arm at Hispano Suiza. Rowledge accepted. A native of Peterborough, like Henry Royce, he was Napier's most gifted designer and had created the Lion aero engine. At the time (1921), he was being unfairly blamed for the failure of the post-war Napier car. Rowledge designed the Condor III, Kestrel and 'R' engine, as well as motor car components;

he also designed the air-cooled sleeve-valve Exe engine of the mid 1930s. When E.W. Hives created the Aero and Chassis Divisions in 1937, Elliott became chief engineer of the former and Hives appointed Rowledge aero consultant.

ARTHUR A. RUBBRA (Rbr)

The younger son of a Northampton watchmaker, Rubbra read for his BSc at Bristol University along with two other young men who were to play crucial roles in the future success of Rolls-Royce: A.C. Lovesey and R.N. Dorey. Rubbra was recruited into the Experimental Department of Rolls-Royce by E.W. Hives, shortly after Lovesey but before Dorey, in 1925. His first task was to attempt to get more power out of the Eagle, a process which he said caused the engine to 'go out of focus'. He was then asked to concentrate on the development of the first Rolls-Royce aero engine supercharger, which involved working in Derby and at RAE, Farnborough. In the late 1920s, he transferred to Design under A.J. Rowledge, and in that role had further direct contact with Henry Royce. He had first met Royce in 1926, when he had to make a case to build a supercharger test rig in Derby. In 1934, when Colonel Barrington was appointed chief designer Aero, Rubbra became his deputy. In reality, he bore the load.

In 1940, when Packard took on the manufacture of the Merlin, Barrington was seconded to them, along with J.E. Ellor and J.M. Reid. It was then that Rubbra was given total responsibility for Merlin design, and A.C. Lovesey for its development. In due course, Rubbra additionally took responsibility for the design of the Griffon and Eagle 22. When Dr. S.G. Hooker, who had been the third in the Merlin triumvirate responsible for supercharging, moved to Barnoldswick in 1943 as chief engineer on the gas turbines, Rubbra also became involved in their design. He was involved particularly on the turboprops – Trent, Clyde, Dart and Tyne. In 1951 he became deputy chief engineer, and then in 1954 technical director of Rolls-Royce, with a seat on the main board. Before retiring in 1968 he was chief technical advisor for two years, and in retirement he remained a consultant into the 1970s. With his old colleagues, Hooker and Lovesey, he returned to help get the RB211 right.

Rubbra died in 1982. He was a gentle giant. Self-effacing in the extreme, he gave others credit he could rightly have claimed himself. Quiet and calm, even in crises, he was possessed of a good sense of humour, and his integrity was total. Rubbra had a deep understanding of good engineering practice, and great technical tenacity. His dedication to the task in the war years broke his health. Arthur Rubbra was awarded the CBE for his work on aero engineering. His older brother, Edmund, was also awarded a CBE for his musical composition.

CAPTAIN THE LORD HERBERT SCOTT (LHS)

Recruited to the board as a salesman in Rolls-Royce's first year to add social standing to the company, Lord Herbert Scott had been with the Irish Guards and became the longest-serving director in the company's history. A cousin of Lord Montagu, he was Chairman from 1936 until his death in 1944.

CAPTAIN R.T. ('Ronnie') SHEPHERD (Shep)

Shepherd's early working life was spent in the gun department of Vickers. In 1916 he volunteered for the Army, where his determination to fly led to his posting to the Royal Flying Corps a year later. Having undergone pilot training, he flew FE2b aircraft with 102 Squadron in France. Late in the war, he returned to England on night operations against Zeppelins with 37 Squadron. When the war ended he left the service, but eighteen months of civilian life led to his rejoining.

In due course, Shepherd left the RAF and became chief flying instructor with Phillips and Powis (later known as Miles). Again, his stay was short, and eighteen months later he became a CFI with the newly formed National Flying Services. His posting was to Tollerton, where he was to control the Nottingham Flying Club branch. In the autumn of 1931, the Installation and Design department of Rolls-Royce began simple flying operations at Tollerton. Flight testing had been seen as desirable for a year or two, but the Schneider Trophy and thoughts of a national test centre had both served to delay the beginning of any work on the project. Captain Shepherd was seconded to do the test flying, which led to the establishment of a permanent base alongside the RAF at nearby Hucknall aerodrome late in 1934. Shepherd was invited to join Rolls-Royce as chief test pilot – although not before Ronnie Harker had become the company's first test pilot through internal transfer.

Ronnie Shepherd remained chief test pilot through the busy war years and into the era of the jet engine. He retired when he stopped test flying in 1951, although he returned to make the first free flights of the world's first jet-powered VTOL machine, the 'Flying Bedstead'. His flying career began in 60 mph Farman Longhorns and ended in 600 mph Canberras. He died in 1955.

(Sir) ARTHUR F. SIDGREAVES (Sg)

Brought in from Napier in 1920 by Basil Johnson as export manager, Sidgreaves succeeded Johnson as Managing Director in 1929. He was at the helm in Royce's last years, and continued without support from 1933 through Wormald's declining years until the appointment of Ernest Hives to succeed Wormald as general manager in 1936. Sidgreaves was, of course, responsible for the appointment of Hives – arguably his greatest decision. Thereafter, the powerhouse of Rolls-Royce was Ernest Hives. To Sidgreaves goes the credit for acquiring the Bentley motor car business, and it was during his stewardship that the Derby Bentley, Phantom III, 20/25 hp, Goshawk, Peregrine, Vulture and Merlin were launched. To have ventured a significant contribution to the launch costs of the prototype Fairey Battle, Hawker Hurricane and Supermarine Spitfire in order to secure the selection of the Merlin remains perhaps the greatest testimony to his stature. He retired shortly after the war.

W. ('Bill') STAMMERS

Stammers trained as a civil engineer and worked on dock construction before serving in the Corps of Royal Engineers in the First World War. He was demobilised with the rank of Captain and became personal assistant to Roy Fedden, technical director of Cosmos Engineering, which had built the Rolls-Royce Falcon and Hawk during the war at Fishponds, Bristol. Fedden had by then begun the design and development of what became the world-renowned Bristol air-cooled radial engine family. Fedden and his team were taken over by Bristol Aeroplane Company, and became their Engine Department in 1920. Stammers was appointed commercial manager of the Engine Department, and remained a key member of the Bristol team for a quarter of a century.

In May 1937 Rotol Airscrews Ltd. was registered as a jointly owned company by Bristol and Rolls-Royce, with the intent of making variable pitch propellers. Stammers was appointed general manager with no seat on the board, and two years on, Rotol still relied on support and direction from the parent companies. It needed galvanising into independent action, and the decision was taken to bring in R.H. Coverley from Derby with a title of his own making: 'controller'. Autocratic in the extreme, Coverley's style relegated Stammers to a minor role, and in March 1945 his services were terminated with compensation for loss of office. Described as 'a perfect gentleman', who would hold a door open for an office boy, it is believed that he became general manager of Lagonda Motors. Stammers was succeeded by John Reid in 1945, and when Coverley was forced to resign late in that year, he was not replaced. It was not until Reid retired in 1951 that his successor as Managing Director had a seat on the Rotol board.

A. JOHN STENT (AJS)

One of Royce's design team, Stent did work on the early designs of the Kestrel supercharger before Ellor was brought in from the RAE to apply his outstanding knowledge of supercharging to bear on the design.

HARRY J. SWIFT (Sft)

One of the big names on production between the wars and throughout the Second World War, Swift served his apprenticeship with the Great Eastern Railway in Norwich. He joined Rolls-Royce in 1908 and became a chargehand in the Transmission Department, rising to become superintendent of the Axle and Gearbox Department. In 1914 he was appointed general superintendent of the Fitting and Assembly Departments, and was in this position during the early days of the war. In 1918, he was made assistant works manager of Nightingale Road. From 1928 until 1936 he was works manager. Effective in an old style of working, he was an exceedingly strong character possessed at times of a colourful vocabulary. He was Wormald's choice as his successor as general manager. E.W. Hives and R.W.H. Bailey mutually agreed that they would resign if Swift were appointed. Happily, Hives was chosen to succeed Wormald, and when he created the Chassis and Aero Division structure in 1937 Swift became production manager of the Aero Division, with R.H. Coverley as his counterpart on the Car Division. Swift rose to the challenge during the war as general manager of Aero Production, covering the huge sub-contract organisation as well as Rolls-Royce facilities throughout the country. His contribution in providing Merlin engines in ever-increasing numbers, and helping others to do so, was outstanding. He remained in this role until 1950, when he became a consultant to Lord Hives. He retired on the same day as T.S. Haldenby in November 1952.

T. ALAN SWINDEN (Sn)

Alan Swinden came from Sheffield, and was one of the first intake of nine graduates in 1937, when Rolls-Royce discontinued premium apprenticeships in favour of what were then called engineering pupils. Swinden was interviewed by R.W.H. Bailey, recently appointed chief engineer of the new Chassis Division, which included a personal tour of the factory. In September of that year, he joined the Experimental Department of the Division on a two-year stint as a 'tester's mate' attached to George Ratcliffe. Initially he tested car engines on the beds, but this grew to include test driving on the road. The year 1938 saw much activity on the carburettors of the new Wraith and Bentley V models, and 1939 saw studies of the absorption of power by tyres at high speed (a dangerous experience!).

With the advent of war, Swinden moved to Clan Foundry, and in due course was taken by W.A. Robotham to London, along with the latter's secretary, Ouida Haroun, when he was appointed Chief Engineer, Tanks, at the Ministry of Supply. At the end of the war, Swinden was appointed personal assistant to E.W. Hives, and took responsibility for 'site services', including what would now be called Human Resources. When Hives became Chairman, Swinden continued his duties under W.T. Gill, finance director, and then under J.D. Pearson, before leaving in 1955. Long thereafter his name was recalled in Derby with the greatest respect.

After leaving Rolls-Royce, he joined the Engineering Employers Federation which, as a result of the country's general industrial relations situation at the time, was in need of a powerful body. There he rose to become director, before moving on in the 1960s to become the first director of the Engineering Industries Training Board. His final executive post was deputy director of the Confederation of British Industry. Since retiring, he has continued with professional rather than managerial interests, and, at the time of writing, lives in Surrey.

J. RAY THOMPSON (JRT)

Thompson was one of the young, capable and energetic team of production engineers who joined Alec McWilliams in 1942 to set up the production of the Meteor engine, the unsupercharged Merlin, for use in tanks. At the end of that year, E.W. Hives proposed the famous 'swap' of Rolls-Royce's work on the Meteor engine for the Rover car company's work on the Whittle jet engine. As a result, production of the Meteor was handed over progressively to Rover in 1943, whereupon the Belper team moved to Newcastle-under-Lyme to produce the Derwent I jet engine.

After the war, Hives moved jet engine production to Derby. Thompson's career progressed, and by the 1950s he was in charge of production engineering in Derby. Following the acquisition of Bristol Siddeley in 1966, he was posted to the Small Engine Division at Leavesden as production director. He left Rolls-Royce in 1971 to pursue his career elsewhere, but retired to live near Derby and became an active member of the Rolls-Royce Heritage Trust.

JOHN FRANCIS ('Jack') WARWICK (JWk)

A member of the long-established Warwick family from Alvaston and later Osmaston Park in Derby, Jack joined Rolls-Royce in 1919 and served his time as a fitter in the Experimental Department. He was involved with the removal of the sparking plugs from the 'R' engine the night before Flt. Lt. H.R.D. Waghorn won the Schneider Trophy in 1929. The discovery of aluminium particles on one plug led to the saga of the overnight cylinder block and piston change. He also worked on the 'R' engine-powered speed record boat, *Miss England III*. Warwick rose to become manager of the Experimental Fitting Shop on Sinfin A site in Derby in the 1950s and 60s. He retired in 1970 and survived to the age of ninety. One of Jack's six sisters married E.W. Hives; another married Roy Speed, who was to succeed Horace Percy Smith as general manager, Experimental, after the latter's tragic death.

HAROLD WHYMAN (Wym)

The name of Whyman first comes to the fore when the Silver Ghost was put back into production after the First World War. Having concentrated all his efforts in the war on aero engine product support, and in 1919 in support of the transatlantic flight challenge, Eric Platford had to re-establish customer support on the car side. It was said that his office in 1920 was like a travel agent's. 'Do you mind going abroad?' 'No – where to?' 'I'll tell you tomorrow when you pick up your tickets.'

The Indian market retained its pre-war importance, and several Maharajahs had so many Rolls-Royces that they required their own resident maintenance engineer. The Maharajah of Patiala was one such, with twenty-seven Rolls-Royces – one for each of his five wives, and more for his numerous concubines. He also had ninety-three cars of other makes for hunting and camping trips. Whyman was posted to Patiala. He had just got married, and the honeymoon became the voyage to India. Shortly after the Whymans' arrival, the Maharajah threw a party to which senior British officers and citizens were invited. The palace ballroom was packed, and one by one, the Maharajah indicated to couples that he wished them to leave the floor. Eventually, only the Whymans were left. Harold was worried, thinking he might have made a social blunder. He became even more worried when he realised that the Maharajah was watching his wife. Happily, it transpired that his interest was in her dancing skills, and he promptly engaged her to teach his wives and concubines the latest European steps – the Black Bottom and Turkey Trot among them.

The Maharajah was hard on his cars, using them for the chase through the bush, and Whyman had to prepare separate cars for morning and afternoon hunts, and even night-time outings. But, work apart, life for the Whymans was never dull, as they were drawn into the social world of Patiala – palace dinners almost nightly, followed by 'men only' entertainment. The Maharajah was also a frequent visitor to the Whymans' bungalow. Anxious to escape his many court 'hangers-on', he would exclaim, 'I've lost the buggers for ten minutes', and gratefully accept a cup of Mrs. Whyman's tea. On one such occasion, the Maharajah was told of the imminent 20 hp model, and Whyman expressed the hope that His Highness would have the first to come to India. He responded by cabling for the first six!

Late in the 1920s, the Whymans returned to Derby, where Harold became an experimental test driver. The first car he tested extensively, together with George Ratcliffe, was 17 EX. When the Chassis Division was created in 1937, he naturally became a part of it, and was put in charge of the Experimental garage. When war came, he was called upon by W.A. Robotham to make Clan Foundry in Belper habitable. Experimental car parts and equipment needed storing in weather-proof conditions, and the old foundry had to be made fit to work in. Whyman had the difficult task under wartime conditions of finding materials and labour to seal the roof and lay a concrete floor over the dirt. He accomplished the task in a remarkably short time, thereafter performing an administration role throughout the war as right-hand man to Robotham. Afterwards, he remained with Robotham, becoming works manager of the Oil Engine Division and finally, after its move to Shrewsbury, assistant general manager. He retired in 1964 on completing fifty years with Rolls-Royce.

ARTHUR WORMALD (Wor)

Joined F.H. Royce & Co. Ltd. in the Tool Room at Cooke Street in 1904. Following Royce's major illnesses and move away from Derby in 1912, Wormald became general works manager and a director. He served the company with commitment until his health broke. He died in 1936. Possessed of a certain cunning, he ruled over his domain through a small band of loyal henchmen, yet he had a deep-seated understanding of the workforce which established excellent and enduring industrial relations.

BIBLIOGRAPHY OF
BOOKS CONSULTED

A S I HAVE SAID, THERE HAVE BEEN many books written on almost every aspect of Rolls-Royce and Bentley cars, and I have read every one I could find, using their research in this volume. Occasionally, they contradict each other, or at least later research has shown that earlier statements were not quite accurate. Wherever possible, I have acknowledged sources. Here is a list of titles from which I have extracted information.

Allen, Warner, *Lucy Houston DBE, one of the few*, Constable, 1947

Banks, F. Rodwell, *I Kept no Diary*, Airlife, 1978

Barker, Ralph, *The Schneider Trophy races*, Chatto & Windus/Random House UK, 1971

Bastow, Donald, *Henry Royce – mechanic*, Rolls-Royce Heritage Trust (Historical Series Vol. 12), 1989

Bentley, W.O., *W.O. – The Autobiography of W.O. Bentley*, Hutchinson, 1961

Birch, David, *Rolls-Royce and the Mustang*, Rolls-Royce Heritage Trust (Historical Series Vol. 9), 1987

Bird, Anthony, and Hallows, Ian, *The Rolls-Royce Motor Car*, B.T. Batsford Ltd., 1984

Bishop, Edward, *Hurricane*, Airlife, 1986

Blake, Robert, and Louis, W. Roger, *Churchill*, Oxford University Press, 1993

Bobbitt, Malcolm, *Rolls-Royce and Bentley*, Sutton Publishing Ltd., 1997

Bowyer, Chaz, *History of the RAF*, Hamlyn, 1985

Bowyer, Michael, *The Spitfire 50 Years On*, Patrick Stephens, 1986

Brabazon, Lord, of Tara, *The Brabazon Story*, private publication

Brendon, Piers, *The Motoring Century: The Story of the Royal Automobile Club*, Bloomsbury, 1997

Brooks, David S., *Vikings at Waterloo*, Rolls-Royce Heritage Trust, 1997

Bruce, Gordon, *Charlie Rolls – pioneer aviator*, Rolls-Royce Heritage Trust, 1990

Bruce, J.M., *The Aeroplanes of the Royal Flying Corps*, Putnam Aeronautical Books, 1992

Buxton, Neil K., and Aldcroft, Derek H. (eds.), *British Industry between the Wars: Instability and Industrial Development 1919–39*, Scolar Press, 1978

Cable, Boyd, *Rolls-Royce Aero Engines and the Great Victory – Aeroplanes*, Rolls-Royce, 1920s

Cable, Boyd, *Rolls-Royce Aero Engines and the Great Victory – Seaplanes, Flying Boats, Airships*, Rolls-Royce, 1920s

Cable, Boyd, *The Soul of the Aeroplane – The Rolls-Royce Engine*, Rolls-Royce, 1920s

Churchill, Winston, *The Second World War, Vols. I–VI*, Cassell, 1951

Clarke, Peter, *Hope, Glory, Britain 1900–1990*, Penguin, 1996

Clarke, Tom, *Ernest Claremont – a Manchester life with Rolls-Royce and W.T. Glover & Co.*, Hulme Press, 1995

Clarke, Tom, *The Rolls-Royce Wraith*, John M. Fasal, 1986

Colvin, Ian, *The Chamberlain Cabinet*, Victor Gollancz, 1971

Cook, Ray, *Armstrong Siddeley, The Parkside Story 1896–1939*, Rolls-Royce Heritage Trust, 1988

De Havilland, Sir Geoffrey, *Sky Fever*, Hamish Hamilton, 1961

Deighton, Len, *Battle of Britain*, Jonathan Cape, 1980

Dibbs, John, and Holmes, Tony, *Hurricane – a Fighter Legend*, Osprey/Aerospace, 1995

Dickey, Philip S. III, *The Liberty Engine 1918–1942*, Smithsonian Institution Press, 1968

Douglas, Sholto, *Years of Command*, Collins, 1966

Driver, Hugh, *Lord Northcliffe and the early years of Rolls-Royce*, Rolls-Royce Enthusiasts Club, 1998

Edmunds, Henry, *Reminiscences of a Pioneer*, private publication, early 1900s

Evans, Michael, *In the Beginning, the Manchester origins of Rolls-Royce*, Rolls-Royce Heritage Trust (Historical Series Vol. 4), 1985

Fasal, John, and Goodman, Bryan, *The Edwardian Rolls-Royce*, Thames View (Holdings) Ltd., 1995

Fasal, John, *The Rolls-Royce Twenty*, Burgess & Son, 1979

Fearon, P., *British Industry between the Wars*, Scolar Press, 1979

Fedden, Sir Roy, *Britain's Air Survival – an appraisement and strategy for success*, Cassell & Co. Ltd., 1957

Gilbert, Martin, *A History of the Twentieth Century, Volume One: 1900–1933*, HarperCollins, 1997

Gilbert, Martin, *A History of the Twentieth Century, Volume Two: 1933–1951*, HarperCollins, 1998

Golley, John, *Whittle, the true story*, Airlife, 1987

Gough, Kevin, *The Vital Spark – the development of aero engine sparking plugs*, Rolls-Royce Heritage Trust, 1991

Gray, Robert, *Rolls on the Rocks*, Panther, 1971

Griffiths, Harry, *Testing Times – Memories of a Spitfire Boffin*, United Writers Publications, 1992

Gunston, Bill, *By Jupiter! – the life of Sir Roy Fedden*, Royal Aeronautical Society, 1978

Gunston, Bill, *Fedden – the life of Sir Roy Fedden*, Rolls-Royce Heritage Trust, 1998

Gunston, Bill, *Rolls-Royce, Aero Engines*, Patrick Stephens, 1989

Harker, R.W., *Rolls-Royce from the Wings*, Oxford Illustrated Press, 1976

Harker, R.W., *The Engines were Rolls-Royce*, Collier Macmillan, 1980

Harvey-Bailey, Alec, *Rolls-Royce, the formative years, 1906–1939*, Rolls-Royce Heritage Trust (Historical Series Vol. 1), 1983

Harvey-Bailey, Alec, and Evans, Michael, *Rolls-Royce, the pursuit of excellence*, Sir Henry Royce Memorial Foundation (Historical Series Vol. 3), 1984

Harvey-Bailey, Alec, *Rolls-Royce – The Derby Bentleys*, Sir Henry Royce Memorial Foundation (Historical Series Vol. 5), 1985

Harvey-Bailey, Alec, *Rolls-Royce – Hives, The Quiet Tiger*, Sir Henry Royce Memorial Foundation (Historical Series Vol. 7), 1986

Harvey-Bailey, Alec, *Rolls-Royce – Twenty to Wraith*, Sir Henry Royce Memorial Foundation (Historical Series Vol. 8), 1986

Harvey-Bailey, Alec, *Rolls-Royce, the sons of Martha*, Sir Henry Royce Memorial Foundation (Historical Series Vol. 14), 1989

Harvey-Bailey, Alec, *Rolls-Royce – Hives' Turbulent Barons*, Sir Henry Royce Memorial Foundation (Historical Series Vol. 20), 1993

Harvey-Bailey, Alec, *The Merlin in Perspective – the combat years*, Rolls-Royce Heritage Trust (Historical Series Vol. 2, 4th edition), 1995

Henshaw, Alex, *Sigh for a Merlin*, John Murray, 1979

Hooker, Sir Stanley, *Not much of an Engineer*, Airlife, 1984

Howarth, Stephen, *August '39*, Hodder & Stoughton, 1953

Howarth, T.E.B., *Prospect and Reality, Great Britain 1945–1955*, Collins, 1985

James, Derek N., *Schneider Trophy Aircraft 1913–31*, Bodley Head, 1981

Kaplan, Philip, and Collier, Richard, *The Few*, Blandford Press, 1989

Keegan, John, *The First World War*, Hutchinson, 1998

Keegan, John, *The Second World War*, Hutchinson, 1989

Kirby, Dr. Robert, *Avro Manchester – the Legend behind the Lancaster*, Midland Counties, 1995

Lacey, Robert, *Ford, the men and the machine*, Heinemann, 1986

Lea, Ken, *Rolls-Royce – the first cars from Crewe*, Rolls-Royce Heritage Trust (Historical Series Vol. 23), 1997

Lewis, Gwilym H., and Bowyer, Chaz (eds.), *Wings over the Somme 1916–1918*, Bridge Books, 1994

Lewis, Peter, *British Bomber since 1914*, Bodley Head, 1980

Lewis, Peter, *British Fighter since 1912 – Sixty years of design and development*, Putnam & Co, 1979

Lloyd, Ian, *Rolls-Royce – The Growth of a Firm*, Macmillan, 1978

Lloyd, Ian, *Rolls-Royce – The Merlin at War*, Macmillan, 1978

Lloyd, Ian, *Rolls-Royce – The Years of Endeavour*, Macmillan, 1978

Lumsden, Alec, *British Piston Aero-Engines and their Aircraft*, Airlife, 1994

Marshall, Sir Arthur, *The Marshall Story*, Patrick Stephens, 1994

Mason, Francis, *The Avro Lancaster*, Aston Publications, 1989

McCarthy, Roy, *Rolls-Royce Limited*, Odhams (for Rolls-Royce), 1957

Meynell, Lawrence, *Rolls – Man of Speed*, Bodley Head, 1950s

Miller, William J., *Memoirs*, private publication, 1980s

Minchin, G.R.N., *Under my Bonnet*, G.T. Foulis, 1950

Mitchell, Gordon, *R.J. Mitchell, Schooldays to Spitfire*, Gordon Mitchell, 1986

Mondey, David, *The Schneider Trophy*, Robert Hale, 1975

Montagu, Lord, of Beaulieu, *Rolls of Rolls-Royce*, Cassell, 1966

Morriss, H.F., *Two Brave Brothers*, private publication, 1916

Morton, C.W., *History of Rolls-Royce Motor Cars 1903–1907*, G.T. Foulis, 1964

Nahum, Andrew, Foster-Pegg, R.W., and Birch, David, *The Rolls-Royce Crecy*, Rolls-Royce Heritage Trust, 1994

Nockolds, Harold, *Lucas – The First 100 Years*, David & Charles, 1977

Nockolds, Harold, *The Magic of a Name*, G.T. Foulis, 1959

Oldham, Wilton J., *The Hyphen in Rolls-Royce*, G.T. Foulis, 1967

Oldham, Wilton J., *The Rolls-Royce 40/50 hp – Ghosts, Phantoms and Spectres*, G.T. Foulis, 1974

Pemberton, Sir Max, *The Life of Sir Henry Royce*, Selwyn and Blount, 1930s

Penrose, Harald, *British Aviation – The Adventuring Years 1920–39*, Putnam, 1963

Penrose, Harald, *British Aviation – The Pioneer Years*, Putnam, 1967

Penrose, Harald, *British Aviation – The Great War and Armistice*, Putnam, 1969

Penrose, Harald, *British Aviation – Widening Horizons, 1930–34*, HMSO, 1979

Penrose, Harald, *British Aviation – The Ominous Skies 1935–39*, HMSO, 1980

Penrose, Harald, *Adventure with Fate*, Airlife, 1984

Price, Alfred, *The Spitfire story*, Arms & Armour Press/Cassell, 1992

Quill, Jeffrey K., OBE, *Spitfire, A Test Pilot's Story*, John Murray, 1983

Quill, Jeffrey K., OBE, *The Birth of a Legend*, Quiller Press, 1986

Richie, Sebastian, *Industry and Air Power – the Expansion of British Aircraft Production, 1935–1941*, Frank Cass, 1997

Rimmer, Ian, *Rolls-Royce and Bentley – Experimental Cars*, Rolls-Royce Enthusiasts Club, 1986

Robertson, Bruce, *Spitfire – the story of a famous fighter*, Harleyford Publications, 1973

Robotham, W.A., *Silver Ghosts and Silver Dawn*, Constable, 1970

Rolls-Royce, *Rolls-Royce Armoured Cars and the Great Victory*, Rolls-Royce, 1920s

Rolls-Royce, *Rolls-Royce Cars and the Great Victory*, Rolls-Royce, 1920s

Rubbra, A.A., *Rolls-Royce Piston Aero Engines – a designer remembers*, Rolls-Royce Heritage Trust, 1990

Sarkar, Dilip, *Invisible Thread: Spitfire's Tale*, Ramrod Publications, 1992

Schlaiffer, Robert, and Heron, S.D., *Development of Aircraft Engines and Development of Aviation Fuels*, Harvard Business School, 1950

Shacklady, Edward, and Morgan, Eric B., *Spitfire – The History*, Key Publishing Company, 1987

Sharp, Cecil M., *DH – A History of De Havilland*, Airlife, 1982

Shirer, William, *The Rise and Fall of the Third Reich*, Secker and Warburg, 1963

Sims, Charles, *Royal Air Force, The First 50 Years*, Adam & Charles Black Ltd., 1968

Skidelsky, Robert, *John Maynard Keynes, The Economist as Saviour, 1920–1937*, Macmillan, 1992

Smith, Herschel, *Aircraft Piston Engines*, McGraw, 1981

Sonnenburg, Paul, and Schoneberger, William A., *Allison, Power of Excellence 1915–1990*, Coastline Publishers, 1990

Stait, Bruce, *Rotol, the History of an Airscrew Company, 1937–1960*, Alan Sutton, 1990

Stewart, Adrian, *Hurricane*, William Kimber & Co. Ltd., 1982

Stokes, Peter, *From Gipsy Gem – with diversions 1926–86*, Rolls-Royce Heritage Trust, 1987

Thorne, A., *Lancaster at War*, I. Allan, 1990

Tritton, Paul, *The Godfather of Rolls-Royce – the life and time of Henry Edmunds, MICE, MIEE, Science of Technology's Forgotten Pioneer*, Academy Books, 1993

Tuffen, H.J., and Tagg, A.E., *The Hawker Hurricane, Design, Development and Production*, Royal Aeronautical Society, Historical Group, 1988

Venables, David, *Napier, the first to wear green*, G.T. Foulis/Haynes Publishing, 1998

Wallace, Graham, *The Flight of Alcock and Brown*, Putnam, 1955

Weinberg, Gerhard L., *A World at Arms*, Cambridge University Press, 1994

Whitney, Daniel D., *Vees for Victory! The story of the Allison V-1710, 1929–1948*, Schiffer Military History, 1998

Whittle, Sir Frank, *Jet, the story of a pioneer*, Frederick Muller, 1953

Williams, David E., *A View of Ansty*, Rolls-Royce Heritage Trust, 1998

PHOTO CREDITS

The majority of the photographs have been provided by the Rolls-Royce Heritage Trust.

The photograph of the Rolls-Royce radiator in the group between pages 36 and 37 was taken and lent by Mike Evans.

The photograph of the Rolls-Royce Eagle engine being serviced at the front in the First World War in the group between pages 84 and 85, and the photograph of the Spitfires in action during the Battle of Britain in the group between pages 244 and 245 are reproduced by kind permission of the Imperial War Museum.

The photographs of the Porte Felixstowe F.2A and the Bristol F. 2B in the group between pages 84 and 85 are reproduced by kind permission of the RAF Museum at Hendon.

The photograph of Ivor and Tommy Broom with their Mosquito in the group between pages 244 and 245 is reproduced by kind permission of Air Marshal Sir Ivor Broom.

INDEX